Web Development with Microsoft® Exchange 2000 Server

Alex E. Willis and Paul R. Bebelos

with Robert A. Saccone

M&T Books

An imprint of Hungry Minds, Inc.

Best-Selling Books • Digital Downloads • e-Books • Answer Networks
e-Newsletters • Branded Web Sites • e-Learning

New York, NY • Cleveland, OH • Indianapolis, IN

Web Development with Microsoft® Exchange 2000 Server

Published by
M&T Books
An imprint of Hungry Minds, Inc.
909 Third Avenue
New York, NY 10022
www.hungryminds.com

Library of Congress Control Number: 2001092918

ISBN: 0-7645-4883-2

Printed in the United States of America

10 9 8 7 6 5 4 3 2 1

1B/SV/QT/QS/IN

Distributed in the United States by Hungry Minds, Inc.

Distributed by CDG Books Canada Inc. for Canada; by Transworld Publishers Limited in the United Kingdom; by IDG Norge Books for Norway; by IDG Sweden Books for Sweden; by IDG Books Australia Publishing Corporation Pty. Ltd. for Australia and New Zealand; by TransQuest Publishers Pte Ltd. for Singapore, Malaysia, Thailand, Indonesia, and Hong Kong; by Gotop Information Inc. for Taiwan; by ICG Muse, Inc. for Japan; by Intersoft for South Africa; by Eyrolles for France; by International Thomson Publishing for Germany, Austria, and Switzerland; by Distribuidora Cuspide for Argentina; by LR International for Brazil; by Galileo Libros for Chile; by Ediciones ZETA S.C.R. Ltda. for Peru; by WS Computer Publishing Corporation, Inc., for the Philippines; by Contemporanea de Ediciones for Venezuela; by Express Computer Distributors for the Caribbean and West Indies; by Micronesia Media Distributor, Inc. for Micronesia; by Chips Computadoras S.A. de C.V. for Mexico; by Editorial Norma de Panama S.A. for Panama; by American Bookshops for Finland.

For general information on Hungry Minds' products and services please contact our Customer Care department within the U.S. at 800-762-2974, outside the U.S. at 317-572-3993 or fax 317-572-4002.

For sales inquiries and reseller information, including discounts, premium and bulk quantity sales, and foreign-language translations, please contact our Customer Care department at 800-434-3422, fax 317-572-4002 or write to Hungry Minds, Inc., Attn: Customer Care Department, 10475 Crosspoint Boulevard, Indianapolis, IN 46256.

For information on licensing foreign or domestic rights, please contact our Sub-Rights Customer Care department at 212-884-5000.

For information on using Hungry Minds' products and services in the classroom or for ordering examination copies, please contact our Educational Sales department at 800-434-2086 or fax 317-572-4005.

For press review copies, author interviews, or other publicity information, please contact our Public Relations department at 317-572-3168 or fax 317-572-4168.

For authorization to photocopy items for corporate, personal, or educational use, please contact Copyright Clearance Center, 222 Rosewood Drive, Danvers, MA 01923, or fax 978-750-4470.

 is a trademark of Hungry Minds, Inc.   is a trademark of Hungry Minds, Inc.

About the Authors

Alex E. Willis has a bachelor's degree in Computer Information Systems from New Hampshire College, is a certified MCSE, certified in Exchange 2000, and has seven years' experience working with and designing enterprise e-mail systems. Alex is currently a Technical Account Manager for Research In Motion, creators of the industry-leading BlackBerry wireless e-mail solution. Before joining RIM, Alex was most recently a Messaging Architect for Internosis, a Gold-Level Microsoft Certified Solutions Provider (MCSP), where he led the design and implementation of many Microsoft Exchange projects. Alex also founded SMTPGateway.net and is the creator and Web master for www.bostonbands.com.

Paul R. Bebelos has been in the computer industry since 1994, when he got his start learning computer aided design (CAD). He soon developed a passion for computers and their abilities. He moved his career into the wonderful world of technical support in 1996 and in 1997 began his endeavors as a developer. He achieved his Microsoft Certified Professional status in 1998 and holds certifications in NT 4, VB5, and VB6. He is currently employed full-time as the primary Applications Developer for a large investment firm in Boston, MA. When Paul is not programming he enjoys various sports and spending time with his family.

About the Contributor

Robert A. Saccone, author of Chapters 3–5, is an experienced applications developer and project manager with over 10 years of hands-on experience in information architecture and knowledge management technology. He currently manages a Web development team for Goodwin Procter LLP, Boston, MA and one of the largest law firms in the country, where he designs and develops Web-based enterprise applications using Microsoft IIS, SQL Server, Exchange and other Microsoft server and development tools.

Credits

SENIOR ACQUISITIONS EDITOR
Sharon Cox

PROJECT EDITORS
Andy Marinkovich
Neil Romanosky

TECHNICAL EDITOR
James Kelly

COPY EDITOR
S. B. Kleinman

EDITORIAL MANAGER
Mary Beth Wakefield

VICE PRESIDENT AND EXECUTIVE GROUP PUBLISHER
Richard Swadley

VICE PRESIDENT AND EXECUTIVE PUBLISHER
Bob Ipsen

VICE PRESIDENT AND PUBLISHER
Joseph B. Wikert

EDITORIAL DIRECTOR
Mary Bednarek

PROJECT COORDINATOR
Maridee Ennis

GRAPHICS AND PRODUCTION SPECIALISTS
Beth Books
Sean Decker
Joyce Haughey
Barry Offringa
Laurie Petrone
Jacque Schneider

QUALITY CONTROL TECHNICIAN
Andy Hollandbeck
Charles Spencer

PROOFREADING AND INDEXING
TECHBOOKS Production Services

COVER IMAGE
© Noma/Images.com

Preface

It seems like a long time ago that we all got together and decided we need to write this book. We felt strongly that with our combined experience and perspective that it would specifically answer many of the needs of our peers in the field. Our intent was to create a resource for ourselves and for others who want to get the most out of Web applications on the Exchange 2000 Server platform. We use real-life examples and because we all work in the field, our actual projects and needs were used as inspiration for the content.

Who Should Read This Book?

Anyone who needs information about developing Web-based applications on the Exchange 2000 Server platform needs this book. That statement may sound broad, and the advances in Exchange 2000 Server over previous versions of Exchange make it even broader. Not only developers but administrators will need to become familiar with at least basic Exchange development. And while the experience level for this book is intermediate to advanced, even beginning developers will be able to follow along and use the sample code. As best we could, we made each code sample useable as-is or with little customization.

What This Book Contains

This book is separated into five sections with a total of 18 chapters and four appendixes.

Part I: Introduction to Exchange 2000

This version of Exchange is particularly well equipped to support robust development. But, as with any platform, you need to know what it is capable of before you can create applications that use it to its fullest potential. This section discusses what makes Exchange 2000 Server a robust platform for your applications and what tools you can use to develop with.

Part II: The Web Storage System

If there is one major enhancement to Exchange 2000 Server, this is it. The Web Storage System is what allows Exchange to be as open as it is. This section introduces you to the architecture of the Web Storage System, its security, and its management.

Part III: Extending Your Data to the Web

This is the fun section. It discusses how to bring your data to life by displaying and manipulating it in your Web site. Using familiar technologies such as ADO, CDO, and XML you can access Exchange Server as you would any other database. We also discuss customization of the Outlook Web Access experience.

Part IV: Collaboration and Messaging

The introduction of Exchange 2000 Server brings the new CDO. CDO provides you with direct access to items in the Web Storage System. This section helps you create applications that provide features similar to those that make Exchange 2000 a corporate standard, such as messaging, calendaring, and contacts.

Part V: Workflow Applications

This advanced section dives into creating rich workflow applications. After all, Exchange 2000 isn't just an e-mail server anymore. Workflow applications enable you to create applications that automate business tasks.

Appendixes

Here's where we tell you what's on the Web site and where to get more information. We also provide reference material here, and talk about an issue very important to the success of any project – the deployment of the applications that you create.

Companion Web Site

All sample code in the listings in this book are available for download from the companion Web site. In addition to the listings, we also included a couple bonus applications for you. The Web site is available at `http://www.hungryminds. com/extras/`.

Styles and Conventions

This is a technical book. As you'd expect, it contains many code examples. For the most part, you won't need help deciphering the code from the text, but to make it easier to spot while skimming, all code is set in `monospaced` type. For example:

```
set NewMsg = createobject("CDO.Message")
```

The margins in this book sometimes made it necessary to split a code line into two lines. Rather than letting it wrap where it may, we use the underscore (_) to denote the continuation from one line onto another. For example:

```
set NewMsg = __
createobject("CDO.Message")
```

VBScript allows the use of the underscore to break a line, so you can use it in your live working code.

When a sample piece of code is used outside a code listing, as in reference to a function name or a piece of code, it will be also be displayed in a monospaced type. For example, you might see us refer to the `CreateHTMLBody` method.

We also use icons in this book to highlight important information and helpful tips. You can pick out icons by looking for the following symbols in the text.

Acknowledgments

I must first thank the team at Hungry Minds. There is no way I would have completed this book without the support of Sharon Cox, Neil Romanosky, and the many people behind the scenes. I don't see completing this book itself as the important milestone, but I am thankful to have reached a place in my professional career where I have something to contribute. I owe a great deal to many people for helping in one way or another to get me to this place. For that, I would like to thank all who made a contribution, large or small, to my personal and professional growth. Ronald Jacobs Sr., Kristy Glynn, Eric Miyadi, Wayne Pauley, Ivan Kousidis, Mark DiNino, Michael Walker, Anthony T. Mann, Ric Anderson, Sunni Shepherd, my family, and the nicest people I know, Jeanie and Clarence Savoie.

— Alex E. Willis

I would like to thank the editorial staff — Neil Romanosky, Andy Marinkovich, Jim Kelly, and S. B. Kleinman — for their patience, effort, and expertise. A book just isn't a book without you guys. Thank you Sharon Cox for giving me the opportunity to participate in the publication of this book and for buying time when I needed it. Thanks to my compadre and co-author Alex Willis, for considering me when searching for a second co-author, and thanks to Rob Saccone for contributing. You both are very talented individuals and it was a pleasure working with you on this project. Truly, without your contributions this book would not have been possible. To Rob B., Tom K., and Steven A., thanks! You guys were there when I needed you the most. Thank you to the people that most influenced me, Leonard, Mom and Dad, Aunty Joanne and Grandma: Your support and motivation has a lasting impression. Last but certainly not least, thank you to my wonderful wife Melissa. Thank you for your understanding, patience, support, and love. There really are no words to express how grateful I am to be married to a woman like you.

— Paul R. Bebelos

I would like to thank my son Justin and my wife Linda, who both made many sacrifices to allow me to work on this book. Without their understanding, I would have never made it through those late nights toiling over the keyboard. I'd also like to thank the people at Hungry Minds for their flexibility and support throughout this project. Despite the book's many changes and demanding schedule, they somehow managed to keep me on track and on time. I extend my gratitude to everyone who contributed their time, effort and expertise to make my small contribution a part of a great book. Most of all, I'd like to thank Alex Willis for convincing me to work with him on this book. Even after many years and many projects, his energy and motivation never cease to amaze me. Without his encouragement (and persistence!), I don't think I could have made it through this book. Thanks Alex!

— Robert A. Saccone

Contents at a Glance

Contents

Part I

Introduction to Exchange 2000

CHAPTER 1
Exchange 2000 as a Web-Development Platform

CHAPTER 2
Development Tools and Environments

Chapter 1

Exchange 2000 as a Web-Development Platform

EXCHANGE 2000 SERVER is the perfect development platform for your organization's Internet, intranet, or business application. Out of the box, Exchange 2000 is a powerful standards-based messaging platform complete with contact management, scheduling, and built-in workflow functionality. Development is easy because it supports several different programming technologies already in use today. In fact, you can use any programming language that supports the COM Object Model to develop collaborative applications with Exchange 2000. Developers benefit from enhanced security, replication, and Active Directory features because of Exchange 2000's integration with Windows 2000. The value of Exchange 2000 is that you can use as much or as little as it has to offer.

Exchange 2000 is also the first BackOffice product to be extended to the Web using the new Web Storage System. This means that every item stored in Exchange 2000 has its own URL and can be directly accessed from a Web browser. This makes extending your data to the Web easy. You can build a static Web site with links to variable data with no code at all. This chapter will introduce you to these features and show you how you can use this new technology to build powerful, collaborative applications on top of Exchange 2000.

The Active Directory

A major enhancement in the Exchange 2000 architecture is the absence of a directory service. Microsoft took the best features of the directory service found in previous versions of Exchange and added security features and scalability, resulting in the Active Directory. This is why Exchange 2000 cannot run in a pure Windows NT 4.0 (or earlier) domain. Exchange administrators will recognize characteristics such as an extensible schema, hierarchical structure of organization, sites, and X.500 standards, but Active Directory offers more. For example, replication is performed at the item level, which makes for more efficient replication. Security has also been enhanced, enabling granular administrative delegation. The addition of administrative and routing groups is another major enhancement.

For the developer, the major difference is that any directory-related interaction will be done against the Active Directory rather than an Exchange directory. Applications that create Exchange accounts, for example, will be directed to the Active Directory. Another difference is the ability to dynamically create custom attributes and classes for use in development. You can also replicate these attributes and classes to other sites in the Active Directory, providing a robust environment in which to manage your collaborative applications.

Distribution lists have also changed. Accounts in the Active Directory can be grouped into two types, *security groups* and *distribution groups*. Security groups control access to resources in the Windows 2000 environment, much like Local and Global groups in Windows NT. Distribution groups create e-mail distribution lists. Exchange Distribution lists are now managed in the Active Directory Users and Computers Microsoft Management Console (MMC) snap-in along with other account information (see Figure 1-1).

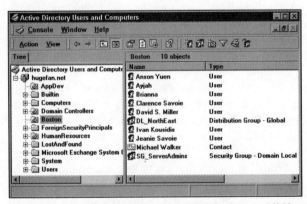

Figure 1-1: The Active Directory Users and Computers MMC snap-in

Active Directory accounts

You manage accounts in Active Directory programmatically using the Active Directory Services Interface (ADSI). ADSI is a set of COM objects used to interface with Lightweight Directory Access Protocol (LDAP) to manage the Active Directory users, groups, and so on. You might already be familiar with LDAP as a directory search tool: Exchange 5.5 supported the use of LDAP to search against its Global

Address Book. Similarly, LDAP is used to search against and manipulate the Active Directory. However, unlike in Exchange 5.5, in which you can use any LDAP query tool and query `LDAP://server.domain.com`, in Exchange Server 2000 you must use the proper Active Directory name space for the server you are querying. Since Web browsers do not support the use of name spaces in LDAP queries, you cannot use them. You must use either the Windows 2000 address book (Start → Search → For People, and set the Look In: field to Active Directory) or a tool such as `ldp.exe` that ships with the Windows 2000 Resource Kit.

Active Directory NameSpaces

Active Directory is built on a hierarchical directory structure – LDAP – that enables you to group the enterprise directory geographically and organizationally. Objects in Active Directory are separated into *containers*. Each object contains other, more specific, objects until you reach individual and shared resources such as printers. When developing applications that manipulate Active Directory information, you first make a connection to an Active Directory object, and then either request information about or manipulate an object's item. To demonstrate this LDAP syntax, Listing 1-1 makes a connection to the Active Directory RootDSE object and requests the name of the `RootDomainNamingContext`.

 All example code in the listings that follow was developed in VBScript for Active Server Pages (ASP). These examples are complete and can be copied to and run from your Exchange 2000 server without modification.

Listing 1-1: Displaying the RootDomainNamingContext

```
<%@ LANGUAGE = VBScript %>
<%
Dim TopLevelDomain
Dim RDNC

'Make the connection
set TopLevelDomain = Getobject("LDAP://RootDSE")

'request the name of the rootDomainNamingContext
rdnc = TopLevelDomain.get("rootDomainNamingContext")

'display the result
response.write RDNC
%>
```

You can use this method to create portable applications that do not have to be hard-coded with information specific to the domain for which they were developed.

The Web Storage System

It wasn't too long ago that e-mail administrators around the world would seek out and destroy (so to speak) users storing files and other data in their mailboxes. The common practice was not to allow the mail system to be used for file storage or file transfers. The Web Storage System encourages the opposite, and actually makes it quite inviting. It is now conceivable – and actually beneficial – to use Exchange 2000 server for storage purposes such as document management and data archiving.

The Web Storage System was designed as a flexible and extensible platform for storing, accessing, and organizing information, thereby supporting a variety of data access APIs and protocols. But most importantly, the Web Storage System was designed as a platform for sharing information by making it available to a wide range of clients through Web-based standards and protocols. With little or no code at all, you can make your data accessible across the Web through standard HTTP by exposing secure virtual directories, and by allowing clients access to your information using supported client tools such as Windows 2000 Web Folders, Office 2000, or the Outlook Web Access client. While you can provide access without any programming, you can use the Web Storage System as a powerful development platform for creating and deploying custom Web applications. With the Web Storage System, you can:

♦ Host Web sites and Web applications by storing your HTML, ASP, and other files in Web Storage System folders, making them accessible to the Web through IIS virtual directories.

♦ Create and register Web Storage System forms that are bound to your data and are rendered automatically when you access a specific folder or type of item, or when you issue a specific type of request for a resource.

♦ Use components of the Outlook Web Access client in combination with your own forms, views, or ASP applications to create a custom user interface that can be accessed via the Web.

♦ Build dynamic ASP pages that access Web Storage System data programmatically using the ActiveX Data Objects (ADO) or Collaboration Data Objects (CDO) object models, and are displayed automatically when a client requests certain items.

♦ Build powerful client-side applications using Distributed Authoring and Versioning (WebDAV) and eXtensible Markup Language (XML) to request and retrieve data, or even update data, from the Exchange server, and dynamically render the requested data to the user.

The Web Storage System offers a variety of choices to Web developers who want to build dynamic, data-driven Web applications that can be accessed by a wide range of clients.

The Web Storage System represents a single point of storage for all types of structured and semi-structured data, including messages, documents, audio/video files, and even databases and complete Web sites. Organizations storing data in several, often disparate, systems can now consolidate information storage into fewer servers and benefit from the new features of Exchange 2000, such as built-in collaboration tools, security, enterprise replication, and Web access.

From a development perspective, this means that applications can be created more quickly. You can collect data for storage from Microsoft Office and other products by using Web Folders, Web Sites using WebDAV, or Outlook 2000 using Public Folders to custom applications. You can access and manipulate data stored in the WSS using existing APIs such as ADO/OLEDB 2.5, CDO 2.0, XML, and even MAPI 1.2. No matter what kind of data you want to store, be they documents, databases, or audio files, they are all items in the store that you can access in the same way (see Figure 1-2).

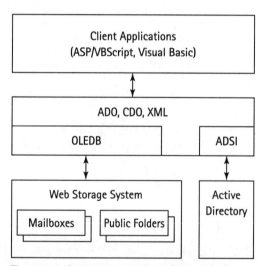

Figure 1-2: Exchange 2000 Data Access Model

Public Folder Trees

Exchange 2000 now supports the creation of multiple public folder trees. You can create additional trees with the Exchange System Administrator or by using code (see Chapter 6). Multiple public folder trees enable developers to store different types of folders on the same server while separating MAPI-type folders from folders that host applications. MAPI clients such as Outlook can access only the default public-folder tree, while Web browsers and IMAP clients can access data in additional public-folder trees as well as being able to access the default public-folder tree.

Accessing the Web Storage System

You can access data stored in the WSS in several ways. The next sections will introduce three common development methods for accessing data: CDO, ADSI, and ADO. (See Parts III and IV for more detailed information.)

CDO for Exchange

CDO has been completely remodeled for Exchange 2000. Although in their day the previous versions of CDO were invaluable for developing messaging applications, each consisted of a single library that was somewhat limited in functionality. While CDO 1.2 is still supported for backward compatibility with your existing applications, the version of CDO that ships with Exchange 2000 contains new features. The DLL's are listed in Table 1-1.

TABLE 1–1 CDO 2.0 DLLS

CDO	File Name	Description
CDO for Exchange 2000	Cdo.dll	Used for messaging, contacts, and scheduling
CDO for Exchange Management	Cdoexm.dll	Used for creating and managing mailboxes, and for managing security
CDO Workflow for Exchange	Cdowf.dll	Used for building workflow applications

Unlike previous versions of CDO, CDO for Exchange does not require a MAPI profile to make its connection to the server. Developers were previously forced to use CDO for NT Server (CDONTS) to develop messaging applications for the Web. CDONTS was useful, but limited to sending messages via SMTP (Simple Mail Transport Protocol); you couldn't validate an e-mail address against the Global Address book, for example. CDO for Exchange enables developers to create Web-based e-mail applications without CDONTS (see Listing 1-2) and offers full functionality to Web applications.

Listing 1-2: Example CDO Code that Creates and Sends E-mail

```
<%@ Language=VBScript %>

<html>
<head>
```

```
</head>
<body>

<%
'CDO Sample. Create and send an e-mail

'dim your variables
Dim rcpt
Dim from
Dim Subj
Dim body

'populate your variables
rcpt = "recipient@company.com"
from = "sender@company.com"
subj = "Sample: Create and send an e-mail using CDO"
body = "This is a test message"

'create the CDO object
Set Msg = CreateObject("CDO.Message")

'set the object properties and send the message
With Msg
   .To   = rcpt
   .From = from
   .Subject  = subj
   .TextBody = body
   .Send
End With

'display a success message
response.write "Message successfully sent to: " & rcpt

%>
</body>
</html>
```

You can use CDO in conjunction with ADSI to manipulate directory information specific to Exchange, such as by creating mailboxes for Active Directory users or creating public folders. ADSI features enable you to develop portable code so you won't have to hard-code domain names and other variables such as username in your applications. Listing 1-3 demonstrates querying LDAP for the root domain and then using the results to create a public folder in the appropriate place.

Listing 1-3: Using CDO to Create a Public Folder

```
<html
<body>
'CDO Sample. Creating public folder

<%@ Language=VBScript %>
<%

Dim sURL
Dim oLDAP
Dim sDomain

Set oLDAP = GetObject("LDAP://rootdse")
sDomain = oLDAP.Get("rootDomainNamingContext")
'result will be something like DC=DOMAIN, DC=.com

'convert DC=DOMAIN, DC=.com to domain.com
sdomain = replace(sdomain, "DC=", "")
sdomain = replace(sdomain, ",", ".")

'build the URL to  //domain.com/public folders/FolderName
sURL = "file://./backofficestorage/"
sURL = sURL & sDomain
sURL = sURL & "/public folders/FOLDERNAME/"

'create the CDO connection
set con = CreateObject("cdo.folder")

'set the folder properties then save new folder
with con
 .Description = "Test Folder"
 .contentclass = "urn:content-classes:folder"
 .Fields("http://schemas.microsoft.com/exchange/_
outlookfolderclass") = "IPF.Note"
 .Fields.Update
 .DataSource.SaveTo sURL
end with

response.write "Folder Successfully Created!"
%>

</body>
</html>
```

ADO 2.5

ActiveX Data Objects (ADO) has been around for some time, and it provides an easy-to-understand interface to databases such as Microsoft Access and SQL Server. Developers have grown used to using ADO for data access and can now use the skills they have learned to access data stored in the Exchange 2000 Web Storage System. Inthe same way you can use ADO to access an SQL database, you can use it to make a connection to the store and create recordsets for data manipulation. Furthermore, you can now make connections using an item's specific URL. Listing 1-4 demonstrates making a connection to a user's inbox using its URL.

Listing 1-4: Using ADO to Make a Connection to a User's Inbox

```
<HTML>
<BODY>
'ADO Sample. Data binding to a user mailbox

<%@ LANGUAGE = VBScript %>
<%

URL = "http://servername/exchange/useralias/inbox"

set conn = createobject("ADODB.connection")
conn.provider = "exoledb.datasource"
conn.open URL
response.write "Successful Connection!"

%>

</body>
</html>
```

File-system access to the Web Storage System

Applications using file-system storage can also be modified to access files stored in the Web Storage System (WSS). When Exchange 2000 server is installed, a drive mapping (usually M:\) is created automatically on the server. Administrators can share this directory, allowing users to browse their mailboxes as personal directories. Users can make a connection to this area and browse as they can on any other file server share or local drive (see Figure 1-3). Exchange configures security automatically so users can only browse public folders and their own mailboxes.

Before you can develop applications using these new technologies, you must fully understand the collaborative capabilities of Exchange Server 2000. The sections that follow introduce new features of Exchange 2000 that provide out-of-the-box collaboration. Once you know what you can do with Exchange 2000, you can create applications that automate and enhance those capabilities.

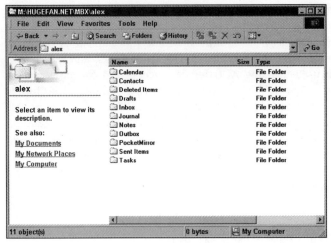

Figure 1–3: A user's mailbox displayed as a network drive

Web Folders

Web Folders enable you to save and edit files on a Web server from any application that supports the use of Web Folders, such as FrontPage, Word, or Excel.

Connectivity is also possible over the Internet through the Distributed Authoring and Versioning (WebDAV) protocol. WebDAV is a standard that extends the HTTP protocol to provide read and write access over the Internet to items in the WSS. This is especially convenient for users behind firewalls, because WebDAV uses port 80 just like any other Web site.

One benefit of storing items in the WSS and accessing them via Web Folders is that Microsoft Office documents are automatically cataloged when they are stored in the Web Store, which enables users to search for specific documents by their document properties. Since all information is stored in one central place, search results will also include documents, messages, and posts – potentially from public as well as private folders. See Chapter 5 for information on setting up search pages.

To give you an idea of how fast you can get started with collaboration, create a Public Folder called Marketing using the Exchange System Manager or the Outlook client. Now set the permissions on the folder, giving the anonymous user Author permissions. You now have the foundation for collaboration. Users can drag and drop items into this folder by way of browsing to http://<yourservername>/public/Marketing.

If you want users to be prompted for a username and password when accessing this folder, set the anonymous client permissions to none, and then assign appropriate permissions to users or groups.

Users can also edit and create data in this folder directly from Office 2000 products, such as Word or Excel, by creating a Web Folder. You can create a Web Folder by following these steps:

1. Open "My Network Places" from the client desktop.

2. Click "Add Network Place."

3. Enter the location of the Network Place (`http://<yourservername>/ public/marketing`).

4. Click Next and finish the Wizard.

Once created, the Web Folder looks like what is shown in Figure 1-4.

Figure 1–4: URL used to create a Web Folder named Marketing for Exchange 2000 Public Folder

After you complete these steps, your Web Folder is listed in My Network Places and is available for browsing (see Figure 1-5).

Figure 1–5: A Web Folder listed in My Network Places along with any drive mappings

Hosting Web Applications

Without the WSS, Web applications are stored in a directory on the Web server. This limits connectivity by requiring FTP access to add files, and a Web browser to view the data. Further, updating HTML files requires downloading them, editing them, and then uploading them again, unless of course you edit the Web site from the server itself. Since the WSS can host complete Web sites – including ASP – users can create and edit HTML and ASP pages directly from any application that supports the use of Web Folders. This technology reduces the cost of owning an intranet. Take, for example, an organization that has an intranet comprised of the following parts:

- ◆ A telephone directory that pulls information from the Human Resources SQL database

- ◆ An area where employees can read Human Resource information, such as policies and procedures manuals, online

- ◆ An area where employees can read Marketing material

While updating the telephone directory manually after its creation will most likely not be necessary, updating the Human Resources and Marketing areas requires several manual steps. Someone has to create the documents. Then someone else has to post the information to the Web site. Unless personnel in the Marketing and HR departments are trained in HTML editing and FTP software, this usually means that the administrator has to accept the documents, convert them to HTML, and upload them to the Web site.

With Exchange 2000 you can remove administrators from this scenario after creating the public folder. The administrator creates a public folder called, say, Main, and two subfolders beneath it, one called HR and one called Marketing. An HR designee is assigned the permissions to read and write to the HR folder, and a Marketing designee is assigned the permissions to read and write to the Marketing folder. Everyone is assigned read permissions to Main, HR, and Marketing.

The administrator creates any HTML and/or ASP pages, containing references to the HR and Marketing folder files, that are needed for the Main folder.

HR and Marketing can create Web Folders and use familiar applications such as Word or FrontPage to create and update HTML files in their respective folders with no assistance from the administrator. Users can open, edit, and save files to their current locations with no need for FTPing or administrator intervention.

Outlook Web Access (OWA)

Outlook Web Access (OWA) is Microsoft's Web client for Exchange 2000. The new OWA is closer to being a full-featured client then ever before, and it is a perfect example of the powerful development capabilities of Exchange 2000 Server. In many cases, OWA will be the client of choice, because it requires no software installation other than a Web browser and because it provides cross-platform support. Roaming users don't need to set up a MAPI profile to use OWA, and it is extended to Internet users easily.

One of the most exciting new characteristics of OWA is that each item has its own URL. Furthermore, each container has its own URL. This enables you to break OWA into pieces and display the information you want in the layout you want. You can use the URLs listed in Table 1-2 to access specific information.

TABLE 1-2 OUTLOOK WEB ACCESS DIRECT URLS

URL	Description
`http://server/exchange/alias/inbox?cmd=contents`	Opens the Inbox and displays contents
`http://server/exchange/alias/contacts?cmd=contents`	Opens Contacts and displays contents
`http://server/exchange/alias/notes?cmd=contents`	Opens Notes and displays contents
`http://server/exchange/alias/tasks?cmd=contents`	Opens Tasks and displays contents
`http://server/exchange/alias/calendar?cmd=contents`	Opens Calendar and displays contents
`http://server/exchange/alias/inbox?cmd=new`	Starts a new message from the Inbox

If you leave off the command, for example, `http://server/exchange/alias/calendar`, OWA will render the display in the familiar frameset containing the navigation menu on the left, as if you had started OWA normally and then navigated to your calendar. If you want to see the contents of any container in a window alone, you must type `?cmd=contents` at the end of the URL. You can use these URLs to create your own version of OWA as shown in Figure 1-6.

One thing missing from the new version of OWA is the login form. When a user logs into the default OWA Web site, his or her mailbox is displayed automatically based on the username used for authentication. I for one miss the old-style login page; fortunately, it's easy to recreate. You can create an HTML page that looks like the old login page, as shown in Listing 1-5.

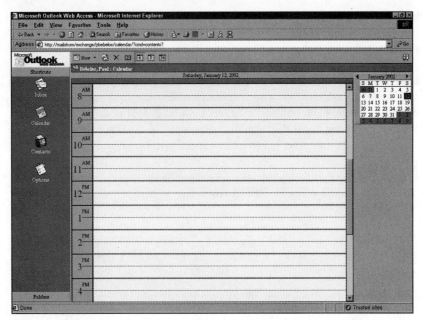

Figure 1-6: Contents of public folder without the Outlook bar on the left

Listing 1-5: Old-Style OWA Login Page

```
<HTML>
<HEAD>
   <TITLE>OWA Login Page</TITLE>
</HEAD>

<BODY>

<input type="text" name="Alias" size="25">
<br>
Enter your alias and then
<a href="http://server/exchange">Click here</a>.

</BODY>
</HTML>
```

In fact, if you have customized your OWA from Exchange 5.5, you can reuse that login.asp page. Just take out all the code and replace it with the href from Listing 1-5. In this case, it doesn't really matter what the user enters into the Alias box, since OWA will prompt for a username and password and find the correct mailbox based on that information.

However, if users have access to multiple mailboxes, it's convenient to allow them to type in an alias name before entering OWA. To do this, build an HTML page with a form that asks for the user's alias name and passes that information to an ASP page. The ASP page will build the correct URL and redirect the browser to the user's mailbox. OWA will again prompt for a username and password for authentication, and then open the mailbox requested. To make your own OWA login page, follow steps 1-3 below:

1. Create a directory under the `wwwroot` folder on the Exchange Server called OWA.

2. Create the login page that asks for the user's alias and call it `default.htm`:

```
<HTML>
<HEAD>
     <TITLE>OWA Login Page</TITLE>
</HEAD>

<BODY>

<FORM METHOD="GET" ACTION="exchange.asp">
<input type="text" name="Alias" size="25">
<input type="submit" value="Login">
</form>



</BODY>
</HTML>
```

3. Create an ASP page called `exchange.asp` to accept the user alias, and start OWA:

```
<%@ LANGUAGE = VBScript %>
<%
Dim alias
Dim sURL

alias = request.querystring("alias")
sURL = "http://servername/exchange/" & alias
response.redirect (sURL)
%>
```

Web Storage System Events

System events are actions that can trigger other actions. Scripts can be made to run every time a contact is updated, for example. You may also want to send an e-mail to a distribution list automatically when that contact information is changed. Or you may want to make sure the contact's phone number is in the proper format *before* saving the data.

System events were not accessible in earlier versions of Exchange, which made certain types of applications difficult to develop. Everything that happens in Exchange is an event. WSS events allow you to write code that will react to events without user intervention. The process of interacting with these events is known as creating a *system event sink*. System event sinks enable developers to create more robust applications that are client-independent.

Events are synchronous or asynchronous. Synchronous events happen *before* the change is committed to the store — actually, they happen once before (the *begin phase*) and once after (the *abort phase*). You can use synchronous events to validate or change data before the data are committed. This is more efficient than validating the data after they've been committed, and then deleting them if necessary and starting over. Consider an application that adds a disclaimer to each e-mail that is sent. The synchronous event can intercept the message, add the disclaimer to the message body, and then allow the message to continue.

Asynchronous events happen *after* data are committed, so they are best used to trigger notifications. You can also use them when it isn't necessary to stop the data from being committed. For example, you may want to send an e-mail notification when a folder is changed. You don't need to send the notification before the folder is changed, or at the exact moment that the change takes place; just promptly thereafter.

Summary

Exchange 2000 heralds a new era in the evolution of the e-mail administrator. The line between Exchange developers and Exchange administrators is getting thin. It won't be long before an Exchange administrator will be expected to be able to create at least moderately complex collaborative workflow applications. Administrators will have to change the way they think of messaging systems. The good news is that Exchange 2000 does a lot to make it easy.

Chapter 2

Development Tools and Environments

IN THIS CHAPTER

◆ Visual Basic 6.0

◆ The IIS 5.0 Environment

◆ Visual InterDev

◆ FrontPage 2000

EXCHANGE 2000 SERVER LENDS ITSELF quite well to development in the Active Server Pages (ASP) environment; however you do have choices. The kind of applications that you develop may dictate, or at least sway you towards, one development environment or another. This chapter will introduce some of the popular development tools and how to prepare them for Exchange 2000 development.

Visual Basic 6.0

Visual Basic (VB) is a powerful development environment with which many developers have become very familiar. However, if you're new to VB, you need to know certain things before you begin.

Exchange 2000 Server Development Kit (SDK)

The DLLs you need in order to program on the Exchange 2000 platform are installed automatically on the server on which Exchange 2000 Server is installed. If you plan to develop your code on a different computer, you need to obtain the DLLs and install them on your development workstation. These DLLs can be found in the Exchange 2000 SDK, which you can download at `http://www.microsoft.com/exchange`. The files included in the Exchange 2000 SDK are `codex.dll`, `cdoexm.dll`, and `cdowf.dll`. You may also need to distribute these files with your applications, so include them in the Application Setup Wizard.

Project references

Once the Exchange 2000 SDK is installed on your computer, you must add a reference to the DLL in your project before you can use it. To add the reference in VB 6.0, choose Project → References and select the appropriate DLLs (see Figure 2-1).

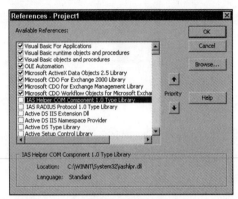

Figure 2–1: Visual Basic 6.0 project references

DLL's located in the c:\winnt\system32 are loaded automatically, but you can use the Browse button to include DLLs located elsewhere.

Sample application

The easiest way to understand Exchange 2000 development in VB 6.0 is to walk through an example. The following sample application will take you through the entire process of creating an application that makes a connection to your inbox and lists the subject of each message therein.

After starting Visual Basic, the first step is to create the new project file. To do this, choose File → New Project. When the New Project dialog box appears, choose Standard EXE and click OK.

The next step is to create the user interface – the part of the program that the user interacts with. For this application you will need a text box to list the subjects and a command button to start the application (see Figure 2-2).

Now you are ready to set the references for your project. Since this application will be enumerating records in the mailbox as a database, you will need the Microsoft ActiveX Data Objects 2.5 Library. To add the reference, choose Project → References. Refer to Figure 2-1.

At this point, the project is ready for coding. To get to the code area, double-click the Command button to expose the code window, shown in Figure 2-3.

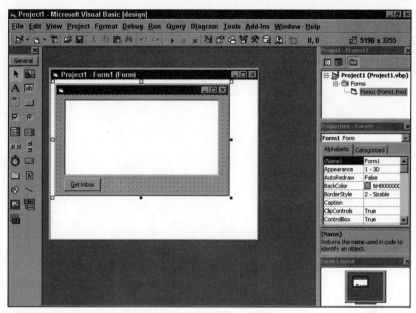

Figure 2-2: Sample application's user interface

Figure 2-3: Visual Basic 6.0 code window

Any code placed between the lines `Private Sub Command1_Click()` and `End Sub` will be executed when the user clicks the Command button. Here you want a subroutine to be executed. Listing 2-1 contains the subroutine that will make the connection and retrieve the messages from the inbox. Place this subroutine just below the `Private Sub Command1_Click()` and `End Sub` lines.

Listing 2-1: VB 6.0 example — Using ADO to connect to a users' inbox

```
Sub Get_Inbox()

Dim conn As ADODB.Connection
Dim rec As ADODB.Recordset
Dim URL As String
Dim strSQL As String

'Build the URL
URL = "http://<servername>/exchange/<alias>/inbox"

'Open a Connection
Set conn = New ADODB.Connection
 With conn
   .Provider = "exoledb.datasource"
   .Open URL
 End With

'Build the SQL Statement
strSQL = "SELECT  ""urn:schemas:httpmail:subject"""
strSQL = strSQL & " FROM SCOPE('shallow traversal of """ & _
URL & """')"
strSQL = strSQL & " where ""DAV:isfolder"" = false"

'Create the recordset
Set rec = New Recordset
 With rec
   .Open strSQL, conn
 End With

'Populate the Listbox
Do Until rec.EOF
 List1.AddItem rec.Fields("urn:schemas:httpmail:subject") & ""
 rec.MoveNext
Loop

rec.Close
conn.Close
Set conn = Nothing
Set rec = Nothing
End Sub
```

After creating this subroutine, you'll be left with the following:

```
Private Sub Command1_Click()

End Sub

Sub Get_Inbox()
...code
End Sub
```

Now, connect the Command button with the execution of this subroutine. Type the Call command in the Command1_Click() subroutine:

```
Private Sub Command1_Click()
  Call Get_Inbox()
End Sub
```

You are now ready to test your application. Press F5 to run the application (see Figure 2-4). There's no error handling in this example, so you'll be alerted to any errors that occur.

Figure 2-4: Running the application

Table 2-1 outlines the pros and cons of Visual Basic 6.0.

TABLE 2-1 VISUAL BASIC 6.0 PROS AND CONS

Pros	Cons
Early binding (speed)	Requires client installation
COM component development	You have to buy the software
Richer user interface	You must upgrade clients when you upgrade code
Less server processing	Only for Windows clients

The IIS Environment

Internet Information Server (IIS) 5.0 is the foundation on which ASP Web pages are built. ASP programming is probably the easiest code to develop in, in terms of preparation, because your Exchange 2000 Server is already going to have everything you need: IIS 5.0 and Exchange 2000 SDK DLLs. This section will introduce you to some of the environment settings in IIS 5.0 that you will need to know.

IIS management

IIS is managed with the Internet Service Manager MMC snap-in from the administration tools group. It is here that you will perform administration tasks related to permissions, auditing, and other settings.

Virtual directories

Virtual directories enable you to store Web content in a folder other than the default Web folder (usually `c:\inetpub\wwwroot`). The default installation of Exchange 2000 includes four virtual directories that OWA uses (see Table 2-2).

TABLE 2-2 EXCHANGE 2000 VIRTUAL IIS DIRECTORIES

Web Virtual Directory	Function
/exchweb	Stores graphics and other ancillary files that OWA uses
/exadmin	Used by the Exchange Administration tool to administer public folders
/exchange	Stores the mailbox root
/public	Contains the default public folders tree

A virtual directory named Public is created automatically when you install Exchange 2000, and any public folders that you create in that tree are accessible via the URL `http://<servername>/Public/<foldername>`. However, if you create additional Public Folder trees, you will have to create your own virtual directory to access them. You may also want to use a different URL to access the default public folders, such as `http://<servername>/<foldername>`. There are two ways to create virtual directories, each with different results. First, you can create a virtual directory directly from the Internet Services Manager. Second, you can create a virtual directory from the Exchange System Manager.

CREATING VIRTUAL DIRECTORIES WITH THE INTERNET SERVICES MANAGER

Most often, you will create and manage virtual directories from the Internet Services Manager. Virtual directories interact differently with Exchange Public Folders. Manually created virtual directories are not rendered by Outlook Web Access, and therefore behave more like FTP directories than like public folders. In some cases, this may be desirable, for instance if you want to set up a download area wherein clients can download files. In this case, your user only has to save files to the public folder using Outlook or Outlook Web Access, and then use a Web browser to download the files.

To create a virtual directory from the Internet Services Manager, use the Virtual Directory Creation Wizard:

1. Open the Internet Services Manager and right-click Default Web Site. Then choose New → Virtual Directory, as illustrated in Figure 2-5.

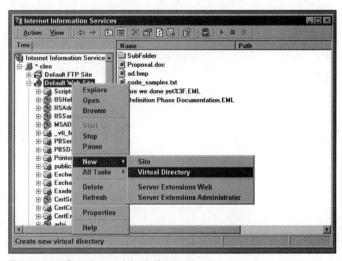

Figure 2-5: Creating a virtual directory

2. Click Next on the Welcome screen and you'll be prompted to name your virtual directory. Type a name in the alias box and then click Next.

3. Browse to the directory containing your public folder (see Figure 2-6).

4. After locating the public folder, click OK.

5. You'll be prompted to select permission settings. You must select at least Read and Browse. If you are hosting a Web site you may also need script permissions. Complete the wizard, by clicking the Finish button.

Figure 2-6: Browsing public folders

Your public folder is now viewable from any Web browser, just as if it were any other Web site. This folder can store any kind of data (see Figure 2-7).

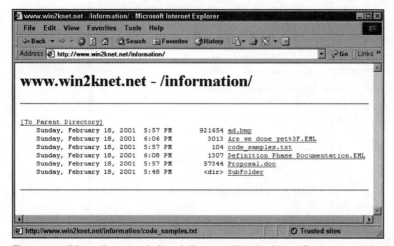

Figure 2-7: Manually created virtual directory linked with an Exchange public folder

 You need to set permissions to read and browse in order to view files in a public folder with this method. You can manage permissions on the public folder and select Allow anonymous access if you choose.

Notice that when you're viewing this folder, Outlook Web Access doesn't take over and render the page. This is because the virtual directory was not created from the Exchange System Manager. Virtual directories created through the Exchange System Manager are configured so that all files are parsed through the `Davex.dll`

file before being sent to the browser. `Davex.dll` is the Exchange implementation of WebDAV.

You can also store a Web site in this folder, by creating a default.htm Web page and posting it to the folder.

CREATING A VIRTUAL DIRECTORY FROM THE EXCHANGE SYSTEM MANAGER

In order to view the public folder with Outlook Web Access, you must create and manage the virtual directory using the Exchange System Manager. Refer to the "Creating a New Public Store" section in Chapter 3 for instructions on creating Exchange public-folder virtual directories.

Permissions

You can manage security to your Web site in one of four ways in IIS. Table 2-3 lists them and their descriptions.

TABLE 2-3 IIS SECURITY MANAGEMENT METHODS

Security Method	Explanation
IP and Domain Security	You can allow or deny access based on IP address or domain of client. For example, you can allow all users on a local IP segment to access a Web site, while giving users on the Internet no access.
IIS Authentication	You can control access based on the type of authentication you configure. Types of authentication are anonymous access, clear text, integrated Windows authentication, and Secure Sockets Layer (SSL).
IIS Permissions	You can control what actions are allowed — for example, reading, writing, running scripts, and directory browsing.
NTFS Permissions	Make use of NTFS. Using NTFS provides a higher level of security because only authenticated users who have been given explicit permissions can access.

Exchange 2000 public folders use NTFS permissions, so you can allow anonymous connections. Users will be prompted for usernames and passwords for NTFS security. However, if you are hosting ASP pages in your public folder, you need to also set the execute permissions to at least scripts only. You configure security management on the Properties page of the specific resource, as illustrated in Figure 2-8.

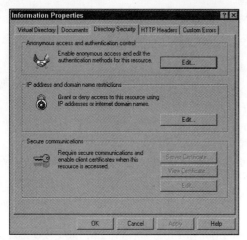

Figure 2-8: Directory Security Properties page

WWW applications

A WWW application is defined as the collection of directories, files, and sub-directories within them, designated as the starting point of your virtual directory. A WWW application enables you to control how your applications run and interact with the server and client. Configuring your application involves mapping filename extensions to the programs that interpret them. For example, an `.asp` file is mapped to the `asp.dll` located in the server's c:\winnt\system32 directory. Other settings include application options (Table 2-4) and application debugging (Table 2-5).

TABLE 2-4 APPLICATION OPTIONS SETTINGS

Setting	Description
Enable Session State	Causes ASP to create a session for each user so that you can identify each user across multiple Web pages
Session Timeout	Automatically ends a session if a user does not send or request information within the timeout period
Enable Buffering	Causes ASP to send information to the browser after it is collected, rather than as it is processed
Enable Parent Paths	Enables you to use relative paths in your ASP scripts
Default Language	States the default ASP language that will be used (ASP or JScript)
ASP Script Timeout	Specifies the length of time ASP will allow a script to run

TABLE 2-5 APPLICATION DEBUGGING SETTINGS

Setting	Description
Enable ASP server-side script debugging	Enables you to examine scripts during processing, but causes ASP to run in single-threaded mode
Enable ASP client-side script debugging	Reserved for future use; has no effect
Send detailed error messages	Sends detailed error information to client, including filename, error, and line number
Send text error message to client	Enables you to replace default error message with custom text message

When you use the Exchange System Manager to create your virtual directory, an application is created automatically. You can manage the application settings from the Internet Services Manager by right-clicking your virtual directory and choosing Properties. If an application has been created for this virtual directory, the Configuration button will be available, as shown in Figure 2-9.

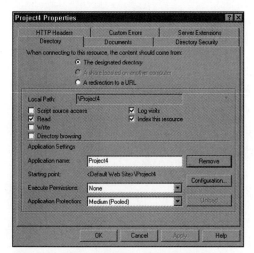

Figure 2-9: ASP application configuration

When you create a virtual directory using the Internet Services Manager, an application is not automatically created along with it. You need to create one yourself by clicking the Create button on the Virtual Directory tab.

You must create an application in order to use a global.asa file in your virtual directory's application. Otherwise IIS will use the configuration in the global.asa file.

Managing COM+ objects

COM+ objects enable you to take advantage of the benefits of Visual Basic in your ASP Web pages. These objects can also be shared between multiple ASP applications. The management of COM+ objects has been moved from the IIS Manager to the Windows 2000 Component Services Manager (see Figure 2-10), located in the Administration Group.

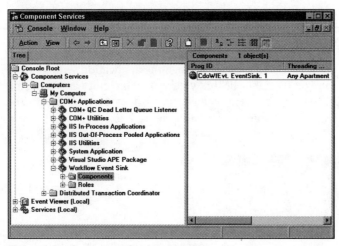

Figure 2-10: Component Services Manager

Creating your own COM+ objects requires extensive knowledge of Visual Basic and is a topic outside the scope of this book. While COM+ objects are very useful for designing Web-based applications, their use is not compulsory. Refer to the Microsoft Web site (http://msdn.microsoft.com) for more information about creating your own COM+ objects.

Visual InterDev

Visual InterDev (VI) is a Web site–editing tool with advanced features such as WYSIWYG (What You See Is What You Get), IntelliSense-enabled script development for statement completion, and step-through debugging. These features mimic those of the Visual Basic development environment more than any other editor's.

Visual InterDev is project-based, so while you can edit an existing ASP Web page by double-clicking it, to create one you must create either a new project or a new ASP Web page in an existing project.

The benefit of working with Visual InterDev is that you don't have to work on the server console to create and edit ASP Web-site applications. You can use Visual InterDev to connect to the Web server and create and edit files directly. Visual InterDev also enables you to create and edit Web sites locally, and then synchronize them with your production Web server.

As in Visual Basic 6.0, setting project references in Visual InterDev enables you to make use of the statement-completion feature (see Figure 2-11). To add a project reference, choose Project → Project References and select the components you wish to work with.

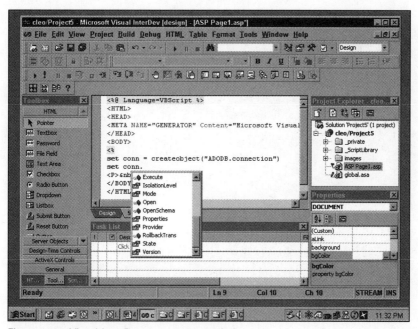

Figure 2-11: Visual InterDev statement completion

Also note that project references are automatically added to the project's global.asa file and can be used with other IntelliSense-enabled editors.

FrontPage 2000

FrontPage 2000 is another editing tool that has been enhanced for building Web sites on the IIS 5.0 platform. While it doesn't offer as many features as Visual InterDev, it does provide other editing and hosting features. Some of these features require processing on the Web server, which requires the installation of server extensions. The FrontPage Server Extensions are programs that run on the Web server to do the server-side processing.

You install the server extensions by installing FrontPage on your server and selecting Install Server Extensions from the FrontPage Installation Wizard. You do not need Server Extensions to develop applications with Exchange, but as with any development tool, using FrontPage can come in handy when you need to rapidly develop applications.

FrontPage enables you to connect directly to your Web server and create and manage Web sites. When you use FrontPage to create the Web site on your server, the Web site is marked as a FrontPage-enabled Web site. FrontPage adds a tab to the Web site's property page in IIS that enables you to configure the server extensions, as illustrated in Figure 2-12:

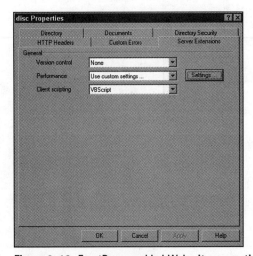

Figure 2-12: FrontPage-enabled Web-site properties

To create a new Web site using FrontPage, start the New Web Wizard (see Figure 2-13) by choosing File → New → Web.

In the Location drop-down box, type in the URL of your server plus the name of the new Web site (http://<servername>/new_Web_site_name). FrontPage will then create the directory on the server, create the IIS virtual directory, and enable the Web site for FrontPage server extensions.

Now create a Web page by going to File → New → Page. FrontPage features a normal view for WYSIWYG editing, and an HTML view for writing script.

Do not install FrontPage server extensions on a virtual directory created with the Exchange System Manager. Exchange System Manager configures files to be parsed through WebDAV, which interferes with FrontPage server extensions.

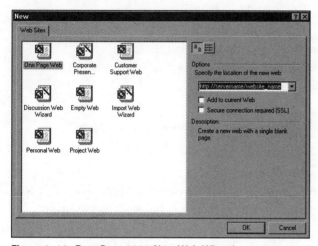

Figure 2-13: FrontPage 2000 New Web Wizard

Type Libraries and Constants

You need the Exchange 2000 SDK DLLs to provide access to Exchange 2000's constants. Constants are variables that represent values that you can use in your scripts. For example, you may need to access the CDO constant cdoActiveConnection. To access this and other constants, you need to make project references.

Type libraries assist with editing in Visual Basic 6.0 and Visual InterDev (as well as other IntelliSense-enabled editors). Each Exchange SDK DLL (codex.dll, cdoexm.dll, cdowf.dll,) has a built-in type library. When in the course of editing you make a reference to the Type Library in either the global.asa file or the specific ASP page you are working on, the Type Library displays all available datatypes or objects that are available. After typing ADODB followed by a period (.), for example, you will be prompted with available enumerations that you can use with ADODB.

To include the type libraries in your ASP page, add the following metadata lines to the ASP page after the `<HTML>` tag:

```
<!-METADATA
TYPE="TypeLib"
NAME="Microsoft CDO For Exchange 2000 Library"
UUID="{CD000000-8B95-11D1-82DB-00C04FB1625D}"
VERSION="1.0"-->

<!--METADATA TYPE="TypeLib"
NAME="Microsoft CDO for Exchange Management Library"
UUID="{25150F00-5734-11D2-A593-00C04F990D8A}"
VERSION="6.0"-->

<!--METADATA TYPE="TypeLib"
NAME="Microsoft CDO Workflow Objects for Microsoft Exchange"
UUID="{CD001000-8B95-11D1-82DB-00C04FB1625D}"
VERSION="1.0"-->
```

These metadata lines will include the CDO Type Libraries. You may also want to include the libraries for ADO or any other component you want to work with.

Summary

In the world of e-commerce, more and more applications are being developed for the Web environment: You will likely do some programming with ASP/VBscript. However, Visual Basic still beats VBscript when it comes to performance and features (like the ability to develop COM+ objects and DLLs). The fact that you can choose your development environment enables you to create powerful and robust applications more easily than before.

Part II

The Web Storage System

Chapter 3

Overview of the Web Storage System

OF THE MANY NEW TECHNOLOGIES introduced in Exchange 2000, one of the most innovative is the Web Storage System. Using the Web Storage System, developers can use advanced data-storage and information-sharing capabilities to enhance their existing applications, extend the out-of-the-box functionality of Exchange and Outlook, or create powerful new collaborative applications.

In this chapter, I provide an overview of the Web Storage System, describe its features and architecture, and explain the many ways in which you can use it to develop your own custom applications.

Introducing the Web Storage System

The Web Storage System is an advanced data storage technology that gives you a new way to store, manage, and interact with your data. It is a multi-purpose platform, combining the functionality of a traditional file system, a collaboration server, and a Web server in one package. Using the Web Storage System, you can store almost any type of information, from e-mail messages to documents to streaming multimedia data, and access this information using a variety of different clients and data-access tools. All data within the Web Storage System are organized into a hierarchy of folders and sub-folders, much as a traditional file system is organized. However, the Web Storage System provides many more capabilities that a traditional file system cannot. For example, the Web Storage System enables you to:

- ◆ Store and access data of any type, from simple documents and messages to multimedia data such as streaming audio and video

- ◆ Further identify, organize, and search for your data using numerous pre-defined properties, or by using an unlimited number of custom properties

- ◆ Access your data and properties through a wide variety of data-access protocols and interfaces, including access to all Web Storage System folders and items via URLs using HTTP/WebDAV

- ◆ Build queries that quickly search for information based on property values or the Web Storage System's powerful full-text search capabilities

- ◆ Host Web applications by storing your Web files in the Web Storage System, or build dynamic views to your data by creating Web Forms that integrate your application and data in the same location

- ◆ Secure your data with a comprehensive security model that is tightly integrated with Windows 2000 security – down to the item or even the property level

- ◆ Respond to events in the Web Storage System, such as an item being saved or a message being sent, by building Web event-sink components

In addition to offering many new features for developers, the Web Storage System is also used by Exchange 2000 to store and manage information. In previous versions of Exchange, all data were stored in either a single public or private information store; Exchange 2000 now uses the Web Storage System to manage both stores. Developers can access all the information managed by Exchange using the same data-access tools and technologies that they would use to access other Web Storage System data.

Although introduced with Exchange 2000, the Web Storage System is a data-storage technology that future Microsoft products, such as the Microsoft SharePoint Portal Server, will continue to use. SharePoint, formerly known as Tahoe server, will build upon the Web Storage System to provide advanced business-portal, document, content-management, and publishing features. As more products begin to incorporate Web Storage System technology, developers will be able to further take advantage of the features it offers.

Storing Your Data

Out of the box, the Web Storage System provides you with a wide variety of methods for storing and accessing your data. In addition to using the familiar Microsoft Outlook client, you can use Microsoft Office 2000 applications to directly access the Web Storage System via URL or by creating Web folders; you can use Windows Explorer through the Web Storage System's Installable File System (IFS) functionality; or you can use a Web browser to access items via URL using Outlook Web Access (OWA). This flexibility, in addition to the many options provided to developers for building custom data-access applications, is what makes the Web Storage System an ideal platform for collaboration and information sharing.

To demonstrate the flexibility of using different clients to manage the same data, Figures 3-1 through 3-4 show the contents of a public folder using Outlook, Office 2000, Windows Explorer, and Internet Explorer using Outlook Web Access (OWA), respectively.

In Figure 3-1, you can see several items, stored in a shared public folder named PublicInfo, as displayed using Microsoft Outlook. Through Microsoft's Messaging API (MAPI), Outlook interacts with the Web Storage System by enabling you to view folders and files, edit information, and post new items to folders — either by dragging and dropping or by sending them as e-mail attachments. Note the different types of items listed — Word documents, text files, e-mail messages, and a bitmap graphic. You can also see the properties of each item, such as the subject or file size, displayed in columns.

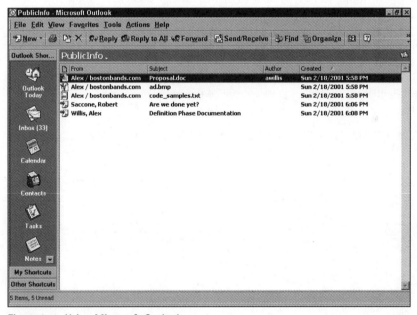

Figure 3-1: Using Microsoft Outlook

Figure 3-2 shows the contents of the same folder, this time from the File → Open dialog box in Word for Windows 2000. As you can see, you can type the URL to a folder directly in the dialog box. Additionally, you can click the My Network Places icon and create a Web folder, which is a shortcut to a Web Storage System folder that you can use to access documents with Office or Windows Explorer.

Figure 3-2: Using Microsoft Office 2000

You can also access the Web Storage System using Windows Explorer through the Exchange Installable File System (IFS) interface. On each Exchange server is mounted an M: drive, which gives access to each Web Storage System store as a file-system directory. The M: on the host server can either be accessed locally on the server or shared to network clients, who will view it as just another network drive. You can then use all the typical Explorer functionality to interact with Web Storage System data, such as dragging and dropping or copying and pasting. Figure 3-3 shows the PublicInfo folder on the M: drive of the Exchange server.

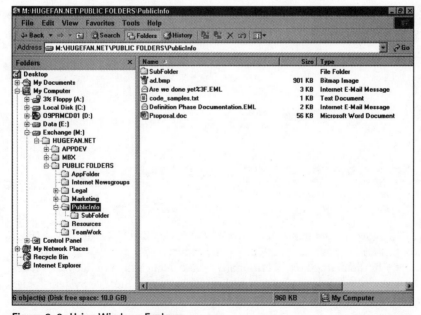

Figure 3-3: Using Windows Explorer

You can use a Web browser to access the Web Storage System remotely using Outlook Web Access. OWA with Exchange 2000 provides you with virtually the same functionality as the Outlook client, but communicates with the Web Storage System using the HTTP protocol, which is ideal for passing through Internet firewalls.

Figure 3-4 illustrates how to access the same folders and files using Internet Explorer and the OWA client.

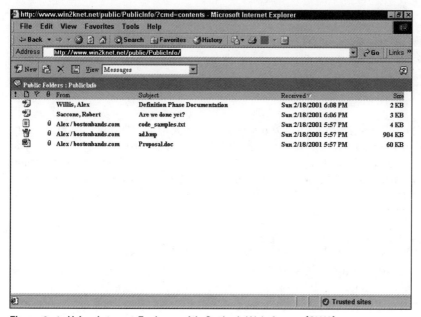

Figure 3-4: Using Internet Explorer with Outlook Web Access (OWA)

As you can see, the Web Storage System offers broad support for client access to the data it stores, giving users and developers alike many ways to access and manage their data.

The Web Storage System Architecture

The Web Storage System, first introduced with Exchange 2000, is a new data-storage technology designed to store any type of data and give you access to them from a wide range of clients and data-access technologies. It is a smart database that can easily evolve to meet your and your application's needs, and that uses industry-standard protocols and APIs to enable developers to leverage their existing skills when building custom applications.

Almost any type of data can be stored in the Web Storage System, including items that define the Web Storage System itself. In addition to storing data items such as documents and messages, the Web Storage System also stores properties associated with these items and makes them accessible to clients and data-access tools. These properties are defined in schemas that you can extend to create your own custom properties; the properties and schemas are stored as items themselves. Custom properties are defined and stored in the Web Storage System natively using XML.

 To learn more about item-properties schemas, see Chapter 4.

The Web Storage System is tightly integrated with the Windows 2000 security model and Active Directory services. Each item has a security descriptor that you can access in XML format, and that is based on the security-descriptor format defined by Windows 2000. You can set permissions on Web Storage System folders, items, or even on individual properties, and all permissions are based on user or group accounts maintained in the Active Directory.

The Web Storage System and Exchange 2000

The introduction of the Web Storage System has changed the storage architecture of Exchange 2000 quite a bit from previous versions. Exchange itself now uses the Web Storage System to store and manage all information in both public folders and each user's mailbox. As a result, many limitations of previous versions have been removed.

To better understand the architecture of the Web Storage System, you must first understand some key concepts and terms you use when administering Exchange. Exchange contains storage groups, each of which contains one or more information stores, which in turn contain the public folders and private mailboxes of each user. And unlike previous versions of Microsoft Exchange, which had only one public-information store and one private mailbox store per server, Exchange 2000 now supports multiple public and private stores, which can make identifying what is stored where even more confusing. Table 3-1 lists some terms and definitions that you should become familiar with before working with the Web Storage System.

TABLE 3-1 EXCHANGE 2000 KEY TERMS AND DEFINITIONS

Term	Definition
Information store	The storage technology used by Exchange 2000 to store mailboxes and public folders. Two types of specific stores exist in the Information store: Public stores and private (mailbox) stores.
Storage group	A collection of one or more public stores and mailbox stores. Each storage group uses a common set of transaction logs, and runs in its own server process.
Public folder store	A part of the information store that contains information in public folders. A public folder store consists of an .edb file, which contains rich-text data, and an .stm file, which contains streaming data. This is the equivalent of a Web Storage System store.
Private store (mailbox store)	A part of the information store that contains information in user mailboxes. A public folder store consists of an .edb file, which contains rich-text data, and an .stm file, which contains streaming data.
Database	A physical file storing information in the Information store. Two types of database files exist — an .edb file, which contains rich-text data, and an .stm file, which contains streaming data such as audio or video files.
Public folder tree	A single hierarchy of public folders. One public folder tree exists per public folder store.
Mailbox	The location where mail is delivered. User mailboxes are stored in private mailbox stores.

Exchange 2000 stores all information in one of two types of information stores — a public-folder store, which contains all the information in public folders, or a mailbox store, which contains all the information in user mailboxes. By default, Exchange creates a single public-folder store and a single mailbox store. Each of these stores consists of two database files, which physically contain the information in each store — an .edb file, used to store rich-text data, and an .stm file, used to store streaming data and Web content. Both the default public-folder store and the default mailbox store are contained in a single default storage group, which allows you to administer both stores together, and configures them to run in the same server process and to share the same transaction logging. Figure 3-5 describes the relationship between storage groups and stores, and shows how the groups are physically stored.

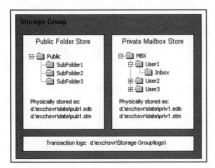

Figure 3-5: The relationship between storage groups, information stores, and databases.

In Exchange 2000 you can create new public or private stores, or new storage groups, in addition to the default stores. This is a significant improvement over previous versions, which only supported one public store and one private store per server. Now you can create additional top-level public-folder trees that can be shared by different groups of users, such as departments, or additional mailbox stores to split up the number of user mailboxes per store.

It is important to note, however, that the default public and private stores created by Exchange are the only stores configured for access by MAPI clients such as Microsoft Outlook. Unfortunately, Outlook users cannot access any new stores you create. However, these new stores are accessible through other clients, such as Outlook Web Access (OWA), or applications developed with ADO, CDO, or HTTP/WebDAV.

Also, Exchange 2000 now uses a *single-instancing* storage model to optimize data storage. For example, if the same message appears in more than one user's mailbox, the message item is physically stored only once in the Web Storage System. All mailboxes will point to this single instance of the item.

Each of the information stores in Exchange, public or private, is actually an individual Web Storage System store, with all of the functionality the Web Storage System provides. Whereas previous versions of Exchange used a somewhat limited data-storage architecture, Exchange 2000 is built upon and takes advantage of the robust data-storage capabilities of the Web Storage System. As a result, all the messaging and file information managed by Exchange is now accessible through the many data-access options that the Web Storage System provides. For example, you can access any mailbox, public folder, or item directly through a Web browser via URL, and the Web Storage System will automatically render the appropriate Web forms to display the information.

In addition, the Web Storage System's full-text indexing capabilities enable high-performance searching of all types of information in Exchange, such as e-mail messages or documents. This enables users to quickly find the information they need, using familiar tools such as the Outlook client, or custom applications using ADO and Web Storage System SQL queries.

Creating a New Public Store

Exchange 2000 provides you with the Exchange System Manager, an easy-to-use interface for managing storage groups and information stores. You can use it to create and manage Web Storage System stores and storage groups, create folders and mailboxes, set permissions, and create virtual directories to allow access to your data via HTTP and the Web.

In this section, I'll walk you through the process of creating a new public store using the Exchange System Manager. I'll also walk you through the process of creating a virtual directory to allow clients to access the new folder tree via the Web. The process is fairly straightforward, and can be summarized in the following basic steps:

1. Create a new public folder tree.

2. Create and mount a new public store, and associate it with the new folder tree.

3. Optionally define one or more virtual directories referencing a folder or folders.

You must create a new public folder tree before creating a new public store. If you attempt to create a new public store without first creating a new folder tree, you will receive an error. Open the Exchange System Manager and find Folders, as shown in Figure 3-6. Right-click Folders, select New, and then select Public Folder Tree. Enter the folder-tree name in the Properties dialog box and then click OK.

Figure 3-6: Creating a new public-folder tree

Next you must create a new public store and associate it with the folder tree you just created. (In this example we will also create a new storage group to contain the new public store.) In the Exchange System Manager, right-click the server icon, select New, and then select Storage Group. In the Properties dialog box that appears, enter a name for the new storage group and specify a location for transaction logs and system files. Click OK when you are finished. Figure 3-7 shows the new storage-group dialog box.

Figure 3-7: Creating a new storage group

Next you will create a new public store in the new storage group. Right-click the storage group, select New, and then select Public Store. Note that you can also create a new private Mailbox Store here as well. After entering a name for the store, you must associate it with the folder tree you created. Click the Browse button next to the "Associated public folder tree" text box to view all available folder trees, and select the folder tree you just created. (You should also look at the other tabs located in the Properties dialog box. Note the physical database-file locations displayed under the Database tab.) Click OK when you have finished. You will be prompted to mount the new store. Click Yes to mount the store – you will be alerted when the store has been successfully mounted. Figure 3-8 shows the new public-store dialog box.

The final step is to create a new virtual directory to give clients access to your new public-folder tree through OWA or other clients and data-access tools. You do this by first expanding the Protocols folder under the server, and then expanding the HTTP and Exchange Virtual Server groups. Listed below Exchange Virtual Server you will see all the registered virtual directories already created. Right-click Exchange Virtual Server, select New, and then select Virtual Directory. The Virtual Directory Properties dialog box will appear. Enter a name and then select the public folder you want to publish as a virtual directory. Here you can select any public folder in any public-folder tree – you are not limited to the top-level folder. This is useful when you are creating separate virtual directories for each of your applications, regardless of where they are physically located in the folder structure.

Figure 3-8: Creating a new public store

 Do not use the Internet Services Manager to create virtual directories; you must follow the steps listed for the Exchange System Manager. Although it is possible, by pointing to the M: drive of the Exchange Server, to create a virtual directory using the Internet Services Manager, you will not be able to access the Web Storage System correctly using this method.

You can test your new public folder by launching Internet Explorer and entering the URL to your new virtual directory – for example, `http://www.your-domain.com/AppFolder/`. Using OWA, the default Web form registered, the Web Storage System will display your new folder and its contents. You can then post items to the folder using OWA, create a Web folder using Windows Explorer and drag items into the folder, or save documents directly to the folder using the Microsoft Office Save As dialog box and entering the URL to the folder directly.

Developing with the Web Storage System

As you can see, the Web Storage System, with all of its client access methods, metadata management, and security features, can meet most of your data-storage requirements without requiring that you write any code at all. Its ability to efficiently store and organize almost any type of data makes it a powerful tool. The ability to effectively manage information and knowledge is critical to the success of any business, and the out-of-the-box features of the Web Storage System can facilitate the knowledge management process.

But in addition to the robust features the Web Storage System provides by default, it provides a rich set of tools and technologies that developers can use to extend its functionality and build powerful applications that manage and interact with the data stored in it.

Data-access APIs and protocols

The Web Storage System supports many data-access APIs and protocols, which make the information it stores available to a wide range of clients. Whereas previous versions of Exchange provided access to items through only the Messaging API (MAPI) interface, Exchange 2000 and the Web Storage System now support the following API interfaces in addition to MAPI:

- ◆ You can use the Exchange OLEDB interface along with ActiveX Data Objects (ADO) 2.5 to navigate and manage folders and items through server-side ASP applications or COM+ components.

- ◆ You can use Collaboration Data Objects (CDO) for Exchange 2000 to develop collaborative applications that use the messaging, calendaring, or contact-management features of Exchange. You can even use CDO to build powerful workflow applications that respond to events generated by the Web Storage System, or to create applications that administer Exchange using CDO for Exchange Management.

- ◆ You can access the Web Storage System using the industry-standard HTTP protocol. You can use the HTTP protocol, enhanced through the Web Distributed Authoring and Versioning (WebDAV) specification, to create or modify folders and items, or to search for items by specifying specific commands and parameters using eXtensible Markup Language (XML).

- ◆ You can access Web Storage System data through the Exchange Installable File System (IFS) interface, which enables you to view and modify information using Windows Explorer or the Win32 file-system API.

- ◆ The Web Storage System also gives you access to data using other industry-standard protocols, such as POP3 or IMAP4, although these protocols are primarily used to access private mailbox information.

By providing many ways to access and store information, the Web Storage System gives developers the opportunity to leverage their existing skills and use their preferred methods to access the same data. If you are a database developer, you can use familiar ADO Connection and Recordset objects to navigate and search for information. If you are a Web developer, you can use HTTP/WebDAV and XML to access and manipulate data. You can use the new CDO for Exchange objects to send messages and manage contacts or calendar information. In most scenarios, you will find that you can use a combination of any or all of the data-access technologies to build robust applications that will meet your requirements.

Web forms

To effectively manage and secure your data, you can design and use Web forms, Web pages that are automatically displayed by the Web Storage System when you access a specific folder or item. For example, you can create and register an HTML or ASP page that displays the custom properties of items designated by a custom content class. Whenever a user accesses an item of the content class you defined, your custom page appears instead of the default Outlook Web Access form.

The Web Storage System can also detect the type of browser you are using and use this information to determine the appropriate form or forms to display. This eliminates the need to develop for particular browsers or browser versions – the Web Storage System will simply render the appropriate form for the client.

All Web forms are registered in the forms registry, and each form registration is actually an item stored in the Web Storage System with specific properties set to identify the parameters defining the form, such as the folders or items the form is associated with. You can create form registrations programmatically by using code, or graphically by using tools provided with the Web Storage System SDK.

For more information regarding Web forms and form registrations,
see Chapter 10.

Web Storage System events

Whenever an item is saved, deleted, moved, or copied within the Web Storage System, a Web Storage System event is triggered that can be monitored and responded to by specialized COM+ components called *event sinks*. You can build complex logic within these components that can set item properties, check the validity of items, or notify users as certain actions occur that involve your data. And with the help of the CDO Workflow object model and the graphical Exchange Workflow Designer, you can create powerful workflow applications with which to track items as they move through the workflow process.

You can also monitor events that are triggered when a store is mounted or dismounted or when a certain amount of time has elapsed, and respond to these events either synchronously or asynchronously.

For more information regarding Web Storage System events and creating
workflow applications, refer to Part V, "Workflow Applications."

With all of this flexibility and all of these advanced features, what types of applications can you build using the Web Storage System? The following are some examples.

DOCUMENT OR KNOWLEDGE MANAGEMENT SYSTEMS

With its ability to store and organize almost any type of information, it's easy to see how the Web Storage System can effectively manage a company's electronic information. And because most businesses' information and knowledge is stored in documents, you can leverage the Web Storage System to create powerful knowledge-management applications that make it easy for users to organize, find, secure, and access the business's information.

WORKFLOW APPLICATIONS

You can use the Web Storage System's event model, along with the CDO Workflow object model and the workflow engine, to create complex workflow applications that track the state of documents. The workflow engine enables you to control the various state transitions of documents as they advance through a workflow process and respond to the events triggered by various actions by checking the current state of the document. It reacts according to a user-definable list of actions, which you can create easily using tools such as the Workflow Designer for Exchange.

WEB APPLICATIONS

As its name implies, the Web Storage System is tightly integrated with Web protocols and technology, such as the industry-standard HTTP protocol and the Extensible Markup Language (XML). The Web Storage System's ability to host Web sites, to automatically render custom Web forms or components of Outlook Web Access, and to support multiple protocols and server-side technologies, make it an ideal platform for developing robust Web applications.

Summary

The Web Storage System is a powerful new data storage engine that gives developers an entirely new set of tools to develop robust data-driven applications. In the following chapters, we will examine the Web Storage System in more detail, describing how data is stored and how you can customize it to meet your needs.

Chapter 4

The Web Storage System Schema

THE WEB STORAGE SYSTEM can store a multitude of items consisting of many different types and formats, and can organize these items and make them available to a wide range of clients or data-access tools. The Web Storage System also stores a wide range of properties for each of the items stored within it. All of these properties, and the definitions of the items themselves, are stored in Web Storage System schemas.

Not only does the Web Storage System use properties to store and maintain information about items in addition to the contents of the items, but it also uses some predefined properties to identify certain types of items or folders, such as schema folders, or even the items stored in schema folders that define the properties themselves.

The Web Storage System schema provides a means for defining the properties of each item, and also enables you to create your own custom properties to be used by individual items or shared among items in folders. This chapter describes the architecture of schemas, content classes, and properties, and how you can use them to extend the functionality of the Web Storage System. Later in the chapter I will walk you through creating your own schema and defining custom content classes and properties.

Web Storage System Schemas

The Web Storage System uses schemas to define the various types of items and their properties stored within it. In more traditional database terms, you can think

51

of the schema as a data dictionary, defining all of the columns or fields in a table. The Web Storage System, however, is not as strictly defined as a traditional relational database. The schema is completely extensible: It enables you to add additional custom properties without restructuring the way data are stored. This flexibility is what enables the Web Storage System to store and organize so many disparate types of data.

Schema folders

Schema information is stored in one or more folders in the folder tree. Each folder in the Web Storage System references at least one schema folder, but may reference an unlimited number of additional folders to gain access to more properties. By default, the Web Storage System creates a single hidden global-schema folder in which all predefined properties and classes are stored. The URL to the global schema is `http://www.your-domain.com/public/non_ipm_subtree/schema/`.

All new folders created in the Web Storage System reference this folder and have access to all the predefined properties and content classes stored in it.

In folders that reference more than one schema folder, property definitions are searched for starting in the default schema stored in the folders's `urn:schemas-microsoft-com:exch-data:schema-collection-ref` property. Any additional schema references, which are stored in an array in the folder's `urn:schemas-microsoft-com:exch-data:baseschema` property, are then searched in the order in which they were defined. All of the schemas referenced by a folder are referred to as the folder's *schema scope*; each folder in the Web Storage System can have a different schema scope — ranging from a simple reference to the global schema, to a long list of schema-folder URLs.

Property definitions

Each item stored in the Web Storage System has a rich set of predefined properties describing various attributes of the item, such as the display name of the item, its content class and type, and its security settings. Although items can share common properties defined in the schema, each item can conceivably have a completely different set of properties. For example, a document might have author or editor properties and a contact item might have an e-mail address or a contact-name property, but both items can share a display-name property. You can also extend an item's properties by defining your own custom properties and using them to further identify, organize, and search for items. All predefined and custom properties and property values are saved in the Web Storage System along with each item, and you can access these values specifically by property name.

Defining your own item properties is extremely useful for storing information about an item in a structured fashion, as opposed to relying solely on the contents of the item. For instance, suppose you create a Microsoft Word proposal that must be reviewed and ultimately approved by several people. You can create a custom `Status` property that can be updated at various points in the review process to reflect the document's current status (such as reviewed, rejected, or approved). You can then examine this property value to determine where you are in the approval process, and update the value at each point in the process. This is one approach to making powerful workflow and state-management applications. (Please refer to Part V, "Workflow Applications," for detailed coverage of using Exchange 2000 and the Web Storage System for workflow applications such as this.)

Creating properties item by item is limiting. You cannot use properties added to an individual item to search for information, or share these item properties among multiple items. Only property definitions defined in a schema and associated with a content class are searchable, but all custom properties are available individually: You can examine each item using a data-access API or client software (including MAPI clients such as Outlook).

It's important that you understand schemas and properties if you're going to build applications that will query the Web Storage System, because you will use properties for search criteria or sorting results. I'll discuss querying and sorting items in Chapter 5.

Properties and Namespaces

Each of the properties defined in a Web Storage System schema is further organized into namespaces. Namespaces are simply string values that group related properties together. For example, different types of items, such as documents or contacts, use different namespaces to organize their properties in a logical way. You can also use namespaces to ensure that property names are unique. A property named `value` in one namespace may have an entirely different meaning from a property named `value` in another namespace. For these reasons, property names are always comprised of both the namespace and the property name, according to the Uniform Resource Identifier (URI) naming conventions. The URI syntax is an Internet standard convention for identifying resources on the Internet – either by location, using a Uniform Resource Locator (URL), or by unique name, using a Uniform Resource Name (URN). The names of all properties, including custom namespaces and properties, follow this convention.

Items can use a combination of predefined and custom properties from several namespaces at the same time, including both built-in and custom namespaces. Figure 4-1 illustrates how properties and namespaces are stored and shared.

Various vendors and Internet standards groups have defined many existing namespaces. The prefix to the name of the namespace usually identifies the source or purpose of the namespace. For example, namespaces beginning with `http://schemas.microsoft.com/` are specific to Microsoft products, and namespaces beginning with `urn:schemas` are registered and defined in accordance with various

Internet standards. Exchange 2000 uses both Microsoft-specific namespaces and non-product-specific standard namespaces; developers can take advantage of both. Table 4-1 lists some of the most common namespaces in the Web Storage System.

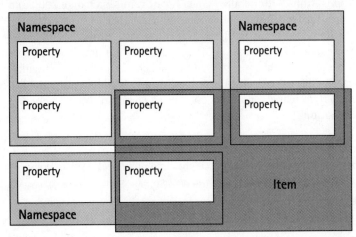

Figure 4-1: Web Storage System items can use properties from several different namespaces.

TABLE 4-1 WEB STORAGE SYSTEM NAMESPACES

Namespace	Description
DAV:	Properties used by the Web-based Distributed Authoring and Versioning (WebDAV) protocol. WebDAV properties generally include information used for storing and accessing data.
http://schemas.microsoft.com/exchange/	Properties specific to the Web Storage System and Exchange 2000. Related namespaces include the http://schemas.microsoft.com/exchange/events/ and http://schemas.microsoft.com/exchange/security/ namespaces.
urn:schemas:microsoft-com:office:office	Properties specific to Microsoft Office documents.

Namespace	Description
`urn:schemas-microsoft-com:office:forms`	Properties used by HTML forms in the Web Storage System.
`urn:schemas:microsoft-com:datatypes:`	Definitions for data types used to create custom schemas and properties.
`urn:schemas:microsoft-com:exch-data:`	Definitions for specific data types used by Exchange in the Web Storage System.
`urn:schemas:microsoft-com:xml-data:`	Definitions for eXtensible Markup Language (XML) namespaces.
`urn:schemas:calendar:`	Properties used by calendaring items.
`urn:schemas:contacts:`	Properties used by contact items.
`urn:schemas:httpmail:`	Properties used to define the body of an e-mail message.
`urn:schemas:mailheader:`	Properties used in the header of an e-mail message.

Defining custom namespaces and properties

When creating custom properties, you will also need to define your own namespaces to organize them. It is important to note that the names you choose for your namespaces must not only be unique among those you have already defined, but may also need to be unique across the Web, depending on your application. Here are some naming guidelines to keep in mind when defining your own namespaces:

◆ To avoid confusion and to distinguish your custom properties from predefined properties, don't use names that have already been defined, or that are similar to the names of existing namespaces.

◆ To ensure uniqueness, use your registered domain name in the namespace, such as `urn:schemas-your-domain:` or `http://schemas.your-domain.com/your-schema/`.

◆ If you cannot use a registered domain name, you can use a Globally Unique Identifier (GUID), which you can generate through several utilities and which are guaranteed to be unique. Keep in mind that GUIDs are quite long and may be difficult to read in your code.

Specific guidelines also exist for naming your custom properties and constructing fully qualified property names. Properties are always referenced by their full names, which consist of the namespace and the local property name together, separated by a specific separation character. The separation character is dependent on the characters that appear at the end of the namespace URI: For example, if the namespace name ends with the character /, :, or ?, the property name is simply appended to the namespace URI, as follows:

```
"DAV:" & "contentclass" = "DAV:contentclass"
"urn:schemas:mailheader:" & "sender" = urn:schemas:mailheader:sender
```

If the namespace name ends in any other character, append the # character to the namespace URI to separate the namespace from the property name, as follows:

```
"urn:schemas-microsoft-com:office:office" & "Title" =
"urn:schemas-microsoft-com:office:office#Title"
```

Using these naming guidelines is especially important when you're referencing properties using HTTP/WebDAV or XML, because if you neglect to use the correct separator character between a namespace URI and a property name, a # character is automatically inserted, which may cause you to inadvertently set or create the wrong property!

The Exchange Explorer

The Exchange Explorer, included with the Exchange SDK, is an invaluable tool for browsing and viewing folders and items and their properties. Using this tool, you can become familiar with the property settings used by the different types of items, including content class and property definition items that you've created.

In addition to being an extremely useful tool for exploring the various items and properties in the Web Storage System, the Explorer enables you to create new folders, items, content classes, and property definitions, which can make defining your own properties and content classes in custom schema folders much easier. You can also use the Exchange Explorer to easily register Web forms and Web Storage System event sinks through the provided registration wizards.

Figure 4-2 shows the Exchange Explorer interface.

I'll discuss Web forms and Web Storage System Events in detail in Chapter 10, "Web Storage System Forms," and in Chapter 18, "Web Storage System Events," respectively.

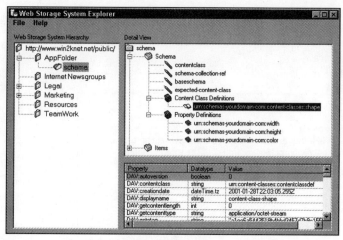

Figure 4-2: The Exchange Explorer interface

Content Classes

You can use content classes to identify the purpose of an item within a folder or application, and also to define the properties used by items in the class. Content classes do not define what kind of item it is associated with, such as a Microsoft Word document or e-mail message; rather they define the way in which the item should be interpreted or processed by an application.

One example that illustrates using content classes is an expense report content class. Suppose you are building an expense-report submission application that must be able to accept both Microsoft Word and Microsoft Excel expense reports. These are very different types of items, but as expense reports both share common properties, such as date submitted and total expense amount. You can create an expensereport content class and associate properties with the class, and then set each expense report item's DAV:contentclass property to the expensereport class. By doing so, you enable your application to process any expense report, regardless of what type of item it is. Figure 4-3 shows how many different items can be of the same content class.

Content classes identify not only the purpose of an item, but also the properties shared by each item in the content class. This does not mean that an item of a specific content class is limited to the properties defined by the content class. You can think of the content class as a template of properties for an item, or a starting point from which you can add more properties. As I mentioned earlier in this chapter, custom property definitions must be associated with a custom content class defined in a folder's schema if you want them to be shared by multiple items in that folder. Each schema stores property and content-class definition items, and also associates properties with each content class. This does not mean that every custom property must be associated with a content class – you can create individual item-level properties that are not associated with a content-class definition.

"ExpenseReport" content class

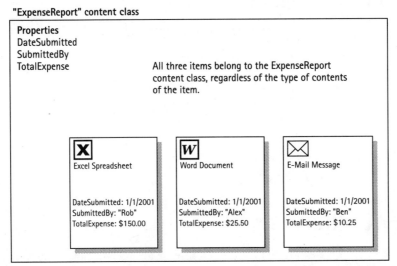

Figure 4–3: Many items can be assigned the same content class, regardless of the type of item.

Instead of creating entirely new content classes and sets of properties, in some situations you may simply want to extend the properties of an existing content class. For example, a content class defining basic document properties such as "author" might be adequate for storing simple documents, but you may want to define a few additional properties to enhance your document-management capabilities. You can create a new content class that *inherits* all the properties of the existing document-content class, plus any additional properties you create, without your having to define the existing properties again. Content classes are able to accomplish this by setting the urn:schemas-microsoft-com:xml-data#extends property of the new class to the name of the existing content class you are extending. This concept may seem familiar to many experienced software developers, as many object-orientated programming languages support class or object inheritance. Figure 4-4 illustrates how content classes can inherit the properties of other content classes.

Folders can also be assigned a content class, which will identify the default class of items that the folder will store. A folder with a specifically defined content class can still store any type of item, but the folder will essentially be optimized to store items of the defined content class. By default, folders are assigned a content class of urn:content-classes:folder, which identifies them as general-purpose folders that can store any type of item. Table 4-2 lists additional folder-content classes used by Exchange 2000.

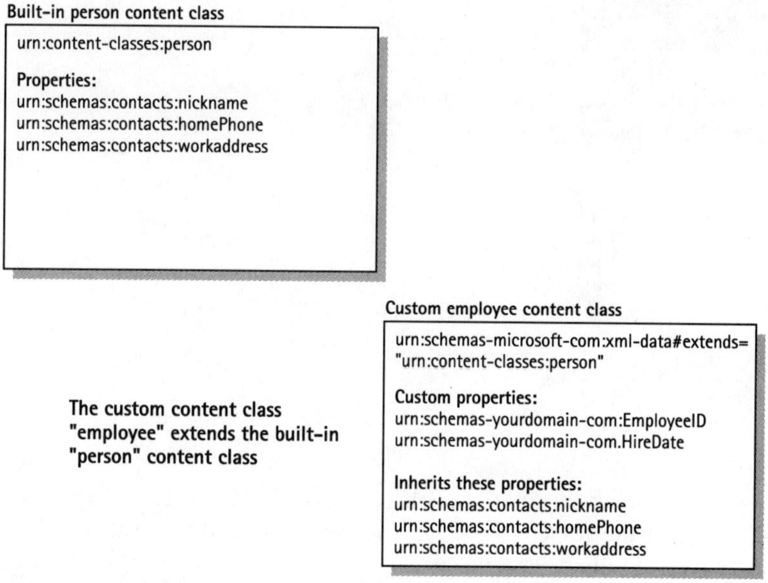

Built-in person content class

```
urn:content-classes:person

Properties:
urn:schemas:contacts:nickname
urn:schemas:contacts:homePhone
urn:schemas:contacts:workaddress
```

The custom content class
"employee" extends the built-in
"person" content class

Custom employee content class

```
urn:schemas-microsoft-com:xml-data#extends=
"urn:content-classes:person"

Custom properties:
urn:schemas-yourdomain-com:EmployeeID
urn:schemas-yourdomain-com.HireDate

Inherits these properties:
urn:schemas:contacts:nickname
urn:schemas:contacts:homePhone
urn:schemas:contacts:workaddress
```

Figure 4-4: Content classes can contain their own properties in addition to inheriting the properties of other content classes.

TABLE 4-2 SOME PREDEFINED FOLDER-CONTENT CLASSES USED BY EXCHANGE

Folder Content Class	Description
urn:content-classes:contactfolder	Contacts folder
urn:content-classes:mailfolder	Folder that store e-mail messages
urn:content-classes:taskfolder	Tasks folder
urn:content-classes:calendarfolder	Calendar folder
urn:content-classes:notefolder	Notes folder
urn:content-classes:journalfolder	Journal folder

Note that the folder content classes listed above correspond with the default mailbox folders in Exchange. In fact, Exchange explicitly sets the DAV:contentclass property for each mailbox folder and also when new folders are created using Microsoft Outlook. See Figure 4-5 to see Outlook's new folder dialog box and how the folder-creation options correspond to the folder-content classes.

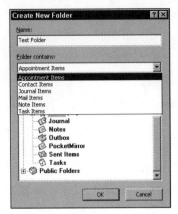

Figure 4-5: Content classes listed in Microsoft Outlook's New Folder dialog box

You can also define a set of other content classes that the folder will typically store. This set is called the folder's *expected content class*, and you can set it by assigning one or more content-class names to the `urn:schemas-microsoft-com:exch-data:expected-content-class` property of the folder item. This property is important for searching a folder's contents, as the list of properties available to queries is constructed by the Web Storage System by gathering the properties of all of the expected content classes of the folder.

Defining Content Classes and Properties

Before creating your own content classes and properties, it is a good idea to create a custom-schema folder for your application. Although you can add content classes and properties to the default schema, it is a better practice to create your own schema in which to store all the properties specific to your application. You can always reference both the default schema and your custom schema from any folder you create.

 You do not have to define your custom properties in a schema, as you can simply add properties to an item individually. But if you do not define your properties and associate them with content classes, you will not be able to search for items using those properties.

In the following sections, I'll walk you through the process of creating your own schema folder, defining custom-content classes, and defining new custom properties.

You will also discover how to reference your new schema from your application folders, and how to set item properties within these folders.

Creating a schema folder

Before you can use your created content classes and properties, you must first create a custom-schema folder. This folder will store all your custom-property and content-class definition items and will be referenced by any folders that contain items that use your custom properties.

The first step in defining a custom schema is to create a new folder item in which to store schema information. This schema is essentially a folder like any other, but with a few changes to specific property values. After creating the new folder item, set its `urn:schemas-microsoft-com:exch-data:baseschema` property to the Web Storage System's global-schema folder. (Referencing the global schema from your custom schema will allow applications to use your custom properties as well as the predefined content classes and properties defined in the global schema.) Then set the `DAV:ishidden` property of the new folder item to a value of `True` so the folder will not appear in client applications.

Listing 4-1 provides an example of how to create a schema folder using ADO and ASP/VBScript. First the example defines the URL to the new schema folder, and also defines the URL to the global schema folder. (The example assumes that a folder named `AppFolder` already exists in the public folder.) Next it creates an ADO `Record` object and calls the `Record.Open` method using the `adCreateCollection` parameter to create a new folder item. (Also note the `adModeReadWrite` and `adModeShareExclusive` parameters, where `adModeReadWrite` requests read/write access in order to create the new folder, and the `adCreateCollection` parameter indicates that you are creating a folder, not a single item.) After setting the appropriate properties, the example saves the changes and closes the connections.

It is not uncommon to encounter locking and sharing errors when using the ADO `Record` object to create folders or items, especially in production systems with active users and connections. It is a good idea to include the `adModeShareExclusive` parameter when creating a new item, as it will prevent other users or processes from accessing the item until the item is created.

Also, before you can use ADO and other constants such as `adModeShareExclusive` in your ASP or VBScript applications, you must either define all constants or reference the type libraries that define these constants. ASP can use the new `METADATA` tag to directly reference the type library of an ActiveX component. The code examples in this book exclude these references for simplicity, but you can see how this is accomplished in the code examples included on the CD-ROM.

Listing 4-1: Using ADO to Create a New Schema Folder

```
Dim sNewSchemaURL
Dim sGlobalSchemaURL

' URL to the new folder item
sNewSchemaURL = "http://www.your-domain.com/public/AppFolder/schema/"

' URL to the global schema folder
sGlobalSchemaURL = "http://www.your-domain.com/public/non-ipm-subtree/schema/"

Dim Rec
Set Rec = CreateObject("ADODB.Record")

Dim Conn
Set Conn = CreateObject("ADODB.Connection")
Conn.Provider = "ExOLEDB.DataSource"

' open a connection
Conn.Open sNewSchemaURL

' create the new folder and set properties to reference
' the global schema and to hide the new folder from client applications
With Rec
    .Open sNewSchemaURL, Conn, adModeReadWrite Or adModeShareExclusive, _
adCreateCollection
    .Fields("urn:schemas-microsoft-com:exch-data:baseschema") = _
Array(sGlobalSchemaURL)
    .Fields("DAV:ishidden") = True
    .Fields.Update
    .Close
End With
Conn.Close
```

You can also use the HTTP/WebDAV protocol and XML to create a schema folder. Listing 4-2 creates the same schema folder as the previous example, this time by issuing an HTTP/WebDAV MKCOL request to create the folder item, and by setting the appropriate folder properties using XML in the body of the request.

Listing 4-2: Using HTTP/WebDAV and XML to Create a New Schema Folder

```
MKCOL http://www.your-domain.com/public/AppFolder/schema/ HTTP/1.1
Host: www.your-domain.com
Content-Type: text/xml

<?xml version="1.0"?>
```

```
<d:propertyupdate xmlns:d="DAV:">
    <d:set>
        <d:prop>
            <e:baseschema xmlns:e="urn:schemas-microsoft-com:exch-data:">
                    http://www.your-domain.com/public/non-ipm-subtree/schema/
            </e:baseschema>
        </d:prop>
        <d:prop>
            <d:ishidden>True</d:ishidden>
        </d:prop>
    </d:set>
</d:propertyupdate>
```

For more information on how to use HTTP/WebDAV and XML to create and access folders and items in the Web Storage System, see Chapter 8, "HTTP/WebDav and XML."

Defining properties

After you've created a schema folder, you can then begin to create custom-property definitions. You create property definitions in much the same way that you created the schema folder: First you create a new item in the schema folder, and then you set the appropriate item properties. However, creating a property-definition item requires setting several specific property values, such as the name of the property and the type of data the property stores. Table 4-3 lists the properties used by property-definition items. Note that some property values are required in order to create a new property-definition item; all others are optional.

TABLE 4-3 PROPERTIES FOR CREATING A NEW CUSTOM PROPERTY

Property Name	Description
DAV:contentclass	String value, always set to urn:content-classes:propertydef (required).
urn:schemas-microsoft-com:xml-data#name	String value identifying the name of the custom property; this should include a unique namespace and property name combination, such as urn:schemas-your-domain-com:yourpropertyname (required).

Continued

TABLE **4–3** PROPERTIES FOR CREATING A NEW CUSTOM PROPERTY *(Continued)*

Property Name	Description
`urn:schemas-microsoft-com:` `datatypes#type`	String identifying the data type of the custom property.
`urn:schemas-microsoft-com:` `exch-data#isrequired`	Boolean value indicating whether or not the property is required.
`urn:schemas-microsoft-com:` `exch-data#default`	String indicating the default value for the property, if the value is not explicitly specified.
`urn:schemas-microsoft-com:` `exch-data#isindexed`	Boolean value indicating whether or not the property can be indexed for search performance.
`urn:schemas-microsoft-com:` `exch-data#ismultivalued`	Boolean value indicating whether or not the property can be more than one value. If `True`, the property can contain an array of values of the data type indicated in the `#type` property.
`urn:schemas-microsoft-com:` `exch-data#isreadonly`	Boolean value indicating whether or not the property is read-only.
`urn:schemas-microsoft-com:` `exch-data#isvisible`	Boolean value indicating whether or not the property is visible to client applications.

Listing 4-3 shows how to use ADO to define custom properties. The example uses the custom-schema folder from the previous example, and creates three new custom properties called `urn:schemas-your-domain-com:color`, `urn:schemas-your-domain-com:height`, and `urn:schemas-your-domain-com:width`.

Listing 4–3: Using ADO to Define Custom Properties

```
Dim sSchemaURL
' URL to custom schema folder
sSchemaURL = "http://www.your-domain.com/public/AppFolder/schema/"

Dim Conn
Set Conn = CreateObject("ADODB.Connection")
Conn.Provider = "ExOLEDB.DataSource"
Conn.Open sSchemaUrl

Dim Rec
Set Rec = CreateObject("ADODB.Record")

' create the color property
```

```
With Rec
    .Open sSchemaURL & "color", Conn, adModeReadWrite or _
adModeShareExclusive, adCreateNonCollection, adCreateOverwrite
    .Fields("DAV:contentclass") = "urn:content-classes:propertydef"
    .Fields("urn:schemas-microsoft-com:xml-data#name") = _
"urn:schemas-your-domain-com:color"
    .Fields("urn:schemas-microsoft-com:datatypes#type") = "string"
    .Fields.Update
    .Close
End With

' create the height property
With Rec
    .Open sSchemaURL & "height", Conn, adModeReadWrite or _
adModeShareExclusive, adCreateNonCollection, adCreateOverwrite
    .Fields("DAV:contentclass") = "urn:content-classes:propertydef"
    .Fields("urn:schemas-microsoft-com:xml-data#name") = _
"urn:schemas-your-domain-com:height"
    .Fields("urn:schemas-microsoft-com:datatypes#type") = "int"
    .Fields.Update
    .Close
End With

' create the width property
With Rec
    .Open sSchemaURL & "width", Conn, adModeReadWrite or _
 adModeShareExclusive, adCreateNonCollection, adCreateOverwrite
    .Fields("DAV:contentclass") = "urn:content-classes:propertydef"
    .Fields("urn:schemas-microsoft-com:xml-data#name") = _
"urn:schemas-your-domain-com:width"
    .Fields("urn:schemas-microsoft-com:datatypes#type") = "int"
    .Fields.Update
    .Close
End With

Conn.Close
```

Defining content classes

Content classes, like properties definitions, are actually items created in the schema folder with specific properties and values — the content class and the name being the most important. You also define the property definitions that the content class includes by setting the urn:schemas-microsoft-com:xlm-data#element property. This is a multivalue property that contains a string array of property names. If you want the content class you are creating to inherit all the properties of an existing class or classes, set the urn:schemas-microsoft-com:xlm-data#extends property to the names of one or more existing content classes. The new content class will then inherit all the property definitions from the content class or classes you are extending.

Listing 4-4 demonstrates how to create a custom content class named `urn:schemas-your-domain-com:content-classes:shape`, which extends the `urn:content-classes:item` content class and references the three custom properties from the previous example. Note the convention used in naming the custom content class, which expands on the base `urn:schemas-your-domain-com` namespace you can use when creating the custom properties. Using this naming convention is a good way to logically organize your namespaces, content classes, and property names.

Listing 4-4: Creating a Custom Content Class

```
Dim sSchemaURL
' URL to schema folder
sSchemaURL = "http://cleo.hugefan.net/public/AppFolder/schema/"

Dim Conn
Set Conn = CreateObject("ADODB.Connection")
Conn.Provider = "ExOLEDB.DataSource"
Conn.Open sSchemaURL

Dim Rec
Set Rec = CreateObject("ADODB.Record")

With Rec
    .Open sSchemaURL & "content-class-shape", Conn, adModeReadWrite Or
adModeShareExclusive, adCreateNonCollection

    ' content class name
    .Fields("urn:schemas-microsoft-com:xml-data#name") = _
            "urn:schemas-your-domain-com:content-classes:shape"

    ' set the content class of the new content class
    .Fields("DAV:contentclass") = "urn:content-classes:contentclassdef"

    ' the content class being extended
    .Fields("urn:schemas-microsoft-com:xml-data#extends") = _
            Array("urn:content-classes:item")

    ' array of properties belonging to this content class
    .Fields("urn:schemas-microsoft-com:xml-data#element") = _
            Array("urn:schemas-your-domain-com:color", _
                "urn:schemas-your-domain-com:height", _
```

```
            "urn:schemas-your-domain-com:width")
    .Fields.Update
    .Close
End With
Conn.Close
```

 When creating content classes or property definitions, do not confuse the name of the item you create in the schema folder with the actual name of the property or content class. For example, you can create in the schema a property item named `color` that defines the `urn:schemas-your-domain-com:color` property definition. Applications reference the property name; the item name is irrelevant.

Using custom properties and content classes

Now that you've seen how to create a custom schema, a content class, and several custom properties, take a look at how you can reference the custom schema to make these properties available to your applications. You'll also see examples of retrieving and setting the values of these custom properties on items stored in your application folders.

To use your new custom content classes and properties, you must reference your custom-schema folder from the folders in your application. You do this by setting the `urn:schemas-microsoft-com:exch-data:baseschema` property on each folder in which you want your custom schema to be available to the location of your custom schema folder. Keep in mind that when you created your custom-schema folder, you set its `urn:schemas-microsoft-com:exch-data:baseschema` property to the global-schema folder. As a result, applications referencing your custom schema will also have available to them all predefined properties and content classes from the global schema. Listing 4-5 expands on the previous examples by showing you how to reference a custom schema from a folder.

Listing 4–5: Referencing a Custom Schema

```
Dim sAppFolderURL
Dim sAppSchemaURL

sAppFolderURL = "http://www.your-domain.com/public/AppFolder/"
sAppSchemaURL = "http://www.your-domain.com/public/AppFolder/schema/"

Dim Conn
Set Conn = CreateObject("ADODB.Connection")
Conn.Provider = "ExOLEDB.DataSource"
```

Continued

Listing 4-5 *(Continued)*

```
Conn.Open sAppFolderURL

Dim Rec
Set Rec = CreateObject("ADODB.Record")
With Rec
    .Open sAppFolderURL, Conn, adModeReadWrite
    .Fields("urn:schemas-microsoft-com:exch-data:baseschema") = sAppSchemaURL
    .Fields.Update
    .Close
End With
Conn.Close
```

Now that you've created a custom content class and associated custom properties with the content class, you can use the properties to store additional information about the items in your application folder. In the next example you will learn how to associate the custom content class with an item in the Web Storage System, and how to set the item's property values.

Listing 4-6 shows an example of using VBScript and ASP, first to create a simple text item in the folder named AppFolder, and then to set its content class to the urn:schemas-your-domain-com:content-classes:shape content class created in the previous example. Then the item's custom properties are set, and all the item's properties and values are returned in an HTML table.

Listing 4-6: Setting Content Class and Property Values

```
<HTML>
<HEAD>
<TITLE>Setting custom properties</TITLE>
</HEAD>
<BODY>

<%
Dim sFolderURL
' URL to application folder
sFolderURL = "http://www.your-domain.com/public/AppFolder/"

Dim Conn
Set Conn = CreateObject("ADODB.Connection")
Conn.Provider = "ExOLEDB.DataSource"
Conn.Open sFolderURL

Dim Rec, Fld
```

```
Set Rec = CreateObject("ADODB.Record")

With Rec
    .Open sSchemaURL & "textitem.txt", Conn, adModeReadWrite Or _
        adModeShareExclusive, adCreateNonCollection

    ' set the content class property to our custom content class
    .Fields("DAV:contentclass") = _
        "urn:schemas-your-domain-com:content-classes:shape"

    ' set the custom properties
    .Fields("urn:schemas-your-domain-com:color") = "blue"
    .Fields("urn:schemas-your-domain-com:height") = 3
    .Fields("urn:schemas-your-domain-com:width") = 5
    .Fields.Update

    ' now display all of the properties of the new folder in a table
    %>
    <TABLE border=1 cellPadding=1 cellSpacing=1 width="100%">
    <b><TR><TD>Property</TD><TD>Value</TD></TR></b>

        <%
    For Each fld in .Fields
        Response.Write "<TR>"
        If Not IsArray(fld.value) Then
            Response.Write "<TD>" & fld.name & "</TD><TD>" & _
                fld.Value & "</TD>"
        Else
            Response.Write "<TD>" & fld.name & "</TD><TD>"
            Response.Write "mulitvalue</TD>"
        End If
        Response.Write "</TR>"
    Next

    Response.Write "</TABLE>"

    .Close
End With
Conn.Close
%>


</BODY>
</HTML>
```

Summary

The ability to create custom content classes and properties in your own schemas is yet another powerful tool for creating applications provided by Exchange 2000 and the Web Storage System. You can extend the data-storage capabilities of your applications to include any type of information, and make your information easier to organize and find.

Understanding the Web Storage System schema is important, not only for designing your application's data-storage requirements, but also for developing applications that access the Web Storage System's data. The schema defines all the data elements that you can use to search for and organize items, and the more you understand how the schema works and what you can do with it, the easier it will be for you to develop powerful applications.

Chapter 5

Searching the Web Storage System

THE WEB STORAGE SYSTEM can contain a vast amount of information consisting of many different types and formats, and can organize your information in an almost infinite structure of folders and sub-folders. But as the amount of information and the complexity of your storage system grow, how can you easily find the specific information you are looking for? The Web Storage System provides robust search capabilities that enable you to locate items based on item properties, or by using the powerful full-text search engine to find information based on the text in a document or message body of an item.

This chapter will describe the various methods of searching for information, as well as how to create dynamic search folders and how to optimize the Web Storage System's search capabilities.

Searching for Information

Although the Web Storage System provides you with an enhanced means of storing and organizing your data, as the volume of this data grows you may find it increasingly difficult to locate the specific information you are looking for. As many network or Exchange administrators have learned, the number of e-mails, contacts, documents, and other items, as well as the complexity of the folder structure storing these items, grow exponentially over time, especially when users begin to realize the benefits of using the Web Storage System to organize their own information.

Fortunately, the Web Storage System provides robust search capabilities, enabling you to query for information based on item properties, the contents of an item, or both. And unlike with a structured database, which you would query by specifying a table and specific search criteria, you can search the contents of a folder or folders and optionally search all sub-folders at the same time.

You can search for information using ADO, OLEDB, or WebDAV using the Web Storage System Structured Query Language (SQL), which is based on standard ANSI SQL syntax, with which many developers are already familiar. Additionally, the version of SQL used by the Web Storage System also supports full-text query syntax, such as the CONTAINS and FREETEXT predicates, which are based on the syntax defined by the Microsoft Indexing Service.

For more details on how to use ADO or WebDAV to execute SQL statements and return results, refer to Part III, "Extending your Data to the Web."

In addition to performing ad-hoc queries against your data, HTTP/WebDAV can programmatically create dynamic search folders that appear as standard folders, but return a collection of items that are the results of an SQL statement. This is a powerful feature that enables you to hide the complexity of SQL queries from users, yet provide them with dynamic views of their information.

All of these search capabilities are tightly integrated with the Web Storage System's security model. Searches are executed by the Microsoft Indexing Service, which runs under a system account that has access to all the information in the Web Storage System, including private mailbox stores and other private folders. To enforce security, each item returned in the results of an SQL query is evaluated against the item's Access Control List (ACL) and the privileges of the current user; any items that the user does not have access to are eliminated from the results.

Web Storage System SQL

You can search for items in the Web Storage System by using a version of SQL that is based on standard SQL syntax already known and used by many developers. This version of SQL uses standard elements such as the SELECT, FROM, and WHERE keywords. The basic structure of a Web Storage System query is as follows:

```
SELECT property_list | *
FROM folder_url | SCOPE(folder_scope)
[WHERE criteria]
[ORDER BY property_list]
[GROUP BY property_list]
```

As you can see, the basic SELECT statement syntax is easy to understand and construct. First, you specify the list of properties you want returned, and then you identify the folder or folders you want to search and optionally specify any search criteria to narrow the results. Following are several examples of simple SELECT statements:

```
SELECT "DAV:displayname",
       "DAV:href"
FROM   "http://www.your-domain.com/public/AppFolder/"
```

The following example is the same as the previous example, but uses the file://./backofficestorage URL syntax instead of http://:

```
SELECT "DAV:displayname",

"DAV:href"
FROM   "file://./backofficestorage/your-domain.com/ ...
public/AppFolder/"
```

In the next example, the results are limited to non-folder items only by specifying DAV:isfolder =False in the WHERE clause, and the results are ordered by item content class using the ORDER BY clause:

```
SELECT "DAV:displayname",
       "DAV:href",
       "DAV:contentclass"
FROM   "http://www.your-domain.com/public/AppFolder/"
WHERE  "DAV:isfolder" = False
ORDER BY "DAV:contentclass"
```

You can also use SELECT * to return all the properties in your results, but this method has several disadvantages. The list of properties returned when you issue a SELECT * query is determined by several factors: the folder(s) you are searching, the schema scope of each of those folders, and the expected content class of the folder(s). For each folder specified in the FROM clause, the query processor first looks at the expected content classes defined for the folder to determine which sets of properties to include. The query processor then searches the schema scope of each folder for definitions of these properties, which may point to one or more schema folders. The list of properties is constructed after all properties from all expected content classes in all folders have been gathered, and it is then returned in your query's results. As you might imagine, query performance can be greatly affected if you select all properties; therefore, you should always try to limit the properties in your SELECT property list to those you need in your results.

For more information on schema scope and expected content classes,
see Chapter 4, "The Web Storage System Schema."

When building WHERE clauses in your SQL statements, you will sometimes have
to use the CAST function. The CAST function explicitly assigns a data type to a
property in a returned recordset or to a value used as a search criterion. Data-type
issues generally do not occur with any built-in properties, but are common when
custom properties are used as search criteria. In the following example, the SQL
statement should return all items where the custom property isthere is set to true,
but because the CAST function is not used, an error may be returned indicating
incorrect SQL syntax.

```
SELECT "DAV:displayname"
FROM   "file://./backofficestorage/your-domain.com/public/AppFolder"
WHERE  "urn:your-domain.com:isthere" = True
```

Here is a better form of the same SQL statement, this time using the CAST function:

```
SELECT "DAV:displayname"
FROM   "file://./backofficestorage/your-domain.com/public/AppFolder"
WHERE  "urn:your-domain.com:isthere" = CAST("True" as "Boolean")
```

CAST can also be used on properties, as in the following example:

```
SELECT "DAV:href"
FROM   "http://your-domain.com/public/AppFolder"
WHERE  CAST("urn:your-domain.com:numericvalue" AS "int") >= 123.45
```

The CAST function only supports XML data types, which are listed in Table 5-1
along with the equivalent OLEDB data types.

TABLE 5-1 XML DATA TYPES AND EQUIVALENT OLEDB DATA TYPES

XML Data Type	OLEDB Data Type
boolean	DBTYPE_BOOL
	string
mv.string	DBTYPE_WSTR, DBTYPE_STR
	DBTYPE_ARRAY | DBTYPE_WSTR
	DBTYPE_ARRAY | DBTYPE_STR
	int
mv.int	DBTYPE_I4
	DBTYPE_ARRAY | DBTYPE_I4
	float
mv.float	DBTYPE_DOUBLE
	DBTYPE_ARRAY | DBTYPE_DOUBLE
	dateTime.tz
mv.dateTime.tz	DBTYPE_FILETIME
	DBTYPE_ARRAY | DBTYPE_FILETIME
	fixed.14.4
mv.fixed.14.4	DBTYPE_CY
	DBTYPE_ARRAY | DBTYPE_CY
	i2
mv.i2	DBTYPE_I2
	DBTYPE_ARRAY | DBTYPE_I2
	i8
mv.i8	DBTYPE_I8
	DBTYPE_ARRAY | DBTYPE_I8
	r4
mv.r4	DBTYPE_R4
	DBTYPE_ARRAY | DBTYPE_R4
	uuid
mv.uuid	DBTYPE_GUID
	DBTYPE_ARRAY | DBTYPE_GUID
	bin.base64
mv.bin.base64	DBTYPE_BYTES
	DBTYPE_ARRAY | DBTYPE_BYTES

Search scope

In the WHERE clause, you specify the folder or folders you want to include in your search. The collection of folders you specify is called the *search scope*, which identifies not only the specific folders, but also whether or not each folder's sub-folders should be included in the search. By using the SCOPE keyword in the WHERE clause, you can specify a SHALLOW TRAVERSAL search, which excludes any sub-folders, or a DEEP TRAVERSAL search, which searches all of the specified folders and their sub-folders.

By default, if you specify a URL in the FROM clause but do not use the SCOPE keyword, the Web Storage System query processor will assume a *shallow traversal* and will not include sub-folders. If you use the SCOPE keyword but do not specify either a *shallow* or *deep traversal*, the query processor will perform a *deep traversal*, including all sub-folders in the search. Following are examples of how you can specify different search scopes in your queries.

◆ This example searches the documents folder and its sub-folders for any document that was authored by "Linda," and returns the title, comments, and date created, sorted in descending order by date created. Note that document items are identified by a content class of urn:content-classes:document.

```
SELECT  "urn:schemas-microsoft-com:office:office#Title",
        "urn:schemas-microsoft-com:office:office#Comments",
        "urn:schemas-microsoft-com:office:office#Created"
FROM    SCOPE('deep traversal of "http://www.your-
domain.com/public/documents/"')
WHERE   "DAV:contentclass" = "urn:content-classes:document"
        AND "urn:schemas-microsoft-com:office:office#Author" =
"Linda"
ORDER BY "urn:schemas-microsoft-com:office:office#Created"
DESC
```

◆ This example issues a shallow traversal search for all mail messages in a specific user's inbox with the word "memo" in the subject line. Note that a shallow traversal is not explicitly specified, but is assumed by the query processor because the SCOPE keyword is not used.

```
SELECT  "urn:schemas:mailheader:date",
        "urn:schemas:mailheader:sender",
        "urn:schemas:mailheader:subject",
        "urn:schemas:httpmail:textdescription"
FROM    "http://www.your-domain.com/mbx/alex/inbox"
WHERE   "DAV:contentclass" = "urn:content-classes:message"
        AND "urn:schemas:mailheader:subject" LIKE "%memo%"
```

◆ This example searches two folders, including all sub-folders, for any item last modified after January 1, 2001, and returns the name of the item's parent folder, its display name, and the date it was modified.

```
SELECT  "DAV:parentname",
        "DAV:displayname",
        "DAV:getlastmodified"
FROM    SCOPE('deep traversal of "http://www.your-
        domain.com/public/folderA/"',
        'deep traversal of "http://www.your-
        domain.com/public/folderB/"')
WHERE   "DAV:getlastmodified" > '1/1/2001'
```

◆ This example introduces the GROUP BY clause and the built-in DAV: visiblecount property to get a count of items by content class. Using GROUP BY and the DAV:visiblecount property together is very useful for constructing SQL queries to gather statistics about the data stored in your folder trees. It is also important to mention here that the Web Storage System does not support standard SQL aggregate functions, such as AVG, MIN, MAX, COUNT, or SUM, that are normally used with the GROUP BY clause.

```
SELECT  "DAV:contentclass",
        "DAV:visiblecount"
FROM    SCOPE('deep traversal of "http://www.your-
domain.com/public/folderA/"')
GROUP BY "DAV:contentclass"
```

You cannot perform a deep traversal search in the default MAPI public store, which is created by default by Exchange for MAPI clients such as Outlook. The query processor will return an error if you attempt such a search, either explicitly or implicitly, by using the SCOPE keyword.

Full-text searching

In addition to searching for items with specific property values, you can also execute full-text searches to find items based on their contents. Using a variety of search options, such as wildcards, pattern matching, and and/or logic, you can create powerful searches that you can use alone to find information or in combination with other search criteria based on property values. You can even perform full-text searches on specific properties other than the actual contents of an item, such as the subject of an e-mail message.

For full-text indexing and storage Web Storage System uses the Microsoft Search Service – the same service used by Microsoft SQL Server or Index Server – and standard full-text search syntax. To execute a full-text search you use the

CONTAINS or FREETEXT predicates in the WHERE clause of your SQL statement, and specify the full-text indexed properties you want to search and the words or phrases you are searching for. Both the CONTAINS and FREETEXT predicates use the following syntax:

```
...WHERE CONTAINS( [propertyname | * ], search_criteria)
...WHERE FREETEXT( [propertyname | * ], search_criteria)
```

- ◆ propertyname is where you optionally specify the full-text indexed property you want to search; alternately, you can specify an asterisk (*) to search the body of an item and all full-text indexed properties at the same time. If you omit propertyname, only the body of each item will be searched.

- ◆ search_criteria is the word(s) or phrase(s) you are searching for. The criteria can be simple, such as a single word, or a complex string of words and phrases, such as:

```
CONTAINS(' (lunch OR dinner) AND NOT "baked apple pie" ')
```

Note the use of single and double quotes in the preceding example. The query processor expects the entire set of search criteria to be enclosed in single quotes, and any phrases or words containing non-alphanumeric characters must be contained in double quotes inside the single quotes.

 TIP The use of quotes in search criteria can be very confusing, especially when you are building very complex full-text queries or constructing SQL statements in code. When building search criteria, start simple, and then add criteria piece by piece, making sure that each component is quoted correctly. If you are having difficulty, test the query as you add each piece of criteria to pinpoint the trouble spots.

The CONTAINS and FREETEXT predicates differ in the way in which your search criteria are processed by the query engine. When you use CONTAINS, the query engine performs a more precise search, matching words and phrases in your search criteria specifically. When you use FREETEXT, the query engine performs a search based more on the meaning of the words or phrases in your criteria, based on inflections and various forms of the words you provide, than on the exact words themselves. In other words, FREETEXT performs a looser search, enabling you to provide more generic search criteria in your queries.

In addition to indexing the contents of items in the Web Storage System, the full-text indexer also includes certain item properties in the indexing process. This enables you to perform full-text searches on these properties instead of, or in addition to, searching the contents of each item. Table 5-2 lists the properties that are full-text indexed by default by the Web Storage System's full-text indexer.

Table 5-2 DEFAULT PROPERTIES THAT ARE FULL-TEXT INDEXED

MAPI Properties	DAV/OLEDB Properties
PR_SUBJECT, PR_SUBJECT_W	urn:schemas:httpmail:subject
PR_BODY, PR_BODY_W	urn:schemas:httpmail:textdescription
PR_SENDER_NAME, PR_SENDER_NAME_W	urn:schemas:httpmail:sendername
PR_SENT_REPRESENTING_NAME, PR_SENT_REPRESENTING_NAME_W	urn:schemas:httpmail:fromname
PR_DISPLAY_TO, PR_DISPLAY_TO_W	urn:schemas:httpmail:displayto
PR_DISPLAY_CC, PR_DISPLAY_CC_W	urn:schemas:httpmail:displaycc
PR_DISPLAY_BCC, PR_DISPLAY_BCC_W	urn:schemas:httpmail:displaybcc
PR_SENDER_EMAIL_ADDRESS, PR_SENDER_EMAIL_ADDRESS_W	urn:schemas:httpmail:senderemail

---

Creating Search Folders

Not only can you use Web Storage System SQL to create ad-hoc queries to search for data, but you can also persist SQL queries as dynamic search folders. Search folders are created programmatically, and appear as normal folders but actually contain items that are the results of an SQL statement. Like any other folder in the Web Storage System, a search folder can be accessed via a client or data-access protocol, or queried using SQL; yet the search folder contains a dynamic collection of items based on the results of an SQL statement defined when the search folder was created.

By creating search folders, you eliminate the need to code using SQL to retrieve and save search results, and you therefore create dynamic views to your data without having to re-execute static queries. Creating search folders is similar in concept to creating views in a structured database: A view consists of the results of an SQL statement and looks like a table to clients, and can be accessed and queried like a table. However, the contents of the view are not physically stored with the view; they are created dynamically from the contents of the underlying table or tables, based on the search criteria in the underlying SQL statement. Like views, search folders do not actually store items or copies of items; rather, they contain links to items stored in other folders.

Currently, you can only create search folders programmatically using the HTTP/ WebDAV protocol, and you can create search folders only in private or public stores other than the default MAPI public-folder tree. This obviously puts a restriction on who can create and maintain search folders, but clearly search folders can greatly enhance how your applications organize and present information.

Listing 5-1 demonstrates how to create a search folder by submitting an HTTP/ WebDAV MKCOL request. The MKCOL command is normally used to create a collection, or folder, but when creating a search folder you set the searchrequest of the folder to an SQL statement to indicate to the Web Storage System that the contents of the folder will be dynamically gathered based on the results of the SQL query.

Listing 5-1: Creating a Search Folder Using MKCOL

```
MKCOL http://www.your-domain.com/AppFolder/Memos/ HTTP/1.1
Content-type: text/xml

<?xml version="1.0"?>
<a:propertyupdate xmlns:a="DAV:" >
    <a:set>
        <a:prop>
            <a:searchrequest>
              <a:sql>
                    SELECT "DAV:displayname"
                    FROM SCOPE('deep traversal of "/AppFolder"')
                    WHERE "urn:schemas:mailheader:subject" LIKE "%memo%"
                </a:sql>
            </a:searchrequest>
        </a:prop>
    </a:set>
</a:propertyupdate>
```

This example creates a search folder named Memos, which is located under the AppFolder folder. In the body of the request, XML is used to set the folder's searchrequest property to an SQL statement that will search AppFolder and all of its sub-folders for every item with a subject containing the word "memo." Note that when setting the searchrequest property, you specify the SQL statement in an sql child element of the searchrequest property.

For more information on creating and issuing HTTP/WebDAV requests to Exchange Server, see Chapter 8, "HTTP/WebDAV and XML."

When you are specifying the SQL statement in the `searchrequest` property of a search folder, it is not important what properties you list after `SELECT`. This is because the search folder will only use the `WHERE` portion of the statement to determine which items to return.

Once a search folder is created, it behaves just like a normal folder – it can be accessed, queried, and deleted – but the items contained in the search folder are not actually stored there; only links to the original items are. Search folders do have some specific additional properties that are automatically set by the Web Storage System when the folders are created – the `DAV:searchtype` property is set to `dynamic`, and the `DAV:resourcetype` property is set to `DAV:collection/DAV:searchresults`. And you cannot add items to a search folder as you can to a normal folder. If you attempt to add an item or create a sub-folder, an error will be generated.

 Search folders cannot be created in the default MAPI public-folder tree; only in new non-MAPI public folders.

Enabling Full-Text Searching

In order to perform full-text searches on your data, you must first create a full-text index for your information store. This is a fairly straightforward operation, which you can accomplish in a few steps using the Exchange System Manager. First you must create an initial full-text index, or catalog, by right-clicking the information store on which you want to perform a full-text search and then select Create Full-Text Index from the pop-up menu. You are then prompted for the location of the catalog. Enter the path of a local directory and click OK. Figure 5-1 shows the Create Full-Text Index menu option in the Exchange System Manager.

After creating the initial index, you must then run a full population, also called a *crawl*, to fill it with full-text data. This will begin a process that will catalog every word in every item in the store, as well as certain properties included by default in the full-text index. To begin the full population, right-click the information store and select Start Full Population from the pop-up menu. Depending on the volume of data and number of items in the store, the initial indexing process may take a significant amount of time to complete. However, this process is run in the background and should not affect the normal operation or performance of your Exchange server. On a large amount of data, it would be ideal to run the initial index overnight or over a weekend.

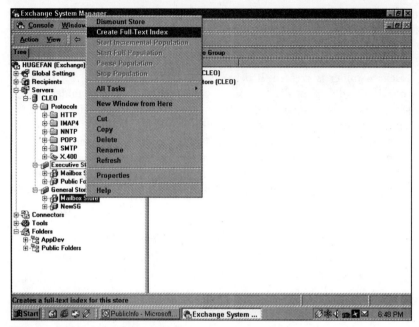

Figure 5-1: Creating a full-text index

Once the initial index is populated, you can perform full-text searches on your data. However, you need to periodically update the full-text catalog as data are changed or added to the Web Storage System. You do this by performing an incremental update, which will update only the existing full-text catalog with new or changed information. You can start an incremental update manually by right-clicking the information store and selecting Start Incremental Population, or automatically by scheduling the incremental update to run at set intervals. To schedule the update, right-click the information store, select Properties, and then select the Full-Text Indexing tab. Two scheduling options are available to you: an Update interval, to schedule an incremental population of the full-text catalog, and a Rebuild interval, to schedule a periodic complete rebuild of the full-text catalog. You can select from a list of pre-defined options for scheduling, or you can click the Customize button to select your own specific days and times to run the catalog updates. Figure 5-2 illustrates the scheduling options available in the full-text indexing Properties dialog box.

At any time you can view the status of an index population, as well as other summary information, by expanding the information store and clicking Full-Text Indexing. As shown in Figure 5-3, you can view indexing statistics, such as the last date and time the index was updated, the number of documents indexed, or the size and location of the index. More importantly, you can view the current index status, which will tell you whether or not an index population has completed.

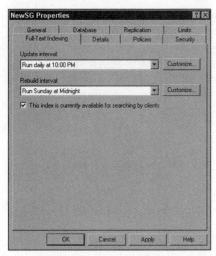

Figure 5-2: Scheduling updates using the full-text indexing Properties dialog box

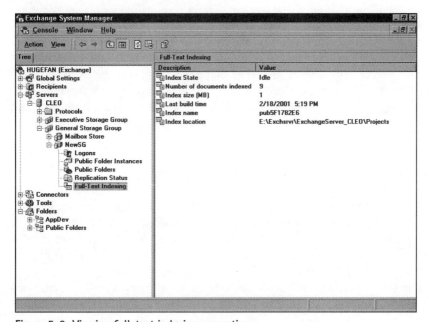

Figure 5-3: Viewing full-text indexing properties

Customizing Full-Text Indexing

You can customize the full-text indexing process by creating your own list of additional properties to index in addition to the default HTTPMAIL properties listed in Table 5-2. First you must create a text file listing the properties that you want to be indexed – one property name on each line – and then you must edit the registry to reference this text file. To edit the registry, run the `regedt32` utility from the command prompt and navigate to the `HKEY_LOCAL_MACHINE\Software\Microsoft\Search\1.0` key. If it doesn't already exist, create a key under 1.0 called `ExchangeParameters`; under the `ExchangeParameters` key, add a key called `SchemaTextFilePathName`. Add a string value to this key indicating the full path and filename of the text file containing the properties you want to be full-text indexed, such as `C:\EXCHSRVR\FTPROPS.TXT`. Rebuild your full-text catalog, and these properties will now be indexed for full-text searching.

 The predefined `DAV:href` and `DAV:displaynames` cannot be full-text indexed, even if included in the full-text properties text file specified in the registry.

In addition to customizing the list of properties to be indexed, you can also customize the list of "noise" words that Exchange recognizes. Noise words are common words such as "the" or "and" that are excluded from full-text searches by the MSSearch service. By default, these words are listed in the `noise.eng` file, located in the \Program Files\Common Files\System\MSSearch\Data\Config directory on the Exchange server. Noise words in other supported languages are listed in separate files with different extensions according to the language. If you want to include additional words, you can simply edit these files in a text editor such as Notepad. These words will be excluded after you stop and then restart the MSSearch service.

Optimizing Your Searches

By implementing full-text indexing, you can enable powerful full-text search capabilities in addition to the default property-searching abilities of the Web Storage System. When using your own custom properties as search criteria, you can further improve search performance by creating an index on these properties. Creating a property index does not enable full-text searching on custom properties, but it does greatly improve search performance when you are using any custom properties as search criteria. However, in order to create a property index you must meet some specific criteria:

◆ The property cannot be a predefined property; it must be a custom property.

◆ The custom property definitions `isindexed` property must be set to `true`. This setting does not create the index itself, but it does enable the custom property to be indexed.

♦ The custom property must be defined in a schema and associated with a custom content class.

♦ The custom content class must be included in a folder's list of expected content classes.

If one or more properties meet all of the preceding criteria you can use the CREATE INDEX SQL statement to index all custom properties in a specific folder. Note that this will create an index on *all* suitable custom properties that are part of the folder's expected content classes. You cannot create an index on a single custom property.

The syntax for the CREATE INDEX statement is as follows:

```
CREATE INDEX * ON "folder_URL" (*)
```

The asterisk (*) after INDEX and the asterisk after the folder URL are both required, and *folder_URL* must be enclosed in double quotes.

 You cannot delete a property index once it has been created, because the Web Storage System SQL does not support DROP INDEX. The only way to delete an index in a folder is to move the items in the folder to another folder, delete and recreate the folder, and move the items back.

Besides using indexing properly, there are several other ways to improve search performance in the Web Storage System. First you should ensure that your Exchange server's hardware configuration is appropriate for the number of users and volume of data it is supporting. As a rule of thumb, you should add at least 256MB of RAM to the recommended amount of memory for your Exchange server if you plan on running full-text indexing. In addition, you should use a RAID disk configuration to make sure that you have adequate disk performance and adequate disk space to store the full-text index files.

You can also further optimize the full-text indexing process, especially with very large information stores, by rearranging the location of the various disk files used by the MSSearch service. The files used by indexing fall into four categories:

♦ *Catalogs*, which store the index data

♦ *Property stores*, which contain various properties of items indexed in the catalog

♦ *Gatherer logs*, which contain logging information for the indexing service

♦ *Temporary files*, which are used by the indexing service

By default, the property stores and gatherer logs are located on the same drive as the Exchange Server, and temporary files are located on the system drive. You can improve indexing performance by moving the property stores and temporary files to a different drive, preferably located on a RAID array. You can move the property-store files to a different location by using the `PSTOREUTL` utility located in the Program Files\Common Files\System\MSSearch\Bin directory. The `PSTOREUTL` utility is run using the syntax as follows: where `<servername>` is the name of your Exchange Server, `C:` is the default drive where the Exchange Server software is installed, and `D:` is the drive to which you want to move the property store files.

```
PSTOREUTL.EXE exchangeserver_<servername>
-M "c:\exchsrvr\ExchangeServer_<servername>.edb"
-L "d:\exchsrvr\ExchangeServer_<servername>"
```

To change the location of the indexing-service temporary files, you use the `SETTMPPATH.VBS` utility, also located in the Program Files\Common Files\System\ MSSearch\Bin directory. This is a VBScript utility, which you run using the following syntax (where `d:\temp` is the new drive and directory where temporary files will be created):

```
cscript settemppath.vbs d:\temp
```

You should perform these steps before you populate a full-text index for the first time, because of the potentially large size of a fully populated catalog, and you should stop the MSSearch service.

Summary

In addition to offering advanced data storage capabilities, the Web Storage System provides robust search capabilities to provide quick access to the data you need. By using data-access technologies such as ADO or HTTP/WebDAV and XML, you can create queries to locate items based on their properties, their contents, or both. You can even persist these queries as search folders that you can use to create dynamic views of your Web Storage System data. These search capabilities, along with the multitude of data-access options available, make the Web Storage System an ideal platform for developing advanced data-centric applications.

Chapter 6

Web Storage System Management and Security

IN THIS CHAPTER

- ◆ Configuring the Web Storage System
- ◆ Understanding the Exchange Security model and permissions
- ◆ Working with the security descriptor
- ◆ Managing Exchange virtual servers
- ◆ Using COM+ security

MANAGEMENT AND SECURITY CONCEPTS within the Web Storage System are an import part of developing Web applications for Microsoft Exchange. In this chapter we will introduce you to key concepts in setting up a new Web Storage System, either through the Exchange System Manager or programmatically through ASP. We will also show you how security and permissions work within the Exchange System Manager, how you can programmatically control an object's permissions with the security descriptor, how Internet Information Server (IIS) integrates with Exchange, and how you can set up a COM+ application for use from your ASP applications.

Configuring the Web Storage System

When Exchange is first installed it creates a storage group called the first storage group. The first storage group is the main storage group, in which the public folder store and the mailbox store are created. Before you begin to build your applications on the Web Storage System, you should configure a separate public storage group, public folder tree, and public folder store. This isolates your applications from the main storage group, and is helpful in terms of disaster recovery. It is much easier to back up individual storage groups if they are smaller in size. You can use the Exchange System Manager to create storage groups, public folder trees, and public folder stores.

You can also programmatically configure the Web Storage System using the Collaborative Data Objects for Exchange Management (CDOEX) or Active Directory Services Interface (ADSI). Both of these APIs enable developers to manage the

Active Directory. CDOEX is a server-side API and does not exist on client machines. ADSI, however, is installed as part of a standard Windows 2000 installation.

The process for configuring a new Web Storage System is as follows:

1. Create a public storage group

2. Create a public folder tree

3. Create a public folder store

4. Mount the public folder store

5. Create a public folder application root

6. Create an Exchange Virtual Server for Web access

7. Assign Web, folder, and directory permissions

Building LDAP Connection Strings

When connecting to Exchange programmatically through ADSI or CDOEX, you will use the Lightweight Directory Access Protocol (LDAP) specifier. LDAP is the standard protocol used to communicate between Active Directory and client applications in the Windows environment. The LDAP binding string consists of the LDAP specifier followed by the server name (the domain controller that contains the Active Directory) and the *distinguished name* of the object. The distinguished name consists of the complete path through the hierarchy and is made up of any number of the attributes listed in Table 6-1.

TABLE **6-1** DISTINGUISHED NAME (DN) ATTRIBUTES

Attribute	Description
CN	Common name of the object
OU	Organizational Unit. An individual part of an organization, such as Human Resources or Finance.
DC	Domain Controller identifier, used for each part of your domain (for example, `starship.enterprise.com` is `dc=starship,dc=enterprise,dc=com`)

Here are several examples of what LDAP binding strings may look like:

◆ Binds to the server mailstrom:

```
LDAP://mailstrom
```

- Binds to the user Joe User in the Recipients container:

```
LDAP://mailstrom/cn=Joe User,cn=Recipients
```

- Binds to the First Storage Group in the Exchange Server:

```
LDAP://mailstrom/First Storage Group,
cn=InformationStore,cn=MAILSTROM,cn=Servers,cn=First
Administrative Group,cn=Administrative Groups,cn=Enterprise,
cn=Microsoft Exchange,cn=Services,
cn=Configuration,dc=starship,dc=enterprise,dc=com
```

The LDAP specifier is case-sensitive — that is, `LDAP://` is not the same as `ldap://`. The correct specifier is all upper case.

CDO for Exchange Management

At the root of the CDOEX API is the Exchange Server object (`ExchangeServer`), used to bind to the domain computer. To bind to an Exchange Server, use the `Open` method and pass the name of the domain computer. When the `Open` call completes, you can examine the `DataSource` object and view the `SourceUrl` property to see the LDAP specifier. From the specifier you can use the pieces of the string to build new LDAP binding strings. It is good practice to avoid hard-coding LDAP strings within code: The more dynamic the routines are, the more useful they will be. Refer to Figure 6-1 for the complete CDO for Exchange object model.

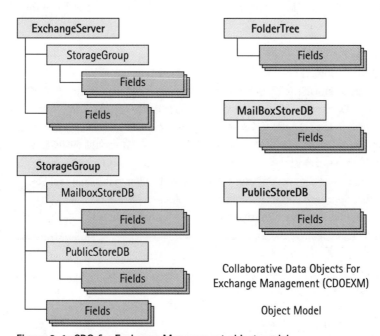

Figure 6-1: CDO for Exchange Management object model

Creating a Public Storage Group

To Create the Public Storage Group using the Exchange System Manager, follow these steps:

1. Open the Exchange System Manager by selecting Start → Programs → Exchange → System Manager.

2. Navigate to the Servers container and choose your server name from within the container.

3. Right-click on your server name and choose New → Storage Group.

4. In the Properties dialog box, enter the name of the Storage Group as **Applications** for the purposes of this example. You can also change the location of the transaction logs if necessary.

5. Click OK and the new Storage Group is created.

To programmatically create the storage group from an ASP Application using VBScript, you need to create an Exchange Server object and a storage group object. You then use the Exchange Server object to open a connection to the Exchange Server, create an LDAP binding string with the new storage group name, and use the storage group object to save the binding string back to the directory. Refer to Listing 6-1 for a complete code example using CDOEX objects. Figures 6-2 and 6-3 show the Watch window for the Exchange Server object (objExServer) and the Storage Group object (objExSG) after creation of and connection to the Exchange Server by means of the LDAP specifier.

 The CDOEX objects need to execute under a security context that has the necessary permissions to perform management tasks within the Active Directory Exchange metabase. You can approach this problem in three ways. The first is to log onto the server as the administrator. The second is to wrap your routines in COM objects, install your objects as COM+ applications, and then create a security role that has the necessary permissions. (For a complete explanation, see the section "Using COM+ security" later in this chapter.) For the third approach you may implement NT Authentication on the IIS Web and grant the user administrative rights to the Exchange Server.

Listing 6-1: Creating a Public Storage Group with CDOEX

```
Sub CreatePSGroup(strSGName, strCmptrName)

Dim objExServer    '* Exchange Server object
Dim objExSG    '* Storage Group object
```

```
'* Create Exchange Management Objects
Set objExServer = _
Server.CreateObject("CDOEXM.ExchangeServer")
Set objExSG = Server.CreateObject("CDOEXM.StorageGroup")

'* Set the Storage Group Name
objExSG.Name = strSGName
  '* Connect to Exchange
  objExServer.DataSource.Open strCmptrName

  '* Build the URL to the StorageGroup using the StorageGroups array property
  myVar = objExServer.StorageGroups

  strTmp = MyVar(0)
  strTmp = Mid(strTmp,Instr(2,strTmp,"cn="))
  '* this line is returned
  '* cn=InformationStore,cn=MAILSTROM,cn=Servers,
  '* cn=First Administrative Group,cn=Administrative
  '* Groups,cn=Enterprise,
  '* cn=Microsoft Exchange,cn=Services,
  '* cn=Configuration,dc=starship,dc=enterprise,dc=com
  '* protocol specifier & Directory Server Property & strTmp
  strSGUrlOut = "LDAP://" & objExServer.DirectoryServer & "/cn=" & strSGName &
"," strTmp

  '* Save Storage Group Back to Exchange
  objExSG.DataSource.SaveTo strSGUrlOut

  '* Clean Up
  Set objExServer = Nothing
  Set objExSG = Nothing
End Sub
```

Name	Value	Type
⊟ objExServer		Object
⊟ DataSource		Object
— SourceClass	"IADs"	String
— Source		Object
— IsDirty		Boolean
— SourceURL	"LDAP://mailstrom.starship.enterprise.com:389/cn=MAILSTROM,cn=Serv	String
⊞ ActiveConnection		Object
⊞ Fields		Object
— Name	"MAILSTROM"	String
— ExchangeVersion	"Version 6.0 (Build 4417.6)"	String
⊟ StorageGroups		Variant
— StorageGroups[0]	"cn=First Storage Group,cn=InformationStore,cn=MAILSTROM,cn=Serv	String
— SubjectLoggingEnabled	False	Boolean
— MessageTrackingEnabled	False	Boolean
— DaysBeforeLogFileRemoval	7	Long
— ServerType	0	Object
— DirectoryServer	"MAILSTROM.starship.enterprise.com"	String

Figure 6-2: Watch window illustrating the CDOEXM ExchangeServer object

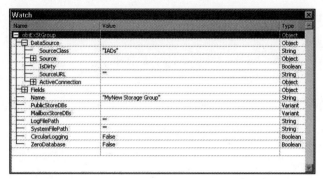

Figure 6-3: Watch window illustrating the CDOEXM storagegroup object

Now that you have created a new storage group, go ahead and create a public folder tree.

Creating a Public Folder Tree

To create a Public Folder Tree using the Exchange System Manager, follow these steps:

1. Open the Exchange System Manger by selecting Start → Programs → Exchange → System Manager.

2. Navigate to the Folders container.

3. Right-click Folders and choose New → Public Folder Tree.

4. In the Properties dialog box, enter the name of the Public Folder Tree as IntranetApplications.

5. Click OK and the new Group is created.

To programmatically create a Public Folder Tree from an ASP Application using VBScript, you need to create an Exchange Server object and a Public Folder Tree object. You then use the Exchange Server object to open a connection to the Exchange Server, create an LDAP binding using the GetFolderTreeURL to return the LDAP string for a Public Folder Tree, and finally use the Public Folder Tree DataSource object to save the binding string back to the Exchange directory. Refer to Listing 6-2 for a complete code example using CDOEX objects.

Listing 6-2: Creating a Public Folder Tree Using CDOEX

```
Sub CreatePFTree(strCmptrName, strFolderName, strFolderOutURL)

    On Error Resume Next

    Dim objExServer    '* Exchange Server Object
```

```
    Dim objExTree       '* Public Folder Tree object

    Set objExServer = Server.CreateObject("CDOEXM.ExchangeServer")
    Set objExTree = Server.CreateObject("CDOEXM.FolderTree")

    '* Bind to the Exchange Server
    objExServer.DataSource.Open strCmptrName

    '* Build the URL to the PublicFolderTree Using the GetFolderTree
    '* Routine The GetFolderTreeUrl Takes the Domain Computer Name
    '* and an FHTRoot output variable
    Call GetFolderTreeUrl(strCmptrName,FHTRoot)
    strFolderOutURL = "LDAP://" & objExServer.DirectoryServer & "/cn=" &
strFolderName & "," & FHTRoot

    '* Set the name of the PublicFolderTree
    objExTree.name = strFolderName

    '* Save the PublicFolderTree
    objExTree.DataSource.SaveTo strFolderOutURL

    If Err.number <> 0 Then
      Call LogError("Error:" & Err.number & "<BR>" & "Description: " &
Err.description & "ADSI Path: " + strFolderOutURL)
      Err.Clear
    End If

    '* Cleanup
    Set objExServer = Nothing
    Set objExTree = Nothing

End Sub
```

Creating a Public Folder Store and mounting it

To create a Public Folder Store and mount it using the Exchange System Manager,
follow these steps:

1. Open the Exchange System Manager by selecting Start → Programs →
   Exchange → System Manager.

2. Navigate to the Applications storage group.

3. Right-click and choose New → Public Store.

4. In the Properties dialog box, enter the name of the public folder tree as
   IntranetApplications.

5. Next, associate the IntranetApplications public folder tree by clicking the Browse button and selecting IntranetApplications from the list of available Public Folder Trees.

6. Choose OK and then Apply.

7. After you choose OK and close the Properties dialog box, you will be prompted with a message asking if you would like to mount the newly created store. Choose Yes and Exchange will mount the store. After a few seconds you will be notified that the IntranetApplications store was mounted successfully.

To programmatically create a public folder store from an ASP application using VBScript, you need to create an Exchange Server object and a Public Folder Store object. Next, use the Exchange Server object to open a connection to the Exchange Server, create an LDAP binding string using the GetFolderTreeURL routine to retrieve the LDAP string for a Public Folder Tree, and then use the public folder store FolderTree property to map the Public Folder to the Public Store. Then ensure that the Storage Group exists where the Public Store is going to be created. To do this, check the strSG name variable against the Storage Group array to see if the name exists in the array. If the Storage Group name doesn't exist or is blank, bind to the First Storage Group and then use the DataSource object of the Public Store to save the new store back to the server. Finally, use the Public Store object's mount method to tell Exchange to mount the new store. Refer to Listing 6-3 for a complete code example.

Listing 6-3: Creating and Mounting a Public Folder Store Using CDOEX

```
Sub CreatePStore(strCmptr,strPSName,strFldr,strSG, blnMount, strPSOutUrl)
   Dim iServer
   Dim iPbStoreDB

   Set iServer = Server.CreateObject("CDOEXM.ExchangeServer")
   Set iPbStoreDB = Server.CreateObject("CDOEXM.PublicStoreDB")

   Dim arrSGroup
   Dim i
   Dim strTemp
   Dim strFldrURL
   Dim strFHName

   '* Bind to the Exchange Server
   iServer.DataSource.Open strCmptr
```

```
'* Get the FolderTreeHierarcy to build the URL to the Public Folder
GetFolderTreeURL strCmptr, strFTHName

'* Build the URL to the PublicFolderTree
strFldrURL = "LDAP://" & iServer.DirectoryServer & "/CN=" & strFldr & "," &
strFTHName

'* Set the variant array to the array of StorageGroups from Server object
arrSGroup = iServer.StorageGroups
'* Start to build the URL to the PublicStore - first part
strTemp = "LDAP://" & iServer.DirectoryServer & "/CN=" & strPSName & ","

'* Set the name of the PublicStoreDB
iPbStoreDB.Name = strPSName
'* Set the name of the PublicFolderTree
iPbStoreDB.FolderTree = strFldrURL

' Verify if the StorageGroup strSG exist in the StorageGroups array
If strSG = "" Then
  '* Finish building the URL to the PublicStoreDB - add last part
  strPSUrl = strTemp & iServer.StorageGroups(0)
Else
  For i = 0 To UBound(arrSGroup)
    If InStr(1, arrSGroup(i), strSG) <> 0 Then
      ' Finish to build the URL to the PublicStoreDB - add last part
      strPSUrl = strTemp & arrSGroup(i)
    End If
  Next
End If

' Save the PublicStoreDB
iPbStoreDB.DataSource.SaveTo strPSUrl

' Mount the PublicStoreDB if thr blnMount is True
If CBool(blnMount) = True Then
  iPbStoreDB.Mount
End If
' Cleanup
Set iServer = Nothing
Set iPbStoreDB = Nothing
End Sub
```

Removing Public Folder Stores, Public Folder Trees, and Storage Groups from Exchange Programmatically

To programmatically remove Public Folder Trees, Storage Groups, or Public Folder Stores, you follow the same steps shown for Listings 6-1, 6-2, and 6-3, but work in reverse order. First, unmount and remove the Public Folder Store; next, remove the Public Folder Tree; and finally, remove the Storage Group.

For a Public Folder Store, make sure that the store is unmounted by using the `Dismount` method of the public store object, and perform the same process of build an LDAP binding URL to the resource using the `StorageGroups` array property from the Exchange Server object. Once you build the LDAP string, bind to the Public Store and use the `DataSource.Delete` method to remove the item.

For Public Folder Tree, modify the `GetFolderTreeURL` to return the name of a folder and its LDAP binding string, create a Public Folder Tree object, use the `DataSource.Open` method to bind to the object, and then use the `DataSource.Delete` method to remove it.

For a Storage Group, create the LDAP binding string using the `StorageGroups` array property, bind to the Storage Group with the `StoreGroup` object's `DataSource.Open` method, and use the `DataSource.Delete` method to remove the Storage Group.

Setting up for the Web

The next steps in configuring Exchange are creating an application root folder in the newly created IntranetApplications Public Folder Tree, and then creating a virtual server to expose that application root folder to the Web. To create a new root folder called WebManagement, follow these steps:

1. Open the System Manager by selecting Start → Programs → Exchange → System Manager.

2. Navigate to the IntranetApplications Public Folder Tree and select it.

3. Right-click and choose New → Public Folder (Figure 6-4).

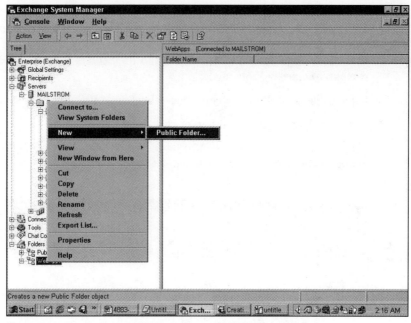

Figure 6-4: Creating a new Public Folder called WebManagement

4. In the Properties dialog box, enter **WebManagement** in the Name field.
5. Click the OK button (Figure 6-5).

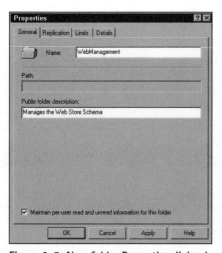

Figure 6-5: New folder Properties dialog box

Now that you have created the root folder, try creating an Exchange Virtual Server so that you can access the WebManagement folder from your Web browser.

1. In the Exchange System Manager, expand the Servers container → *<your computer name>* → Protocols.

2. Expand the HTTP Protocol container → Exchange Virtual Server container.

3. Select the Exchange Virtual Server container.

4. Right-click and choose New → Virtual Directory (Figure 6-6). The Properties dialog box will appear (Figure 6-6).

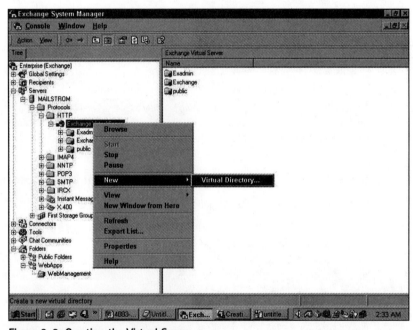

Figure 6-6: Creating the Virtual Server

After the Properties dialog box displays, you must name the directory and change the path to point to your Public Folder, as described in the following steps:

1. In the Name field, enter **WebManagement**.

2. In the Exchange Path frame, change the setting to Public Folder by checking the Public Folder checkbox.

3. Click Modify. This displays the Public Folder Selection dialog box.

4. In the Public Folder Selection dialog box, choose the Public Folder Tree that you created by navigating the tree to the IntranetApplications tree and the WebMangement folder.

5. Click OK when done (Figure 6-7).

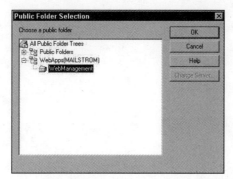

Figure 6-7: The Public Folder Selection dialog box

Now you can change the security permissions to allow anonymous access and give users execute permissions for ASP pages, as shown in the following steps:

For more detailed instruction on the IIS security settings and Exchange, please refer to the "IIS and Exchange Integration" section later in this chapter.

1. Choose the Access tab in the Properties dialog box.

2. On the Access tab, change the Execute Permissions to Scripts by checking the Scripts checkbox.

3. Click Modify. The Authentication Methods dialog box will appear.

4. In the Authentication Methods dialog box, uncheck Basic Authentication and Integrated Windows Authentication.

5. Check the Anonymous Access checkbox. This enables the Anonymous Account field. In this field enter the name of the anonymous IIS user. This is usually **IUSR_machinename** (i.e. IUSR_MAILSTROM).

6. Click OK and then OK again (Figure 6-8).

You'll notice the new Virtual Directory under the Exchange Virtual Server. To test the directory, do the following:

1. Open Internet Explorer.

2. Enter the name of the server, followed by the directory name (i.e. **http:// mailstrom/webmanagement/**).

Figure 6-8: Setting anonymous access

You should get the Exchange default OWA display, as shown in Figure 6-9.

In a production environment, you would not enable the anonymous user account for Web-enabled management tools. This is done strictly for demonstration.

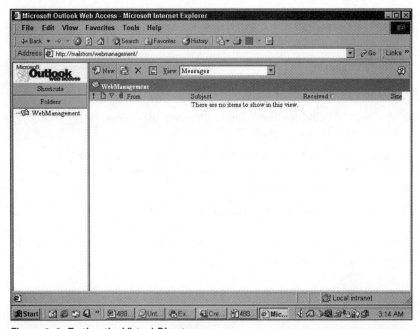

Figure 6-9: Testing the Virtual Directory

Web Storage System Security

The Web Storage System is tightly coupled with the Windows 2000 security model and the Active Directory. If you are familiar with NT 4.0 security, the Active Directory shouldn't be too unfamiliar to you. With the introduction of Exchange 2000 and the Active Directory, Exchange no longer maintains a separate user database. Exchange 2000 is an extension of the Windows 2000 Active Directory schema. You can use Active Directory Service Interface (ADSI) objects to access users, groups, and computers within the directory.

The Exchange 2000 security model is a departure from the role-based security used in Exchange 5.5; it uses NTFS permissions and additional Exchange-specific permissions to grant or deny users access to folders and files. You can still apply the standard Exchange 5.5 roles by using the `DACLLegacyRoles` template to assign the appropriate bitmask for the standard roles used in Exchange 5.5.

How security works

When a user logs on and is authenticated by the domain, he or she is granted an *access token* containing his or her Security Identifier (SID). A SID relates a user or group with an object being granted or denied access. Every Exchange object stored in the Web Storage System contains a Security Descriptor (SD). An SD stores information about the security attributes for a Web Storage System object.

The Security Descriptor contains the Access Control List (ACL) and the ACL contains Access Control Entries (ACE), which contain individual user or group SIDs. The ACL is a list of users and groups that have been granted or denied permissions to the object in question. The ACE is the individual entry in the list identifying the user of the group and its permissions. The Security Descriptor is stored as a property of the Exchange object and the property is stored in binary format.

Using Active Data Objects or WebDAV, you can access the Security Descriptor. When you access the Security Descriptor, Exchange returns it in XML form and the SD contains a Discretionary Access Control List (DACL) and Entity objects. The DACL can contain multiple Entity objects. The Entity objects describe a list of users or groups and SIDs with an *access mask*. The access mask is comprised of hexadecimal bitmasks of permissions.

WebDAV will be discussed in detail in Chapter 8.

Security identifiers (Role SIDS)

The Web Storage System introduces a new concept called a *Role SID*. A Role SID is a security identifier property and contains a list of ACE's for a particular object.

Role SIDs can be grouped into two different types, "mailing and document management" and "security." Role SIDs can be compared to Discretionary Access Control Lists (DACLs) to grant or deny access to objects in the Web Storage System. Role SIDs are accessed through the `http://schemas.microsoft.com/exchange/security/` name space. The properties are in XML format, as shown in Listing 6-4.

Listing 6-4: Example of the XML Creator Role SID Property

```
<S:sid xmlns:S="http://schemas.microsoft.com/security/"
xmlns:D="urn:uuid:c2f41010-65b3-11d1-a29f-00aa00c14882/"
D:dt="microsoft.security_identifier">
<S:string_sid>S-1-5-18</S:string_sid>
<S:type>user</S:type>
<S:nt4_compatible_name>NT AUTHORITY\SYSTEM</S:nt4_compatible_name>
</S:sid>
```

Table 6-2 lists all the Role SIDs from the `http://schemas.microsoft.com/exchange/security` name space.

TABLE 6-2 ROLE SID PROPERTIES

Role SID	Schema Property	Description
Creator	creator	Security identifier of the creator of the item
Last Modifier	lastmodifier	Security identifier of the last modifier of the item
Original Author	originalauthor	Security identifier of the original author of the item
Original Sender	originalsender	Security identifier of the original sender of the item
Original Sent Representing	originalsentrepresenting	Reserved for future use
Originator	originator	Not implemented
Read Receipt From	readreceiptfrom	Security identifier of the originator of the item
Received By	receivedby	Security identifier of the reader of the item
Received Representing	receivedrepresenting	Security identifier of the recipient of the item
Report Destination	reportdestination	Not implemented

Role SID	Schema Property	Description
Report From	reportfrom	Not implemented
Sender	sender	Security identifier of the sender of the item
Sent Representing	sentrepresenting	Not implemented
Admin Security Descriptor	admindescriptor	Security descriptor for a folder or collection. Identifies the object's owner and primary group. Can also contain a DACL that controls access to the object, and a System Access-Control List (SACL) that controls the logging of attempts to access the object.
Security Descriptor	descriptor	Security descriptor for an item. Same as the Admin Descriptor.

Managing security

To manage security on an object, you can either use the Exchange System Manager or programmatically access the object's Security Descriptor through the `http://schemas.microsoft.com/exchange/security/descriptor` property using ADO or WebDAV. This section covers both options.

PERMISSIONS

Because of the security integration between the Web Storage System and the Active Directory, when you modify users' permissions from the Exchange System Manager, Exchange is automatically updating the NT File System (NTFS) folder permissions in the IFS (Installable File System), typically set to drive mapping. This integration gives the Web Storage System more flexibility and control over how clients interact with your applications.

 When setting permissions on public folders, never set the permissions directly from the Installable File System (IFS).

Permissions are grouped into two categories, *Active Directory standard permissions* and *Exchange Extended permissions*. The Active Directory permissions are permissions used by the NT File System. Examples of Active Directory standard permissions are Modify, Read/Execute, and Full Control. Exchange Extended Permissions are permissions that Exchange adds to the standard Active Directory Permissions. Examples of Exchange Extended permissions are Administer Information Store, Create Public Folder, and Full Store Access. You can set Exchange Extended permissions through the Security tab of public folder trees or the Administrative button of Public Folders.

When you are viewing an object's permissions, Active Directory permissions are listed first, followed by Exchange Extended permissions. Table 6-3 lists the Exchange Extended permissions and their descriptions.

TABLE 6-3 LISTING OF EXCHANGE EXTENDED PERMISSIONS

Permission	Description
Add PF to admin group	Indicates which users are allowed to add a public folder to an administrative group
Administer information store	Used by the Information Store service to determine if a user has permissions to perform various operations.
Create named properties in information store	Used by the Information Store service to determine if a user has permissions to create named properties. A named property is a store attribute that can be accessed by name. Examples include display name, locale, deleted-item flags, and activation schedule.
Create public folder	Indicates which users are allowed to create a public folder under the specified folder.
Create top-level public folder	Indicates which users are allowed to create a top-level public folder on the specified public-folder hierarchy.
Full store access	Indicates which users are allowed full access to the Information Store.
Mail-enable public folder	Indicates which users can make a public folder mail-enabled.
Modify public-folder ACL	Used to determine if a user has permission to modify a public-folder Access Control List (ACL).

Permission	Description
Modify public-folder admin ACL	Used to determine if a user has permission to modify a public-folder administrative ACL.
Modify public-folder deleted-item retention	Indicates which users are allowed to modify the length of time (in days) that items deleted from the public folder are retained.
Modify public-folder expiration	Indicates which users are allowed to modify the expiration date of content in the public folder.
Modify public-folder quotas	Indicates which users are allowed to modify the size limit of the public folder.
Modify public-folder replica list	Indicates which users are allowed to modify the replica list. An administrator must be given this permission on the administrative group to which this public folder points and the public database to which the replica should be added.
Open mail send queue	Used by Information Store to determine if a user has permission to open the Mail Send queue used for queuing messages to and from Information Store. Typically only the Exchange Servers account is granted this permission.
Read all metabase properties	Indicates which users are allowed to read the Internet Information Services (IIS) metabase, the database that stores configuration values for IIS.
Remove PF to admin group	Indicates which users are allowed to remove a public folder to an administrative group.
View information-store status	Used by the Information Store service to determine if a user has permission to view Information Store data, such as logon information and resources.

You can use the Exchange System Manager to change permissions on public folder trees as follows:

1. Open the Exchange System Manager (Start → Programs → Exchange → Exchange System Manager).

2. Navigate to the Folders container.

3. Right-click the public folder tree you want to set permissions on.

4. Choose Properties to display the AppDev Properties dialog box, with the General, Details, and Security tabs across the top. Select the Security tab to display the current security settings for this folder (Figure 6-10).

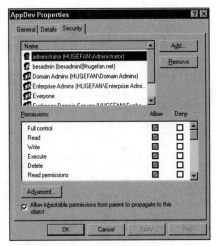

Figure 6-10: Folder Properties dialog box showing the security tab selected.

When the Folder Properties dialog box is displayed, you'll notice a permissions listing, an Advanced button, and, at the bottom of the dialog box, the "Allow inheritable permissions from parent to propagate to this object" checkbox. To differentiate between permissions explicitly set at this level and permissions that are inherited, the latter are shaded gray. These permissions cannot be modified.

Permissions by default are inherited from the parent object. In order to change inherited objects' permissions and explicitly set permissions on objects at this level, you must uncheck the "Allow inheritable permissions from parent to propagate to this object" checkbox. When you uncheck this box you will be prompted by a Security information dialog box to remove, copy, or cancel the current action.

By clicking the Remove button, you are removing all inheritable permissions from the parent object and keeping only those permissions that were explicitly set at this object level. By clicking the Copy button, you are explicitly copying all inherited permissions to this object level and keeping permissions that were explicitly set. Clicking the Cancel button aborts the current action and re-checks the checkboxes. Figure 6-11 shows the Security information dialog box.

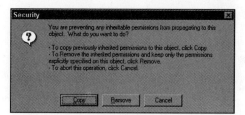

Figure 6-11: Security Information dialog box

ADDING USERS OR GROUPS TO THE SECURITY TAB
To add a user or group, do the following:

1. Click the Add button from the folder Properties dialog box (Figure 6-10). The Select Users, Computers, or Groups dialog box will appear.

2. Select the user or group and click Add. Repeat if necessary to add multiple users.

3. Click OK when finished.

You'll notice that the user or group will inherit all the permissions from the parent and that these checkboxes are un-shaded, meaning that these permissions were explicitly set at this level (see Figure 6-10).

Looking at the permissions window, you should see the deny column. By checking this column for any of the permissions, you are explicitly denying rights to this user or group. The deny permission takes precedence over any other permissions, so be careful when denying access for a particular permission.

You can also set any Exchange extended permissions by checking the appropriate permission. Clicking the Advance button will bring up the Access Control Settings dialog box, which shows the permissions that have been denied or granted. If a user or group has been denied or granted extended permissions, he or she will have one entry for each extended permission denied or granted. All of the denied Active Directory permissions will be listed first, followed by the denied Exchange extended permissions.

In the Access Control Settings dialog box, you'll also notice bold or shaded icons, which indicate the permissions that were explicitly added at this level or propagated from the parent level. The "Allow inheritable permissions to propagate to this object" checkbox works exactly like the one on the Permissions tab. Figure 6-12 shows the Access Control Settings dialog box.

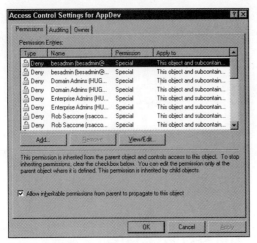

Figure 6-12: Access Control Settings dialog box

PERMISSION ENTRIES

To view or set the way in which an extended permission or NT standard permission applies to child objects, click the permission in the Permissions Entries window in the Access Control Settings dialog box and click the View/Edit button. The Permissions Entry dialog box will display, showing which NT Standard or Exchange extended permission is granted or denied and how it propagates to child objects. Propagation to child objects is controlled by the "Apply onto" drop-down list. Table 6-4 shows a listing of the "Apply onto" drop-down list options. Figure 6-13 illustrates the Permission Entry dialog box.

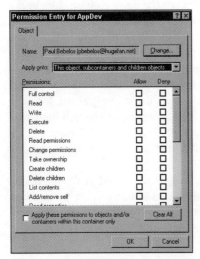

Figure 6-13: Permission Entry for AppDev dialog box

TABLE 6-4 APPLY ONTO DROP-DOWN LISTING

Option	Description
This Folder only	Only applies to current folder. No propagation occurs.
This Folder and subfolders	Applies to current folder and subfolders. No propagation to folder items.
This Folder and items	Applies to this folder and its items. No propagation to sub-folders.
Subfolders only	Applies to sub-folders. No propagation to folder or sub-folder items.
Items only	Applies to all items in folders and sub-folders. No propagation to sub-folders.
This folder, subfolder, and items	Applies to all folders, sub-folders, and items. Full propagation. (Default.)
Subfolders and items only	Applies to sub-folders and subfolder items but not to current folder.

OVERLAPPING PERMISSIONS
When permissions overlap, the most restrictive permission takes precedence. For example, if a user is granted permissions to view a folder's contents, but belongs to a group that is not explicitly granted permissions to view the contents of that folder, he or she will be denied access. If a user is explicitly denied view permissions and belongs to a group that has view permissions, he or she will be denied viewing permissions.

MODIFYING NON-MAPI CLIENT PERMISSIONS (PUBLIC FOLDERS)
To modify Non-MAPI folder permissions under your Public Folder Tree, follow these steps:

1. Open System Manager (Start → Programs → Exchange → System Manager).

2. Navigate to the Folders container.

3. Select the Public Folder.

4. Right-click the Folder.

5. Click Properties to open the Properties dialog box, which features the General, Replication, Limits, Details, and Permissions tabs across the top.

6. Select the Permissions tab to display the current permissions for this folder. Figure 6-14 shows the Non-MAPI Client Folder Permissions pane.

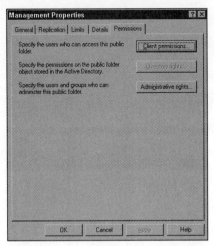

Figure 6-14: Non-MAPI Client Folder Permissions pane

On this pane you'll notice three buttons: Client permissions . . . , Directory rights, and Administrative rights. . . . The Directory rights option will be disabled. This button is only available when you're setting permissions for MAPI client access, such as in Outlook. Since no public folder tree but the default, public folders, can be accessed by Outlook, this option is disabled. The Client permissions . . . button enables you to set the Active Directory Standard permissions. The Administrative rights . . . button enables you to set Exchange extended permissions. (For a review of standard permissions versus extended permissions, please review the "Permissions" section earlier in this chapter.) Table 6-5 lists the extended properties, which must be set at the public folder tree level.

TABLE 6-5 EXTENDED PROPERTIES NOT ON ADMINISTRATIVE TAB

Extended Property Name

Add PF to admin group

Create named properties in Information Store

Create top-level public folder

Mail-enable public folder

Open mail send queue

Remove PF to admin group

Read all metabase properties

Create public folder

The permissions on Public Folders work identical to public folder trees. Permissions can be grouped into two categories: *Standard NT Permissions* and *Exchange Specific Permissions*. Permissions can be applied to Folders and Non-Folders in the same manner in which they would on Public Folder Trees. Here are the steps to change or set permissions on a non-MAPI Public Folder:

1. From the Permissions dialog box, click the Advanced button.

2. Add a user or group, or choose an existing user or group.

3. Click the View/Edit button.

4. Use the "Apply onto" drop-down list to set the way in which a permission or set of permissions applies to child objects.

Inheritable and overlapping permissions work the same way Public Folder Trees do, and the least restrictive permissions have precedence. Table 6–6 lists the permissions for Public Folders.

TABLE **6–6** PUBLIC FOLDER PERMISSIONS

Permission	Applies to	Bitmask (Hex)
Delete	NT Standard	&H00010000
Read Permission	NT Standard	&H00020000
Change Permission	NT Standard	&H00040000
Take Ownership	NT Standard	&H00080000
Synchronize	NT Standard	&H00100000
Read Property	Non-folder and folder	&H00000010
Write Property	Non-folder and folder	&H00000008
Read Attributes	Non-folder and folder	&H00000080
Write Attributes	Non-folder and folder	&H00000100
*Write Own Property	Non-folder and folder	&H00000200
*Write Own Item	Non-folder and folder	&H00000200
*View Item	Non-folder and folder	&H00000800
Read Body	Non-folder item	&H00000001
Write Body	Non-folder item	&H00000002

Continued

TABLE 6-6 PUBLIC FOLDER PERMISSIONS *(Continued)*

Permission	Applies to	Bitmask (Hex)
Append Message	Non-folder item	&H00000004
Execute	Non-folder	&H00000020
List Contents	Folder	&H00000001
Create Container	Folder	&H00000002
*Owner	Folder	&H00004000
*Contact	Folder	&H00008000

Rights marked with an asterisk are Exchange-specific.
Bitmasks are listed for use when working with the Security Descriptor.

Working with the Security Descriptor

Client Permissions can also be accessed, modified, deleted, and set programmatically through the Security Descriptor property: `http://schemas.microsoft.com/exchange/security/descriptor`.

You can access the Security Descriptor through World Wide Web Distributed Authoring and Versioning (WebDAV) or Active Data Objects (ADO) using the Exchange OLEDB Provider.

The minimum required rights to access the security descriptor are:

◆ `READ_CONTROL` — Equates to the NT Standard Permission Read

◆ `WRITE_DAC` — Equates to the NT Standard Permission Change Permission

◆ `WRITE_OWNER` — Equates to the NT Standard Take Ownership

The Security Descriptor is returned in XML format, an example of which is provided in Listing 6-5 (an asterisk indicates that a node is optional).

Listing 6-5: Security Descriptor XML Structure Example

```
<security_descriptor xmlns="http://schemas.microsoft.com/security/">
<revision>...</revision>
<owner>...</owner>
<group>...</group>
<dacl>
<effective_aces>...</effective_aces>
*<subcontainer_inheritable_aces>...</subcontainer_inheritable_aces>
```

```
*<subitems_inheritable_aces>...</subitems_inheritable_aces>
</dacl>
<sacl>...<sacl>
</security_descriptor>
```

The Discretionary Access Control List (DACL) is divided into three groups of Access Control Entities (ACEs). Each group maps to the way in which an item's security affects containers and objects below it and `Effective ACES` applies to the current object. The `subcontainer inheritable ACEs` and `subitems inheritable ACEs` refer to folder and non-folder objects below this object. This would come into effect primarily when you're setting permissions for containers.

Each container consists of one or more ACEs, and each ACE contains an access mask and Security Identifiers (SIDs), which are comprised of at least the `nt4_compatible_name`. ACEs at the `effective aces` level have an attribute called `inherited`. The `inherited` attribute identifies whether or not the current mask is inherited form the parent level. When setting new masks, set the `inherited` attribute to 0 (false). ACEs at the next two levels also have an `inherited` attribute, and a `no_propagate_inherit` attribute, which indicates whether `inherit these permissions to objects and/or containers within this container only` is checked.

The Access Mask is a hexadecimal bitmask of the granted or denied rights. (For a list of rights and bitmask values see Table 6-6.) To create a mask, simply add the hex values. For example, to grant someone full standard NT access rights, you add 0x00010000 + 0x00020000 + 0x00040000 + 0x00080000 + 0x00100000 = 0x1f0000. Listings 6-6 and 6-7 provide examples of an allowed ACE XML and a denied ACE XML structure, respectively.

Listing 6-6: Allowed ACE XML Example

```
<access_allowed_ace inherited>
<access_mask>...</access_mask>
<sid>
<string_sid>...</string_sid>
<type>...</type>
<nt4_compatible_name>...</nt4_compatible_name>
<ad_object_guid>...</ad_object_guid>
<display_name>...</display_name>
</sid>
</access_allowed_ace>
```

Listing 6-7: Denied ACE XML Example

```
<access_denied_ace inherited>
<access_mask>...</access_mask>
<sid>
```

Continued

Listing 6-7 *(Continued)*

```
<string_sid>...</string_sid>
<type>...</type>
<nt4_compatible_name>...</nt4_compatible_name>
<ad_object_guid>...</ad_object_guid>
<display_name>...</display_name>
</sid>
</access_allowed_ace>
```

READING THE SECURITY DESCRIPTOR WITH ADO

To read the Security Descriptor of an object using ADO, first bind to the object and then read the http://schemas.microsoft.com/exchange/security/descriptor property. Listing 6-8 uses ADO to read the Security Descriptor property.

 When loading an XML Security Descriptor into the XMLDOM using either load or loadXML methods, set the validateOnParse property to false before reading the XML or you will receive a "Data Type 'Microsoft.Security Descriptor' is not supported" error.

Listing 6-8: Reading the Security Descriptor Using ADO

```
Const SDNAMESPACE = "http://schemas.microsoft.com/exchange/security/"
Const BASEPATH =
"file://./backofficestorage/starship.enterprise.com/webapps/webmanagement/webfil
es/"

Public Function ReadSD() as String
  Dim oRec As New ADODB.Record
  Dim xmlSD As String
  On Error Goto ErrTrap
  oRec.Open BASEPATH & "myfilename.eml", , adModeReadWrite, adOpenIfExists

  ReadSD = oRec.Fields(SDNAMESPACE & "descriptor").Value

  '* Clean Up
  oRec.Close
  Set oRec.ActiveConnection = Nothing
  Set oRec = Nothing
Exit Function
ErrTrap:
  Err.Raise Err.Number, "[ReadSD]",Err.Description
End Function
```

You can also use WebDAV to read the Security Descriptor of an object. First create the XML request string, and then create an `MSXML2.XMLHTTP` object to issue a `PROPFIND` request on the object. Next, issue the request and read the result into an XMLDOM object. Listing 6-9 illustrates how to use WebDAV to read an object's Security Descriptor.

Listing 6-9: Reading the Security Descriptor Using WebDAV

```
'* Create an XMLhttp Request XML String
strxml = "<?xml version='1.0'?>"
strxml = strxml & "<d:propfind xmlns:d=""DAV:"" & _

xmlns:a=""http://schemas.microsoft.com/exchange/security/"">"
strxml = strxml & "<d:prop>"
strxml = strxml & "<a:descriptor/>"
strxml = strxml & "</d:prop>"
strxml = strxml & "</d:propfind>"

'* Create an XMLHTTP object
Set xmlhttp = Server.CreateObject("MSXML2.XMLHTTP")

'* use propfind XMLHttp Request
xmlhttp.Open "PROPFIND", "http://mailstrom/security/sd.txt",False
xmlhttp.setRequestHeader "Content-Type","text/xml"
xmlhttp.setRequestHeader "Depth","0"
xmlhttp.setRequestHeader "Translate", "f"
'* Send request
xmlhttp.send strxml
'* Check response
If xmlhttp.status <> 207 Then
  '* Handle Error
  Response.Write xmlhttp.status & "<BR>" & xmlhttp.statustext
Else
 Set xmldom = Server.CreateObject("MSXML2.DOMDocument.3.0")

'* If this is not set to false we will receive
'* a data type microsoft.security_descriptor not supported error
xmldom.validateOnParse = False

xmldom.load xmlhttp.responseXML

'* Process Descriptor Here

 Set xmldom = nothing
End If

Set xmlhttp = nothing
```

MODIFYING AN OBJECT'S SECURITY DESCRIPTOR USING ADO

When modifying an object's Security Descriptor, you'll need to create the entire Security Descriptor XML Shell. Bind to the object and set the `http://schemas.microsoft.com/exchange/descriptor` property. By default, the Security Descriptor property appends to the existing security. When creating the XML SID, the most efficient element to specify is `string_sid`; however, if you don't know the SID you can specify at least one of the following (listed in ascending order of efficiency): `Nt4_compatible_name`, `object_guid`, and `displayname`. Listing 6-10 illustrates an example of how to modify an object's Security Descriptor using ADO.

TIP To avoid tricky permission issues with IIS when accessing the Security Descriptor from ASP, use a COM+ component.

Listing 6-10: Updating the Security Descriptor Using ADO

```
  Const FLD_SEC_DESC =
"http://schemas.microsoft.com/exchange/security/descriptor"
  Dim strxml
  strxml = strxml & "<S:security_descriptor
xmlns:data='urn:uuid:c2f41010-65b3-11d1-a29f-00aa00c14882/'
xmlns:S='http://schemas.microsoft.com/security/'
data:dt='microsoft.security_descriptor'>"
  '* DACL starts Here
  strxml = strxml & "<S:dacl defaulted=""0"" protected=""0""
autoinherited=""1"">"
  '* Effective Aces applies to current object
  strxml = strxml & "<S:effective_aces>"
  '* inherit means this ACE is not inherited from previous level.
  '* no propagation sets the propagate of this folder and child
objects only check box
  '* create the XML access allow ace
  strxml = strxml & "<S:access_allowed_ace S:inherited=""0"">"
  '* mask should reflect object type ie Folder or Non-Folder
  strxml = strxml & "<S:access_allowed_ace inherited=""0"">"
  strxml = strxml & "<S:access_mask>1fc9ff</S:access_mask>"
  strxml = strxml & "<S:sid>"
  strxml = strxml &
"<S:nt4_compatible_name>starship\spock</S:nt4_compatible_name>"
  strxml = strxml & "</S:sid>"
  strxml = strxml & "</S:access_allowed_ace>"
  strxml = strxml & "</S:effective_aces>"
  strxml = strxml & "</S:dacl>"
```

```
strxml = strxml & "</S:security_descriptor>"

Set oRec = Server.CreateObject("ADODB.Record")
oRec.Open
"file://./backofficestorage/starship.enterprise.com/intranetapps/sec
urityfolder/secinherit",,adModeReadWrite
'* set the security descriptor property
oRec.Fields(FLD_SEC_DESC).Value = strXml
'* update the fields collection
oRec.Fields.Update

oRec.close
Set oRec.ActiveConnection = nothing
Set oRec = Nothing
```

You can also use WebDAV to modify the Security Descriptor of an object. First create the XML request string and then create an MSXML2.XMLHTTP object to issue a PROPPATCH request on the object. Next, issue the request and read the result into an XMLDOM object. Listing 6-11 illustrates how to use WebDAV to modify an object's Security Descriptor.

Listing 6-11: Updating the Security Descriptor Using WebDAV

```
strxml = "<?xml version='1.0'?>"
strxml = strxml & "<d:propertyupdate xmlns:d='DAV:'
xmlns:S='http://schemas.microsoft.com/security/'
xmlns:exsec='http://schemas.microsoft.com/exchange/security/'>"
strxml = strxml & "<d:set><d:prop>"
strxml = strxml & "<exsec:descriptor>"
strxml = strxml & "<S:security_descriptor
xmlns:data='urn:uuid:c2f41010-65b3-11d1-a29f-00aa00c14882/'
data:dt='microsoft.security_descriptor'>"

'* DACL starts Here
strxml = strxml & "<S:dacl
xmlns:S=""http://schemas.microsoft.com/security/"" defaulted=""0""
protected=""0"" autoinherited=""1"">"
'* Effective Aces applies to current object
strxml = strxml & "<S:effective_aces>"
'* inherit means this ACE is not inherited from previous level.
'* no propagation Sets the propagate to this folder and child
object only check box
strxml = strxml & "<S:access_allowed_ace S:inherited=""0"">"
'* mask should reflect object type ie Folder or Non-Folder
```

Continued

Listing 6-11 *(Continued)*

```
  strxml = strxml & "<S:access_allowed_ace inherited=""0"">"
  strxml = strxml & "<S:access_mask>1fc9ff</S:access_mask>"
  strxml = strxml & "<S:sid>"
  strxml = strxml &
"<S:nt4_compatible_name>starship\spock</S:nt4_compatible_name>"
  strxml = strxml & "</S:sid>"
  strxml = strxml & "</S:access_allowed_ace>"
  strxml = strxml & "</S:effective_aces>"

  '* Close DACL
  strxml = strxml & "</S:dacl>"
  strxml = strxml & "</S:security_descriptor>"
  strxml = strxml & "</exsec:descriptor>"
  strxml = strxml & "</d:prop></d:set>"
  strxml = strxml & "</d:propertyupdate>"

  Set xmlhttp = Server.CreateObject("MSXML2.XMLHTTP")

  xmlhttp.Open "PROPPATCH",
"http://mailstrom/security/secinherit/",False
  xmlhttp.setRequestHeader "Content-Type","text/xml"
  xmlhttp.setRequestHeader "Depth","0"
  xmlhttp.setRequestHeader "Translate", "f"

  xmlhttp.send strxml

  If xmlhttp.status <> 207 Then
    Response.Write xmlhttp.status & "<BR>" & xmlhttp.statustext
  Else
    Set xmldom = Server.CreateObject("MSXML2.DOMDocument.3.0")

    '* If this is not set to false we will receive
    '* a data type microsoft.security_descriptor not supported error
    xmldom.validateOnParse = false

    xmldom.load xmlhttp.responseXML
    m_secdesc = xmldom.xml

   Set xmldom = nothing
  End If

  set xmlhttp = nothing
```

To remove security from an item, read the item's Security Descriptor into the XMLDOM, use the XMLDOM to manipulate the Security Descriptor, and then save the entire XML string back to the object the same way you would modify an object's Security Descriptor.

When working on or enumerating through the Security Descriptor in the XML-DOM, you can use the XPath query syntax to retrieve nodes. For example, if you want to retrieve all the effective ace allowed nodes, you can bind to an object, read the responseXML property into an XMLDOM object, and use XPath syntax to return a NodeList object to enumerate. Listing 6-12 provides an example of this.

Listing 6-12: Retrieving All of the access_allowed_ace and Enumerating Them

```
Dim oNodeList
Dim oNode
'* Use code to Bind to object and read the Security descriptor
into the xmldom.

oNodeList =
xmldom.selectNodes("//s:security_descriptor/s:effect_aces/s:
access_allowed_ace")
  For each nNode in oNodeList
    Response.write nNode.nodeText
  Next
```

IIS and Exchange Integration

IIS integrates with Exchange via the Virtual Server Protocol. IIS stores all its configuration information in its metabase until Exchange is installed, whereupon the IIS metabase information is copied into the Active Directory and Exchange modifies it's metabase to allow the Exchange 2000 Server Metabase Update service to replicate Exchange information into it. The Exchange 2000 Server Metabase Update service will override any information in the IIS metabase. For this reason it is critical not to change permissions for an Exchange Virtual Server outside the System Manager.

Controlling IIS Security

You control IIS Security from the Exchange Virtual Server container and the IIS MMC snap-in. In order for a non-MAPI Public Folder Store to be accessible from a Web browser, you need to create an Exchange Virtual Server that maps to the Web Storage System Public Folder. No programmatic way to set up an Exchange Virtual Server exists.

IIS Security is split into two categories, Web permissions and authentication settings (NTFS). Web permissions apply to all users accessing your Web, whereas NTFS permissions apply to a specific user or group in the Active Directory.

If Web permissions and NTFS permissions differ for a directory or file, the more restrictive settings take precedence.

Managing the Exchange Virtual Server

The Exchange Virtual Server root, which maps to the default Web site in the IIS MMC snap-in, is the only server managed outside the System Manager. To manage the Exchange Virtual Server's security settings, open the IIS MMC snap-in with the following steps:

1. Select Start → Programs → Administrative Tools and select Internet Information Server. The MMC console will open.

2. Navigate to the Exchange Virtual Server container, indicated in IIS as the Default Web Site.

3. Right-click Default Web Site and then choose Properties.

4. Select the Directory Security tab (under anonymous access and authentication control) and click Edit.

5. Choose one of the following options (Figure 6-15 illustrates the Security Authentication Methods):

   ■ **Anonymous access:** Logs the user onto the server with the username IUSR_machinename.

   ■ **Basic authentication:** Requires a user to enter a valid Windows username and password. Authenticates against the NTFS permissions assigned to the Web folder. The username and password are sent in clear text.

   ■ **Digest authentication for Windows domain servers:** Same as Basic Authentication, using a challenge-response mechanism. No username and password are sent to the server.

   ■ **Integrated Windows Authentication:** Uses the user's logged-on user credentials to validate against the server. The server gets the user's credentials from a request to the browser. The password is encrypted.

Figure 6–15: IIS Security Authentication methods

Managing Virtual Servers

To manage all other Virtual Servers, complete the following steps. Figure 6-16 illustrates the Exchange Virtual Servers container in the Exchange System Manager.

1. Open the Exchange System Manager.

2. Expand the Servers container.

3. Expand your *server name.*

4. Expand the Protocols container.

5. Expand the HTTP container.

6. Expand the Exchange Virtual Server container.

7. Right-click the Virtual Server.

8. Select Properties to display the WebManagement Properties dialog box.

9. Choose the Access tab to display the IIS Security settings. The Access pane is split into three sections: Access Control, Execute Permissions, and Authentication Settings.

♦ **Access Control:** The Access Control settings pertain to Web permissions and control how users interact with the Web site. You can choose from the following four options:

   ■ **Read** grants the user read permission (this is the default setting).

If you uncheck Read Access you will restrict all users from viewing content regardless of their NTFS permissions. If you leave this option checked you will allow users to view files if NTFS permissions are not set.

- **Write** grants the user write permission. You can allow remote authors to create, move, search, or delete files and directories on your server. The *Write* permission is part of the Web Distributed Authoring and Versioning (WebDAV) HTTP 1.1 extension.

- **Script Source Access** allows a user to view script source code. If Read is selected the user can read source; if Write is selected the user can write source back to the server. This option is not available if neither Read nor Write is checked.

> If *Script Source Access* is selected, you may be exposing sensitive information, such as usernames and passwords from ASP applications, to your users. This option should be used with Windows user accounts and high-level authentication such as integrated security.

- **Directory browsing** allows a user to view the directory contents when a default page is not set.

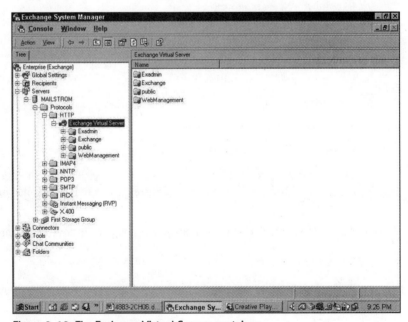

Figure 6-16: The Exchange Virtual Servers container

◆ **Execute Permissions:** Controls script-execution level and Web permissions. Choose from the following three options:

- **None** gives the user execute permissions. ASP applications and executables will not execute.

- **Scripts Only** gives the user only ASP applications to execute.

- **Script and Executables** allow both executables and ASP applications to execute.

◆ **Authentication Settings:** Controls anonymous access and NTFS permissions. To open the Authentication Methods dialog box (Figure 6-17), click the Authentication button on the Access Control tab. The Authentication tab is very similar to the IIS MMC snap-in. The major difference is that you don't have the Digest Authentication. The other options on this dialog box work identically to their counterparts in the IIS MMC snap-in, which was explained earlier in this chapter in the "Managing the Exchange Virtual Server" section.

Figure 6-17: The Authentication Methods dialog box

Typical Virtual Server configurations

To enable Anonymous Access for your Virtual Server, complete the following steps:

1. Open the Exchange System Manager to the Virtual Server root.

2. Open the Virtual Server Properties dialog box.

3. Click the Authentication button.

4. Uncheck the Basic Authentication and Integrated Security checkboxes.

5. Check the Allow Anonymous Access checkbox.

6. In the Anonymous Account text box, enter the **IUSR_machinename** account.

To enable Integrated or Basic Authentication, or both, complete the following steps:

1. Open the Exchange System Manager to the Virtual Server root.

2. Open the Virtual Server Properties dialog box.

3. Click the Authentication button.

4. Check the Basic Authentication checkbox and/or the Integrated Security checkbox.

5. Uncheck the Allow Anonymous Access checkbox.

6. Set up NTFS permissions on the folder.

 Refer to the "Web Storage System Security" section earlier in this chapter.

To enable your Web server to execute ASP scripts, complete the following steps:

1. Open the Exchange System Manager to the Virtual Server root.

2. Navigate to the Virtual Server.

3. Open the Virtual Server Properties dialog box.

4. Under the Access Control section , check the Read Permissions checkbox.

5. Under the Execute Permissions section, choose Scripts.

COM+ applications

For a more robust and reusable approach to developing Web applications, you may want to consider building COM components instead of VBScripts. A COM component is a reusable object–based approach to development, otherwise known as *middle-ware*. COM components expose interfaces via properties and methods, and as a developer you are not concerned about how the interface is implemented, just about what is exposed. Building COM components has several advantages:

- ◆ *Encapsulation* — Common code is isolated.

- ◆ *Faster execution* — Code is compiled instead of interpreted. VBScript is interpreted by the ASP engine and therefore executes slower than compiled code.

- ◆ *Reusability* — You can reuse the same objects in other scripts.

- ◆ *Tighter security* through COM+ applications. ASP security model integrates with the standard NT security model and is page, directory, or application specific. COM+ applications allow for role checking at the code level.

You can build COM components in several languages, including C++, VB, Visual J++, and the Microsoft .NET platform. For a more comprehensive discussion on building COM components, see the Microsoft Platform SDK (`http://msdn.microsoft.com/library/default.asp?url=/library/en-us/cossdk/htm/betaintr_6qan.asp?frame=true`).

USING COM+ SECURITY

When processes need to execute under a security context other than that of the current user, you can wrap your code into a COM component and use COM+ roles. A COM+ role enables you to apply role-based security at the code level using *role checking*, which refers to limiting code execution to a particular role defined by the COM+ application. For example, you may have an object with several methods exposed, and yet you may not want every user to be able to call every method and you may therefore need to grant administrative access to the objects executing code. Complete the following steps to integrate your custom objects into a COM+ application and enable role checking:

1. Open the Component Services MMC snap-in (Start → Programs → Administrative Tools → Component Services).

2. When the MMC opens, navigate to the COM+ Applications container (Component Services → Computers → My Computer → COM+ Applications).

3. Right-click the COM+ Applications container and choose New → Application (Figure 6-18) to start the COM+ Application Wizard (Figure 6-19).

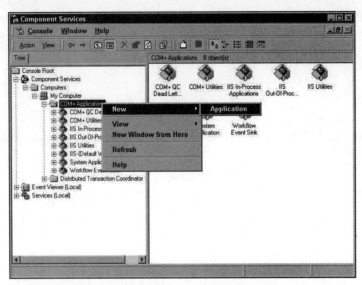

Figure 6-18: Creating a New COM+ Application package

Figure 6-19: COM+ Application Wizard

4. Click the Next button in the COM+ Application Wizard to open the Install or Create a New Application screen (Figure 6-20).

5. Choose the Create an empty application option.

6. In the Create Empty Application screen, enter the name of the COM+ application as **CDOEX Management**.

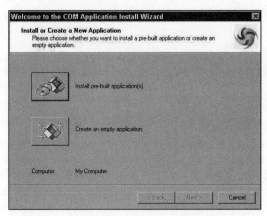

Figure 6-20: The Install or Create a New Application screen

7. In the Activation Type section of the Create Empty Application screen, choose one of the following two options:

- Library Package will execute the object within the creator's process; that is, if you have enabled anonymous access for your site, when the COM component executes it will use the identity of the *IUSR_*machinename. You will not be able to enable role checking.

- Server Application will enable you to execute the code under a dedicated identity. This identity can have whatever permissions you choose. You will also be able to perform role checking.

8. Choose the Server application and then click the Next button (Figure 6-21). The Set Application Identity screen will open.

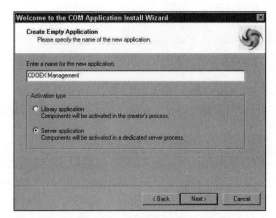

Figure 6-21: Creating a New Server application

9. The Set Application Identity screen provides you with the following two choices:

- **Interactive user:** The interactive user is identified as the user logged onto the machine. If no one is logged in, the process cannot execute. This setting also limits the security context to the context of the logged-in user. If your object needs administrative rights and the current user is not granted these rights, the process cannot execute.

- **This user:** Enables you to set an identity from the domain or local computer. The best approach for this type of process execution is to create a user account on the domain and grant that account the necessary permissions. If you need a user to make management changes to Exchange, create an Exchange Admin account on the domain, grant the appropriate permissions, and use that account as the identity for your COM+ application.

10. Choose the This user option and set the identity by clicking Browse and selecting the appropriate user account from the domain list (Figure 6-22).

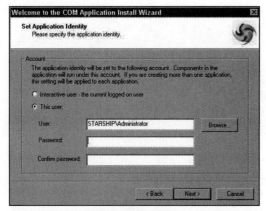

Figure 6-22: Choosing user identity

11. On the last screen, click Finish and complete the Wizard (Figure 6-23).

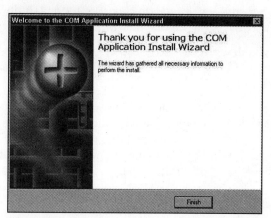

Figure 6-23: Completing the COM+ Application Wizard

COM+ creates a new application package under the COM+ Applications container. Expand your new Application package and you will see a Components folder and a Roles folder. The Components folder is where your COM component will be installed and the Roles folder is where you create roles and associate them with users.

We've gone ahead and converted the ASP script for creating a Public Storage Group to a COM component called CDOEXMGMT.clPublicStorageGroup. The component exposes one method called CreatePSGroup and takes one parameter, the name of the Storage Group strSGName. The function uses a private function called getServerInfo to retrieve the local server name so you can bind to the server and create the LDAP specifier. You will also use the same object to set up a user role called Admin and implement role checking on this function. The COM component and code for this example can be downloaded from this book's public Web site.

Follow these steps to install the COM object and create the Security role:

1. Right-click the Components folder of the package you just created and choose New → Component. This will start the Component Install Wizard. Click the Next button.

2. On the Import or Install New Component screen, you have the following three options:

- **Install new components** enables you to choose a DLL or TLB file. COM+ will take care of registering the files with the registry.

- **Install components that already exist** displays a list of Prog IDs for you to choose from. If the component is already registered you can choose this option.

- **Install new event class** COM+ events is a loosely-coupled events (LCE) system. For a more in-depth explanation, see the COM+ documentation.

For this example, choose the Install New Components option, which will open the Install New Components dialog box. Follow these steps to install the COM object:

1. Click the Add button.

2. Using the Open dialog box, navigate to the folder where the CDOEXMGMT.dll exists.

3. Choose the file DLL. CDOEXMGMT.dll.

4. Click the Open button. COM+ will import and read the object's interface.

5. Click the Next button and the Finish screen should display.

6. Click the Finish button. The COM+ Application should now contain the object (see Figure 6-24).

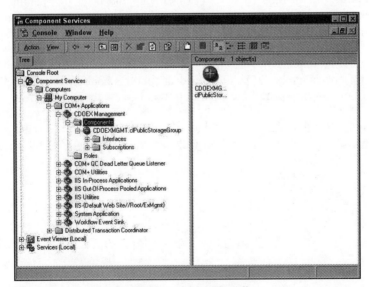

Figure 6-24: Completed COM+ component install

Now that the component is installed, create an Admin role and assign users to it. Here's how:

1. Right click the Roles folder and choose New → Role.

2. In the Role dialog box, enter the name of the role as **Admin** and choose OK. The role will be created in the Roles container.

Follow these steps to add users to the role:

1. Expand the Admin Role container to expose the Users container.

2. Right-click the Users container and choose New › User.

3. In the Select Users or Groups dialog box, choose the appropriate users from the domain in which you wish to give access to this object.

For this example choose the *IUSR_machine* account. This is the anonymous user for Web access. You should add the Local Machine Administrator as well as yourself. You can also assign Groups from the domain to the role, such as Administrators or Exchange Admins. This will make it easier for you to manage the accounts assigned to the role if the role is tied back to a Domain Global Group.

 You will also need to configure IIS to use either Integrated Windows authentication or Basic authentication. Then you will need to configure the Public Folder with the accounts that need to access the Web page. They will be the same as the accounts you add to the Admin Role users list.

Now that you have added the object and created the role, follow these steps to set the appropriate properties on the object to enforce role checking:

1. Right-click the component and choose Properties from the pop-up menu. This will display the Properties dialog box of the component.

2. Choose the Security tab at the top.

3. Under Authorization, make sure that the Enforce Component Level Access Checks checkbox is selected.

4. In the Roles explicitly set for selected item section, check the roles on which you want to enforce checks. If you have created more than one role, check the roles that apply to this object (Figure 6-25).

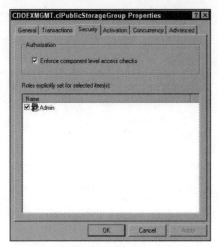

Figure 6-25: CDOEXMGMT Object Properties dialog box

5. Click the OK button.

To enforce role checking in the COM object, your object needs to attach to the COM+ ObjectContext using the GetObjectContext function. Then you would use the IsUserInRole function, passing the role to compare against. The IsUserInRole function checks to see if the current user is in the role specified. Listing 6-13 provides a full code example.

Listing 6-13: COM+ role checking

```
Option Explicit
Private m_MtxObjCtx As COMSVCSLib.ObjectContext
Public Function CreatePSGroup(ByVal strSGName As String) As Boolean
'* Use the Mtx ObjectContext IsUserInRole to validated
'* against Com+ Role
  If m_MtxObjCtx.IsCallerInRole("Admin") Then
    '* Your Code Here
  Else
    '* Return False
    CreatePSGroup = False
    '* Call SetAbort on the Object Context
    m_MtxObjCtx.SetAbort
    '* Raise Error back to calling routine indicating that
'*Authorization Failed
    Err.Raise -9999, "[CDOEXMGMT][CreatePSGroup]", & _
    "User is not Authorized."
  End If
```

```
End Function

Private Sub Class_Initialize()
  '* Get Object Context on Class Initialize
  Set m_MtxObjCtx = GetObjectContext()
  If m_MtxObjCtx Is Nothing Then Err.Raise 5
End Sub

Private Sub Class_Terminate()
  '* Release Context when SetAbort or SetComplete are Called
  Set m_MtxObjCtx = Nothing
End Sub
```

Summary

In this chapter we have shown you ways to configure, manage, and apply security to your applications through the use of tools, such as the Exchange System Manager, Microsoft Management Console snap-ins for IIS, and COM+, as well as programmatically, through the use of APIs such as CDOEX, ADSI, ADO, and WebDAV. You have seen how the Exchange Security model has matured since Exchange 5.5 and have examined its robust features and integration with the Windows 2000 Active Directory. You have also seen how Exchange uses XML within its security model, allowing for ease of access through the Security Descriptor, and have examined the potential for building and implementing middle-tier COM components. You have also seen how Exchange manages its integration with IIS, allowing for the Web Storage System's accessibility over the HTTP protocol. With this rich set of features, you can build upon your own ideas in using Exchange 2000 as a Web-development environment.

Part III

Extending Your Data to the Web

Chapter 7

ActiveX Data Objects

IN THIS CHAPTER

◆ ActiveX Data Objects (ADO)

◆ Using ADO with CDO

◆ Data binding

◆ Searching the Web Storage System

YOU MAY HAVE ALREADY USED previous versions of ADO to connect to Microsoft Access databases or Microsoft SQL databases. Exchange 2000 ships with a new version of ADO (ADO 2.5), which includes the OLEDB 2.5 provider for Exchange server called ExOLEDB. An important new feature of ExOLEDB is that it enables you to bind directly to a URL. (Remember, each item in the Web Storage System has its own unique URL.) This makes connecting to the Exchange data store even easier, because you do not have to write the code to build the connection. ExOLEDB also provides record and stream support, which are used to manipulate message parts of complex messages.

Binding to Data in the Web Storage System

To use the OLEDB provider to access an item in a database, you first must bind to the item. Once the binding is established you can edit the item, or in the case of binding to a container such as a public folder or inbox, you can create an item in that container. To make this binding easy, Exchange 2000 now supports binding directly to a URL. You provide the URL to the item in the Web Storage System and OLEDB configures the connection info and handles the security for you. You can then build your recordset from the data source.

The URL you provide can be in the form of `file://./backofficestorage` or `http://`. When you use the `file://./` name space to connect, Exchange knows that you want to use the ExOLEDB provider because Exchange registers the `file:` OLEDB URL name-space provider with the OLEDB root binder. If you use the `http://` name space, you have to explicitly specify ExOLEDB as the provider, as follows:

```
Set conn = CreateObject("ADODB.Record")
Conn.open "http://servername/public/foldername"
Set conn = conn.ActiveConnection
Conn.Provider = "ExOLEDB.DataSource"
```

When using a `file://` name space, you simply have to specify the URL to open the connection:

```
...
Set rs = CreateObject("ADODB.Record")
Rs.open "file://./backofficestorage/domain/_
Public folders/folder
...
```

Binding to an item in the WSS is only the beginning. Doing something with your connection means using ADO objects. The following objects are exposed by OLEDB and used to access and manipulate items:

◆ **The record object:** Use the `record` object for full access to any item property in the Web Storage System. For example:

```
Set Rec = createobject("ADODB.Record")
Set Conn = creatobject("ADODB.Connection")
Conn.Provider = "ExOLEDB.DataSource"
Conn.Open "http://server/folder"
Rec.Open "http://server/folder/item.txt"
```

◆ **The recordset object:** Use the `recordset` object to issue SQL commands in folders. For example:

```
Set Rec = createobject("ADODB.Record")
Set Conn = createobject("ADODB.Connection")
Dim Rs = createobject("ADODB.Recordset")
Conn.Provider = "ExOLEDB.DataSource"
Conn.Open "http://servername/foldername"
Set Rs.ActiveConnection = Conn
"select ""DAV:displayname"" " _
& "from scope('shallow traversal of ""URL""')" _
& "Where ""DAV:ishidden"" = False"
```

◆ **The connection object:** Use the `connection` object to bind to a particular public or private container. Once you have established a connection, you can reuse the existing connection to access items in that container. For example:

```
Dim Conn as New ADODB.Connection
Conn.Provider = "ExOLEDB.DataSource"
Conn.Open "http://servername/foldername"
Rec.Open "item.eml"
```

◆ **The Fields/Field Object:** When you use an ADO `record` or `recordset` object, the properties are automatically copied into the ADO object. To then make changes to the properties, you make changes to the fields collection and then save the changes back to the Web Storage System using the `Fields.Update` method. CDO keeps the item properties and the associated stream synchronized automatically after saving the item, but when using ADO you must save the data separately using the `_Stream.Flush` method, and resync the stream with the item properties using the `Fields.Resync` method. For example:

```
Dim Rec as New ADODB.Record
Dim Conn as New ADODB.Connection
Conn.Provider = "ExOLEDB.DataSource"
Conn.Open Url
Dim Flds as ADODB.Fields
Dim Fld as ADODB.Field
Rec.Open Url, Conn, adModeReadWrite
Set Flds = Rec.Fields
For Each Fld in Flds
   Response.write fld.value
Next Fld
```

Searching the Web Storage System

Many applications use some type of searching functionality to locate and then bind to an item, but sometimes you wish to search. With Exchange 2000, you can create powerful applications that include search capabilities. You use ADO to navigate the Web Storage System and bind to the search results, just as you do when connecting to a SQL database and searching records. Listing 7-1 illustrates how to search through a public folder for messages sent by a specific user:

Listing 7-1: Searching the Web Storage System Using ADO

```
<HTML>
<HEAD>
     <TITLE>Searching with ADO</TITLE>
</HEAD>

<BODY>
<%
Set info   = CreateObject("ADSystemInfo")
Set infoNT = CreateObject("WinNTSystemInfo")
cName = infoNT.ComputerName
```

Continued

Listing 7-1 *(Continued)*

```
dName = info.DomainDNSName

Set Conn = CreateObject("ADODB.Connection")
Conn.Provider = "Exoledb.DataSource"

cURL = "http://" & cName & "." & dName & "/public/"
Conn.Open cURL

relURL = "folder to be searched"
sender = "Sender's Display Name"

Set rs = CreateObject("ADODB.Recordset")
strQ = "select "
strQ = strQ & " ""urn:schemas:mailheader:date"""
strQ = strQ & ", ""urn:schemas:mailheader:sender"""
strQ = strQ & ", ""urn:schemas:httpmail:sendername"""
strQ = strQ & ", ""urn:schemas:mailheader:subject"""
strQ = strQ & ", ""DAV:contentclass"""
strQ = strQ & ", ""DAV:href"""
strQ = strQ & " from scope ('shallow traversal of "
strQ = strQ & Chr(34) & relURL & Chr(34) & "') "
strQ = strQ & " WHERE ""urn:schemas:httpmail:sendername"" _
= '" & sender & "'"

'build table to display results
Rs.Open strQ, Conn
Response.write "<Table width=600><tr>"
Response.Write "<td><b>Sender:</b></td>"
Response.Write "<td><b>Subject:</b></td>"
Response.Write "<td><b>Date:</b></td>"
Response.write "<tr>"

'loop through and display results
Do Until Rs.EOF
 Response.Write "<td>" &_
 Rs.Fields("urn:schemas:httpmail:sendername").Value & "</td>"
 Response.Write "<td>" &_
 Rs.Fields("urn:schemas:mailheader:subject").Value & "</td>"
 Response.Write "<td>" & _
 Rs.Fields("urn:schemas:mailheader:date").Value & "</td>"
 Response.write "</tr>"
 Rs.MoveNext
Loop
```

```
response.write "</table>"

Rs.Close

%>
</BODY>
</HTML>
```

Sample Applications

We used ADO extensively to create the sample intranet application included on this book's public Web site. An intranet application may include many types of information. For our intranet, we include such examples as a listing of unread messages, a listing of status reports from a public folder, and a listing of the corporate calendar. Download the sample intranet application and experiment on your own with the sample code.

Accessing the inbox

The code example that lists the unread messages from a user's inbox is a good example of using ADO 2.5 and SQL to search and list items in the Web Storage System. The code in Listing 7-2 lists only the unread messages from a user's inbox. This list is useful because it also requests each item's URL so the user can click on an item to read the message.

Listing 7-2: Listing Unread Inbox Messages

```
<%@ Language=VBScript %>
<%
Dim Rec
Dim Rs
Dim strURL
Dim SQL
Dim strSubj
Dim DomainName
Dim strLocalPath
Dim UnreadCount

Set Rec = CreateObject("ADODB.Record")
Set Rs = CreateObject("ADODB.Recordset")
DomainName = "company.com"
UserID ="insert your Exchange alias here"
```

Continued

Listing 7-2 *(Continued)*

```
strLocalPath = "MBX/" & UserID & "/inbox"

strURL = "file://./backofficestorage/" & DomainName & "/" & strLocalPath
Rec.Open strURL

SQL = "select "
SQL = SQL & ", ""urn:schemas:mailheader:from"""
SQL = SQL & ", ""urn:schemas:mailheader:subject"""
SQL = SQL & ", ""urn:schemas:httpmail:read"""
SQL = SQL & ", ""DAV:contentclass"""
SQL = SQL & ", ""DAV:href"""
SQL = SQL & " from scope ('shallow traversal of "
SQL = SQL & Chr(34) & strURL & Chr(34) & "') "
SQL = SQL & " WHERE ""urn:schemas:httpmail:read"" = false"

Rs.Open SQL, Rec.ActiveConnection
Rs.MoveFirst

response.write "<font size=-1>You have unread messages from:<br><ol>"

Do Until Rs.EOF
'change file://./backoffice/ into http:// URL
link = Rs.Fields("DAV:href").Value
newlink = Replace(link, "file://./backofficestorage_
/", "http://www.")
newlink = Replace(newlink, "MBX", "exchange")
itemname = Rs.Fields("urn:schemas:mailheader:from").Value

Response.write "<li><a target=new_window href='" & _
newlink & "'>" & itemname & "</a></li></font>"

Rs.MoveNext
Loop

' close the record and recordset
Rs.Close
Rec.Close

%>
```

Listing 7-2 uses only some of the possible properties available to you. Each message contains many properties that you can query. For example, the code sample in Listing 7-3 examines the first message in the inbox and lists each property and associated value of that message.

Listing 7-3: Enumerating Item Properties

```
<HTML>
<BODY>
<%@ LANGUAGE = VBScript %>
<%

'Bind to the container URL
URL = "http://cleo.hugefan.net/exchange/alex/inbox"
set conn = createobject("ADODB.connection")
conn.provider = "exoledb.datasource"
conn.open URL

'Use the recordset object to execute SQL commands
strQuery = "SELECT *"
strQuery = strQuery & " FROM SCOPE('shallow traversal _
of """ & URL & """')"
strQuery = strQuery & " where ""DAV:isfolder"" = false"

Set Rec = CreateObject("ADODB.Recordset")
Rec.Open strQuery, Conn

'enumerate and display each item property
for each iProp in rec.fields
  response.write "<b>" & iProp.name & "</b>: "
  if not isarray(iProp.value) then
   response.write iProp.value
  else
   response.write "multi-value"
  end if
response.write "<p>"
next
%>
</script>

</BODY>
</HTML>
```

Accessing public folders

Working with public folders is essentially the same as working with an inbox container. Once the connection has been made, you can enumerate the contents of that container — which may include more public folders — or create or delete items from the container. Listing 7-4 illustrates how to list a public folder's contents.

Listing 7-4: ADO Example: Enumerating Public Folder Contents

```
<HTML>
<BODY>

<%
Dim Rec
Dim Rs
Dim strURL
Dim SQL
Dim link
Dim newlink
Dim itemname

Dim DomainName
Dim strLocalPath

DomainName = "company.com"
strLocalPath = "public folders/foldername"

Set Rec = CreateObject("ADODB.Record")
Set Rs = CreateObject("ADODB.Recordset")

'build the URL using variables
strURL = "file://./backofficestorage/" & DomainName _
& "/" & strLocalPath

Rec.Open strURL
'build the SQL command
SQL = "select "
SQL = SQL & " ""urn:schemas:mailheader:content-class"" "
SQL = SQL & ", ""DAV:href"" "
SQL = SQL & ", ""DAV:displayname"" "
SQL = SQL & " from scope ('shallow traversal of "
SQL = SQL & Chr(34) & strURL & Chr(34) & "')"
SQL = SQL & " where ""DAV:ishidden"" = False _
and ""DAV:isfolder"" = False"
SQL = SQL & " ORDER BY ""DAV:displayname"" "

Rs.Open SQL, Rec.ActiveConnection
Rs.MoveFirst

response.write "Folder Contents:<br>"
While Not Rs.EOF

  itemname = Rs.Fields("DAV:displayname").Value
```

```
link = Rs.Fields("DAV:href").Value

'change file://./backoffice/public folders/foldername into
'www.servername.com/public/foldername
newlink = Replace(link, "file://./_
backofficestorage/", "http://www.")
newlink = Replace(newlink, "public folders", "public")

response.write "<ol>"
Response.write "<li><a href='" & newlink & _
"'>" & itemname & "</a></li>"

Rs.MoveNext
Wend
Rs.Close
Rec.Close

%>
</BODY>
</HTML>
```

The practical application for Listing 7-4 is creating an intranet Web site that lists technical documents, or marketing material saved to public folders by Microsoft Outlook users. When you use this method, you create a Web site that is inherently dynamic. The Web site is created each time a Web user visits, so it will include information recently saved there by Outlook users.

Accessing calendar items

You can access calendar containers just like any other container, but they have unique properties, of course, including start time, end time, attendees, location, and so forth. The example we use in our sample intranet application displays the corporate event schedule, as illustrated in Listing 7-5.

Listing 7-5: ADO Example: Listing Calendar Items

```
<HTML>
<HEAD>
<TITLE>Calendar Listing</TITLE>
</HEAD>
<BODY >

<%

Set Rec = CreateObject("ADODB.Record")
```

Continued

Listing 7-5 *(Continued)*

```
Set Rs = CreateObject("ADODB.Recordset")

strURL = "file://./backofficestorage/company.com/_
public folders/corporate calendar/"
Rec.Open strURL
Set Rs.ActiveConnection = Rec.ActiveConnection

Rs.Source = "SELECT ""DAV:href"", " & _
" ""urn:schemas:httpmail:subject"", " & _
" ""urn:schemas:calendar:dtstart"", " & _
" ""urn:schemas:calendar:dtend"" " & _
"FROM scope('shallow traversal of """ & strURL & """')"
Rs.Open
Rs.MoveFirst

%>

<br><br>
<TABLE border=0>
<tr>
<td align=center bgcolor="blue" width=200>Subject</td>
<td align=center bgcolor="blue">Start</td>
</tr>

<%

Do Until Rs.EOF
response.write "<tr><td>"
Response.Write Rs.Fields("urn:schemas:httpmail:subject").Value
response.write "</td>"

response.write "<td align=right>"
Response.Write Rs.Fields("urn:schemas:calendar:dtstart").Value
response.write "</td>"

Rs.MoveNext
Loop
%>
</tr>
</table>
</BODY>
</HTML>
```

Accessing contacts with ADO

In database terms, contacts are probably the closest thing in Exchange 2000 to what people normally think of when they think of a database. Use ADO to access and enumerate the contacts container, as illustrated in Listing 7-6.

Listing 7-6: Listing Contacts

```
<%@ Language=VBScript %>
<html>
<body>

<%
Dim Rs
Dim Rec
Dim strURL

DomainName = "company.com
strLocalPath = "MBX/User_alias/Contacts"

Set Rec = CreateObject("ADODB.Record")
Set Rs = CreateObject("ADODB.Recordset")
strURL = "file://./backofficestorage/" & _
DomainName & "/" & strLocalPath

Rec.Open strURL
Set Rs.ActiveConnection = Rec.ActiveConnection

Rs.Source = "SELECT ""DAV:href"", " & _
" ""urn:schemas:contacts:email1"", " & _
" ""urn:schemas:contacts:nickname"", " & _
" ""urn:schemas:contacts:title"" " & _
"FROM scope('shallow traversal of """ & strURL & """') "
Rs.Open
%>

<br><br>
<TABLE cellspacing=0 cellpadding=4>
<%
Do Until Rs.EOF
response.write "<tr><td>"
Response.Write "Nickname : " &
Rs.Fields("urn:schemas:contacts:nickname").Value
```

Continued

Listing 7-6 *(Continued)*

```
response.write "</td><td>"

Response.Write "Email1 : " &
Rs.Fields("urn:schemas:contacts:email1").Value
response.write "</td><td>"

Response.Write "Title : "
&Rs.Fields("urn:schemas:contacts:title").Value
response.write "</td><td>"

Rs.MoveNext
Loop
%>
</table>
</body>
</html>
```

When to Use CDO or ADO

You will learn in Part IV, "Collaboration and Messaging," that the syntax and uses for CDO for Exchange are similar to those for ADO. In fact, they were developed by Microsoft to complement each other – ADO to navigate the Web Storage System and CDO to manipulate the items properties.

Specifically, ADO objects are used for:

◆ Searching folders and folder hierarchies for messages

◆ Setting custom properties for messages

CDO objects are used for:

◆ Creating new message items

◆ Sending messages

◆ Modifying existing message items

For example, if you want to create an application that deletes a message from a mailbox, use ADO to connect to the mailbox folder and bind to the message stored in the Web Storage System. You then use CDO to delete the message.

Using both objects, however, does not necessarily mean that you need to make two connections to the Web Storage System. CDO can bind directly to the ADO datasource using the `IdataSource.OpenObject` or `IDataSource.SaveToObject` methods, so you don't have to make two connections. For example:

```
Dim Stm
Dim iMsg
Dim iDsrc
Dim Path
fPath="c:\myfile.doc"

Set Stm = CreateObject("ADODB.Stream")
Stm.Open
Stm.LoadFromFile fPath
Set iMsg = CreateObject("CDO.Message")
Set iDsrc = iMsg
iDsrc.OpenObject Stm, "_Stream"
Set LoadMessageFromFile = iMsg
```

Item manipulation

You can also use ADO for simple management operations, such as copying messages between folders. Listing 7-7 illustrates how to use ADO to copy a message from one folder to another.

Listing 7-7: Copying Folder Items Using ADO

```
<HTML>
<HEAD>
      <TITLE>ADO Copy Sample</TITLE>
</HEAD>

<BODY>
<%

Dim Rec, Info, InfoNT, sUrlRoot, sUrl, sUrlDest
Set Info   = CreateObject("ADSystemInfo")
Set InfoNT = CreateObject("WinNTSystemInfo")

SUrlRoot = "http://" & InfoNT.Computername & "." &
Info.DomainDNSName & "/public/"
sUrl     = sUrlRoot & "folder1/item1.txt"
SurlDest = sUrlRoot & "folder2/item2.txt"

Set Conn = CreateObject("ADODB.Connection")
Conn.Provider = "ExOLEDB.DataSource"
Conn.Open sUrl

Set Rec = CreateObject("ADODB.Record")
```

Continued

Listing 7-7 *(Continued)*

```
Rec.Open sURL, Conn, adModeReadWrite
Rec.CopyRecord ,sUrlDest
Rec.Close

%>
</BODY>
</HTML>
```

Summary

ADO gives you access to raw data in the Web Storage System (WSS). Use common ADO syntax to access items in the Web Storage System as you would access items in any database. Then navigate, search, and modify the properties of items using ADO objects. Navigation is made easy by using URL's. URL's allow you to bind directly to an object in the WSS without having to bind to a parent object first. ADO also lets you query the WSS using SQL-like syntax for fast and more direct searching. You will find ADO to be your best method for searching and navigating through folders and files in the WSS.

Chapter 8

HTTP/WebDAV and XML

THE WEB STORAGE SYSTEM supports the HTTP 1.1 World Wide Web Distributed Authoring and Versioning (WebDAV) extensions. The WebDAV extensions are a powerful technology used to offload server processing to the client and reduce stress on the server. The purpose of this chapter is to provide an overview of the main WebDAV methods, XML and XSLT, for creating and processing WebDAV responses. In addition, we will examine the general method of creating a WebDAV request, as well as XML transformations with XML style sheets.

An Overview of WebDAV

WebDAV is an extension of the HTTP 1.1 protocol specification. WebDAV, as described in Request For Comment RFC2518, provides a standard set of HTTP protocol extensions with which clients can remotely edit and publish (write) to WebDAV-aware HTTP servers.

WebDAV enables seamless integration and collaboration among teams because it is operating system–independent (OS-independent), as long as the client can communicate over HTTP. The mechanism for communication between client and server, as described in RFC2518, is XML. XML was chosen because of its internationalization support and its extensibility.

The WebDAV specification identifies key methods for *name-space manipulation, locking* (collision avoidance), *remote resource management,* and *resource properties.*

◆ *Name-space manipulation* refers to the ability to move and copy resources.

◆ *Locking* prevents users from overwriting each others work. The WebDAV specification forces a compare or merge before files can be published.

◆ *Remote resource management* enables full management of resources within the file system: You can *create*, *delete*, *view*, *edit*, and *publish* (write) resources and folders (collections).

◆ *Resource properties* are metadata about a given resource on the server. Resource properties can be anything that describes the resource, such as author, title, subject, and publication date. Resource properties can also be used for searching and retrieving resources on the server.

WebDAV server support for the Microsoft platform is incorporated into Windows 2000 and Internet Information Server 5.0. Client support involves Internet Explorer 5.0 and above with the Microsoft XML COM object model (MSXML) and Office 2000. Exchange 2000 integrates with IIS 5.0 through virtual servers exposing the Web Storage System public folder over the HTTP protocol. Clients can then use the XMLHTTP object to build XML WebDAV requests to work with resources within the Web Storage System. Security for WebDAV is controlled though IIS and Exchange.

For the complete WebDAV specification, go to `http://www.webdav.org/ specs/ RFC2518`.

WebDAV: HTTP 1.1 Protocol Extensions

As defined in the RFC2518, the HTTP 1.1 extensions define a set of methods and headers with which to create and process WebDAV requests. Tables 8-1, 8-2, and 8-3, respectively, list the methods, headers, and status codes used in creating and processing WebDAV requests and responses.

TABLE 8-1 WEBDAV METHODS

Method Name	Description
GET	Retrieves an entity identified by the request URI
HEAD	Identical to GET without the response-message body

Method Name	Description
PUT	Creates a non-collection resource. If the parent or ancestors do not exist, the request must FAIL with a 409 (conflict) status.
POST	Used to submit forms. Does not apply to collection resources.
OPTIONS	Discovers the compliant classes of a resource.
COPY	Copies a resource from its current URI to a destination URI specified in the destination header. The destination header must be present. Success is not guaranteed if the resource is locked by another process.
MOVE	Moves a resource from its current URI to a destination URI in a three-step process: COPY, consistency check, DELETE. All three steps are automatic and the destination header must be present. Success is not guaranteed if the resource is in use by another process.
DELETE	Deletes the resource from its current URI and any references to the current URI.
MKCOL	Creates a collection resource (folder).
PROPFIND	Retrieves properties defined on the request URI. May use a depth header of 1, 0, or infinity.
PROPPATCH	Sets or removes properties from the request URI. Must use the propertyupdate, set, and remove XML elements.
LOCK	The resource is unavailable by means of the lockinfo XML element. Must contain a timeout header unless it is a refresh to an existing lock by this resource.
UNLOCK	Removes a lock token as specified in the lock token request header from the requested resource.
SEARCH	Initiates a server-side search. Must use the searchrequest, sql XML elements. Not part of RFC2518. This is a modified version of the SEARCH method defined in Internet-Draft: DAV Searching & Locating, which may be found at, http://www.webdav.org/ dasl/protocol/draft-dasl-protocol-00.html

TABLE 8-2 WEBDAV REQUEST HEADERS

Header	Description
Depth	Used with PROPFIND or SEARCH methods to determine the scope of the search. May except values of 0, 1, or infinity. Depth Infinity is not supported for MAPI-accessible stores.
Destination	Specifies the URI that identifies a destination. Used with MOVE and COPY.
Lock-Token	Used with the UNLOCK method to identify the lock to be removed.
Overwrite	Specifies whether or not to overwrite a destination resource during a COPY or MOVE operation. May pass a value of F for false or T for true.
Status-URI	Used with the 102 (Processing) status code to inform the client of the status of a method.
Timeout	Sets the expiration date and time for the LOCK requests. Clients may include Timeout headers in their LOCK requests.
Content-Type	Organizes media types.
Content-Length	Indicates the size of the entity body.
Expires	Specifies the date/time after which the response is considered stale.
Location	Used to redirect the recipient to a location other than the request-URI for completion of the request or identification of a new resource.
Refer	The address (URI) of the resource from which the request-URI was obtained.
Translate	Indicates if the Web server should perform any "translation" on the file (that is, return the source or the rendered version of the file).
Range	Used in issuing a SEARCH. Returns the specific range: Example: Range: rows=20-39
DAV Header	Indicates that the resource supports the DAV schema and protocol.

Header	Description
If Header	Intended for use with any URI that represents state information, referred to as a *state token*, about a resource, as well as ETags.
No-tag-list Production	Describes a series of state tokens and ETags
Tagged-list Production	Specifies that the lists following the resource specification apply only to the specified resource.

TABLE 8–3 WEBDAV RESPONSE STATUS CODES

Status Codes	Description
100	All 1*xx* level codes are *informational*
200	All 2*xx* level codes indicate *success*
300	All 3*xx* level codes indicate *redirection*
400	All 4*xx* level codes indicate *client errors*
500	All 5*xx* level codes indicate *server errors*

Introduction to XML

Extensible Markup Language (XML) is the mechanism used to send and receive WebDAV requests and process responses. XML is a universal means of describing structured data. Consider the table structure for a personal book collection shown in Figure 8-1.

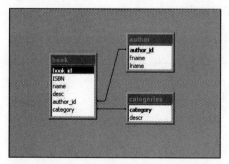

Figure 8-1: Structured data for a personal book collection

XML, when examined by Notepad or other text editors, looks similar to HTML and is stored as plain text with a file extension of .xml. XML makes use of tags and attributes, just like HTML, but XML is well formed, meaning that every tag comes in a pair: an opening and a closing tag. HTML has tags that are not well formed, such as <IMG> and <BR>. These tags do not have closing tags associated with them. Also, XML tags are not defined, meaning, if the tag <B>...</B> is used in an XML document, it does not necessarily indicate boldface type as it would in an HTML document. The tags in a well-formed XML document are delimiters describing the data in the document. Listing 8-1 is an example of an XML string describing the personal book collection shown in Figure 8-1.

Listing 8-1: Book Collection XML Code Example

```
<BOOKS>
  <BOOK id='1'>
    <ISBN>0-1234-5678-9</ISBN>
    <NAME>Pumpkins in the Night</NAME>
    <DESC>This is a scary book</DESC>
    <CATEGORY>Mystery</CATEGORY>
    <AUTHOR id='1'>
      <FNAME>Mr. Old</FNAME>
      <LNAME>Orchard</LNAME>
    </AUTHOR>
  </BOOK>
</BOOKS>
```

Note that each tag in Listing 8-1 has a correlating closing tag, and that some tags also contain attributes. Internet Explorer will display well-formed XML documents using a default style sheet. Figure 8-2 shows how Internet Explorer will display the books.xml document.

You can include XML in your Web pages using XML Data Islands. An XML Data Island is used to allow client-side scripting against an XML document, and is made up of an open <XML> tag, a closing <XML> tag, and an id attribute identifying the data island. XML Data Islands can be created inline (Listing 8-2), loaded through the src attribute (Listing 8-3), or included as part of a <SCRIPT> block (Listing 8-4). XML Data Islands do not display as part of your Web page and do not consume physical space on the page. You refer to the data island through its id attribute. When you are using the src attribute, the source is a relative or absolute path to the XML file.

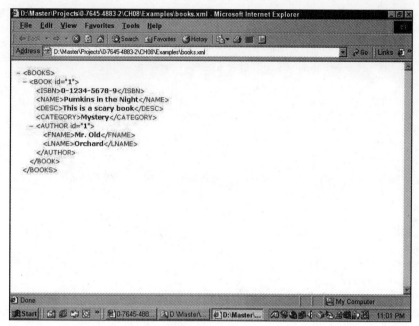

Figure 8-2: Internet Explorer displaying books.xml

Listing 8-2: Including an Inline XML Data Island on a Web page

```
<HTML>
  <HEAD>
  <TITLE>XML Data Island, inline</TITLE>
  </HEAD>
  <BODY>
  <XML id='xmlBooks'>
    <BOOKS>
     <BOOK id='1'>
       <ISBN>0-1234-5678-9</ISBN>
       <NAME>Pumpkins in the Night</NAME>
       <DESC>This is a scary book</DESC>
       <CATEGORY>Mystery</CATEGORY>
       <AUTHOR id='1'>
         <FNAME>Mr. Old</FNAME>
         <LNAME>Orchard</LNAME>
       </AUTHOR>
     </BOOK>
    </BOOKS>
  </XML>
  </BODY>
</HTML>
```

Listing 8-3: Including an XML Data Island on a Web Page Using the src Attribute

```
<HTML>
  <HEAD>
  <TITLE>XML Data Island, using the src attribute</TITLE>
  </HEAD>
  <BODY>
  <XML id='xmlBooks' src='books.xml'></XML>
  </BODY>
</HTML>
```

Listing 8-4: Including an XML Data Island on a Web Page Using the <SCRIPT> Tag

```
<HTML>
  <HEAD>
  <TITLE>XML Data Island, using the SCRIPT block</TITLE>
  </HEAD>
  <BODY>
  <SCRIPT language='xml' id='xmlbooks'>
    <BOOKS>
     <BOOK id='1'>
        <ISBN>0-1234-5678-9</ISBN>
        <NAME>Pumpkins in the Night</NAME>
        <DESC>This is a scary book</DESC>
        <CATEGORY>Mystery</CATEGORY>
        <AUTHOR id='1'>
          <FNAME>Mr. Old</FNAME>
          <LNAME>Orchard</LNAME>
        </AUTHOR>
      </BOOK>
    </BOOKS>
  </SCRIPT>
  </BODY>
</HTML>
```

XML elements can also use name spaces. A name space is used to uniquely identify the element across the Internet so it cannot be confused with another XML element of the same name. XML structures can contain multiple name spaces. A name space can be a Uniform Resource Identifier (URI), Uniform Resource Number (URN), or Uniform Resource Locator (URL). Each type must adhere to the W3C rules for that particular type. To use a name space with an XML structure, use the xmlns attribute and assign an abbreviation to your name space. Then use the abbreviation to define your elements. Listing 8-5 demonstrates the <BOOKS> XML structure using the name space URL http://starship.enterprise.com.

Listing 8-5: Using an XML Name Space with Your XML Structure

```
<sec:BOOKS xmlns:sec='http://starship.enterprise.com'>
 <sec:BOOK id='1'>
   <sec:ISBN>0-1234-5678-9</sec:ISBN>
   <sec:NAME>Pumpkins in the Night</sec:NAME>
   <sec:DESC>This is a scary book</sec:DESC>
   <sec:CATEGORY>Mystery</sec:CATEGORY>
   <sec:AUTHOR id='1'>
     <sec:FNAME>Mr. Old</sec:FNAME>
     <sec:LNAME>Orchard</sec:LNAME>
   </sec:AUTHOR>
 </sec:BOOK>
</sec:BOOKS>
```

You can also use XML Schemas and Document Type Definition (DTD) to define your XML structures. XML also has support for data types. While these concepts are beyond the scope of this book, the following resources can aid you in a more comprehensive study of XML:

Microsoft MSDN   `http://msdn.microsoft.com/library/`
                          `default.asp?url=/nhp/`
                          `default.asp?contentid=28000438`

Microsoft XML SDK 3.0 `http://msdn.microsoft.com/downloads/`
                          `default.asp?url=/downloads/sample.asp?url=/`
                          `msdn--files/027/000/542/`
                          `msdncompositedoc.xml&frame=true`

DEVX XML-Zone   `http://www.xml-zone.com/`
                          `default1.asp?Area=XML`

W3C   `http://www.w3.org/XML/`

TOPXML   `http://topxml.com/`

XSLT   `http://xslt.com/`

The Microsoft XML parser (MSXML)

The Microsoft XML parser (MSXML) is a parser for working with XML documents in the Windows environment. The MSXML parser is distributed free from Microsoft and can be downloaded from the MSDN Web site at: `http://msdn.microsoft.com/downloads/default.asp?URL=/code/topic.asp?URL=/msdn-files/028/000/072/topic.xml`.

MSXML provides a set of properties and methods for loading, persisting, filtering, and sorting XML documents. This set of methods and properties are known as the Document Object Model (DOM).

The examples in this chapter are meant as an introduction to the DOM. For more examples using the DOM, as well as detailed information on the DOM objects and methods, please refer to the XML 3.0 SDK. The most recent release of MSXML (as of this writing) is Microsoft XML Core Services 4.0 RTM. The examples in this chapter will work with the MSXML Parser 3.0 sp1 release and the MSXML parser needs to be installed in Replace Mode. (Please refer to the Microsoft documentation for installing and configuring the MSXML parser in Replace Mode.) You can download the Replace Mode tool from Microsoft at `http://msdn.microsoft.com/downloads/default.asp?url=/downloads/sample.asp?url=/msdn-files/027/001/469/msdncompositedoc.xml&frame=true`. Table 8-4 lists the MSXML parser's core objects and descriptions.

TABLE 8-4 MSXML DOM CORE OBJECTS

Object	Description
DOMDocument	The top-level node of the XML tree
IXMLDOMDocument2	An extension to the DOMDocument. Supports schema caching, runtime validation, and a way to switch on XML Path Language (XPath) support.
IXMLDOMNamedNodeMap	Provides access to node attributes
IXMLDOMNode	A single node in the XML tree
IXMLDOMNodeList	Represents a collection of XML nodes
IXMLDOMParseError	Represents error information
IXMLHTTPRequest	Enables client-side communication with HTTP servers
IXTLRuntime	Enables interaction from within XSLT style sheets

WORKING WITH THE MSXML PARSER

At the root of the XML DOM is the DOMDocument object. Once a new DOMDocument is created, you can use the load or loadxml methods to load XML Data Islands or XML streams into the DOM. The load method takes an XML source as its parameter and the loadxml method takes an XML string as its parameter.

After loading an XML structure into the DOM object, you can use the parseError object to determine whether the XML structure is well formed. If a parseError exists, read the parseError.reason and parseError.srcText properties to get additional parse-error information. Under certain circumstances you may not want to allow the DOM object to parse the XML when loading. In these cases, you can set the validateOnParse property to false and the XMLDOM object will load the invalid XML source, for example, an unsupported data type. In this case, the DOM may not support the data type but you may still want to load the XML source. Listing 8-6 demonstrates how to create and load an XML Data Island into an XMLDOM using client-side JScript.

Listing 8-6: Creating and Loading an XML DOMDocument with an XML Data Island

```
<HTML>
<HEAD>
<TITLE>Creating and Loading an XML DOMDocument</TITLE>
</HEAD>
<BODY>
<!--XML Books Data Island -->
<XML id='xmlbooks' src='books.xml'></XML>
<!—Script Block -->
<SCRIPT language='JScript'>
  // Create the xml DOMDocument
  var xmldom = new ActiveXObject("DOMDocument.3.0");
  // if this is set to false there is no need to check the
  // parseError object
  xmldom.validateOnParse = true;
  /* Load the Data Island into the DOM Object
     using the xml data island id as the source for the load
     method */
  xmldom.load(xmlbooks.src);
  //check to ensure that there is not a parseError
  if (xmldom.parseError) {
    err = xmldom.parseError;
    alert(err.reason + "\n" + err.srcText);
    return;
  }
  //display the xml using the xml property of the xmldom object
  alert(xmldom.xml);
  xmldom = null;
</SCRIPT>
</BODY>
</HTML>
```

You can also use the DOM to create XML elements and add the XML to a Data Island. First create an xmldom object. Then create the individual elements using the createElement method (use the createElement method because you need to use the setAttribute method to set attributes for the book and author elements). Then use the append Child method to append each element to its parent node. The last step is to load the XML into the Data Island using the loadXML method. Listing 8-7 demonstrates how to use the DOM to create an XML document and load it into an XML Data Island.

Listing 8-7: Using the DOM to Create XML Elements and Load Them into a Data Island

```
<HTML>
<HTML>
<HEAD>
<TITLE>Creating and Loading an XML DOMDocument</TITLE>
</HEAD>
<BODY>
<!--XML Books Data Island -->
<XML id='xmlbooks'></XML>
<!--Script Block -->
<SCRIPT language='JScript'>
  // Create the xml DOMDocument
  var xmldom = new ActiveXObject("MSXML2.DOMDocument.3.0");
  var nodebooks;
  var nodebook,nodeisbn,nodename,nodedesc,
  var nodecat,nodeauth,nodefname,nodelname;

  //Create Each Node Element
  nodebooks = xmldom.createElement("BOOKS")
  nodebook = xmldom.createElement("BOOK")
  nodebook.setAttribute("id",1)
  nodeisbn = xmldom.createElement("ISBN")
  nodeisbn.text = "0-1234-5678-9"
  nodename = xmldom.createElement("NAME")
  nodename.text = "Pumpkins in the Night"
  nodedesc = xmldom.createElement("DESC")
  nodedesc.text = "This is a scary book"
  nodecat = xmldom.createElement("CATEGORY")
  nodecat.text = "Mystery"
  nodeauth = xmldom.createElement("AUTHOR")
  nodeauth.setAttribute("id",1)
  nodefname = xmldom.createElement("FNAME")
  nodefname.text = "Mr. Old"
  nodelname = xmldom.createElement("LNAME")
  nodelname.text = "Orchard"

  // Append each element to the appropriate Node
  nodebook.appendChild(nodeisbn)
  nodebook.appendChild(nodename)
  nodebook.appendChild(nodedesc)
  nodebook.appendChild(nodecat)
  nodebook.appendChild(nodeauth)
  nodeauth.appendChild(nodefname)
  nodeauth.appendChild(nodelname)
  nodebooks.appendChild(nodebook)
```

```
// Append to the xmldom
xmldom.appendChild(nodebooks)

//display the xml using the xml property of the xmldom object
//alert("xmldom:" + "\n" + xmldom.xml);

/*
    Load the XML from the DOM to the Data Island through the
    loadXML method of the Data Island
*/
xmlbooks.loadXML(xmldom.xml)
xmldom = null;

//display the xml using the xml property of the data island
//alert("xmlbooks:" + "\n" + xmlbooks.xml);
</SCRIPT>
</BODY>
</HTML>
```

After loading the DOM object with an XML structure, you can search the DOM object for an individual node using the selectSingleNode method, or filter the DOM object for a list of nodes using the selectNodes method. The MSXML parser provides support for the XML Path Language (XPath) version 1.0 (http://www.w3.org/TR/1999/REC-xpath-19991116), which is the query language used in building queries against the populated XML DOM object. XPath is pattern-driven and works much like the hierarchy of a tree. You start with the topmost branches in the tree and work your way down to the element you are searching for. Table 8-5 illustrates several examples of the XPath query language.

TABLE 8–5 XPATH LANGUAGE EXAMPLES

Query	Description
BOOKS or ./BOOKS	Finds all BOOKS elements from the current context. (Use the dot . as the current context.)
BOOKS/BOOK[@id = '1']	Finds the BOOK element whose attribute is id = '1'. (Use the / as a path separator and the [ ] as a pattern or filter and the @ to locate attributes.)
BOOKS/BOOK//NAME	Finds all the NAME elements that are descendents of the BOOK element. (Use // to search each element below the current element.)

Continued

TABLE 8–5 XPATH LANGUAGE EXAMPLES *(Continued)*

Query	Description
BOOKS/BOOK//AUTHOR[@id = '1']	FINDs the AUTHOR element with attribute id = '1' whose parent is BOOK.
BOOKS/BOOK//AUTHOR/*	Finds all the child elements of the AUTHOR element whose parent is BOOK. (Use the * as a wildcard.) Returns all elements.
c:BOOKS	Finds all the BOOKS elements from the c: name space. (Use : as a name-space separator.)

Please refer to Listing 8-1 as a guide for these examples.

 For complete syntax and functionality provided by the XPath language, please refer to the Microsoft XML 3.0 SDK. The Web reference is listed in Table 8-4.

The MSXML parser also supports XML Style Sheets (XSL), a language for expressing style sheets, and XSL Transformations (XSLT), a transformation language for transforming XML documents that is the predecessor to XSL. XML alone has no mechanism for formatting XML data in a presentable way. XSL, XSLT, and XPath provide ways to query, filter, search, and merge or transform XML into HTML or other XML documents.

Listing 8-8 illustrates an example of an XML/XSL transformation for paging and filtering the data. The example transforms an XML Data Island using the tansformNode method of the DOM document object. Figures 8-3 and 8-4 show the HTML Web-page output in Internet Explorer. The complete sample can be downloaded from the books public Web site.

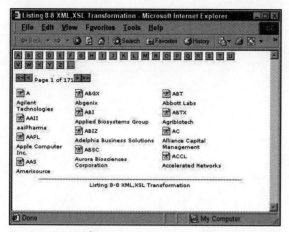

Figure 8-3: XML/XSL transformation example, illustrating the Filter function

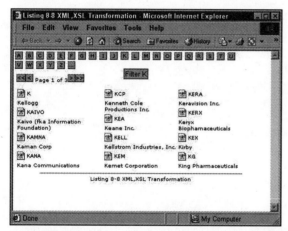

Figure 8-4: XML/XSL transformation example, illustrating the Paging function

Listing 8-8: Using an XSL Style Sheet and the XML transformNode Method

```
<HTML>
<HEAD>
  <TITLE>Listing 8-8 XML,XSL Transformation</TITLE>
</HEAD>
<STYLE>
...
</STYLE>
<SCRIPT language='JScript'>
  function doInitDoc() {
```

Continued

Listing 8–8 *(Continued)*

```
// Use the parseError object to check for parse errors
  if(tickerXML.parseError.errorCode != 0) {
    pErr = tickerXML.parseError;
    alert(pErr.reason + "\n" + pErr.srcText);
    return;
  }
  else {
    /* Using the data id set the innerhtml to the results
       of the transformation */
    data.innerHTML = tickerXML.transformNode(tickerXSL.documentElement);
  }
}
// dofilter
// param letter to filter on
function dofilter(ltr) {
  var fltr1 = "";
  var fltr2 = "";
  // Select the whichpage parameter from the XSL style sheet
  wp = tickerXSL.selectSingleNode("//xsl:param[@name = 'whichpage']");
  // Select the filter parameters from the XSL style sheet
  // these are active live nodes when selected, that is when they
  // are modified they are modified in the style sheet
  fltr1 = tickerXSL.selectSingleNode("//xsl:param[@name='filter1']");
  fltr2 = tickerXSL.selectSingleNode("//xsl:param[@name='filter2']");

  // reset whichpage to 1
  wp.text = 1;

  if (ltr != "...") {
  // set the text property of the filter to upper case and lower case letters
  fltr1.text = ltr.toUpperCase();
  fltr2.text = ltr.toLowerCase();
  }
  else {
    // if this is the ... letter reset the filters to ""
    fltr1.text = "";
    fltr2.text = "";
  }
  // call the transform function
  doInitDoc();
  // unselect the letters
  doUnselect();
  // use the srcElement to change the style
```

```
      window.event.srcElement.className = "selltr";
      // return the call
      return;
    }
// -------- Scrolling Functions ---------//
...
</SCRIPT>
<BODY topmargin='0' leftmargin='0' onLoad='doInitDoc()'>
<!-- XML and XSL Data Islands -->
<XML id='tickerXML' src='rawxml.xml'></XML>
<XML id='tickerXSL' src='abcsort.xsl'></XML>

<TABLE style='BACKGROUND-COLOR: White' border='0' width='500'>
  <TR>
    <TD align='left' id='abc' width='450'>
    <!--call the dofilter function passing the id of the letter -->
      <SPAN onClick='dofilter(this.id)' title='Filter A' class='ltr' id='A'
>A</SPAN>
      <SPAN onClick='dofilter(this.id)' title='Filter B' class='ltr' id='B'
>B</SPAN>
...
    </TD>
  </TR>
  <TR>
    <TD>
      <TABLE style='BACKGROUND-COLOR: white' border='0' width='500'>
        <TR>
          <!-- Location of transformed XML -->
          <TD valign='top' width='450' id='data'></TD>
        </TR>
      </TABLE>
    </TD>
  </TR>
...
</TABLE>
</BODY>
</HTML>
```

All XSLT style sheets begin with an `<?xml version="1.0"?>` processing instruction, followed by the `<xsl:stylesheet>` tag, which defines the XSLT name space `http://www.w3.org/1999/XSL/Transform` and any custom name spaces. XSLT style sheets can consist of as many templates as you like, and can be called by name or through the `match` attribute. Although Listing 8-9 does not make use of this feature, templates can also be imported with the `<xsl:import>` tag.

In Listing 8-9, the first XML template matches the root of the XML document and processes the data according to parameters that are set by JScript from the HTML page and then uses different templates within the style sheet to output the HTML. The style sheet ends with the closing XSL style-sheet tag, </xsl:stylesheet>.

XSL style sheets must also conform to the rules of well-formed XML, which means stricter syntax. Listing 8-9 shows the general outline of the XSL style sheet.

TIP Several XSL debuggers are on the market. We have used Xselerator by MarrowSoft (http://www.marrowsoft.com/), which comes complete with an XPath query analyzer and which we highly recommend. You can download a free 30-day trial. Other XSLT resources can be found at http://xslt.com and http://topxml.com.

Listing 8–9: XSL Style-Sheet General Code Outline

```
<?xml version="1.0"?>
xsl style sheets are well formed just like xml structures
<xsl:stylesheet xmlns:xsl='http://www.w3.org/1999/XSL/Transform'
xmlns:a='DAV:' xmlns:b='bwawe-2000:' version='1.0'>
<xsl:output method='html'/>
...
<xsl:template match='/'>
...
</xsl:template>
<xsl:template name='vcardheader'>
    <xsl:param name="numpages"/>
...
</xsl:template>
<xsl:template name='vcardfooter'>
...
</xsl:template>
<xsl:template match='a:response'>
...
</xsl:template>
<xsl:template name='tickervcard'>
...
</xsl:template>
</xsl:stylesheet>
```

Creating WebDAV Requests Using the XMLHTTP Object

Part of the MSXML parser is the `MSXML2.XMLHTTP` object you use when creating and processing WebDAV HTTP requests. The typical steps in creating a request are as follows:

1. Use the `open` method on a resource, setting the `execute` method and authentication settings.

2. Set any custom headers using the `setRequestHeader`.

3. Use the `send` method to send the request.

4. Process the response by reading one of the four response properties:

   - `responseBody`

   - `responseStream`

   - `responseText`

   - `responseXML`

Table 8-6 lists the properties of the XMLHTTP object model.

TABLE 8-6 XMLHTTP PROPERTIES DESCRIPTION

Property	Description
onreadystatechange	Set this property to the event handler of a synchronous request. Allows the request to call the event handler during the statechange.
readyState	Returns the state of the event
responseBody	Returns the response body as a byte array
responseStream	Returns the response body as an IStream object
responseText	Returns the response body as a string
responseXML	Returns the response body as an XML structure
status	HTTP status code returned by the response
statusText	HTTP status text returned by the response

Table 8-7 lists the methods of the XMLHTTP object model.

TABLE 8–7 XMLHTTP METHODS DESCRIPTION

Method	Description
abort	Cancels the current request
getAllResponseHeaders	Retrieves all the HTTP headers
getResponseHeader	Retrieves a single HTTP header
open	Initializes the MSXML2.HTTP object and determines the method to use, the resource, and the authentication information for the request
send	Sends the HTTP request and receives the response
setRequestHeader	Sets a value for a HTTP header when sending a request to the Web server with the send method

Creating and updating items using WebDAV

Following the typical steps to create an XML HTTP request, to create a new non-collection item in the Web Storage System using WebDAV you use the WebDAV PROPPATCH method, specifying the name of a new or existing item. Set the content-type and translate headers. Next, send an XML requestBody using the <propertyupdate> <set/> <prop/>...</propertyupdate> XML structure. Lastly, check the status returned from the request for success or failure. When constructing the XML requestBody structure, remember to specify the content-class of the item you are creating.

The main difference between updating an item and creating an item is that when you are updating an item the source URI exists, which is what causes the item to be updated rather than created. Listing 8-10 provides an example of how to create a new non-collection item with a fictitious Oriental-rug company's rug content-class. To update an item, pass the URI of the item. When creating the bstrxml, set only the properties you want to update.

Listing 8–10: Creating a Non–collection Item by Using the PROPPATCH WebDAV Method

```
<SCRIPT language='JScript'>
  xmlhttp = new ActiveXObject("MSXML2.XMLHTTP.3.0");
  function dosendreq(bstrURIResource, bstrxml, bstrDAVMethod) {
    // Initialize the http object with the DAV request Method
    // resource and async parameter to false.
```

```
xmlhttp.open(bstrDAVMethod, bstrURIResource, false);
// set the content headers using the setRequestHeader
xmlhttp.setRequestHeader("content-type","text/xml");
xmlhttp.setRequestHeader("translate","f");
//send the request
if(bstrxml != "") {
  xmlhttp.send(bstrxml);
}
else {
  xmlhttp.send();
  }
//Check the status code to see if the request was successful
// any status other than a 200 level code is an error
if(xmlhttp.status >= 200 && xmlhttp.status < 300) {
  return true;
}
else {
  return false;
}
}


// this function will show the error, because the xmlhttp object
// is global to these functions just read the status and
// statusText if return is false
function showError() {
  alert(xmlhttp.status + "\n" + xmlhttp.statusText);
  return;
}
</SCRIPT>
```

The `bstrxml` parameter is an XML structure (shown in Listing 8-11) and is generated by the `createUpdateRugXML` function. The only tricky part of the structure is the XML name spaces. When creating `propertyupdate` XML structures, you need to incorporate at a minimum the `DAV:` name space. You do this by defining an XML name space using the `xmlns:` attribute and the alias, followed by the name space. For example, to include the `DAV:` name space, you include the following in your `propertyupdate` tag:

```
xmlns:a="DAV:"
```

Then refer to the `propertyupdate` with the alias `<a:propertyupdate>`. (See Listing 8-5 for more information on name spaces in XML.)

When working with multivalued properties or a data type other than a string, you need to ensure that you define the Microsoft XML data-type name space `urn:uuid:c2f41010-65b3-11d1-a29f-00aa00c14882/` as a valid XML name-space alias. You must then use the alias on the appropriate properties with the correct data type. To reference the data-type name space within each property, use the data type name-space alias and then dt='*data type*'. Notice in Listing 8-11 that the data type name-space alias is using b; therefore, when referring to the name space you would use b:dt='mv.string', which indicates that this is a multivalued string property. Each value of the property is then referenced by the XML name-space alias (<c:v>) within the property tag.

Listing 8–11: bstrXML Parameter Structure

```
<a:propertyupdate xmlns:b='urn:uuid:c2f41010-65b3-11d1-a29f-
00aa00c14882/' xmlns:c='xml:' xmlns:a='DAV:'
xmlns:s='starship-enterprise-com'>
  <a:set>
    <a:prop>
      <a:contentclass>starship-enterprise-com:content-
classes:rug</a:contentclass>"
      <s:id>9995869</s:id>
      <s:name>Kazak</s:name>
      <s:desc>Every Kazak rug is unique.</s:desc/>
      <s:country>Russia</s:country/>
      <s:price>$3000</s:price/>
      <s:size>10x12</s:size/>
      <s:colors b:dt='mv.string'>
        <c:v>red</c:v>
        <c:v>green</c:v>
        <c:v>blue</c:v>
      </s:colors>
      <s:instock b:dt='boolean'>1</s:instock>
      <s:qty>100</s:qty>
    </a:prop>
  </a:set>
</a:propertyupdate>
```

When updating an existing item, set only the properties you want to update.

Creating collections (folders)

To create a folder or collection object within the Web Storage System, use the WebDAV MKCOL method and pass the name of the folder URI. If you pass a requestBody you can set properties on the folder, such as the DAV: displayname.

If no `requestBody` is passed then no properties will be set. The `requestBody` XML consists of the `<propertyupdate><set/><prop/>...<propertyupdate>` XML structure. Refer to Listing 8-11 as a reference for an example of how to use the `propertyupdate` XML structure. You can use the `dosendreq` function we used in Listing 8-10. The function accepts a `requestBody`, folder uri and a WebDAV method. To reuse the function, pass your `propertyupdate` XML structure as the `bstrxml` (optional) parameter, folder URI, and `MKCOL` as the `bstrDAVMethod` parameter.

Retrieving properties from a resource

To retrieve properties from a resource, issue a `PROPFIND` WebDAV request with a `<propfind><prop>...</propfind>` XML structure. You can also submit a `depth` header as part of the request. The `depth` header can be 1, 0, or `infinity` (by default, the `depth` header is `infinity`). If the `depth` header is 1, the `PROPFIND` request will not return custom properties that are not part of the content-class of the item. If you issue a `PROPFIND` request with a `depth` header of 0, the request will return all properties.

After a `PROPFIND` request is submitted, and if a successful response was returned, you will receive a `status` of 207 and a `statusText` of *multistatus* response. You can then read the `xmlResponse` property to retrieve the result. The `xmlResponse` property will return a `<multistatus>..</multistatus>` XML structure that can be loaded directly into an XMLDOM object for further processing. Listing 8-12 shows a `PROPFIND` WebDAV request and Listing 8-13 shows a sample `<multistatus>` XML structure.

Listing 8-12: Issuing a PROPFIND WebDAV Request

```
<SCRIPT language='JScript'>
  xmlhttp = new ActiveXObject("MSXML2.XMLHTTP.3.0");
  var xmldom = new ActiveXObject("MSXML2.DOMDocument.3.0");

  function dopropfind(bstrURIResource) {
    var szXML = "";
    //propfind xml structure
    szXML += "<a:propfind xmlns:a='DAV:' xmlns:s='starship-enterprise-com'>"
    szXML += "<a:prop>"
    szXML += "<s:id/>"
    szXML += "<s:name/>"
    szXML += "<s:desc/>"
    szXML += "</a:prop>"
    szXML += "</a:propfind>"
    // Initialize the http object with the DAV request Method
    // resource and async parameter to false.
```

Continued

Listing 8–12 *(Continued)*

```
xmlhttp.open("PROPFIND", bstrURIResource, false);
// set the content headers using the setRequestHeader
xmlhttp.setRequestHeader("content-type","text/xml");
xmlhttp.setRequestHeader("translate","f");
xmlhttp.setRequestHeader("depth","0");
//send the request
xmlhttp.send(szXML);
//Check the status code to see if the request was successful
if(xmlhttp.status == 207) {
  // Load the response into the xmldom
  xmldom.load(xmlhttp.responseXML);
  alert(xmldom.xml)
  return;
}
else {
  alert(xmlhttp.status + "\n" + xmlhttp.statusText);
}
}
```

Listing 8–13: A <multistatus> XML Structure for Listing 8-12

```
<a:multistatus xmlns:b="urn:uuid:c2f41010-65b3-11d1-a29f-
00aa00c14882/" xmlns:c="xml:" xmlns:s="starship-enterprise-com:"
xmlns:e="urn:schemas-microsoft-com:office:office" xmlns:a="DAV:">
  <a:response>
    <a:href>http://mailstrom/examples/rugstore/kazak.eml</a:href>
    <a:propstat>
      <a:status>HTTP/1.1 200 OK</a:status>
        <a:prop>
          <s:id>6568F69</s:id>
          <s:name>Kazak</s:name>
          <s:desc>Every Kazak rug is unique.</s:desc>
        </a:prop>
    </a:propstat>
  </a:response>
...
</a:multistatus>
```

Although this is not illustrated in Listing 8-13, it is possible to get multiple statuses within each response. For example, you may receive a property not found (<propstat>) or a data type not supported (<propstat>), followed by a list of the properties.

Creating search requests

Creating a search request is a little different from updating or retrieving an item using the PROPPATCH or PROPFIND methods. Instead of initializing the HTTP object with the URI of an item, you initialize it with a collection or folder URI. In creating a search request, you use the WebDAV method SEARCH and the new XML structure `<searchrequest><sql/>... </searchrequest>`, which is also part of the DAV: name space. The SEARCH request method also returns a `<multistatus>` XML structure.

Embedded within the `<searchrequest>` XML structure is a `<sql>` tag. Embedded within the `<sql>` tag is the Structured Query Language (SQL) that is sent to the server. The SQL statement is a standard SQL SELECT statement and has the following syntax:

```
SELECT select-list | *
FROM SCOPE(resource-list)
[WHERE search-condition]
[order-by-clause]
```

The SELECT statement list items are embedded within double quotes. For example:

```
SELECT "DAV:displaname", "starship-enterprise-com:id"
```

The FROM clause sets a scope, which can be one of the following:

```
'shallow traversal of "/rugs/"'
```

or

```
'deep traversal of "/rugs/inventory/"'
```

You can also specify the scope by setting the requestHeader depth to 1, 0, or infinity. On the depth header you can use a noroot option to exclude the root from the search. The syntax for this setting is as follows:

```
setRequestHeader("depth","1,noroot")
```

If a scope is not set, a shallow traversal is assumed. As in Listing 8-12, by modifying the szXML and changing the WebDAV method to SEARCH, you can create a search request. Listing 8-14 shows these changes.

For a review of SQL within the Web Storage System, please refer to Chapter 5, "Searching the Web Storage System."

Listing 8–14: A <searchrequest> WebDAV Request

```
...
szXML += "<a:searchrequest xmlns:d="DAV:"
xmlns:s='starship.enterprise.com'>"
szXML += "<a:sql>
szXML += "SELECT " + quoteSQL("DAV:displayname") + ", "
szXML += quoteSQL("starship-enterprise-com:id ") + ", "
szXML += quoteSQL("starship-enterprise-com:name ") + ", "
szXML += quoteSQL("starship-enterprise-com:price ") + ", "
szXML += "FROM scope('shallow traversal
of("http://mailstrom/example/rugstore/"')"
szXML += "WHERE " + quoteSQL("DAV:contentclass") + " = "
szXML += "'starship-enterprise-com:rug'"
szXML += "</a:sql>"
szXML += "</a:searchrequest>"


...
//modify the request Method
xmlhttp.open("SEARCH", bstrURIResource,false)
// process everything else the same.
...
```

Moving and copying items

To move and copy items in the Web Storage System, issue the MOVE or COPY
WebDAV request. Both methods use the destination requestHeader to the URL of
the new location for the item. Then send the request with an empty requestBody.
If the request is successful, your status property will be a 201 success. Listing
8-15 illustrates a MOVE and COPY function that accepts the fromURL and toURL and
then issues the WebDAV request.

Listing 8–15: Issuing a MOVE and COPY WebDAV Request

```
<SCRIPT language='JScript'>
  var xmlhttp = new ActiveXObject("MSXML2.XMLHTTP");

  function doMoveItem(fromURL, toURL) {
    // Initialize HTTP object
    xmlhttp.open "MOVE", fromURL, false
    xmlhttp.setrequestHeader("destination", toURL);
    xmlhttp.send();

    if(xmlhttp.status != 201) {
      alert(xmlhttp.status + "\n" + xmlhttp.statusText);
    }
  }
```

```
function doCopyItem(fromURL, toURL) {
  // Initialize HTTP object
  xmlhttp.open "COPY", fromURL, false
  xmlhttp.setRequestHeader("destination", toURL);
  xmlhttp.send();

  if(xmlhttp.status != 201) {
    alert(xmlhttp.status + "\n" + xmlhttp.statusText);
  }
}

fromURL = "http://mailstrom/examples/inventory/kazak.eml"
toInbox = "http://mailstrom/examples/inbox/kazak.eml"
toOutbox = "http://mailstrom/examples/outbox/kazak.eml"

doCopyItem(fromURL,toInbox);
doMoveItem(toInbox,toOutbox);
</SCRIPT>
```

Deleting items from the Web Storage System

To delete items from the Web Storage System, issue a WebDAV DELETE request. Pass the URL to the item and leave the requestBody empty. Listing 8-16 illustrates the DELETE method.

Listing 8-16: Deleting Items from the Web Storage System Using the DELETE Method

```
<SCRIPT language='JScript'>
  var xmlhttp = new ActiveXObject("MSXML2.XMLHTTP");

  function doDeleteItem(itemURL) {
    // Initialize HTTP object
    xmlhttp.open "DELETE", itemURL, false
    xmlhttp.send();

    if(xmlhttp.status != 201) {
      alert(xmlhttp.status + "\n" + xmlhttp.statusText);
    }
  }
</SCRIPT>
```

Creating a synchronous request

So far, all the requests we have created in this chapter have been asynchronous. The MSXML.XMLHTTP object has support for a synchronous request. A synchronous request returns control immediately to the caller before the request is complete; an asynchronous request does not return control to the caller until the request is complete.

To create a synchronous request, set the varAsync parameter to true on the open method. If the varAsync parameter is not set, the default is an asynchronous request.

Next, set the onreadystatechange property to a function to handle the event callback. To determine the state of the request, read the readyState property. Table 8-8 lists the possible values for the readyState property.

TABLE 8–8 POSSIBLE VALUES OF THE READYSTATE PROPERTY

Value	Description
(0) UNINITIALIZED	Indicates that the object has been created, but not initialized. The open method has not been called.
(1) LOADING	Indicates that the object has been created and initialized, but that the send method has not been called
(2) LOADED	Indicates that the send method has been called, but that the response is not yet available
(3) INTERACTIVE	Indicates that responseBody and responseText are available for partial data reads, but that full response is not yet available
(4) COMPLETED	Indicates that the request has been completed and that full response is available

The onreadystatechange is available only to scripting languages. This property cannot be used from Visual Basic or C++. Listing 8-17 illustrates how to create a synchronous request.

Listing 8–17: Creating a Synchronous WebDAV Request

```
<SCRIPT language='JScript'>
  var xmlhttp = new ActiveXObject("MSXML2.XMLHTTP");
  //Call Back Function to handle synchronous request
  function handleMe() {
    alert(xmlhttp.readyState)
    if(xmlhttp.readState == 4) {
      alert("Complete!")
    }
  }
```

```
function doDeleteItem(itemURL) {
  // Initialize HTTP object and set the Async parm to true
  // for a synchronous request
  xmlhttp.open "DELETE", itemURL, true
  // set the call back function
  xmlhttp.onreadystatechange = handleMe
  xmlhttp.send();
}
</SCRIPT>
```

Using an XML style sheet to transform a WebDAV response

The WebDAV methods PROPFIND and SEARCH return an xmlResponse in the form of a *multistatus* XML structure (Listing 8-13). Using the technique of an XML Data Island (refer to the "Introduction to XML" section earlier in this chapter), you can load the XML *multistatus* response into an XML DOMDocument object or an XML Data Island, and then transform the data using an XSL style sheet.

Loading the WebDAV XML response into an existing XML Data Island enables you to reuse the response without requiring a new request to the server and also makes for better performance during filtering and sorting. To demonstrate this, start by re-examining Listing 8-8, XML/XSL transformations: You can build upon this example by making the XML Data Island dynamic using the WebDAV SEARCH method with a depth header of 1,noroot and then loading the *multistatus* XML response into an XML Data Island. Listing 8-18 shows you how to do this by modifying the InitDoc() function to initiate a SEARCH WebDAV request and then loading the response into the tickerXML data island.

Listing 8-18: Modifying the InitDoc() Function with a WebDAV PROPFIND Request

```
<SCRIPT language='JScript'>
<HTML>
<HEAD>
  <TITLE>Listing 8-8 XML,XSL Transformation</TITLE>
</HEAD>
<STYLE>
...
</STYLE>
<SCRIPT language='JScript'>
  var xmldom = new ActiveXObject("MSXML2.DOMDocument.3.0");
  var xmlhttp = new ActiveXObject("MSXML2.XMLHTTP.3.0");
// AddQuotes function
function AddQuotes(str) {
  var tmpStr;
```

Continued

Listing 8-18 *(Continued)*

```
    tmpStr = "\"" + str + "\"";
    return tmpStr;
}
  // New function to load data
  // Only needs to be called once.
  function loadXML(uri) {
    szXML = ""
  //Create the XML search string
szXML = "<?xml version='1.0' ?>";
szXML += "<d:searchrequest xmlns:d='DAV:'>";
szXML += "<d:sql>";
szXML += "SELECT " + AddQuotes("starship-enterprise-com:ticker-id")
+ "," + AddQuotes("starship-enterprise-com:ticker-symbol") + "," +
       AddQuotes("starship-enterprise-com:co-name") + "," +
       AddQuotes("starship-enterprise-com:phone")
szXML += " FROM " + AddQuotes(uri)
szXML += " WHERE " + AddQuotes("DAV:contentclass") + " = 'starship-
enterprise-com:content-classes:tickers'"
szXML += "</d:sql>";
szXML += "</d:searchrequest>";

    //Initialize the WebDAV Request.
    xmlhttp.open("SEARCH",uri,false);
    xmlhttp.setRequestHeader("content-type","text/xml");
    xmlhttp.setRequestHeader("depth","1,noroot");
    //send the request passing the sxXML
    xmlhttp.send(szXML);
    //successful multistatus response
    if(xmlhttp.status == 207) {
      // first load into DOM
      xmldom.load(httpxml.responseXML)
      // next load into data island
      tickerXML.loadXML(xmldom.xml)
      // Call the new transformData function
      transformData();
    }
    else {
      showerrors();
    }
  }

  function transformData() {
data.innerHTML = tickerXML.transformNode(tickerXSL.documentElement);
  }
```

```
...
Modify the Body onLoad event to reflect the new function
<BODY topmargin='0' leftmargin='0'
onLoad='loadXML("http://mailstrom/examples/tickers/")'>
//modify the XML Data Island to reflect no src.attribute
<XML id='tickerXML'></XML>
<XML id='tickerXSL' src='abcsort.xsl'></XML>
...
</HTML>
```

Remember also to modify the `dofilter` function with the name of the new function, `transformData`. This is the main transformation routine at this point in the code example.

Summary

In this chapter we have explored the following topics:

♦ WebDAV

♦ The MSXML parser and the MSXML XMLHTTP object

♦ XML and XSLT

♦ How to leverage data islands and use them to transform XML into HTML using XSL style sheets

♦ How to build requests using the WebDAV methods with the MSXML XMLHTTP object and process those requests using XSL style sheets

♦ A complex XML transformation for scrolling and filtering an XML document

With the evolution of the World Wide Web and the wide acceptance of XML as a means for describing data, and of XSLT style sheets as a means of processing XML, it is easy to get a feel for the importance of these technologies. Not only do they make it easier for you to sort, search, and filter, but they provide standardization for describing and processing data.

The Web Storage System's support for these technologies is highly dependent on the WebDAV HTTP 1.1 extensions. The purposes of these technologies are to provide a mechanism for building collaborative applications by offloading server processing without degrading network bandwidth, in order to provide standardization for the act of communicating with a Web server regardless of OS — all without downloading bloated add-ins. WebDAV, XML, and XSLT truly bring collaborative applications to life.

Chapter 9

Active Directory Service Interfaces

ACTIVE DIRECTORY SERVICE INTERFACES (ADSI) gives you access to the underlying directory services. Since Exchange 2000 has no directory, the underlying directory service I'm talking about here is the Microsoft Windows 2000 Active Directory (AD). AD is built on the standard X.500 directory scheme and, as such, can be identified by its hierarchical structure of domains, organizations, containers, and objects. You can use the Lightweight Directory Access Protocol (LDAP) to access the AD (and many other X.500–based directory services), and both ADSI and LDAP are supported natively in the Windows 2000 environment.

ADSI gives you access to AD through a set of LDAP COM interfaces. You can use Active Server Pages (ASP) to access these COM interfaces to create users and distribution lists, and to search for resources throughout the Active Directory. This chapter will examine the use of ADSI to complete the following tasks:

- ◆ Create, delete, and manage users, distribution lists, and organizational units

- ◆ Search the Active Directory

LDAP Structure

It is critical to provide proper syntax when building LDAP query strings. Think of an LDAP query string as a URL. If you type one incorrect character in a URL, you will not get the results you expect. LDAP query strings are the same way.

Name-space review

Recall that the Active Directory is broken into logical separations called *name spaces*. Think of a name space as an organizational chart. Each organization is broken down into divisions, then groups and people. A typical name space for a user named Thomas McMahon in the ESS Organizational Unit might look like this:

```
CN=Thomas McMahon, OU=ESS, DC=Yourdomain, DC=Com
```

Where:

- ◆ CN is the common name of the object (in this case Thomas McMahon).

- ◆ OU is the organizational unit (in this case ESS).

- ◆ DC is the domain identification, broken into two parts for first- and second-level domain information. Yourdomain.com would be DC=yourdomain, DC=com.

While none of these fields are mandatory, you want to use enough of them to make the object you are binding to unique. If you are going to query for a list of all users in the Active Directory, you need to specify only the root domain, as follows:

```
LDAP:// DC=Yourdomain, DC=Com
```

However, if you are going to enumerate the child objects of an organizational unit, you need to include the OU in the LDAP query string:

```
LDAP:// OU=ESS,DC=Yourdomain, DC=Com
```

Querying the Active Directory

ADSI is not only used for querying for Exchange-related information; you can use it to query any information stored in the AD. This is helpful when you're writing portable code that does not depend on hard-coded domain-specific information. When you query the AD, you need a starting point for reference, such as yourcompany.com. So that you don't have to edit your code when moving your application from domain to domain, you'll start your application by searching for the root domain being used. Listing 9-1 illustrates querying the AD for the RootDSE.

Listing 9-1: Displaying the RootDomainNamingContext

```
<%@ LANGUAGE = VBScript %>
<%
Dim RootPath
Dim Path
```

```
'Make the connection
set Rootpath = Getobject("LDAP://RootDSE")

'request the name of the rootDomainNamingContext
path = rootpath.get("rootDomainNamingContext")

'display the result
response.write path
%>
```

Listing 9-2 goes further by connecting to the resulting `RootDSE` and queries for a list of users in that container. Since this container is the Root, the query will return all users in the AD.

Listing 9-2: Example That Queries the AD for a List of Users

```
<%@ LANGUAGE = VBScript %>
<%

dim domain
dim path
dim strADOSQL
dim Rec
dim objconn
dim objcom

'Set up variables
path = "LDAP://DC=yourdomain,DC=com"

'Define SQL query string
strADOSQL = "<" & path _
& ">;(&(objectCategory=Person)(objectClass=User))_
;samaccountname,name"

'Create the ADO connection
Set objconn = Server.CreateObject("ADODB.Connection")
objconn.Provider = "ADSDSOObject"
objconn.Open "ADs Provider"

Set objcom = Server.CreateObject("ADODB.Command")
Set objCom.ActiveConnection = objconn

objcom.commandtext = strADOSQL
Set Rec = objcom.execute
```

Continued

Listing 9-2 *(Continued)*

```
response.write "<table border=1 cellspacing=0>"
response.write "<tr><td><b>Alias</b></td><td>_
<b>Display Name</b></td></tr>"

While Not Rec.EOF
  Response.write "<tr><td>"
  Response.Write Rec.Fields(0)
  Response.write "</td><td>"
  Response.Write Rec.Fields(1)
  Response.Write "</td>"
  Response.write "</tr>"
  Rec.MoveNext
Wend

response.write "</table>"
rec.Close
objconn.Close
Set rec = nothing
Set objcom = nothing
Set objconn = nothing

%>
```

ADSI is often used in conjunction with some other technology. Remember that ADO is used to search and navigate the AD, so you can use ADO and ADSI together, first to navigate to a specific object in the AD, and then to manipulate the object in some way. ADO is also used to access Exchange information. Listing 9-3 illustrates how to query for all objects that have mailboxes. One way to know if a user object has an associated mailbox is to make a query to determine whether it has a home server. Listing 9-3 searches for all user objects that have a home server equal to anything (not blank).

Listing 9-3: Querying for List Users with Mailboxes

```
<HTML>
<HEAD>
</HEAD>
<BODY>
<%@ LANGUAGE = VBScript %>
<%
Dim path
path = "LDAP://host.yourdomain.com"

set rs = createobject("ADODB.connection")
```

```
rs.provider = "adsDSOobject"
rs.open path

strSQL = _
"SELECT adspath, cn, whencreated " & _
"FROM '" & strcon & "' " & _
"WHERE objectcategory='person' AND msExchHomeServername = '*'"
'use an asterisk to search for anything
set cmd = createobject("ADODB.Command")

Cmd.ActiveConnection = rs
Cmd.CommandText = strSQL
Cmd.CommandType = 1
Set Rec = Cmd.Execute

response.write "<table border=1><tr>"
response.write "<td><b>CN</b></td>"
response.write "<td><b>ADSPath</b></td>"
response.write "<td><b>WhenCreated</b></td>"
response.write "<tr>"

  Do Until rec.EOF
    response.write "<td>" & rec.Fields("cn") & "</td>"
    response.write "<td>" & rec.Fields("adspath") & "</td>"
    response.write "<td>" & rec.Fields("whencreated")
    response.write "</td><tr>"
    rec.MoveNext
  Loop
response.write "</table>"

rec.Close
rs.Close
Set rec = Nothing
Set cmd = Nothing
Set rs = Nothing

%>
```

Speeding up searches

Listing 9-1 is a simple illustration of querying the AD for information. You first bind to an item in the AD (even if it's the root), and then query that item. If you bind to the root, the search will be throughout the entire AD. To make searches faster, you can bind directly to either a sub-container or an object itself. Using the example in Listing 9-3, you can query to find out the ADSPath to a specific user.

Once you know the `ADSPath`, you can bind directly to it rather than parsing through the entire AD. Listing 9-4 illustrates how to bind directly to a user and then list its field values:

Listing 9-4: Binding to a User Object

```
<HTML>
<HEAD>
</HEAD>
<BODY>
<%@ LANGUAGE = VBScript %>

<%

Dim Path
Path = "LDAP://host.yourdomain.com/_
CN=DisplayName,OU=Org,DC=YourDomain,DC=com"

set rs = createobject("ADODB.connection")
rs.provider = "adsDSOobject"
rs.open Path

strSQL = "Select * from '" & path & "'"
set cmd = createobject("ADODB.Command")

Cmd.ActiveConnection = rs
Cmd.CommandText = strSQL
Cmd.CommandType = 1
Set Rec = Cmd.Execute

response.write "<tr>"
for each f in rec.fields
 response.write "<b>" & f.name & "</b>: "
 if not isarray(f.value) then
   response.write f.value
 else
   response.write "multi-value"
 end if
 response.write "<p>"
next

response.write "</table>"
rec.Close
rs.Close
Set rec = Nothing
Set cmd = Nothing
```

```
Set rs = Nothing

%>
```

In Listing 9-4, you binded directly to an object and queried for its property values. Another use of this is to bind to a parent object and query for a list of child objects in that container. For example, Listing 9-5 binds to a folder and queries for all files or folders within it.

Listing 9-5: Binding to a Container and List All Child Objects

```
<%@ LANGUAGE = VBScript %>
<%
Dim OU
Dim OUObject

Set OU = GetObject("LDAP://OU=Test_OU, _
DC=yourdomain, DC=com")
response.write "<table border=1><tr>"
response.write "<td>Name</td><td>Class</td></tr>"

For each OUObject in OU
 response.write "<td>" & OUObject.Name & "</td><td>" _
 & OUObject.class & "</td><tr>"
Next

response.write "</table>"
%>
```

Searching the Active Directory can be as easy as looping through all objects until you find the one you want. You can modify the example code in Listing 9-5 to do this, as follows:

```
For each OUObject in OU
 If OUObject.Name  = "John Smith" then
   <some code here>
 Next
```

However, this type of search can be very taxing on resources in a large directory. The best approach is to use the indexing power of the Active Directory and create a SQL query that is specific down to the container level, or even down to the user-object level. Remember, you can use ADSI in conjunction with ADO methods to create queries to the Web Storage System, as you would with any other database. Listing 9-6 illustrates the use of a specific query to show each user and its associated Exchange home server.

Listing 9-6: Searching for Exchange Home Server

```vbscript
<%@ LANGUAGE = VBScript %>

<FORM METHOD="GET" ACTION="this_page.asp">
Please enter last name: <input name="strLName" size=30> _
use * for ALL USERS)
<input type="submit" value="Search">
</form>

<%
Set conn = CreateObject("ADODB.Connection")
Set cmd = CreateObject("ADODB.Command")

conn.Provider = "ADsDSOObject"
conn.Open "Active Directory Provider"
Set Cmd.ActiveConnection = conn
strng = request.querystring("StrLName")

If strng <> "" then
 Cmd.CommandText = "select name,msexchhomeservername _
 from 'LDAP://DC=yourdomain,DC=com' _
 WHERE objectCategory='Person' _
 AND objectClass = 'user' _
 AND sn = " & "'" & strLName & "'"

 Set rs = Cmd.Execute

 response.write "<hr>"
 response.write "Search results for: " & strLName & "<p>"
 response.write "<Table border='1'><tr>"
 response.write "<td><b>Name</b></td><td><b>Home
Server</b></td><tr>"
  While Not rs.EOF
   response.write "<td>" & rs.Fields("name") & "</td>"
   response.write "<td>" & rs.Fields("msExchHomeServerName") _
   & "</td><tr>"
   rs.MoveNext
  Wend
end if
response.write "</table>"

%>
```

The scope of the query in Listing 9-6 is actually the entire directory. To narrow the scope to a particular organizational unit, change the `Cmd.CommandText` to include the organizational unit you want to search, as follows:

```
Cmd.CommandText = "select name,msexchhomeservername _
  from 'LDAP://OU=Test_OU,DC=yourdomain,DC=com' _
  WHERE objectCategory='Person' _
  AND objectClass = 'user' _
  AND sn = " & "'" & strLName & "'"
```

Managing the Active Directory with ADSI

ADSI not only supports searching the AD, but also provides interfaces with which you can make changes. For example, with ADSI you can create organizational units (OU) and users. First you make a connection to the container (either the root or another container), and then you use LDAP commands to create and save the new item. Listing 9-7 illustrates how to create an OU.

Listing 9-7: Creating an Organizational Unit

```
<%@ LANGUAGE = VBScript %>
<%
Dim path
Dim cname
Dim crdate
Dim NewOrg

'Make the connection
set path = Getobject("LDAP://DC=yourdomain,dc=com")

'Create New Organizational Unit
Set NewOrg = path.Create("OrganizationalUnit", "OU=Test_OU")
NewOrg.SetInfo
response.write "OU Created Successfully!"

%>
```

If you want to create an OU inside another OU instead of at the root, you can bind directly to the parent OU, as follows:

```
set path = Getobject("LDAP://OU=Test_OU, DC=yourdomain,dc=com")
```

This is especially important in the case of creating users, since you'll want to create users inside OUs rather than at the root in order to maintain an organized directory. Creating users is a little more advanced than creating OUs, simply because you have more fields to populate, including Exchange-mailbox information (see Part IV, "Collaboration and Messaging"). When you create a user, you do not need to populate all fields, but some are mandatory. Listing 9-8 illustrates how to create a user in the Test_OU you created in Listing 9-5, with the mandatory fields samaccountname and userprinciplename.

Listing 9-8: Creating a User in the Active Directory

```
<%@ LANGUAGE = VBScript %>
<%

Set OU = GetObject("LDAP://OU=Test_OU,DC=yourdomain,DC=com")
Set Ousr = OU.Create("user", "CN=Sunni Shepherd")
Ousr.Put "samAccountName", "SShepherd"
Ousr.Put "givenname", "Sunni" 'creates firstname
Ousr.Put "sn", "Shepherd" ' creates lastname
Ousr.Put "DisplayName", "Shepherd, Sunni"
Ousr.Put "userPrincipalName", "sshepherd@yourcompany.com" _
'used for win2k log on
Ousr.SetInfo 'must save user before you can set password

Ousr.SetPassword "password"
Ousr.AccountDisabled = False
Ousr.SetInfo
response.write "User Created Successfully!"

%>
```

To delete a user, bind to the OU that contains the user and use the delete command, as shown in Listing 9-9.

Listing 9-9: Deleting a User from Active Directory

```
<%@ LANGUAGE = VBScript %>
<%

Set OU = GetObject("LDAP://OU=Test_OU,DC=yourdomain,DC=com")
OU.delete "user", "CN=Ivan Kousidis"

response.write "User Deleted Successfully!"

%>
```

Creating groups is something else you'll probably have to do. Creating a group using LDAP is as easy as creating a container. The hardest part is deciding which type of group you need. Windows 2000 supports two: *Security Groups* and *Distribution*

Groups. Security Groups are for assigning permissions. Distribution Groups are, as you might expect, for e-mail distribution. You cannot assign permissions to a Distribution Group – only to a Security Group. Listing 9-10 illustrates creating either group type.

Listing 9-10: Creating a Group in the Active Directory

```
<%@ LANGUAGE = VBScript %>
<%
Dim OU
Dim Ogrp

Set OU = GetObject("LDAP://OU=Test_OU,DC=yourdomain,DC=com")
Set Ogrp = OU.Create("group", "CN=new_security_group")
Ogrp.Put "samAccountName", "sec_group"

'Use 2 is for Distribution, -2147483644 for Security
Ogrp.Put "groupType", -2147483644

Ogrp.SetInfo
response.write "Group Created Successfully!"

%>
```

Next, you'll want to add users to your new group, although the process is not what you might expect. The change is actually made to the group, rather than to the user. When adding users to a group manually, you open the properties of the group and add the user as a member. Similarly, when adding a user programmatically, you bind to and change the properties of the group. Listing 9-11 shows how to add a user to a group.

Listing 9-11: Adding a User to a Group

```
<%@ LANGUAGE = VBScript %>
<%
Dim Ogrp

Set Ogrp = GetObject("_
LDAP://CN=Marketing, OU=Test_OU, DC=yourdomain, DC=com")
Ogrp.Add ("LDAP://CN=Sunni Sheperd, _
OU=Test_OU, DC=yourdomain, DC=com")

Ogrp.SetInfo
response.write "User Added to Group Successfully!"

%>
```

Summary

ADSI provides the interface you need to search and manage the Active Directory (AD). LDAP is the underlying technology used by ADSI to connect to and manipulate the Active Directory. Use ADSI in your Active Server Pages to create and modify users, groups, and organization units, as well as to delete users. Search the Active Directory using a query language similar to the familiar SQL.

Chapter 10

Web Storage System Forms

WHEN YOU'RE VIEWING FOLDERS AND ITEMS within the Web Storage System over an HTTP request, Exchange will automatically render a default Outlook Web Access (OWA) view. Sometimes this view will not be exactly what you desire, or custom schema properties will not be supported on the default view. Using the Exchange Web forms technology, you can build custom forms within the Web Storage System to override default OWA views.

This chapter will show you how Exchange processes Web forms, how to create form-registration items, how to use the Exchange forms-renderer component (`exwforms.dll`), and how to use the FrontPage extensions for Web Storage System (WSS) forms to quickly develop custom forms within a rapid application development (RAD) environment. RAD is the concept of developing a methodology that allows developers to build software as quickly as possible with minimal effort throughout the software's life cycle.

Learning How Exchange Forms Work

The Exchange Web Storage System model differs from traditional client-server-application processing in that when processing data with a traditional client-server application, you are creating links to forms and pages that process requests to retrieve data and then render the results, whereas with the Exchange Web Storage System model, you are creating requests directly to data, meaning that you are binding content classes to custom forms. For example, you may bind to a folder

195

that contains items or bind to an individual item within the folder. When you save a new item, you are posting the data to a folder. In the previous examples mentioned, you are creating requests directly to the data.

Exchange Web forms are comprised of the following three components:

♦ *A form registration* – A set of properties that are registered within the Exchange store that binds a content class to a Form renderer and identifies browser capabilities.

♦ *A form renderer* – The engine that renders the Exchange item. This can be an ASP page that uses ADO, or the Exchange ISAPI DLL `exwforms.dll`.

♦ *A Web page* – A file that can be rendered within a Web browser and conforms to the World Wide Web Consortium (W3C) specifications for HTML 3.2.

Whenever a user requests data from Exchange over HTTP, Exchange processes the request in the following manner:

1. Exchange Virtual Server receives the request and forwards it to IIS.

2. IIS checks the forms registry for a matching form registration using the `ISAPI.dll`.

3. If a matching registration is found, the computer checks the form registration to see how to render the form. Otherwise, the requested information is rendered with a standard form.

4. Before the form is rendered the form registry passes the following two parameters to the form renderer:

   ■ `formurl` – The `formurl` is the value in the `formurl` parameter of the form registration.

   ■ `dataurl` – The `dataurl` returns the URL of the item from the Exchange store.

   The Form renderer can render the form in one of these three ways:

   ■ As a custom ASP page

   ■ As a custom ASP page with the form renderer (`exwforms.dll`)

   ■ As a custom HTML page with the form renderer (`exwforms.dll`)

5. The form renderer binds the data to the form and passes it back to IIS.

6. IIS passes the results of the rendering back to the client. According to browser capabilities, the data will be bound either at the server or at the client.

Figure 10-1 is a graphic representation of the process outlined in the previous steps.

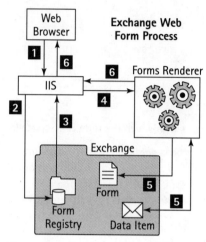

Figure 10-1: Graphic representation of the Web-form process

The Forms Registry and Form Registration

It is in the forms registry that Exchange stores reference information to form-registration items. When you want to associate a custom form with a content class, you create a form-registration item that defines the form's renderer to use in generating the form. When a form-registration item is created, Exchange creates an association to the form's renderer. When the data item is requested, Exchange will read the forms registry, find the form's registration item associated with the content class of the data, and bind the data to the form and render them back to the client. If a custom form-registration item does not exist in the forms registry, Exchange renders the item with the built-in OWA views.

Form-registration items consist of properties from the urn:schemas-microsoft-com:office:forms# name space, which defines the form's renderer used to render the form and also provides information about how to process the form. Form-registration items can be created in any directory, but they are typically created in the directory containing the form or in the application's schema folder. Table 10-1 lists all the properties from the urn:schemas-microsoft-com:office:forms# name space.

TABLE 10-1 FORM REGISTRATION PROPERTIES

Property	Description
binding	Indicates where the binding occurs. Possible values are `server` and `client`.
browser	Indicates the type of browser, such as `Microsoft Internet Explorer`. Use an asterisk (*) as a wildcard.
*contentclass	The name of the content class with which the form is associated.
cmd	String denoting the action or behavior being performed on an object. This is the first parameter after the URL (`?cmd=` part of the URL). Corresponds to the ISAP `QUERY_STRING`. The `QUERY_STRING` is delimited by ampersands (&) that represent modifiers of the action.
contentstate	Refers to the `http://schemas.microsoft.com/exchange/contents` property.
executeparameters	Parameters passed to the rendering engine specified by the `executeurl` field. The parameters must be URL-escaped. Ampersands (&) are used to separate multiple values. Passed on the `QUERY_TRING`.
executeurl*	The URL to execute and render a form. Refers to an ISAPI filter or ASP page.
formurl*	The URL of the form or template being requested and rendered. If the `executeurl` is an ASP, the `formurl` is the same page.
language	The language of the form, automatically provided as part of the HTTP request headers. This attribute corresponds to a case-insensitive ISO language-country/region value in the Accept-Language HTTP header.
majorver	Indicates the major version of the browser supported.
messagestate	Indicates the status of the item. Values include `normal`, `submitted`, `read`, `unread`, and `importance`.
minorver	Indicates the minor version of the browser supported.
platform	Indicates the platform of the browser matched against forms registrations. The platform information is in the same format as in `browscap.ini`. (The platform used is typically `WINNT`.)

Property	Description
request*	Specifies whether the form uses GET or POST requests. The possible values are GET, which queries for information, and POST, which writes information.
version	Major and minor version of the browser supported.

These properties are the minimum required when creating a form registration item.

The contentclass property is the only property required for creating the form-registration item; all other properties are optional.

Creating Form Registrations with ADO and WebDAV

Several methods are available for creating form-registration items. You can pro-grammatically create form-registration items using ADO and WebDAV, or use utilities such as the Web Storage System Explorer and the Web Storage System Builder, a free utility downloadable from this book's Web site. In this section, we are going to briefly look at the Web Storage System Explorer and the Web Storage System Builder, and then show you how to create form-registration items programmatically with ADO and WebDAV.

The Web Storage System Explorer uses a wizard to create form-registration items. To create a form-registration item, simply select the folder in which you wish to create it. Right-click the item's container (located on the right-hand side of the top pane) and then choose the Form Registration Wizard. Use the Wizard to create the item. Figure 10-2 shows the Form Registration Wizard.

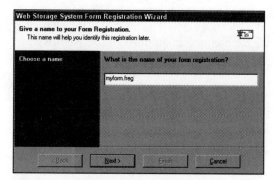

Figure 10-2: The Form Registration Wizard

The Web Storage System Builder uses a form interface that displays a list of properties to fill in. The minimum required properties are listed at the top of the form and additional properties are listed on the bottom of the form. To create a form-registration item, simply select the schema folder from within the Web Storage System Builder, right-click it, and choose New form registration. Fill in the appropriate properties and then choose Save. Figure 10-3 shows the Web Storage System Builder's interface for creating form-registration items.

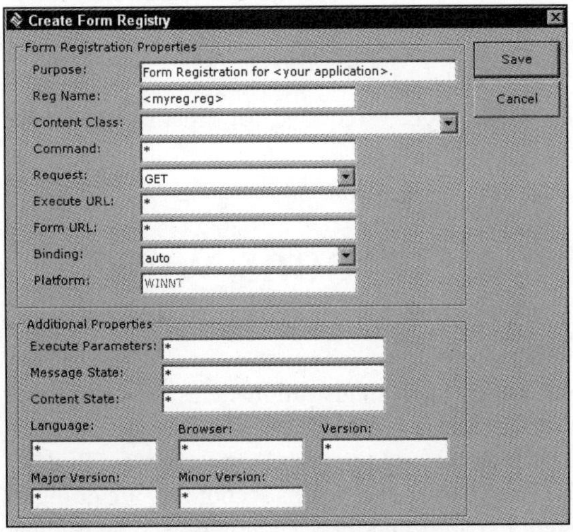

Figure 10-3: The Web Storage System Builder Form-Registration interface

You can also programatically create form-registration items using ADO or WebDAV. You'll need to ensure that you have permissions to modify items in the folder in which you are creating these items.

You do not need to set each property in the urn:schemas-microsoft-com:office:forms# name space; however, in Listings 10-1 and 10-2 each property is set for illustration. Each property must match exactly to identify the form registration item. If a property is not set, the forms registry will treat the property as null. It is good practice to set the property to an asterisk (*), the wildcard character, rather than not setting it at all because Exchange uses an order of precedence when searching properties and trying to resolve conflicting items. The order of precedence for properties is as follows:

1. HTTP request

2. URL action (cmd)

3. Message state

4. Content state

5. Browser capability (browser type and version)

6. Version

7. Platform

8. Major version

9. Minor version

10. Language

The browser capability and version properties, including version, majorver, and minorver, are compared numerically and assigned precedence in the following order, from highest to lowest: =, <=, >=, <, >,*, and null. Therefore, by using a wildcard character you are assigning higher precedence then Null.

The formurl and executeurl properties can use absolute or relative paths. Although absolute path is supported it is not recommended. In listings 10-1 and 10-2, the form-registration items are created using relative path. The registration item is created in the schema folder of the application and Web pages are located in a directory off the root application called webpages. The form-registration item must exist on the same physical server as the item being requested, unless full public-folder replication is active. To programatically create the form-registration item using ADO as the method, complete the following steps:

1. Set a reference to ADO 2.5 in your VB project.

2. Create a new ADODB.Record object.

3. Call the open method with the path and name to the location in which you want to create the registration item. Pass adModeReadWrite for the mode and adCreateNonCollection + adOpenIfExists for the creation options.

4. Set the DAV:contentclass to urn:schemas-microsoft-com:office: forms#registration using the Fields collection of the ADODB.Record object. This identifies the item as a form-registration item.

5. Set the appropriate properties using the Fields collection of the ADODB. Record object and the urn:schemas-microsoft-com:office:forms# schema properties.

6. Call the update method of the ADODB.Record object to save the properties back to the Web Storage System.

7. Clean up by releasing object references.

Listing 10-1 provides an example of how to create a form-registration item using ADO.

Listing 10-1: Creating a Form-Registration Item Using ADO

```
'* Define the urn:schemas-microsoft-com:office:forms# schema
'* properties as constants
Const FORM_SCHEMA = "urn:schemas-microsoft-com:forms#"
Const FORMS_WSS_REG = "registration"
Const FORMS_CALLING_CC = "contentclass"
Const FORMS_REQUEST_TYPE = "request"
Const FORMS_CMD = "cmd"
Const FORMS_BINDING = "binding"
Const FORMS_FORM_URL = "formurl"
Const FORMS_EXE_URL = "executeurl"
Const FORMS_PLATFORM = "platform"
Const FORMS_EXE_PARMS = "executeparameters"
Const FORMS_CONTENT_ST = "contentstate"
Const FORMS_BROWSER = "browser"
Const FORMS_MAJ_VER = "majorver"
Const FORMS_MIN_VER = "minorver"
Const FORMS_VER = "version"
Const FORMS_MSG_ST = "messagestate"
Const FORMS_LANG = "language"
  '* Declare new Record
  Dim oRec as New ADODB.Record
  '* Call Open passing the path using the file: url and name of item
  With oRec
    Open "file://./backofficestorage/starship.enterprise.com/" & _
    "Apps/fpRugStore/Schema/default.freg", , & _
    adModeReadWrite, adCreateNonCollection + adOpenIfExists
    '* Set the DAV Content Class
    .Fields("DAV:contentclass") = FORM_SCHEMA & FORMS_WSS_REG
    '* Set the forms#registration properties
    .Fields(FORM_SCHEMA & FORMS_CALLING_CC) = & _
                        " urn:content-classes:fprugstore-fldr"
    .Fields(FORM_SCHEMA & FORMS_REQUEST_TYPE) = "GET"
    .Fields(FORM_SCHEMA & FORMS_CMD) = "*"
    .Fields(FORM_SCHEMA & FORMS_BINDING) = "server"
    .Fields(FORM_SCHEMA & FORMS_FORM_URL) = &_
                        "/rugstorefp/resources/default.htm"
    .Fields(FORM_SCHEMA & FORMS_EXE_URL) = & _
                        "/ExchWeb/Bin/exwform.dll"
    .Fields(FORM_SCHEMA & FORMS_PLATFORM) = "WINNT"
    .Fields(FORM_SCHEMA & FORMS_EXE_PARMS) = "*"
    .Fields(FORM_SCHEMA & FORMS_CONTENT_ST) = "*"
    .Fields(FORM_SCHEMA & FORMS_BROWSER) = "*"
    .Fields(FORM_SCHEMA & FORMS_MAJ_VER) = "*"
    .Fields(FORM_SCHEMA & FORMS_MIN_VER) = "*"
```

```
    .Fields(FORM_SCHEMA & FORMS_VER) = "*"
    .Fields(FORM_SCHEMA & FORMS_MSG_ST) = "*"
    .Fields(FORM_SCHEMA & FORMS_LANG) = "*"
    '* Call Update
    .Fields.Update
....'* Clean up
    .close
  End With
  Set oRec = Nothing
```

You can create the same form-registration item using WebDAV, by completing these steps:

1. Create an XML `propertyupdate` WebDAV XML request string.

2. Set the `DAV:contentclass` property to the forms-registration name space `urn:schemas-microsoft-com:office:forms#registration`.

3. Set the appropriate name space properties.

4. Open the `xmlhttp` request and set the HTTP header properties.

5. Send the request.

6. Check for errors.

Listing 10-2 shows an example of how to use WebDAV to create a form-registration item.

Listing 10-2: Creating a Form-Registration Item Using WebDAV

```
<SCRIPT Language='JScript'>
var xmldom = new ActiveXObject("MSXML2.DOMDocument.3.0");
var xmlhttp = new ActiveXObject("MSXML2.XMLHTTP.3.0");
function putRegistration() {
  var sXML = ""
  // Create an XML PROPPATCH WebDAV Request
  // define a form namspeace
  // Set the Content Class to the
  // urn:schemas-microsoft-com:office:forms#registration
  // Set the appropriate schema properties
  sXML = "<?xml version='1.0'?>"
  sXML += "<g:propertyupdate xmlns:g='DAV:' +
          "xmlns:form='urn:schemas-microsoft-com:office:forms'>"
  sXML += "<g:set>"
  sXML += "<g:prop>"
  sXML += "<g:contentclass>" +
```

Continued

Listing 10-2 *(Continued)*

```
            "urn:schemas-microsoft-com:office:forms#registration" +
            "</g:contentclass>"
  sXML += "</g:prop>"
  sXML += "<g:prop><form:contentclass>" +
            "urn:content-classes:fprugstore-fldr" +
            "</form:contentclass></g:prop>"
  sXML += "<g:prop><form:cmd>*</form:cmd></g:prop>"
  sXML += "<g:prop><form:request>GET</form:request></g:prop>"
  sXML += "<g:prop><form:executeurl>" +
            "/ExchWeb/Bin/exwform.dll</form:executeurl> </g:prop>"
  sXML += "<g:prop><form:formurl>" +
            "/rugstorefp/resources/default.htm" +
            "</form:formurl></g:prop>"
  sXML += "<g:prop><form:platform>WinNT</form:platform></g:prop>"
  sXML += "<g:prop><form:binding>server</form:platform></g:prop>"
  sXML += "<g:prop><form:language>en</form:language></g:prop>"
  sXML += "<g:prop><form:browser>*</form:browser></g:prop>"
  sXML += "<g:prop><form:majorver>*</form:majorver></g:prop>"
  sXML += "<g:prop><form:minorver>*</form:minorver></g:prop>"
  sXML += "<g:prop><form:messagestate>" +
            "*</form:messagestate></g:prop>"
  sXML += "<g:prop><form:contentstate>" +
            "*</form:contentstate></g:prop>"
  sXML += "</g:set>"
  sXML += "</g:propertyupdate>"
  // open the object and send the request
  xmlhttp.open "PROPPATCH", +
                "http://mailstrom/rugstorefp/schema/default.freg", +
                false
  xmlhttp.setRequestHeader("content-type","text/xml");
  xmlhttp.setRequestHeader("translate","f");
  xmlhttp.send(sXMl)
  // Read status for success
  if(xmlhttp.status >= 200 AND xmlhttp.status < 300) {
    alert("Created!")
  }
  else {
    alert(xmlhttp.status + "\n" + xmlhttp.statusText);
  }
}
</SCRIPT>
```

Now that you have looked at four different ways to create the form-registration item, take a look at how to process the data using two different rendering engines, ASP and the FrontPage forms renderer, `exwforms.dll`.

Building Custom Forms with ASP

The example that we will use for the next two sections is a fictitious inventory system for an Oriental-rug store called Bebian Rugs. Our main goal is to illustrate how to add, edit, delete, list, and page through items using custom forms, Active Server Pages, ADO, and WebDAV. In the first example, we'll use ASP as the rendering engine, while in the second example we will build the entire site using FrontPage extensions for the Web Storage System.

The inventory system tracks the types of rugs in stock, how many of each kind exist, and specific details of each rug, such as color, origin, and size. It uses a custom schema for storing and retrieving the rug data and custom forms for displaying and editing the rug data.

For the purpose of this example, we assume you are familiar with creating and managing custom schema content. If you need to review these concepts, please refer to Chapter 4, "The Web Storage System Schema."

Setting up the Custom Application

The application is set up in its own root application in the Web Storage System. Figure 10-4 shows the directory structure for the application.

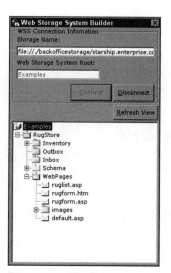

Figure 10-4: The Bebian Rugs directory layout

Table 10-2 lists the description of each directory referred to in Figure 10-4.

TABLE 10-2 BEBIAN RUGS DIRECTORIES

Directory	Description
RugStore	Application root folder
Schema	Application schema directory
Inventory	Inventory folder
WebPages	All Web pages are put in this directory
images	All images for the Web pages are put in this directory.

The content-class and schema information for the application are listed in Table 10-3. You must create the schema folder and all custom properties before experimenting with any examples. You can use any method you wish to create the custom properties and content classes.

TABLE 10-3 BEBIAN RUGS SCHEMA PROPERTIES

Property	Description
starship-enterprise-com:id	ID of the rug
starship-enterprise-com:name	Common name of the rug
starship-enterprise-com:size	Rug dimensions (such as 10 x 12)
starship-enterprise-com:desc	Short description of the rug
starship-enterprise-com:color	Multivalued comma-delimited color listings (such as red,green,blue)
starship-enterprise-com:price	Price of the rug
starship-enterprise-com:qty	Number of rugs in stock

Property	Description
`starship-enterprise-com:instock`	Flag indicating whether a rug is in stock
`starship-enterprise-com:country`	Country of origin of the rug
`starship-enterprise-com:content-class:rug`	Content class defining the rug
`urn:content-classes:inventor-fldr`	Content class defining the Inventory folder
`urn:content-classes:rugstore-fldr`	Content class defining the rug store's root folder

Once the folders, custom properties, and content classes are created, you are ready to begin the next step: laying out the forms, associated Web pages, and form-registration items. The rug system has a default page, a list view page, and a form to edit and add new rugs to the system. The three pages `default.asp`, `rugform.asp`, and `ruglist.asp` are stored in the `webpages` folder. `Rugform.asp` is used for editing and creating new items. `Ruglist.asp` is for deleting rugs from the inventory.

Creating the default.asp form-registration item

`Default.asp` is simply a starting point for the application. No real logic exists on this page; it simply has two links on it, `add` and `view`. Add brings you to the `rugform.asp` page, enabling you to enter new rug information and save the rug back to the inventory folder. View brings you to the `ruglist.asp` page, enabling you to page through all the rugs in the inventory list and to delete rugs. Figure 10-5 shows the finished `default.asp` page.

Take a look at the forms-registration item for the `default.asp` page. To create the form-registration item, you can use any one of the four techniques mentioned earlier in this chapter in the "Creating Form Registrations with ADO and WebDAV" section. Table 10-4 lists the form properties and their values.

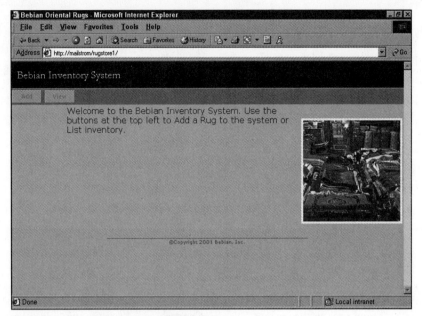

Figure 10-5: The Bebian Rugs default.asp page

TABLE 10-4 BEBIAN RUGS DEFAULT.ASP FORM PROPERTIES

Property	Value
binding	Server
browser	*
contentclass	urn:content-classes:rugstore-fldr
cmd	*
contentstate	*
executeparameters	*
executeurl	../webpages/default.asp
formurl	../webpages/default.asp
language	*
majorver	*
messagestate	*

Property	Value
minorver	*
platform	"WINNT"
request	GET
version	*

Note: Each property is taken from the urn:schemas-microsoft-com:office:forms# *schema.*

Notice the content-class association, from Table 10-4, by setting the contentclass property to urn:content-classes:rugstore-fldr, which tells Exchange to load default.asp whenever the urn:content-classes:regstore-fldr is requested. This content class is associated with the root rug-store folder, rugstore. Also notice the executeurl and formurl properties, in which you identify that you are using Active Server Pages as the renderer and indicate which page to load, respectively. (You'll notice that these two settings are always the same when you're using ASP as the renderer.) Another key thing to notice is the relative path. Because the webpages folder is below the root folder, you need to use a relative path to indicate how to find the default.asp page. All of the form-registration items use this relative path technique to locate the ASP pages linked with a content class. For example: ../webpages/<filename.asp>.

Creating the ruglist.asp form-registration items

Next is the ruglist.asp page. Figure 10-6 shows the completed list view page.

The ruglist.asp page has a lot more functionality then the default.asp page, allowing the user to display a list of rugs and page through all the rugs in the inventory folder. It also provides links back to the default.asp page and to the rugform.asp to edit an existing item or add a new item to the inventory folder. You can also delete an item from the list on this page. Now take a look at the form-registration item for the ruglist.asp page. Table 10-5 lists the form-registration properties and their values.

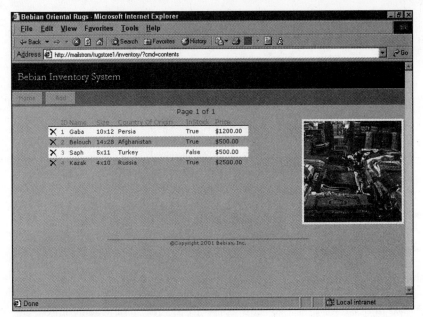

Figure 10-6: The Bebian Rugs ruglist.asp page

TABLE 10-5 BEBIAN RUGS RUGLIST.ASP FORM PROPERTIES

Property	Value
binding	Server
browser	*
contentclass	urn:content-classes:inventor-fldr
cmd	contents
contentstate	*
executeparameters	*
executeurl	../webpages/ruglist.asp
formurl	../webpages/ruglist.asp
language	*
majorver	*
messagestate	*
minorver	*

Property	Value
platform	"WINNT"
request	GET
version	*

Note: Each property is taken from the urn:schemas-microsoft-com:office:forms# *schema*

The form registration for the ruglist.asp page is very similar to the one for the default.asp. It uses ASP pages as the renderer and a relative path to the ASP page, and is bound to the inventory folder through the urn:content-classes: inventor-fldr content class.

You'll notice, though, in this form registration, that the cmd property is set to content. By setting the cmd property, you are identifying that this page is only called when you append a ?cmd=content to the query string of the URL. For example, if you request the URL http://mailstrom/rugstore1/inventory/, when the forms registry compares this value to this registration item's value, you do not get a match. However, if you request http://mailstrom/rugstore1/inventory/ ?cmd=contents, the forms registry finds the match. You can use the cmd property to uniquely identify multiple requests to the same content class, as you will see further on in the rugform.asp registration process.

You also need to create a form registration in order to delete items. When a user clicks the X next to the item in the list, the item must be deleted from the inventory system. In order to set this functionality up you need to create a form registration to support it. Table 10-6 lists the properties and values for this registration item.

TABLE 10-6 BEBIAN RUGS RUGLIST.ASP FORM REGISTRATION PROPERTIES

Property	Value
binding	Server
browser	*
contentclass	starship-enterprise-com:content-classes:rug
cmd	del
contentstate	*
executeparameters	*button=delete

Continued

TABLE 10-6 BEBIAN RUGS RUGLIST.ASP FORM REGISTRATION PROPERTIES *(Continued)*

Property	Value
executeurl	../webpages/ruglist.asp
formurl	../webpages/ruglist.asp
language	*
majorver	*
messagestate	*
minorver	*
platform	"WINNT"
request	GET
version	*

Note: Each property is taken from the urn:schemas-microsoft-com:office:forms# schems

In this form registration you are introducing a new property by setting the executeparameters property to button=delete. The executeparameters property appends itself to the executeurl property. The executeparameters property can hold multiple values separated by ampersands (&) and must be HTML-escaped. You can use the executeparameters property to determine different processes under the same action. For example, your cmd property may be content, and the executeparameters property view=*type*, where *type* may be one of many different views for displaying the content.

Creating the rugform.asp form-registration items

The last page in the inventory system is the rugform.asp page. This page supports two different modes, add and edit. Figures 10-7 and 10-8 show the two different modes for this page. Figure 10-7 shows the Create New screen.

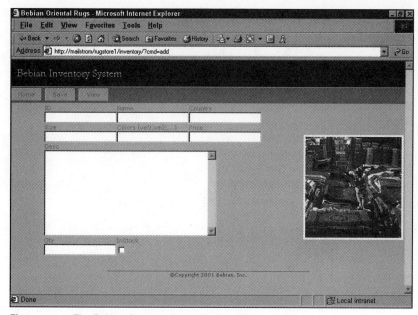

Figure 10-7: The Bebian Rugs rugform.asp Create New page

Figure 10-8 shows `rugform.asp` in edit mode.

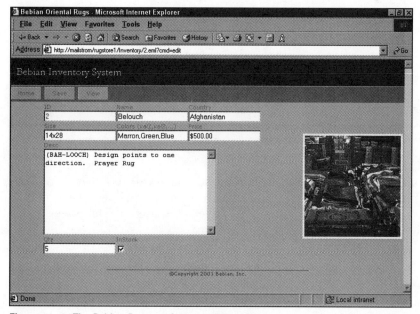

Figure 10-8: The Bebian Rugs rugform.asp Edit mode

Along with the add and edit modes are two different form-registration items. The first binds to the urn:content-class:inventor-fldr with a cmd property set to add. Table 10-7 lists the complete add registration item for this page.

TABLE 10-7 BEBIAN RUGS RUGFORM.ASP FORM REGISTRATION PROPERTIES

Property	Value
binding	Server
browser	*
contentclass	urn:content-classes:inventor-fldr
cmd	Add
contentstate	*
executeparameters	*
executeurl	../webpages/rugform.asp
formurl	../webpages/rugform.asp
language	*
majorver	*
messagestate	*
minorver	*
platform	"WINNT"
request	GET
version	*

Note: Each property is taken from the urn:schemas-microsoft-com:office:forms# schema

The second form-registration item binds to the starship-enterprise-com:content-classes:rug, sets the cmd property to edit, and sets the execute-parameters property to button=edit. Table 10-8 lists the form-registration properties for this page.

TABLE 10-8 BEBIAN RUGS RUGFORM.ASP FORM REGISTRATION PROPERTIES

Property	Value
binding	Server
browser	*
contentclass	starship-enterprise-com:content-classes:rug
cmd	edit
contentstate	*
executeparameters	button=edit
executeurl	../webpages/rugform.asp
formurl	../webpages/rugform.asp
language	*
majorver	*
messagestate	*
minorver	*
platform	"WINNT"
request	GET
version	*

Note: Each property is taken from the urn:schemas-microsoft-com:office:forms# schema

Behind the code – the basic formurl and dataurl

Now that you have seen all the pages in the application, take a look at how the pages get processed. When the Web page is loaded by the Web server, Exchange passes two properties to the Web page: formurl and the dataurl.

formurl is the formurl property from the form registration. Using this property to set the <BASE> HTML tag enables you to set an explicit URL to be used to resolve links and images. For example, if your images folder is under your webpages folder (as in the Bebian Rugs example), you can resolve the images folder by setting the <BASE> tag and then using a relative path from the directory in which the form is located. Listing 10-3 shows an example of setting the <BASE> from the default.asp page. This technique is used exactly the same way in all of the pages used in the Bebian Rugs example.

Listing 10-3: Example of Using the <BASE> Tag and the formurl Property

```
<%@Language='VBScript'%>
<HTML>
<HEAD>
<META NAME="GENERATOR" Content="Microsoft Visual Studio 6.0">
<!-- Use the base href tag to set the base URL for the current page
     for relative path -->
<BASE href='<% =Request("formurl") %>'/>
   ...
</HEAD>
<BODY>
   ...
</BODY>
</HTML>
```

The `dataurl` property is actually the URL to the content class requested – a direct binding to the requested data. This is useful when you're editing, saving, or deleting an item: You can use the `dataurl` to open an item directly without having to search for it or to open a container to list its contents. Listing 10-4 provides an example of how to request the `dataurl` from an ASP page.

Listing 10-4: Requesting the dataurl from an ASP Page

```
<% dataUrl = Request("dataurl") %>
```

The `dataurl` can be used in many ways, as you will see in the next several examples.

Behind the code – building tables with ADO

The `ruglist.asp` page uses Active Data Objects and the `ExOleDb.DataSource` provider to connect to the `dataurl` and build a list of rugs from the `inventory` folder. To do this, you must first build a SQL statement to select the rugs and fields that you want. The reason for using a SQL statement instead of just the `dataurl` is that the `dataurl`, in conjunction with a `Recordset` object, will return every record in the folder without filtering just on the content class of `starship-enterprise-com:content-classes:rug`. When you have a few items and you know that they all have the same content class this is not a big deal, but if you have thousands of items with different content classes it becomes a bigger deal when you're trying to create ADO filters.

Once the SQL statement is built, create a `Connection` object and a `Recordset` object. Use the `dataurl` as a base to open the `ADODB.Connection` object and then use the SQL query and the `Connection` object as the `Recordset` object's `ActiveConnection` to open the `Recordset`. Make sure that both `BOF` and `EOF` are `False` to ensure that you have a valid `Recordset` object.

Next, because you're building the paging routines yourself, you'll want to set the `Recodset.PageSize` property and read the `Recordset.PageCount` property to determine the total number of pages. In the Bebian Rugs example, limit the `PageSize` to 12 records per page and set the bookmark to the page you want to read by setting the `AbsolutePage` property. Then use the `GetRows` method, passing the `PageSize` and the `adBookmarkCurrent` enum as the start position. The `GetRows` function is going to return a two-dimensional array. The reason for using an array is that it improves performance: It's faster to loop through the array than to loop through the `Recordset` and release the `Connection` object as soon as possible.

Once you have the array of records you can simply loop through the array to create the table. You can also use a variable to keep track of which page to load. Listing 10-5 is a partial code listing of `ruglist.asp`. Some things to take note of when looking at the code listing are:

1. How the `dataurl` property is being used

2. How the links are created with the `cmd` property

3. How the use of the `GetRows` method enables you to release the `Connection` and `Recodeset` objects

4. The use of the multi-dimensional array loop (if you are not familiar with it)

Listing 10-5: Creating a Custom Table with ADO and the dataurl Property

```
<%@Language='VBScript'%>
...
'* Create Sql Select Statement
strSql = "SELECT ""DAV:href"" " & _
  ",""starship-enterprise-com:id"" " & _
  ",""starship-enterprise-com:name"" " & _
  ",""starship-enterprise-com:size"" " & _
  ",""starship-enterprise-com:country"" " & _
  ",""starship-enterprise-com:instock"" " & _
  ",""starship-enterprise-com:price"" " & _
"FROM scope('shallow traversal of """ & dataUrl & """') " & _
"WHERE ""DAV:contentclass"" = & _
'starship-enterprise-com:content-classes:rug' " & _
"ORDER BY ""starship-enterprise-com:id"" "

'* open Connection string Set oCn =
Server.CreateObject("ADODB.Connection")
oCn.Provider = "ExOLEDB.DataSource"
oCn.Open dataUrl

'* Open Recordset
```

Continued

Listing 10-5 *(Continued)*

```
Set oRs = Server.CreateObject("ADODB.Recordset")
Set oRs.ActiveConnection = oCn
oRs.Open strSql

'* Check to see if BOF and EOF are true
If Not oRs.BOF And Not oRs.EOF Then
  '* Set ADO Paging to 12 rugs per page
  oRs.PageSize = PAGE
  '* Get total pages
  pgCount = oRs.PageCount
  '* Move to Absolute Page
  oRs.AbsolutePage = iStart
  '* Get Rows aResults = oRs.GetRows(PAGE,adBookmarkCurrent)
  '* Reset Movement
  iNext = iStart + 1
  iBack = iStart - 1
End IF
'*   Clean Up
Set oCn = Nothing
Set oRs = Nothing
%>


...


<!-- Create Table of Results -->
<TABLE border='0' cellpadding='0' cellspacing='0' width='400'>
<TR>
<TD style='font-size: 10pt;padding-bottom: 5px;' align='right'
colspan='6'>Page <% =(iStart) %> of <% =pgCount %></TD>
</TR>
<TR class='HEADERSTYLE'>
<TD Style='BORDER-BOTTOM: black 1px solid;'> </TD>
<TD Align='left' Style='BORDER-BOTTOM: black 1px solid;'>ID</TD>
<TD Align='left' Style='BORDER-BOTTOM: black 1px solid;'>Name</TD>
<TD Align='left' Style='BORDER-BOTTOM: black 1px solid;'>Size</TD>
<TD Align='left' Style='BORDER-BOTTOM: black 1px solid;'>Country Of
Origin</TD>
<TD Align='left' Style='BORDER-BOTTOM: black 1px
solid;'>InStock</TD>
<TD Align='left' Style='BORDER-BOTTOM: black 1px solid;'>Price</TD>
</TR>
<%
```

```
' Process Results
If IsArray(aResults) Then
  For i = lBound(aResults,2) to UBound(aResults,2)
    If i mod 2 <> 0 Then
      sclass = "ROWSTYLE"
    Else
      sclass = "ALTROWSTYLE"
    End If
    Call Response.Write("<TR class='" & sclass & "'>")
    Call Response.Write("<TD><A Title='Delete' href='" & _
    aResults(0,i) & "?cmd=del'><IMG border='0' & _
    src='images/delete.gif'></A></TD>")
    Call Response.Write("<TD><A Title='Edit' href='" & _
    aResults(0,i) & "?cmd=edit'>" & aResults(1,i) & "</A></TD>")
    Call Response.Write("<TD>" & aResults(2,i) & "</TD>")
    Call Response.Write("<TD>" & aResults(3,i) & "</TD>")
    Call Response.Write("<TD>" & aResults(4,i) & "</TD>")
    Call Response.Write("<TD>" & aResults(5,i) & "</TD>")
    Call Response.Write("<TD>" & aResults(6,i) & "</TD>")
    Call Response.Write("</TR>"
  Next
End if
%>
<TR>
<TD align='right' colspan='6' style='padding-top: 5'>
<%
  '* Determine which buttons to show and create link to next or
  '* previous page
  If iBack >= 1 Then
    Response.Write("<A href='../inventory/?cmd=contents&button=" &_
    BTN_BACK & "&iStart=" & iBack & "'>" & _
    "<SPAN title='Move to Prev Page' class='button'><</SPAN></A>")
  End If

  If iNext <= pgCount Then
    Response.Write("<A href='../inventory/?cmd=contents&button=" & _
    BTN_NEXT & "&iStart=" & iNext & "'>" & _
    "<SPAN title='Move to Next Page' class='button'>></SPAN></A>")
  End IF
%>
</TD>
</TR>
</TABLE>
```

Behind the code — add, edit, save, and delete

The `delete` routine relies on the `dataurl` to identify the item to delete. The `delete` routine starts off much like the `list` routine; however, instead of using a `Recordset` object you use an `ADODB.Record` object. Open the item using the `dataurl` and call the `DeleteRecord` method. Then clean up and redirect the request back to the `ruglist.asp` page. Listing 10-6 shows the code for the `delete` routine. To improve the delete process you may want to keep track of the page from which the item was deleted, so as not to reload the first page each time a record is deleted. This could be a bother to the end user.

Listing 10-6: Deleting Items within the ruglist.asp Page

```
Sub DeleteRug
  Dim oRec
  Dim oCon

  On Error Resume Next
  Set oCon = Server.CreateObject("ADODB.Connection")
  Set oRec = Server.CreateObject("ADODB.Record")
  oCon.Provider = "ExOLEDB.DataSource"
  '* This would not typically be hardcode.
  '* You can get the parent url by parsing the dataurl
  oCon.Open "http://mailstrom/rugstore1/Inventory/"

  '* Delete Record
  '* 3 is adReadWrite constant
  oRec.Open dataUrl,oCon,3
  '* Call DeleteRecord
  oRec.DeleteRecord
  '* Check for error
  If Err.number <> 0 Then
    Response.Write Err.description Err.Clear
    Err.Clear
  End If
  '* Close and Release objects
  Set oRec = Nothing
  Set oCn = Nothing
End Sub
```

The next three routines (add, save, and edit) are all in the `rugform.asp` page. Add is a request to load a blank `rugform.asp` page. You can do this by using the `cmd` property and the `executeurl` property (see Tables 10-7 and 10-8 for the form-registration properties and values). Use the same `save` routine for editing and adding new rugs, writing the `save` routine using a WebDAV request. For further information about WebDAV, please refer to Chapter 8, "HTTP/WebDAV and XML" or download the full source code for this example from this book's public Web site.

You control the edit process via the form-registration item. Set the cmd property to edit and the executeparameters to button=edit. When the rugform.asp page loads, request the button item from the querystring. If the button item is set to edit, read the dataurl of the item and retrieve the property values from the Web Storage System. Listing 10-7 shows the edit routine and the request for the executeparameters from the querystring.

Listing 10-7: rugform.asp Edit Routine

```
<%

...

dataUrl = Request("dataUrl")
'* button is passed via the executeparameters
sbutton = Request("button")

Select Case sbutton
  Case BTN_EDIT
  '* Create objectsxfs
  Set oCon = Server.CreateObject("ADODB.Connection")
  Set oRec = Server.CreateObject("ADODB.Record")

  '* Open ADO Connection
  oCon.Provider = "ExOLEDB.DataSource"
  oCon.Open "http://mailstrom/rugstore1/inventory/"
  '* Open Record object Using dataUrl paced form Exchange
  oRec.Open dataUrl,oCon,1

  '* Read Properties
  Id = oRec.Fields("starship-enterprise-com:id").Value
  Rugname = oRec.Fields("starship-enterprise-com:name").Value
  Country = oRec.Fields("starship-enterprise-com:country").Value
  Size = oRec.Fields("starship-enterprise-com:size").Value
  Qty = oRec.Fields("starship-enterprise-com:qty").Value
  Instock = CBool(oRec.Fields("starship-enterprise-
com:instock").Value)
  Price = oRec.Fields("starship-enterprise-com:price").Value
  Desc = oRec.Fields("starship-enterprise-com:desc").Value

If IsArray(oRec.Fields("starship-enterprise-com:colors").Value) Then
  aColor = oRec.Fields("starship-enterprise-com:colors").Value
  For i = lBound(aColor) to UBound(aColor)
    if Len(color) > 0 Then
      color = color & "," & aColor(i)
```

Continued

Listing 10–7 *(Continued)*

```
    Else
       color = aColor(i)
    End If
  Next
End If
  oRec.Close
  Set oRec = Nothing
  Set oCon = Nothing
End Select
```

Typically, you would not hard code the connection URL as in Listing 10-6. You can extract the URL from the `dataurl` passed to the ASP page.

Building Forms with FrontPage and the Forms Renderer

The Microsoft FrontPage Extensions for the Web Storage System enable you to build Web pages quickly using FrontPage 2000 (or FrontPage 2002) and to take advantage of the Web Storage System forms-technology runtime `exwform.dll`, an ISAPI extension for forms rendering. These extensions are installed on top of the existing FrontPage extensions. You can download them from the MSDN download library at the following URL:

```
http://msdn.microsoft.com/downloads/default.asp?url=/downloads/sampl
e.asp?url=/msdn-files/027/001/559/msdncompositedoc.xml&frame=true.
```

 Before you install the FrontPage Extensions for the Web Storage System, you need to make sure that Exchange is running at least Service Pack 1.

For further information about installing the FrontPage Extensions for the Web Storage System, please refer to the documentation provided by Microsoft at the following URL:

```
http://msdn.microsoft.com/downloads/default.asp?url=/downloads/sampl
e.asp?url=/MSDN-FILES/027/001/559/msdncompositedoc.xml&frame=true
```

FrontPage forms renderer with HTML

Once Exchange has been updated and the Extensions have been installed, you must complete the following tasks to enable the extensions on a Web Storage System folder:

1. Create a folder called `fpRugStore` under your Web Storage System root folder.

2. Expose the folder by creating an HTTP virtual server from the Exchange System Manager.

3. Open the Internet Service Manager and locate the virtual folder created in Step 2.

To open the Internet Service Manager, follow these steps:

1.   Select Start → Settings → Control Panel.

2.   When the Control Panel opens, double-click Administrative Tools.

3.   Double click Internet Service Manager.

4. Right-click the folder and select All Tasks → Configure Server Extensions to start the New Sub Web Wizard.

5. Retain all default settings except those for Access Control, for which you should select "Use a different administrator for this web." Uncheck Create local machine groups and in the textbox provided under "Enter a Windows account to use as the web administrator account," enter a username from the domain to add as the account administrator. Then choose the Next button.

6. Click Finish in the last dialog box.

Follow these steps to create a sub-folder in which to store the inventory under the newly-created Web:

1. Right click the Web folder and select New → Server Extensions Web.

2. Enter **inventory** as the name and title.

3. Retain all of the default settings, including the option to "Use the same administrator as the parent web."

Now that you have configured the Web, open the `inventory` folder in FrontPage from the Internet Service Manager by right-clicking the `inventory` folder. Select All Tasks → Open with FrontPage. FrontPage will open with `inventory` as the root. Now create a new folder called `resources` and move the `images` folder below the `resource` folder.

You'll notice that FrontPage will have a new menu item called Web Storage System Forms and a new toolbar at the bottom of the existing toolbars. These items are added by the FrontPage Extensions for the Web Storage System and only show up for Webs configured in the Web Storage System. Figure 10-9 shows the Web setup in FrontPage 2000.

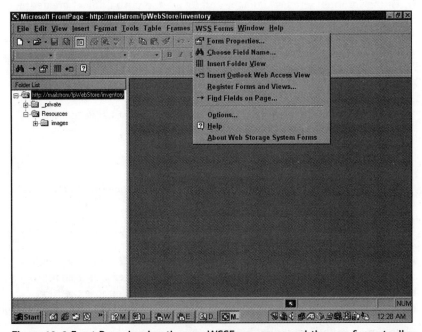

Figure 10-9 Front Page showing the new WSSForms menu and the new forms toolbar

Once you have the Web and sub-Web set up, and have created the `resource` folder, and moved the `images` folder, you are ready to create your rug form.

To create `rugform.htm`, create a new HTML page by selecting the `resources` folder, right-clicking, and choosing New page to open the New page dialog box. Double-click the Form Page Wizard to start creating the form. Figure 10-10 shows the New page dialog box with the Form Page Wizard selected.

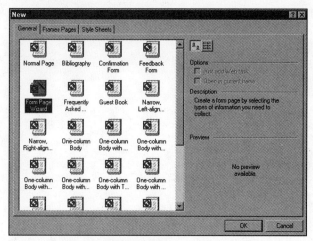

Figure 10-10: The New page dialog

When the Form Page Wizard starts, click Next on the opening screen (Figure 10-11).

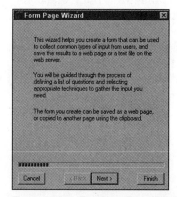

Figure 10-11: The Form Page Wizard opening screen

Repeat the following steps to create each field you will need for the rugform.htm page:

1. Choose the field's data type from the Form Page Wizard's input-type list box.

2. Enter the name of the field.

3. Click Next.

Figure 10-12 shows the Form Page Wizard field-input screen.

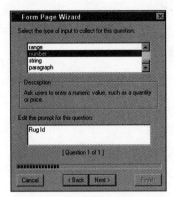

Figure 10-12: The Form Page Wizard field-input screen

On the next screen, enter the field's maximum length (optional) and a variable to store the value of the field. The variable is the name of a custom property that this field will bind to in the Web Storage System so it should follow the rules for naming custom properties. For example, for each field that you need on the rug form, you should use the domain name and property name, which would be *yourdomain*: *<fieldname>*, where *<fieldname>* is the name of the mapped form field and *yourdomain* is the name of your domain. Figure 10-13 shows an example of what the id field looks like.

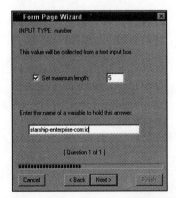

Figure 10-13: Binding the Form field to the Web Storage System custom property

Click Next when you're finished and repeat this process for each field you need to create. Table 10-9 lists all the properties and associated data types for the rugform.htm page.

TABLE 10-9 FIELD LISTINGS FOR RUGFORM.HTM

Field Name	Data Type
Id	Number
Name	String
Country	String
Size	String
Color	String
Price	String
Desc	Paragraph

Once you have created all the fields you want, you'll need to create the rug content class by checking the form properties. To do this, select WSS Forms → Properties to open the Form Properties dialog box (Figure 10-14).

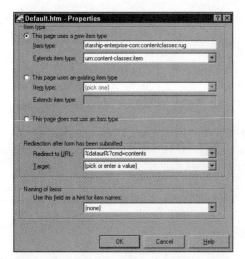

Figure 10-14: The Form Properties dialog box

The Form Properties dialog box has three sections: Item type, Redirection, and Naming.

The Item type section is where you create a new content class for the associated form. (You will need to do this the first time before you save the form.) Make sure the This page uses a new item type button is selected, and then enter the name of the content class as **starship-enterprise-com:rug**. Allow the type to extend the generic Exchange item content class.

The Redirection section determines what happens when the form is posted to the folder. You can use any of four different tokens to determine the redirection after the form is submitted:

- `%dataurl%:`   The URL of the item
- `%datacontainer%:`   The URL of the folder where items are stored
- `%formurl%:`   The URL of the form
- `%formcontainer%:`   The URL of the folder where forms are stored, typically the `resources` sub-folder

You can also use any of these tokens in the forms registry `executeparameters` property by using the `redir=` token to signify a redirection to the forms runtime. For example:

```
execuparameters = redir=%dataurl%
```

You can also append the `?cmd=` property to create a redirection to a particular form action. For example:

```
execuparameters = redir=%dataurl%?cmd=Reply
```

When viewing the full code (downloadable from this book's public Web site), you will notice the `actionspec` attribute, which is only used by the forms runtime and is ignored by standard HTML. When you are using FrontPage, the attribute is set via the redirection section of the forms dialog. When you are coding against the forms runtime `exwform.dll` directly from ASP, you can set this attribute manually, as follows:

```
<FORM method="POST" class="form" id="theform"
actionspec="%dataurl%?cmd=contents" name="theform" target="_self">
```

The next section of the Form Properties dialog box is the Naming section, which is where you pick which filed/custom property on your form will be used to create a name for the item posted. If you leave this section blank, Exchange will use a Globally Unique Identifier (GUID) for the name. When using the file system to read the m: drive, this can be difficult to read. In this example, you can choose the `name` property.

If you have problems saving the form, check your permissions on the inventory folder to ensure that you have administrative rights. Also, make sure that the virtual directories have the write attribute checked.

Once the form properties are set and you are comfortable with them, exit the form properties dialog by clicking OK.

The next step is to save the form back to the Web Storage System under the resource folder. After you select Save, you may get a warning dialog prompting you to save your items to the resource folder. Just ignore it and click OK. Figure 10-15 shows the warning dialog.

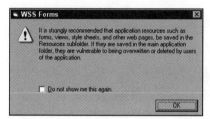

Figure 10-15: The WSS Forms warning dialog

You get this warning because the FrontPage Extensions for the Web Storage System creates all its objects in the resource folder. If your content classes, custom properties, and form-registration items are not saved in the resource folder, your application will not work properly. You can turn the warning off by going to WSSForms → Options to open the Options dialog box and then unchecking the Use resource folder warning when saving a new page option.

When the extensions save the form back to the Web Storage System, they write all the custom properties that you created on your form and create the form-registration items for posting new items, as well as for editing, saving, and viewing items. The Extensions also create a default viewing page using the Folder View Design Time control. Figure 10-16 shows what the directory looks like after the form is saved back to the Web Storage System.

To view the form registrations created by the FrontPage Extensions, select WSS Forms → Register Forms and Views. If you need to modify the default registration items, select the item you need to modify and click Edit. If you need to create a new registration item, select a registration item, clickClone, select the cloned item, and then click Edit. To delete an item, select the item and click Delete. The Add View, Add New, and Add Edit buttons create the default registration items for these actions, respectively. Figure 10-17 shows the Form and View Registrations dialog.

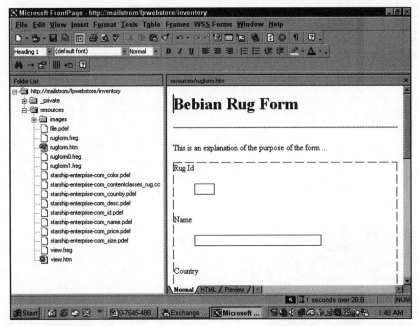

Figure 10-16: Populated Directory after Form is Saved Back to the Web Storage System

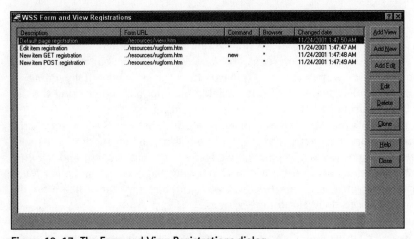

Figure 10-17: The Form and View Registrations dialog

The Folder View Design Time Control (DTC) is an ActiveX control that creates a list view of the Web Storage System folder of your choice. Figure 10-18 shows the view.htm page built by the FrontPage Extensions.

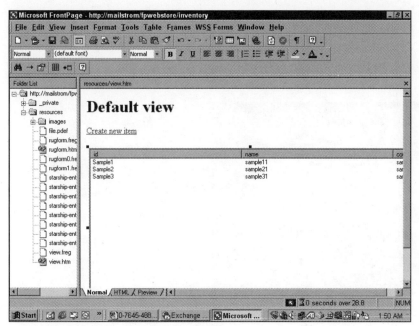

Figure 10-18: List View Design Time Control

Because you are posting your form data to the `inventory` folder, the FrontPage Extensions will set the List View DTC to the `inventory` folder by default. The List View DTC is flexible and useful because all your paging operations are built in, as are your sorting and filter capabilities. You can also control which columns appear in the header and attach custom styles to the rows and headers. To view the List View DTC custom property sheet, right-click the List View DTC and choose Design-Time Control Properties. This will open the Design Time Control Properties dialog. The property sheet is made up of the following four tabs:

◆ *View Data* controls the data displayed in the folder view. You can set the control to do a Deep or Shallow search by checking the "Search subfolders" checkbox. You can also set the filter value to exclude or include data bound to the control. For example:

```
"DAV:ishidden" = false AND "DAV:isfolder" = false AND
"DAV:contentclass" = 'starship-enterprise-com:content-
classes:rug'
```

◆ *View Style* controls the appearance and operation of the entire folder view. Here you can also control the Link Spec, which sets the link action for the list view items. By default, it is the `%dataurl%` token.

◆ *Object Tag* controls properties of the object itself, such as the code base, height, width, name, and alignment, to name a few.

◆ *Parameters* controls the additional parameters for the embedded object PARAM tag.

Figure 10-19 shows the Design-Time Control Properties dialog box.

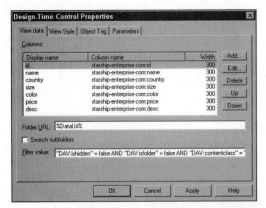

Figure 10-19: The Design-Time Control Properties dialog box

To illustrate the list view control, Figure 10-20 is the complete List View for the Bebian Rug Store System. The List View was built entirely in FrontPage.

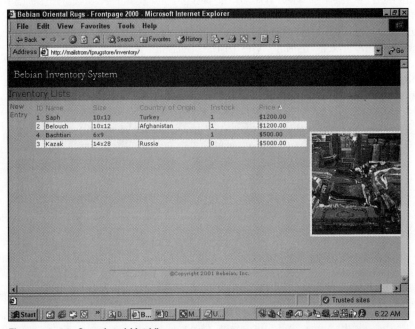

Figure 10-20: Completed List View

The FrontPage Extensions also enable you to insert default Outlook views. To do this, choose the folder and then the view type. You have five different views to choose from:

- *Message Folders* will display e-mail or post items. Three actions are possible:
  - `new` creates a new e-mail
  - `newpost` creates a new post
  - `contents` displays a list view
- *Contact Folders* displays contacts. Two actions are possible:
  - `new` creates a new contact
  - `contents` displays a list of contacts
- *Public Folders* displays a public folder. Two actions are possible:
  - `new` creates a new item to post to the public folder
  - `contents` displays a list view
- *Calendar Folders* displays a calendar view. Two actions are possible:
  - `new` creates a new appointment
  - `contents` displays a list view
- *Link Folders* for all folder types. Can be any folder type.

FrontPage forms renderer with ASP

You can also programmatically use the FrontPage forms renderer (`exwform.dll`) with ASP instead of using static HTML. The DLL exposes an object model that can be used within an ASP page. Using the forms renderer (`exwform.dll`) as an approach to building custom forms will give you the benefit of the forms renderer's ability to bind directly to the data without having to use ADO, as well as the flexibility of writing ASP for form validation and as powerful logic.

The object model for the `WSS.Form` object is listed in Figure 10-21.

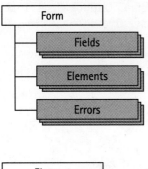

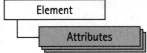

Figure 10-21: WSS Form object model

Table 10-10 lists the properties and methods of the WSS.Form object.

TABLE 10-10 WSS.FORM OBJECT PROPERTIES AND METHODS

Property/Method	Description
CodePage	Identifies the codepage for an Exchange Web form.
DataUrl	Returns the URL of a data item. If the item exists in the Exchange store the DataUrl property returns the URL to the item. The DataUrl property returns an empty string for new items until they are saved to the Exchange store. This property is read-only.
Elements	Returns the collection of all the HTML elements in the page that were named using the name or id attributes. This collection is read-only.
Errors	Returns the collection of all the HTML errors that occur when setting property values in the Fields collection. For example, the conversion of date and time data can cause errors. This collection is read-only.
Fields	Returns the Fields collection of the ADO database (ADODB) object. This collection is read-only.
HasErrors	Returns true if ErrorString has been called on any of the data items and false otherwise. This property is read-only.
IsNew	Returns true if this is a post that creates a new Exchange-store data item and false otherwise. This property is read-only.

Property/Method	Description
LCID	Specifies which local ID to use when rendering an Exchange Web form.
Render	Called at the end of the script block in the combined ASP/EXWFORM pages. This method causes EXWFORM to return the data-bound version of the form and the form's views, including any script. EXWFORM ignores any contents of the page denoted with ASP tags — that is, any text inside <% %> or <script runat="*server*"></script> tags.
Update	Calls on the Fields collection. Changes are updated on the CDO Exchange-store Form object.

Listing 10-8 gives the code for the rugform.asp form using the WSS.Form object.

Listing 10-8: rugform.asp Page Using the WSS.Form Object

```
<%@ Language=VbScript %>
<%
  Dim Wss
  '* Create the Form object
  Set Wss = Server.CreateObject("WSS.Form")

  '* Trap for Post Request
  iF (Request.ServerVariables("REQUEST_METHOD") = "POST") Then
    '* If update is not called for new items the items are not saved
    '* because this form is bound we do not need to set any
    '* properties, just call update.
    Wss.Update()
    '* Redirect to the appropriate location
    Response.Redirect("../fpASP/")
  End If

  '* Always call render to render the form.
  Wss.Render()
%>
```

The WSS.Form object binds to the dataurl of the item being requested. Because the object is bound it is very easy to bind the form fields to it. When creating the form field you need to set the following three properties:

1. class="*field*" indicates that this field is databound.

2. name="*propname*" specifies the custom property to bind to.

3. form="*formname*" specifies the name of the form these fields belong to.

Listing 10-9 gives the code for the rugform.asp form.

Listing 10-9: rugform.asp Binding the Form to the Web Storage System

```
<FORM method="POST" class="form" id="theform" actionspec=""
name="theform" target="_self">
...
  <TD width="112">
    <INPUT type="text" name="starship-enterprise-com:id"
class="field" form="theform" id="fp1" size="14" tabindex="0">
  </TD>
...
  <TD colspan="3" align="right">
<INPUT type="reset" value="Reset" name="Button" tabindex="2">
<INPUT type="submit" value="Save" name="Button" tabindex="1">
</TD>
  </TR>
 </TABLE>
<!-
  Hidden fields for content-class and hinturl for creating new item
-->
  <INPUT type="hidden" name="DAV:contentclass" value="starship-
enterprise-com:content-classes:rug">
  <INPUT type="hidden"
name="http://schemas.microsoft.com/exchange/nosave/hintforurl"
value="starship-enterprise-com:name">
</FORM>
```

For the complete listing of the code in Listing 10-9, you can download the examples from this book's public Web site. Listing 10-9 illustrates the form-tag setup, one bound field, the Submit and Reset buttons and two hidden fields. The hidden fields tell the form's runtime how to create the new item and what content class the item should be.

When creating the form-registration items, set the excuteurl property to the ASP page that is going to process the request. Although you are using the FrontPage form object, the rendering engine is ASP and not the exwform.dll. Table 10-11 shows one of the four form-registration items for this example.

TABLE 10-11 WSS.FORM OBJECT PROPERTIES AND METHODS

Property	Value
contentclass	starship-enterprise-com:rug
executeurl	../webpages/rugform.asp
formurl	../webpages/**rugform.asp**
binding	Server
Platform	WINNT
command	*
executeparameters	*

If you can understand form-registration items, the WSS.Form object shouldn't be very difficult to use. However, if you are struggling with form-registration items and how the Web Storage System processes the request, spend some time studying this concept and observing how the data are always bound to the form via the dataurl. Once you master this concept, you are on your way to creating powerful Exchange Web Applications using the Web Storage System forms technology.

Summary

In this chapter you looked at the Web Storage Systems forms package, how custom forms are processed by the Web Storage System, and what the Web Storage System has to offer to programmers with its ability to customize data.

Of the many different methods for creating Web forms under Exchange, this chapter concentrated on the RAD approach using FrontPage 2000, which is simple and quick, but not very flexible; the more complex method of using ASP and ADO, which is a kind of brute-force method, using a lot of code to do simple tasks but giving you a lot of control; and finally the less complicated and more flexible method of using the WSS.Form object. No matter which approach you take in creating custom forms for the Web Storage System, a method exists to fit your needs.

Chapter 11

Outlook Web Access

IN THIS CHAPTER

◆ Introducing Outlook Web Access (OWA)

◆ Learning OWA components

◆ Understanding form rendering

OUTLOOK WEB ACCESS (OWA) is Microsoft's answer to the need for a Web-based e-mail client. Users can access their Exchange 2000 mailboxes from any browser that supports frames. This of course means that if you allow it, users can access mail from the Internet – anywhere. OWA has actually been around for a while, but the most recent version of OWA offers a rich user interface with features that come close to those offered by Outlook 2000. Users can now, for example, use the preview-pane feature to view message contents without opening the message. Other feature enhancements have been made to the calendar, contacts, and folder areas. The new OWA is important to developers because now you can customize the interface in ways that were not possible in previous versions.

Previous versions of OWA consisted of DLLs, so it was possible to customize only the Welcome screen – because it was an ASP page. The current version of OWA is made of XML pages and is completely open for development. Furthermore, with the introduction of URL addressing, you can access pieces of OWA and rearrange them in your own way. URLs are unique to every object in the information store, so you can add URLs to a Web page that links to folders, items, or mailboxes.

You were introduced to the new OWA in Chapter 1. In this chapter, we will show you how you can customize OWA to meet your own business needs.

OWA Components

Chapter 1 showed you that you can break OWA into pieces and use those pieces separately to create your own version of OWA. An example of this is illustrated on this book's companion Web site. While Outlook Web Access can be used as an e-mail access tool, programmers can also create customized Web sites by using its individual components.

Users often do not use Web sites because they find them to be too cluttered with information. Your intranet is only valuable to your users if it is easy to use and contains valuable information. You don't want to bury the valuable information under clutter, or your users won't use the site. You may want to provide only select information from OWA for your users. Finally, this is possible. You can show your users only their inboxes, only folder information, only calendar information, or any combination of all folders. You can also add information to OWA that isn't there by default. For example, you may want to welcome users with a list of unread messages, plus a list of documents found in a marketing folder. Users faced with one or two containers of information are more likely to stay and read. Table 11-1 lists the components of OWA that can be used together or individually.

TABLE 11-1 OWA COMPONENTS

Container	Container URL	Container Only URL
Inbox	`http://server/exchange/alias/inbox`	`http://server/exchange/alias/inbox/?cmd=contents`
Calendar	`http://server/exchange/alias/calendar`	`http://server/exchange/alias/calendar/?cmd=contents`
User folder	`http://server/exchange/alias/folder`	`http://server/exchange/alias/folder/?cmd=contents`
Public folder	`http://server/public/foldername`	`http://server/public/foldername/?cmd=contents`

By default, OWA starts in a frameset with a list of containers on the left and the user's mailbox on the right. When you use the CMD parameter, you get that container, and only that container, in your browser. When you leave off this parameter, you get the full OWA frameset with the requested container opened, as if the user had entered the site and then opened that container.

Managing components

Each component can be accessed directly by means of its own URL. When you use the basic URL to open a container, OWA renders the information using the default view. You can change this behavior by using the CMD parameter and associated instructional parameter. For example, browsing to `http://server/exchange/public/folder` will display the OWA toolbar across the top, the Outlook bar on the left, and the folder information on the right (see Figure 11-1).

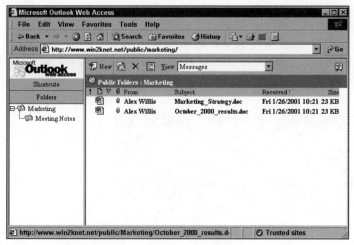

Figure 11-1: Public folder rendered by the OWA default view

This method displays the required information, but doesn't work well in an intranet that is built using frames, because in such an environment it is difficult to get the "look" you are going for. In an intranet, you want to display the container contents without the Outlook bar on the left. This way, you can control the information the user sees and also control the options the user is offered. You can do this using the CMD parameter with the contents instructional parameter, as illustrated in Figure 11-2:

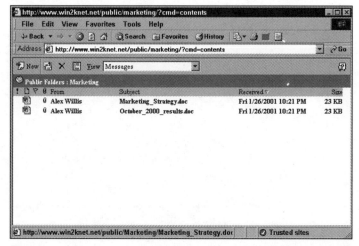

Figure 11-2: Contents of public folder without the Outlook bar on the left

Figure 11-2 illustrates the use of the CMD parameter to display only the container data you wish to display. The user is not permitted to go elsewhere within OWA (except, of course, to delete, open, or create an item in that folder). You can use this method in conjunction with frames to create your own version of OWA. Think about putting your own menu on the left, as shown in Figure 11-3.

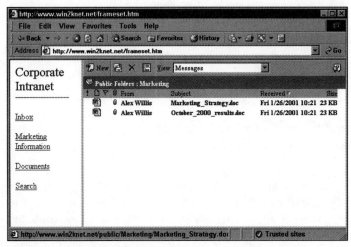

Figure 11-3: Creating a frameset with the contents parameter

The Web site displayed in Figure 11-3 is composed of a single HTML file that uses framesets to include two other files. On the left is a simple HTML file with a list of links that, when clicked, display data in the frame on the right. Listing 11-1 is the source code for the file on the left.

Listing 11-1: Frameset

```
<HTML>
<HEAD>
    <TITLE>Corporate OWA</TITLE>
</HEAD>

<BODY>
<font size=+2>Corporate Intranet</font>
<hr>
<p>
<a href="http://server/exchange/alias/inbox/?cmd=contents"
target="main">Inbox</a>
<p>
<a href="http://server/public/marketing/?cmd=contents"
target="main">Marketing</a>
<p>
```

```
<a href="http://server/public/documents/?cmd=contents"
target="main">Documents</a>
<p>
<a href="http://server/public/search/search.asp"
target="main">Search</a>
</BODY>
</HTML>
```

You can use more instructional parameters, according to the action you want to take. For example, if you wish to create a link that will automatically post an item rather than display the contents of a folder, use the new instructional parameter. Other instructional parameters are listed in Table 11-2.

TABLE 11-2 CMD PARAMETERS

Parameter name	Description
New	Creates a new item
Reply	Replies to a message
Forward	Forwards a message
Save	Saves a message
Send	Sends a message

Several other parameters exist that you can use to further control the data that are displayed. These are shown in Table 11-3.

TABLE 11-3 MORE PARAMETERS

Parameter name	Description
Page=x	Displays page x
View=x	Displays Outlook view named x
Sort=x	Sorts by column x
Date=x	Displays date in calendar

Table 11-4 lists examples of using these parameters with CMD.

TABLE 11-4 CMD EXAMPLES

Use	URL
View a message	http://server/exchange/alias/inbox/item.eml/?cmd=open
Reply to a message	http://server/exchange/alias/inbox/item.eml/?cmd=reply
Display contents	http://server/exchange/alias/inbox/?cmd=contents
Post to a public folder	http://server/public/foldername/?cmd=new

Using the <IFRAME> tag

The <IFRAME> tag is an HTML tag that enables you to include other Web pages within the same HTML file you are displaying. This is similar to but not exactly the same as using framesets. Rather than creating the division of the browsing area that framesets create, the <IFRAME> tag creates a single Web page. You can use the <IFRAME> tag wherever you like in your HTML code to include other Web pages. Figure 11-4 illustrates the use of the <IFRAME> tag:

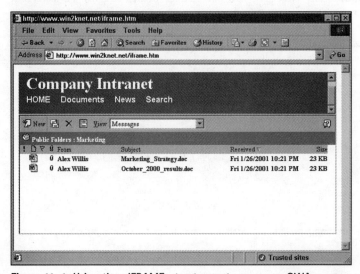

Figure 11-4: Using the <IFRAME> tag to create your own OWA

Listing 11-2 illustrates the use of the <IFRAME> tag to create the Web page displayed in Figure 11-4.

Listing 11-2: Using the <IFRAME> Tag to Create a Customized OWA

```
<html>
<body>
<center>

<IFRAME name='MENU', width = 100%, height = 25%_
, SRC='http://www.win2knet.net/top.htm'>

<IFRAME name='MAIN', width = 100%, height = 70%_
, SRC='http://www.win2knet.net/public/marketing/?cmd=contents'>

</body>
</html>
```

Form Rendering

When you browse information stored in the Web Storage System, OWA renders each request through the ISAPI DLL. This is how OWA knows to display messages with the message form, and posts with the post form. OWA now enables you to change this behavior. Each item in the information store has a tag that describes what it is. This tag is called a *content class*. A message has a content class of `message`, for example. ISAPI knows to display a message using the message form because it checks the content class. This means that no matter where the item exists in the Web Storage System, OWA will correctly display it. You can create your own forms and associate them with certain content classes. OWA will then always render items with that content class using the form you associated with that content class. See Chapter 4 for more details about creating your own custom OWA forms.

Summary

Outlook Web Access is a full-featured e-mail client. In one way or another, you will most likely use some component of OWA in your company's intranet — whether straight Outlook Web Access, direct links to certain public or private folders, or custom forms to be used by OWA when rendering information in the Web Storage System. In any case, you have the tools in OWA to customize as much as you like.

Part IV

Collaboration and Messaging

Chapter 12

Collaborative Data Objects

IN THIS CHAPTER

- ◆ Introducing CDO for Exchange 2000

- ◆ Understanding CDO object models

- ◆ Learning CDO components

- ◆ Using CDO for Exchange management

CDO HAS A LONG HISTORY as an invaluable tool for developing applications for Exchange. Previous versions of CDO were extensions to the MessagingAPI (MAPI), but through its use of OLEDB the current version of CDO provides direct access to items stored in the Web Storage System. This improvement means that you no longer need to make a MAPI connection in your application, which in turn means more stability, because MAPI does not scale well. CDO has also been enhanced to include support for Internet standards such as SMTP, NNTP, MIME, MHTML, vCard, and iCalendar. This chapter will introduce the components and capabilities of the new CDO.

When to Use CDO or ADO for Messaging

First, we must discuss the differences between ADO and CDO. Each provides distinctly different technologies, but they were designed to work together and it's easy to confuse the two. Use the following guidelines to decide whether to use CDO or ADO objects in your messaging applications.

Use ADO objects to do the following:

- ◆ Search for certain types of messages in the Web Storage System

- ◆ Search folders and folder hierarchies for messages

- ◆ Set custom properties for messages

Use CDO objects to do the following:

◆ Create any kind of new message item

◆ Send messages

◆ Modify an existing message item or its properties

CDO Components

Previous versions of CDO included one DLL (Dynamic Link Library); the current version is made up of three DLLs, which are listed in Table 12-1. Each is designed for different aspects of Exchange development. The main components of the CDO object model are messaging, calendaring, contacts, workflow, and management. Within each component are many objects. These DLL's are installed by default with each Exchange 2000 server installation, so you do not need to install any additional software to begin developing Web applications for Exchange. However, the applications must be run from the Exchange server itself.

TABLE 12-1 CDO 2.0 DLLS

CDO	File Name	Description
CDO for Exchange 2000	Cdo.dll	Used for messaging, contacts, and scheduling
CDO for Exchange Management	Cdoexm.dll	Used for creating and managing mailboxes and managing security
CDO Workflow for Exchange	Cdowf.dll	Used for building workflow applications

CDO messaging object model

The CDO object model (Figure 12-1) is the core building block upon which you create messaging applications. Each message is comprised of a hierarchy of content called objects. Each object contains some part of a message's content:

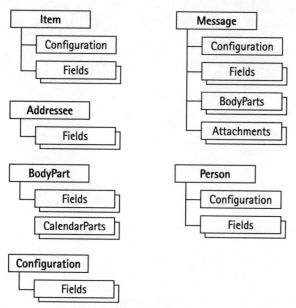

Figure 12-1: CDO messaging object model

CDO objects are similar to ADO objects in that they expose a fields collection that you can access. The fields collection is a great tool that you can use to examine an item. When you request the contents of an item's field collection, you will receive a list of fields and their respective contents. Listing 12-1 illustrates the use of the fields collection by querying a message item for its fields and their respective contents.

Listing 12-1: Enumerating Fields

```
<HTML>
<BODY>
<%
set NewMsg = createobject("CDO.Message")
dim Flds
Set Flds = NewMsg.Fields

response.write "Message has " & Flds.Count & " fields"
response.write "<table border=1><tr>"

for each f in NewMsg.Fields
  response.write "<tr><td><b>" & f.name & "</b></td>"
  if not isarray(f.value) then
    response.write "<td>" & f.value & ".</td>"
```

Continued

Listing 12-1 *(Continued)*

```
  else
    response.write "<td>multi-value.</td>"
  end if
response.write "</tr>"
next

response.write "</table>"
%>

</BODY>
</HTML>
```

Using the DataSource object

CDO objects use the CDO `DataSource` interface `Open`, `Open Object`, `Save`, `SaveTo`, `SaveToContainer`, and `SaveToObject` methods to bind to items stored in the Web Storage System. These methods give CDO direct access to the `Datasource` you are manipulating. For example, the application in Listing 12-2 binds to a public folder and then uses the `SaveTo` method to create a new subfolder.

Listing 12-2: The SaveTo Method

```
'Creating a public folder
<html>
<body>

<%@ Language=VBScript %>
<%
'query for the RootDSE to make this code work on any server
Set oLDAP = GetObject("LDAP://rootdse")
sDomain = oLDAP.Get("rootDomainNamingContext")
'convert DC=DOMAIN, DC=.com to domain.com
sdomain = replace(sdomain, "DC=", "")
sdomain = replace(sdomain, ",", ".")

'build the connection URL
sURL = "file://./backofficestorage/"
sURL = sURL & sDomain
sURL = sURL & "/public folders/ParentFolder/"

'create the object
set cn = CreateObject("cdo.folder")
```

```
cn.Description = "Message Folder"
cn.contentclass = "urn:content-classes:folder"
cn.Fields("http://schemas.microsoft.com/exchange/_
outlookfolderclass") = "IPF.Note"
'update the fields before saving
cn.Fields.Update
cn.DataSource.SaveTo sURL

response.write "Folder Successfully Created!"
%>

</body>
</html>
```

After binding to a data source, such as the AD, use the Save method (Listing 12-3) to commit changes back to the data source:

Listing 12-3: The Save Method

```
<HTML>
<BODY>
'Creating a contact using the Save method<%
Dim strLDAP
strLDAP = "LDAP://cleo.hugefan.net/cn=" & "Nicole Yuen"
strLDAP = strLDAP & ",ou=users,dc=hugefan,dc=net"
Set ppp = CreateObject("CDO.person")
With ppp
  .Fields("objectClass") = "contact"
  .FirstName = "Bolo"
  .LastName = "Yuen"
  .Fields.Update
  .DataSource.Save
  End With
%>

</BODY>
</HTML>
```

Use the SaveToObject method (Listing 12-4) to save data into another object, rather than the Web Storage System. An example of this is embedding a message body part into another message. You do this by binding to the message, then calling the SaveToObject method and passing another body part to it.

Listing 12-4: The SaveToObject Method

```
Dim DS
Set DS = iMsg.DataSource
DS.SaveToObject BP, "IBodyPart"
```

Use the `SaveTo` method (Listing 12-5) when you are saving information to an object in the Web Storage System by passing data to its unique URL. An example of this is posting a message to a public folder or a personal folder.

Listing 12-5: The SaveTo Method

```
<%@ Language=VBScript %>
<%
'Posting to a user's folder
strDomain = "hugefan.net"
strPath = "MBX/alias/inbox"
strURL = "file://./BackOfficeStorage/_
" & strDomain & "/" & strPath


Set iData = createobject("CDO.IDatasource")
Set Conn = createobject("CDO.connection")
Conn.Provider = "ExOLEDB.DataSource"
Conn.Open strURL

Set iMsg = createobject("CDO.message")

With iMsg
  .To = "mdinino@akka.com"
  .From = "ikousidis@vanderweil.com"
  .Subject = "This is the test subject line"
  .TextBody = "This is the test message body"
End With

Set iData = iMsg

iData.SaveTo strURL & "/test.eml", _
Conn, adModeReadWrite
Set CreateAndSaveMessageTo = iMsg
%>
```

The `SaveToContainer` method (Listing 12-6) differs from `SaveTo` in that the name for the resource is automatically generated for you in the collection specified by `strURL`.

Listing 12-6: The SaveToContainer Method

```
<%@ Language=VBScript %>
'Creating a personal appointment using the SaveToContainer Method
<%
Dim strDomain
Dim strPath
Dim strURL
Dim Appt

Set Appt = createobject("CDO.Appointment")
strDomain = "hugefan.net"
strPath = "MBX/alias/Calendar"
strURL = "file://./BackOfficeStorage/_
" & strDomain & "/" & strPath

With Appt
  .Subject = "Insert Subject Here"
  .TextBody = "Insert Body Here"
  .StartTime = "10/06/2001 10:00 AM"
  .EndTime = "10/06/2001 11:00 AM"
  .DataSource.SaveToContainer strURL
End With

Set Appt = Nothing%>
```

Use the Open method (Listing 12-7), which has the same syntax and functionality as other ADO interfaces such as the Record and Recordset, although you cannot use this method to create new items.

Listing 12-7: The Open Method

```
iPerson.DataSource.Open "LDAP://" & Info.UserName
Set iMbx = iPerson.GetInterface("IMailbox")
CN.Provider = "ExOLEDB.DataSource"
CN.Open iMbx.baseFolder
```

Use the OpenObject method (Listing 12-8) to connect to and extract information from an object, rather than the Web Storage System. For example, you can use OpenObject to manipulate encapsulated messages. Extract the embedded message by creating a new Message object and call IDataSource.OpenObject, passing the BodyPart reference containing the encapsulated message.

Listing 12-8: The OpenObject Method

```
Dim msg
Set msg = CreateObject("CDO.Message")
Dim ds
Set ds = Msg.DataSource

ds.OpenObject iBp, "IBodyPart"
Set GetEmbeddedMessage = msg
```

Using the Configuration object

The Configuration object is what you use to set the properties of items such as the sender's address and the message subject. In Listing 12-9, the Configuration object sets the message subject.

Listing 12-9: The Configuration Object

```
<html>
<body>
<%
Dim iMsg
Set iMsg = CreateObject("CDO.Message")

Dim iConfig
Set iConfig = CreateObject("CDO.Configuration")

Set iMsg.Configuration = iConfig

With Imsg
  .To = "recipient@domain.com"
  .From = "you@domain.com"
  .Subject = "Insert subject here"
  .TextBody = "Insert message body here"
  .Send
End With

response.write "Message Sent Successfully!"

%>
</body>
</html>
```

Table 12-2 lists the CDOEX COM+ classes and interfaces with a brief description of each.

TABLE 12-2 CDOEX COM+ CLASSES

CDOEX COM+ Class	Description
Configuration	Used to configure CDO objects
Item	Used to manage items in the Web Storage System
Folder	Used to manage folders in the Web Storage System
Appointment	Used to create and manage appointment items in the Web Storage System
Person	Used to create and manage user and contact information in the Web Storage System and Active Directory
Message	Used to create, send, respond to, and manage message items in the Web Storage System
CalendarMessage	Used to create, send, respond to, and manage messages in the Web Storage System that contain calendar-related information
Addressee	Used to resolve addresses in the Active Directory and retrieve a user's free/busy status
Attendee	Used to add attendees to appointments

Developing messaging applications has always been possible with Exchange server, but now you can also develop applications that automate or assist with the management of the Exchange environment itself. The next section introduces new features and their capabilities.

CDO for Exchange Management

For the developer, collaboration is a big draw to Exchange 2000. For the administrator, however, the ability to automate tasks and build front-ends to management tasks that previously required the installation of administration tools will be very attractive to administrators. Exchange itself is open to development, which enables you to create applications that manage the Exchange environment. CDO for Exchange Management (CDOEXM) is a set of COM objects that you use to create or manage servers, mailbox stores, public stores, public folder trees, storage groups, and users.

CDOEXM is useful for automating such tasks as subscribing to mailing-lists and creating accounts. Imagine users being able to browse an intranet Web site and join mailing lists they are interested in, without having to call the help desk. Also imagine help-desk staff managing Exchange from a Web-management console so that you can allow them to do certain tasks and not others.

Figure 12-2 shows the CDO for Exchange management object model.

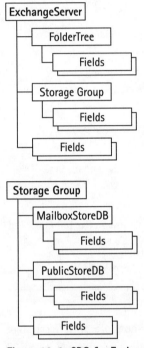

Figure 12-2: CDO for Exchange Management Object Model

Using the ExchangeServer COM+ class

As you might expect, you use the ExchangeServer COM+ class to manage general server-related tasks. You manage the information from the properties dialog of the Server object the Exchange management console. To manage this information in code, use the IExchangeServer interface to query and set information such as server type, server name, and storage groups hosted on the server. You can also set properties such as message tracking and retention policies.

Using the FolderTree COM+ class

The FolderTree COM+ class is for creating, managing, and deleting folder trees. Use the IFolderTree interface to manage folder trees and replicas.

Using the StorageGroup COM+ class

The StorageGroup COM class is for creating, managing, and deleting stores and storage groups. As when you are creating them manually, you must place stores in storage groups.

Using the MailboxStoreDB COM+ class

The MailboxStoreDB COM class is for creating and deleting Exchange 2000 Server mailbox stores. The IMailboxStoreDB interface enables you to mount or dismount a mailbox store, or to access and set its properties.

Using the PublicStoreDB COM+ class

The PublicStoreDB COM class is for managing public stores in Exchange 2000 Server. The IPublicStoreDB interface enables you to create, modify, and delete public stores.

Summary

CDO for Exchange 2000 Server provides the fundamental COM+ components and classes that enable easy Exchange development. These are the building blocks upon which you create items and objects in the Web Storage System. Use the DataSource object to bind to data in the Web Storage System and the Configuration object to set properties.

Chapter 13

CDO Messaging

IN THIS CHAPTER

- ◆ CDO messaging
- ◆ The IBodyPart interface
- ◆ Message object fields
- ◆ The IDropDirectory interface

MESSAGING IS CERTAINLY THE CORE FUNCTIONALITY of Exchange Server. If your Web applications do not include message functionality as the core application, they will at least include it for notifications. CDO messaging enables you to include messaging capabilities in your Web applications. This chapter will show you how to mimic the functionality found in Microsoft Outlook and Outlook Web Access.

Messaging Formats

Exchange Server supports a wide variety of message formats, including plain text, RTF, MIME (Multi-purpose Internet Mail Extensions), and HTML. Depending on the application you're developing, you can get as complex as you need. For example, if you are scripting an event notification, plain text is probably good enough; but if you are building your own Web e-mail application, you will probably want to allow for more robust messaging and file-attachment capabilities. A plain-text message is just that — plain text. No colors, pictures, or fonts are supported. But this is also the simplest of the formats to use. The following is an example of a plain-text message:

```
Message-ID: <000901c14a96$b4e26410$3c00a8c0@rim.net>
From: "Alex Willis" <awillis@best.com>
To: <awillis@win2knet.net>
Subject: Test message in plain-text
Date: Mon, 1 Oct 2001 12:32:48 -0400


This is the body of the text message.
```

Plain text is simple, and is therefore simple to create with code. Basically, you give enough information for Exchange to deliver the message. More complex messages containing colors, font sizes, and so on require a bit more information. Notice how the next example is broken into parts. These parts are called *bodyparts*. When creating a message you can use the IbodyPart interface to add, remove, or manipulate these body parts to suit your needs. A plain-text part is included for e-mail clients that cannot interpret HTML; each of the other parts is contained within sections marked by =_NextPart. Messages are converted this way so they can be transferred over the Internet via SMTP and then converted again when they reach the destination mail server. This next example illustrates a multi-part message in the form in which it travels the Internet:

```
Message-ID: <001401c14a97$2825d650$3c00a8c0@rim.net>
From: "Alex Willis" <awillis@best.com>
To: <awillis@win2knet.net>
Subject: Test in Rich Text Format
Date: Mon, 1 April 2001 12:36:01 -0400
MIME-Version: 1.0
Content-Type: multipart/alternative;
    boundary="-----=_NextPart_000_0011_01C14A75.A10C9530"


This is a multi-part message in MIME format.

------=_NextPart_000_0011_01C14A75.A10C9530
Content-Type: text/plain;
    charset="iso-8859-1"
Content-Transfer-Encoding: quoted-printable


This is the plain text part



------=_NextPart_000_0011_01C14A75.A10C9530
Content-Type: text/html;
    charset="iso-8859-1"
Content-Transfer-Encoding: quoted-printable

<!DOCTYPE HTML PUBLIC "-//W3C//DTD HTML 4.0 Transitional//EN">
<HTML><HEAD>
<META http-equiv=3DContent-Type content=3D"_
text/html; =charset=3Diso-8859-1">
<META content=3D"MSHTML 5.50.4134.600" name=3DGENERATOR>
<STYLE></STYLE>
</HEAD>
```

```
<BODY bgColor=3D#ffffff>
<DIV><FONT face=3DArial color=3D#008000 size=3D5>_
This is the rich text=format</FONT></DIV>
<DIV><FONT face=3DArial size=3D2></FONT> </DIV></BODY></HTML>

------=_NextPart_000_0011_01C14A75.A10C9530--
```

Binary attachments are also supported, but must be converted to a format that can be transferred over the Internet. The following example shows a multi-part message with a very small file attachment:

```
Message-ID: <002001c14a97$873d8e80$3c00a8c0@rim.net>
From: "Alex Willis" <awillis@best.com>
To: <awillis@win2knet.net>
Subject: Test message with file attachment
Date: Mon, 1 April 2001 12:38:41 -0400
MIME-Version: 1.0
Content-Type: multipart/mixed;
    boundary="----=_NextPart_000_001C_01C14A76.001977F0"

This is a multi-part message in MIME format.

------=_NextPart_000_001C_01C14A76.001977F0
Content-Type: multipart/alternative;
    boundary="----=_NextPart_001_001D_01C14A76.001977F0"


------=_NextPart_001_001D_01C14A76.001977F0
Content-Type: text/plain;
    charset="iso-8859-1"
Content-Transfer-Encoding: quoted-printable

Plain text, but file attachment

------=_NextPart_001_001D_01C14A76.001977F0
Content-Type: text/html;
    charset="iso-8859-1"
Content-Transfer-Encoding: quoted-printable

<!DOCTYPE HTML PUBLIC "-//W3C//DTD HTML 4.0 Transitional//EN">
<HTML><HEAD>
<META http-equiv=3DContent-Type content=3D"text/html; =
charset=3Diso-8859-1">
```

```
<META content=3D"MSHTML 5.50.4134.600" name=3DGENERATOR>
<STYLE></STYLE>
</HEAD>
<BODY bgColor=3D#ffffff>
<DIV><FONT face=3DArial size=3D2>plain text, but file =
attachment</FONT></DIV>
<DIV><FONT face=3DArial size=3D2></FONT> </DIV>
<DIV> </DIV></BODY></HTML>


------=_NextPart_001_001D_01C14A76.001977F0--


------=_NextPart_000_001C_01C14A76.001977F0
Content-Type: application/x-msdownload;
    name="test.exe"
Content-Transfer-Encoding: base64
Content-Disposition: attachment;
    filename="test.exe"
```

```
WF7DM8Bew4tEJAhTVldqIItcJBSZWff5i/CLRCQUmff5jTyzV2ofWWoBWCvKO+BQ/zfo
LwsAAIPE
DE54HIO8s4XAdBVXagH/N+gYCwAAg8QMToPvBIX2fedfXlvDVYvsUVGLRQxTVleNeP9q
IFmDZfwA
jV8BaiCLw16Z9/lqH4vIi8OZ9/6LRQheagGJTfiNBIiJRQwr8lqLztPihRBOIUNT/3UI
6BT///9Z
hQ==
```

```
------=_NextPart_000_001C_01C14A76.001977F0--
```

Knowing what these messages look like in raw form will help you understand the development process discussed in this chapter.

Send Messages Using CDO

Sending a message using CDO can be very simple, depending on the complexity of the message itself and the format being used. Exchange supports SMTP messages, as well as complex multi-part messages containing attachments and HTML messages that most mail readers can interpret as Web pages. Using the information in Chapter 12, "Collaborative Data Objects," you can probably imagine the steps involved: Create a new message object, use the configuration object to set the appropriate fields, and then send the message. Listing 13-1 provides an example of this process:

Listing 13-1: Simple Message

```
<html>
<body>
<%

dim imsg
set imsg = createobject("cdo.message")

with imsg
  .to = "awillis@win2knet.net"
  .from = "awillis@win2knet.net"
  .subject = "test message"
  .textbody = "this is the body"
  .send
end with

%>
</body>
</html>
```

You are not likely to include actual values in your code, because this example will send the same message every time you visit the Web page in question. You will probably want to create a form for users to fill out, allowing them to compose a new message. Listing 13-2 is an example of a Web form used to accept input from a user and then send that information to the code in Listing 13-3, which creates and sends the actual message.

Listing 13-2: Web Form

```
<html>
<body>
<form method="post" action="listing13-2.asp">
<P>

<TABLE>
<tr>

<TD>From:</TD>
<TD><INPUT name=sFrom size=50></TD>

<TR><TD>To:</TD>
<TD><INPUT name=sTo size=50></TD>
```

Continued

Listing 13-2 *(Continued)*

```
<TR><TD>Subject:</TD>
<TD><INPUT name=sSubject size=50></TD>

<TR><TD valign=top>Body:</TD>
<TD><TEXTAREA name=sTextBody cols=50 rows=30></TEXTAREA></TD>
</TABLE>

<INPUT type=submit value="Send">
</form>
</body>
</html>
```

Listing 13-3: Accepting the Data and Creating and Sending the Message

```
<html>
<body>
<%

Dim iMsg
Set iMsg = CreateObject("CDO.Message")

Dim iConf
Set iConf = CreateObject("CDO.Configuration")

Set iMsg.Configuration = iConf

With Imsg
.To = Request.Form("sTo")
.From = Request.Form("sFrom")
.Subject = Request.Form("sSubject")
.TextBody = Request.Form.Item("sTextBody")
.Send
End With

response.write "Your Message Was Sent!"

%>
</body>
</html>
```

Add Attachments

Adding attachments can be pretty easy as well. Exchange can automatically generate most of the configuration for you. At its simplest, sending a message with an attachment can be done with few lines of code. For example, Listing 13-4 illustrates sending a message containing an attachment:

Listing 13-4: Adding Attachments to Your Message

```
<%
Dim iMsg
Set iMsg = CreateObject("CDO.Message")

With Imsg
  .To = "awillis@win2knet.net"
  .From = "awillis@win2knet.net"
  .Subject = "This is the Subject Text"
  .TextBody = "This is the Body Text"
  .AddAttachment("c:\internosis.gif")
'or
  .AddAttachment(http://www.myserver.com/image1.jpg)
  .Send
End With
response.write "Message Sent"

%>
```

 The attachment location is local to the server running the Web page. In order for visitors to attach files to their messages, they will first have to upload the files to the server.

HTML Messaging

Listings 13-2 and 13-3 illustrate sending messages in plain text, which usually does the trick, but remember that Exchange supports robust messages. Sending HTML messages with CDO can be as easy as sending simple plain text messages. Simply fill the .HTMLBody field with HTML code that will be translated by the recipient's e-mail client. Listing 13-5 provides an example.

Listing 13-5: HTML Messaging

```
<%

Set iMsg = Createobject("CDO.Message")
Dim sHTMLBody
sHTMLBody = "<HTML><b>This is the body text</b></HTML>"

With iMsg
  .To = "awillis@win2knet.net"
  .From = "awillis@win2knet.net"
  .Subject = "Sample HTML message"
  .HTMLBody = sHTMLBody
  .Send
End With

%>
```

The CreateHTMLBody Method

A really cool feature of the message object is the CreateHTMLBody method. This method accepts a Web site's URL and populates the HTMLBody field with the Web site's contents. This process also creates all the body parts needed to include the graphics contained in the Web site. Listing 13-6 illustrates this process.

Listing 13-6: Embedding a Web Page with the CreateHTMLBody Method

```
<%

Dim iMsg
Set iMsg = CreateObject("CDO.Message")
With iMsg
  .From = "awillis@bostonbands.com"
  .To = "jake@twotonshoe.com"
  .Subject = "Check out this Web site"
  .CreateMHTMLBody "http://www.bostonbands.com"
  .Send
End With

%>
```

If the recipient is using an e-mail client that supports HTML, such as Microsoft Outlook, he or she will see the entire Web page in the message, including all graphics files, as shown in Figure 13-1.

Figure 13-1: Embedded Web page in message

The TextBody Property

In Listing 13-5, it is not necessary to set the `.TextBody` property. Exchange converts the `.HTMLBody` field to plain text and populates the `.TextBody` field for you. You can, however, set the `.TextBody` field to something different so that the `.HTMLBody` and those with clients that support HTML will see the intended HTML message, and those with clients that do not support HTML will see the alternate text. This property is also available in the `urn:schemas:httpmail:textdescription` name space.

Message Object Fields

Alternately, you can manually set the properties on fields in the `urn:schemas` name space. The creation process is essentially the same. To see a list of exposed fields on an object, retrieve and enumerate the Fields Collection. Listing 13-7 illustrates the process of enumerating the Fields Collection of a new message object.

Listing 13-7: Enumerating New Message Fields

```
<%
dim imsg
set imsg = createobject("cdo.message")
```

Continued

Listing 13-7 *(Continued)*

```
dim flds
set flds = imsg.fields

for each f in imsg.fields
    response.write f.name & ": " & f.value & "<p>"
next
%>
```

The code in Listing 13-7 results in the Web page shown in Figure 13-2.

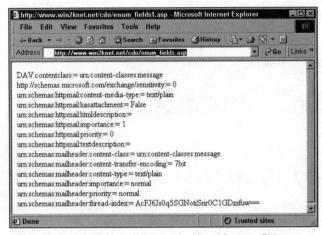

Figure 13-2: The Fields collection of a New Message Object

The IMessage Interface

You can use the method in Listing 13-7 to list the exposed Fields Collection of any object. Listing 13-7 creates a new message and displays the Fields Collection at those times, which are few. Use this example to view the Fields Collection on a message in your inbox to see which fields get populated. When you create a new message, use the IMessage interface to populate its fields as illustrated in Listing 13-8.

Listing 13-8: Manually Setting Fields Properties

```
Dim iMsg
Set iMsg = CreateObject("CDO.Message")

Dim Flds
Set Flds = iMsg.Fields
With Flds
```

```
   .Item("urn:schemas:httpmail:from") = _
"me@mycompany.com"

   .Item("urn:schemas:httpmail:to") = _
"ikousidis@vanderweil.com"

   .Item("urn:schemas:httpmail:subject") = _
"New Designs"

   .Item("urn:schemas:httpmail:textdescription") = _
"The text of the message goes here."

   .Update

End With
```

The IBodyPart Interface

Use the IBodyPart interface to manually create each part of your message. Once you create the message object you can retrieve the IBodyPart interface, and add or remove body parts. When adding data to a body part, write to and flush its data stream as illustrated in Listing 13-9.

Listing 13-9: The IBodyPart Interface

```
<%

Set iMsg = CreateObject("CDO.Message")
Set iBp = iMsg.BodyPart

Set Flds = iBp.Fields
Flds("urn:schemas:mailheader:content-type") _
= "multipart/alternative"
Flds.Update

Set iBp1 = iBp.AddBodyPart
Set Flds = iBp1.Fields
Flds("urn:schemas:mailheader:content-type") _
= "text/plain; charset=""iso 8859-1"""
Flds.Update

Set Stm = iBp1.GetDecodedContentStream
Stm.WriteText "text version of message goes here"
```

Continued

```
Stm.Flush

Set iBp1 = iBp.AddBodyPart

Set Flds = iBp1.Fields
Flds("urn:schemas:mailheader:content-type") = "text/html"
Flds.Update

Set Stm = iBp1.GetDecodedContentStream
Stm.WriteText "<HTML><b>message text goes here</b></HTML>"
Stm.Flush
%>
```

Delete Messages

You can delete messages from Exchange in several ways, ADO being one of them (see Chapter 7, "ActiveX Data Objects"). You can also use CDO and WebDAV. CDO provides this functionality through the use of the IDropDirectory interface and the DropDirectory co-class. You can use the DropDirectory co-class to access a collection of items in a file system, so you might think that it's not for use with Exchange. However, since the Exchange Web Storage System exposes itself as a file system, you can use the DropDirectory co-class and save the message as a file to that location. Once you create the DropDirectory object, use the GetMessages method to create the Message Collection. Listing 13-10 illustrates the use of the DropDirectory co-class to delete the first message in the inbox container.

Listing 13-10: Deleting a Message Using the DropDirectory Co-Class

```
<%
set IDropDir = createobject("cdo.dropdirectory")
Set iMsgs =
iDropDir.GetMessages("M:\hugefan.net\mbx\administrator\inbox\")
imsgs.delete 1
%>
```

Reply to Messages

CDO also enables you to reply to messages using the DropDirectory co-class. Use the Reply or ReplyAll methods to create a reply message. The Reply method exposes the original sender information, and the ReplyAll method includes the original sender info and all addresses on the original To: and CC: fields as well.

Either way, you won't have to address the message. Listing 13-11 illustrates creating a reply message from the first message in the inbox.

Listing 13-11: Replying to a Message

```
<%
Dim iDropDir
Dim iMsgs
Dim iMsg

sPath="file://./_
backofficestorage/hugefan.net/mbx/administrator/inbox"

Set iDropDir = CreateObject("CDO.DropDirectory")
Set iMsgs = iDropDir.GetMessages(sPath)
Set iMsg = iMsgs(1)

Dim iMsg2
Set iMsg2 = iMsg.Reply
imsg2.from = "administrator@win2knet.net"
iMsg2.TextBody = "test reply message" & vbCrLf & iMsg2.TextBody
iMsg2.Send
%>
```

Forward Messages

You can use the DropDirectory co-class to forward messages as well. The .forward method will include the original message information, but you will have to set the .To property yourself. Listing 13-12 illustrates forwarding a message using the DropDirectory co-class.

Listing 13-12: Forwarding a Message Using the DropDirectory Co-Class

```
<%
Dim iDropDir
Dim iMsgs
Dim iMsg

sPath="file://./_
backofficestorage/hugefan.net/mbx/administrator/inbox"

Set iDropDir = CreateObject("CDO.DropDirectory")
Set iMsgs = iDropDir.GetMessages(sPath)
```

Continued

Listing 13-12 *(Continued)*

```
Set iMsg = iMsgs(1)

Dim iMsg2
Set iMsg2 = iMsg.forward

imsg2.to = next_person@somecompany.com
imsg2.cc = "next_person@somecompany.com"
imsg2.from = "administrator@win2knet.net"
iMsg2.TextBody = "forwarding for your review" & vbCrLf &
iMsg2.TextBody
iMsg2.Send

%>
```

Summary

CDO provides messaging functionality similar to, but more extensive than, the messaging functionality found in most messaging applications. In this chapter you learned how to use CDO to delete, read, forward, and reply to messages in mailboxes or public folders. CDO enables you to work with plain-text items as well as with SMTP, NNTP, and HTML messages.

Chapter 14

CDO Calendaring and Contacts

IN THIS CHAPTER

- ◆ Introducing CDO calendaring

- ◆ Creating appointments and meeting requests

- ◆ Processing calendar items

- ◆ Inviting attendees

- ◆ Creating contacts in the Active Directory

- ◆ Creating personal contacts

CALENDARING IS A MAJOR COMPONENT of Exchange 2000 Server. If you are an Outlook user you know that the calendaring features of Exchange are extensive. You can create each of these features in VBScript to add to your Web pages. Calendaring deals with *appointments*, in which there are no attendees, and *meeting requests*, in which others are invited to join. Exchange delivers meeting requests in the same way it delivers any piece of mail, but they have different properties and are stored and manipulated accordingly. This chapter will provide the information you need to create your own calendaring applications as well as contacts applications.

Calendaring Objects and Interfaces

The CDO for Exchange 2000 object library (cdoex.dll) provides the objects and interfaces you need to build calendaring applications with Exchange 2000 Server. The Appointments object is the most common and will be used in all calendar applications, whether for creating or for updating calendar items. The Appointment class contains four collections that you need to use to manipulate a calendar item: Attendees, RecurrencePatterns, Exceptions, and Fields. The calendarParts collection contains the appointment information with which to accept, tentatively accept, or decline a meeting request. The Message object in the calendarmessage object is used for typical messaging actions, such as sending a meeting request.

275

Creating personal appointments

Personal appointments are items in your personal calendar that do not have participants. They just appear on your calendar as reminders, and except for not listing invitees, they look and function exactly like meetings. You can even invite someone later, making the appointment into a meeting. These items are simpler than meeting requests because they do not contain links to other users. They can, however, use some of Exchange's extra features, such as recurrence. You can create a simple appointment in a user's calendar by using the CDO Appointment object, setting the appropriate properties, and saving the item to the user's folder. Listing 14-1 illustrates creating a personal appointment:

Listing 14-1: Creating a Personal Appointment

```
<%@ Language=VBScript %>
<%

Dim strDomainName
Dim strLocalPath
Dim strContainerURL

Set iAppointment = createobject("CDO.Appointment")
strDomainName = "hugefan.net"
strLocalPath = "MBX/alex/Calendar"
strContainerURL = "file://./BackOfficeStorage/" & _
strDomainName & "/" & strLocalPath

With iAppointment
  .Subject = "Halloween Party"
  .Location = "Moms House"
  .TextBody = "You must wear a costume"
  .StartTime = "10/27/2001 10:00 PM"
  .EndTime = "10/27/2001 11:00 PM"
  .DataSource.SaveToContainer (strContainerURL)
End With
Set iAppointment = Nothing

%>
```

Creating meeting requests

Meeting requests are appointments that you create, representing meetings that you invite others to attend. Since multiple users are involved, you also designate a meeting place. Additionally, you can include a file attachment, say an agenda written in Microsoft Word or an Excel spreadsheet to be read in preparation for the meeting. A meeting request must have a meeting organizer who is responsible for changes to the meeting request and for inviting attendees to the meeting. So that attendees are aware of the meeting itself, the organizer has to send them a meeting invitation. The invitation is delivered via an e-mail message. Listings 14-2 and 14-3 illustrate creating a meeting, setting the organizer, and sending a meeting request to the list of attendees.

Listing 14–2: Sending a Meeting Request

```
<%
set iAppt = CreateObject("cdo.appointment")
set iCfg = CreateObject("cdo.configuration")
Set iattendee = createobject("cdo.attendee")
Set iCalmsg = createobject("cdo.calendarmessage")

With cfg
  .Fields("CalendarLocation") = iMbx.Calendar
  .Fields(cdoSendEmailAddress) = "Tfeather@bci.com"
  .Fields.Update
End With

With iAppt
  Set .Configuration = Cfg
  .StartTime = "6/12/2001 10:00:00 AM"
  .EndTime = "6/12/2001 10:30:00 AM"
  .Subject = "Migration Meeting"
  .Location = "Conference Room 3"

  Set iattendee = .Attendees.Add
  iattendee.Address = "MAILTO:RandyGordon@bci.com"
  iattendee.Role = cdoRequiredParticipant

  Set iattendee = .Attendees.Add
  iattendee.Address = "MAILTO:vrobles@buck50.com"
  iattendee.Role = cdoOptionalParticipant

  Set iCalMsg = .CreateRequest
  Set iMsg = iCalMsg.Message
  iMsg.Send
  .Datasource.SaveToContainer iMbx.Calendar
End With

%>
```

Listing 14-3: Inviting Others to a Meeting

```
<%
strDomainName = "hugefan.net"
strLocalPath = "MBX/alex/Calendar"
strContainerURL = "file://./BackOfficeStorage/" & strDomainName &
"/" & strLocalPath

Set iappt = createobject("CDO.appointment")
With iAppt
  .Subject = "Staff Meeting"
  .Location = "Conference Room1"
  .TextBody = "Please bring new ideas"
  .StartTime = "11/25/2001 11:00 AM"
  .EndTime = "11/25/2001 11:30 AM"
  .fields.update
End With

Set iattendee = createobject("CDO.attendee")
Set iAttendee = iAppt.Attendees.Add
with iAttendee
.Address = "awillis@win2knet.net"
.Role = cdoRequiredParticipant
'Other roles include:
'.Role = cdoOptionalParticipant
'.Role = cdoNonParticipant
end with

iappt.fields.update
iappt.DataSource.SaveToContainer strContainerURL

%>
```

Publishing events to a public folder

Using Outlook to create calendar events isn't always possible. You may, for example, wish to allow Internet users to post events, but giving them Outlook access over the Internet is difficult if not impossible in some cases. You can provide this access in a secure and customized way by creating a Web form that accepts data from Internet users and posts to a public calendar folder.

For the most part, the process is the same. For any one of several reasons, you may want to post information to a public folder rather than to create meeting requests to individuals. For example, you may be working with a corporate events calendar where employees may view the calendar on their own time. In this case you don't need attendees to accept a meeting request because attendance is not mandatory, but you may want to notify them of the event nevertheless. Listings 14-4 and 14-5 provide examples of creating an event in a public folder and sending notification of the event to optional attendees.

Listing 14–4: Publishing an Event to a Public Folder

```
<%
Set iappt = createobject("CDO.appointment")
Set iattendee = createobject("CDO.attendee")

strDomainName = "hugefan.net"
strLocalPath = "public folders/corporate calendar/"
strContainerURL = "file://./BackOfficeStorage/" & strDomainName &
"/" & strLocalPath

'Add a required attendee
With iAppt
  .Subject = "Staff Meeting"
  .Location = "Conference Room2"
  .TextBody = "Please bring new ideas"
  .StartTime = "3/21/2001 11:00 AM"
  .EndTime = "3/21/2001 11:30 AM"
  .fields.update
End With

Set iAttendee = iAppt.Attendees.Add
iAttendee.Address = "awillis@win2knet.net"
iAttendee.Role = cdoChair
'iAttendee.Role = cdoRequiredParticipant
'iAttendee.Role = cdoOptionalParticipant
'iAttendee.Role = cdoNonParticipant

iappt.fields.update
iappt.DataSource.SaveToContainer strContainerURL
%>
```

Listing 14–5: Publishing a Calendar Item

```
<%
Domain = file://./backofficestorage/hugefan.net/
FolderURL = "public folders/corporate calendar/"
set iCFG = createobject("cdo.appointment")

With iCfg
.Fields(cdoSendEmailAddress) = "administrator@hugefan.net"
```

Continued

Listing 14-5 *(Continued)*

```
.Fields.Update
End With

With oAppt
  Set .Configuration = iCfg
  .Subject = strSubject
  .StartTime = "8/8/2001 6:00 PM"
  .EndTime = "8/8/2001 9:00 PM"
  .Location = "Function Room"

With .Publish
  .Message.To = oAddr.EmailAddress
  .Message.Fields("bc-hedgefund:send-to") =
"administrator@hugefan.net"
  .Message.Fields("DAV:content-class") = "urn:content-
classes:appointment"
  .Message.Fields.Update
  .Message.Send
End With
.DataSource.SaveToContainer Domain & FolderURL
End With


%>
```

Creating recurring meetings

To create a recurring meeting, you first create a master meeting, and then configure the recurrence pattern and exceptions for that meeting, as shown in Listing 14-6.

Listing 14-6: Creating a Recurring Meeting

```
<%

strDomainName = "hugefan.net"
strLocalPath = "MBX/administrator/Calendar"
strContainerURL = "file://./BackOfficeStorage/" & strDomainName &
"/" & strLocalPath

set cnfg  = createobject("cdo.configuration")
set iappt = createobject("cdo.appointment")

with iappt
  .subject = "Organizational Meeting"
  .location = "15th Floor"
  .starttime = "11/20/2001 3:00 PM"
```

```
   .endtime = "11/20/2001 4:00 PM"
end with

with iappt.recurrencepatterns.add("add")
  .frequency = cdoWeekly
  .interval = 7
  .instances = 52
end with


.datasource.savetocontainer strContainerURL


%>
```

Recurring meetings or events are simply events that happen on a regular basis. The "regular basis" is configurable and CDO provides the configuration parameters. In conjunction with the .interval and .instances properties, use the parameters listed in Table 14-1 to create your recurrence patterns.

TABLE 14-1 RECURRENCE INTERVALS

Constant	Description
CdoSecondly	Occurs every second
CdoMinutely	Occurs every minute
CdoHourly	Occurs every hour
CdoDaily	Occurs every day
CdoWeekly	Occurs every week
CdoMonthly	Occurs every month
CdoYearly	Occurs every year

Setting recurrence exceptions

When you create recurring meetings, you often need to set exceptions. For example, imagine that you create a meeting that is to occur every Monday in the year 2001, except for Monday, June 12. That single Monday is an exception, and rather than create one recurring meeting from January 1 to June 11, and another from June 13 to December 31, you can simply create one recurring meeting with one exception. Listing 14-7 illustrates this process.

Listing 14–7: Recurring Meeting with One Exception

```
<%

strDomainName = "hugefan.net"
strLocalPath = "MBX/administrator/Calendar"
strContainerURL = "file://./BackOfficeStorage/" & strDomainName &
"/" & strLocalPath

set cnfg  = createobject("cdo.configuration")
set iappt = createobject("cdo.appointment")

with iappt
  .subject = "Department Meeting"
  .location = "15th Floor Conf Rm."
  .starttime = "1/1/2001 3:00 PM"
  .endtime = "12/31/2001 4:00 PM"
end with

with iappt.recurrencepatterns.add("add")
  .frequency = cdoWeekly
  .interval = 7
  .instances = 52
end with

with iappt.Exceptions.Add("Add")
  .StartTime = "6/11/2001 3:00 PM"
  .EndTime = "6/11/2001 4:00 PM"
end with
.datasource.savetocontainer strContainerURL

%>
```

Setting time zones

When you schedule a meeting or appointment, the default time zone is that of the server hosting the Web page. To set the time zone in your code, use the Appointment object. If your application is for an intranet site and all users are in a single time zone, along with the server, you can allow the server to set it. However, in some cases you may need to keep track of the time zone for later use. For instance, if this information is going to be displayed to Internet users from multiple time zones, you'll want to be able to convert it. Table 14-2 is a partial list of the time-zone constants you can use.

TABLE 14-2 CDO TIME-ZONE CONSTANTS

Constant	Description
CdoEastern	GMT-05:00
CdoCentral	GMT-06:00
CdoMountain	GMT-07:00
CdoPacific	GMT-08:00

 All time zones are supported. See the SDK help file (available at url:http://www.microsoft.com/exchange) for time zones outside the United States.

The meeting organizer

The meeting organizer is the owner of the meeting and is the only one who can make changes to or cancel the meeting. The meeting organizer is set using the configuration object, as follows:

```
...
Set conf = CreateObject("cdo.configuration")
Conf.fields("cdosendemailaddress") = jim@bostonbands.com
.fields.update
...
```

Process Calendar Items

The ability to create appointments is only one part of a complete calendar application. CDO also enables you to delete, respond to, and forward calendar items.

Deleting appointments

To delete a meeting you use a combination of technologies. In order to delete an object, you first have to find it. Use ADO to find the meeting and make an ADO recordset. Then use the IAppt object to delete the record, as follows:

```
Conn.Provider = "ExOLEDB.DataSource"
Conn.Open iMbx.BaseFolder
```

```
Rec.Open iAppt.DataSource.SourceURL, Conn, adModeReadWrite
Rec.DeleteRecord
Rec.Close
```

This method will delete the appointment, and if no invitees exist you don't have to do anything more. However, if you need to notify invitees of the deletion so that the meeting is also removed from their calendars, you must change the status of the meeting to `cancelled` and send the update message to the attendees. The item will still be stored in the attendees' calendars but not displayed, because the e-mail client will ignore cancelled meetings. Listing 14-8 illustrates changing the status of a meeting to `cancelled`.

Listing 14-8: Cancelling a Meeting

```
Set iCalMsg = iAppt.Cancel
With iCalMsg
    Set Config = .Configuration
    Config(cdoSendUsingMethod) = cdoSendUsingExchange
    Config(cdoMailboxURL) = iMbx.BaseFolder
    Config(cdoActiveConnection) = Conn
    Config.Fields.Update
    .Message.TextBody = "Meeting cancelled"
    .Message.Send
End With
```

Accepting meeting requests

CDO also makes it possible to accept meetings. However, you must find the item first. Use ADO to find the item, and then use CDO to update and save the updates that need to be sent. To be more specific, you need to edit the search query to find a specific calendar request instead of all calendar requests. Listing 14-9 illustrates accepting the first item in a mailbox.

Listing 14-9: Accepting a Meeting

```
<%
Set rs = createobject("ADODB.Recordset")
Set Rec = createobject("ADODB.Record")
Set iCalMsg = createobject("cdo.calendarmessage")
Set iCalMsg2 = createobject("cdo.calendarmessage")
Set iCalPart = createobject("cdo.ICalendarPart")
Set iAppt = createobject("cdo.Appointment")
Set Config = createobject("cdo.Configuration")
Domainname = "yourdomain.com"
Username = "CBurke"
mbxURL = "file://./backofficestorage/" & _
```

```
DomainName & "/MBX/" & Username & "/inbox/"
CalendarURL = "file://./backofficestorage/" & _
DomainName & "/MBX/" & username & "/calendar/"

Config.Fields(cdoSendEmailAddress) = "chrisburke33@hotmail.com"
Config.Fields.Update

Rec.Open mbxUrl
Set Rs.ActiveConnection = Rec.ActiveConnection
Rs.Source = "SELECT ""DAV:href"",""DAV:contentclass"" " & _
  "FROM scope('shallow traversal of """ & mbxURL & """')" & _
  "WHERE (""DAV:contentclass"" = 'urn:content-
classes:calendarmessage')"
Rs.Open

itemURL = Rs.Fields(CdoDAV.cdoHref).Value
iCalMsg.DataSource.Open itemURL
iCalMsg.Configuration = Config

Set iCalPart = iCalMsg.CalendarParts(Index)
Set iAppt = iCalPart.GetUpdatedItem(CalendarURL)
Select Case iCalPart.CalendarMethod
Set iCalMsg2 = iAppt.Accept

iAppt.DataSource.SaveToContainer CalendarURL
iCalMsg2.Message.Send
Response.write "Meeting Accepted"
%>
```

Using Free/Busy searching

Before posting to a calendar, whether it's in a public folder or a user's mailbox, check the Free/Busy status of the desired time to make sure your meeting won't conflict with another appointment. The iAddressee object provides this information. You can query for an exact time, for example when you want to see if a person is available at a specific date and time or, as illustrated in Listing 14-10, you can examine availability over a duration of time. This is useful when you want to create a meeting when the person is next available.

Listing 14-10: Checking Free/Busy

```
<%@ Language=VBScript%>
<%
sStart = #11/20/2001 7:00:00 AM#
```

Continued

Listing 14-10 *(Continued)*

```
sEnd = #11/20/2001 11:00:00 AM#
iInterval = 60

Set iAddr = createobject("CDO.Addressee")
iAddr.EmailAddress = "administrator@win2knet.net"
iAddr.CheckName ("LDAP://" & "Cleo")
sFreeBusy = iAddr.GetFreeBusy(sStart, sEnd, iInterval)
iduration = len(sFreeBusy)

Response.Write "<Table Border=1>"
Response.Write "<TR><TD>" & sStart & "</TD><td></td>"
For i = 2 To iDuration
 Response.Write "<TR>"
 Status(Mid(sFreeBusy, i, 1))
 response.write "</TD>"
Next
Response.Write "<TR><TD>" & sEnd & "</TD><td></td>"
Response.Write "</TABLE>"
Set iAddr = Nothing

Sub Status(sStatus)
 Select Case sStatus
  Case "0"   'Free
    Response.Write "<TD>Free</TD></TR>"
  Case "1"   'Tentative
    Response.Write "<TD>Tentative</TD></TR>"
  Case "2"   'Busy
    Response.Write "<TD>Busy</TD></TR>"
  Case "3"   'Out Of Office
    Response.Write "<TD>Out Of Office</TD></TR>"
  End Select
End Sub
%>
```

When you examine a duration of time, as in the example in Listing 14-10, the resulting Free/Busy value will be listed in a string of numbers. For example, if you examine the hours of 8:00 am to 11:00 am (the duration) with an interval of 60 minutes, and the user is busy the entire time, the result will be 222. The first 2 is 8am–9am (the first interval), the second 2 is 9am–10am (the second interval), and the third 2 is 10am–11am (the third interval). Listing 14-11 illustrates the process of examining a one-hour block with a 60-minute interval.

Listing 14–11: Checking Free/Busy status

```
<%@ Language=VBScript%>
<%
sStartTime = #11/20/2001 9:00:00 AM#
sEndTime = #11/20/2001 10:00:00 AM#

Set iAddr = createobject("CDO.Addressee")
iAddr.EmailAddress = "administrator@win2knet.net"
iAddr.CheckName ("LDAP://" & "Cleo")
sFreeBusy = iAddr.GetFreeBusy(sStartTime, sEndTime, 60)

sStatus = ISBusy(sFreeBusy)
response.write sStatus

Function ISBusy(fb)
 Select Case fb
  Case "0"
    ISBusy = "Free"
  Case "1"
    ISBusy = "Tentative"
  Case "2"
    ISBusy = "Busy"
  Case "3"
    ISBusy = "Out Of Office"
  End Select
End Function
%>
```

Table 14-3 lists the possible results from your query for availability.

TABLE 14-3 FREE/BUSY VALUES

Value	Description
0	Free
1	Tentative
2	Busy
3	Out of office
4	Data not available

CDO Contacts

When dealing with contacts in the Exchange server, you can store data in two areas. You can create contacts in personal contact folders stored on the Exchange server in the user's mailbox, or you can create the contacts in the Active Directory. If many users need access to the contact, create the contact in the Active Directory. The Active Directory can accommodate different types of contacts.

Creating a mail-enabled contact in the Active Directory

CDOEX provides the interfaces you need to create objects in the Active Directory. Mail-enabled contacts are one example of the items you can create. Listing 14-12 demonstrates creating a mail-enabled contact in the Active Directory.

Listing 14-12: Creating a Mail-Enabled Contact

```
<HTML>
<BODY>

<%
fname = "Tracey"
lname = "Dent"
emailaddr = "Tdent@rim.net"
domainDN  = "dc=hugefan"
domainDN  = domainDN & ", dc=net"

Set iPerson = CreateObject("CDO.Person")
With iPerson
    .FirstName = fname
    .LastName  = lname
    .Fields("objectClass") = "contact"
    .Fields.Update
    .DataSource.SaveTo "LDAP://192.168.0.3/cn=" & _
fname & " " & lname & ", ou=users, dc=hugefan, dc=net"

    Set iRecipient = .GetInterface("IMailRecipient")
'use the next line to mail-enable the contact by assigning an SMTP
email address
    iRecipient.MailEnable "smtp:" & emailAddr
    .DataSource.Save
End With
%>

</BODY>
</HTML>
```

See Chapter 9, "Active Directory Service Interfaces (ADSI)," for more information on LDAP (Lightweight Directory Access Protocol).

Creating personal contacts

You create personal contacts not by connecting to the Active Directory, but by connecting to the user's contacts folder using his or her mailbox URL. You still use the CDO.Person object, but not LDAP, so the process is more like creating a message or a post. Listing 14-13 illustrates creating a personal contact.

Listing 14–13: Creating a Personal Contact

```
<%
Set iPer = CreateObject("CDO.Person")

With iPer
  .FirstName = "Ryan"
  .LastName = "Miller"
  .Company = "ABC Enterprises"
  .email = "ryan.s.miller@win2knet.net"
  .workphone = "(555) 555-5555"
  .Fields("objectClass").Value = "contact"
  .Fields.Update
End With

strURL = "file://./backofficestorage/domain/mbx/user/Contacts/"
iPer.DataSource.SaveToContainer strURL
response.write "Personal Contact Created!"

%>
```

You can also use this method to create contacts in a public folder. Running the code in Listing 14-12 will result in the screen shown in Figure 14-1.

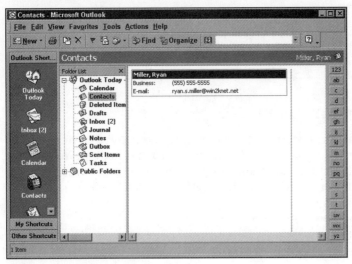

Figure 14-1: Personal contacts

Summary

Adding contact and calendaring functionality to your application means more robust and efficient use of time. In some cases, it may even mean a cost savings. CDO for Exchange provides the interfaces you need to create in one application what some companies get out of two or three applications. When re-engineering your company's workflow process, you can incorporate the best of several disparate applications into one enterprise-scaleable intranet application.

Chapter 15

Real-Time Collaboration with Instant Messaging

IN THIS CHAPTER

- ◆ Overview of Instant Messaging
- ◆ Configuring the Instant-Messaging Service to run
- ◆ Programming with the Instant Messaging components

COLLABORATION COMES IN MANY FORMS, from workflow applications to e-mail to real-time technologies such as the Microsoft Exchange Instant Messaging Service (IM).

This chapter will introduce you to the Instant Messaging Service and demonstrate how to configure it, how to work with the client-side Instant Messaging components, and how to extend Instant Messaging to existing or new Web applications.

Overview of the Instant Messaging Service

The Microsoft Instant Messaging (IM) service is a real-time messaging service that enables contacts to communicate in real-time via a message window and keep track of each other's online status, or *presence information*. A contact's presence information can be one of the following: Offline, Online, Busy, Be Right Back, Away, On The Phone, or Out To Lunch.

IM integrates with Exchange and IIS and communicates over port 80, the standard Internet TCP port.

Configuring Exchange to run the Instant Messenging Service

For the purpose of this section we assume that you have already installed the IM service and that at this point it must be configured in order to work. If you haven't installed the IM service, go back and run the Exchange setup and choose the Add/Remove programs option to add the IM service. If you need further assistance with installing IM, refer to your Exchange documentation or the Exchange Support Web site at http://msdn.microsoft.com.

The first step in configuring Exchange to run IM is to create the IIS Virtual Server from within the Exchange System Manager. Here's how:

1. Open the Exchange System Manager by selecting Start → Programs → Microsoft Exchange → System Manager.

2. After the System Manager opens, navigate to the Instant Messaging container by selecting Servers → Protocols → Instant Messaging.

3. Right-click the Instant Messaging container and choose New Instant Messaging Virtual Server to start the New Instant Messaging Virtual Server Wizard.

4. Click the Next button on the splash screen (Figure 15-1).

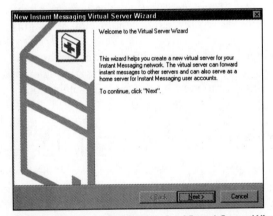

Figure 15-1: The Instant Messaging Virtual Server Wizard

The next screen will ask you to enter a display Name. This is the name that will represent the Virtual Server within the Exchange System Manager. Enter the display Name and click Next (Figure 15-2).

The next screen asks you to choose the associated Web site. If you don't have more than one Web site under IIS, just leave the default option (Figure 15-3). Click Next.

The next screen asks you for the domain name of the Exchange server on which the IM service is going to run. Enter the DNS name and click Next (Figure 15-4).

The next screen asks you to decide whether this server is going to be the home server. If this is the server where user-account information will be stored, then check this box (Figure 15-5) and click Next. If not, just click Next, which will bring you to the last screen where you can click Finish.

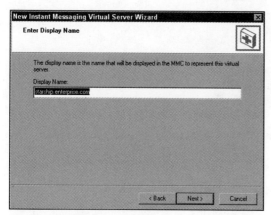

Figure 15-2: Entering a display name in the Instant Messaging Virtual Server Wizard

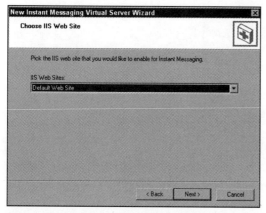

Figure 15-3: Selecting an associated Web site in the Instant Messaging Virtual Server Wizard

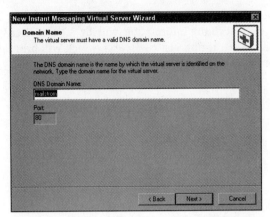

Figure 15-4: Entering the DNS in the Instant Messaging
Virtual Server Wizard

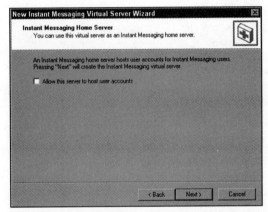

Figure 15-5: Specifying the Instant Message home server
in the Instant Messaging Virtual Server Wizard

If all was successful you will have an IM service Virtual Server under the IM Rendezvous Protocol (RVP) container.

The next step in configuring the IM service is to configure the Domain Name System (DNS) Service-Locator (SRV) resource record. To create the record in DNS, complete the following steps:

1. Start the DNS.

2. Right-click the zone that you want.

3. Select Other New Records → Service Location → Create record.

4. In the Service box, type **_rvp**.

5. In the Protocol box, type _tcp.

6. In the Priority box, type 0.

7. In the Weight box, type 0.

8. In the Port Number box, type 80.

9. In the "Host offering this service" box, type the Fully Qualified Domain Name (FQDN) of the server.

Figure 15-6 shows the completed DNS record.

The FQDN is the same name that you typed in the Domain Name text box of the IM Virtual Server setup. The two must match exactly.

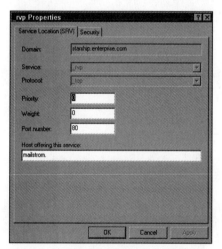

Figure 15-6: Completed Domain Name System (DNS) service-location (SRV) record

The last step in configuring IM is enabling the users to whom you want to allow access to the IM service. Complete the following steps for each user you want to enable:

1. Select Start → Programs → Microsoft Exchange → Active Directory Users and Computers.

2. In the console tree, double-click the domain, and then click Users.

3. Right-click the name of the user, select Exchange Tasks, and click the Next button in the Welcome dialog box.

4. Click the Enable Instant Messaging button, and then click Next.

5. Click the Browse button (next to the "Instant Messaging Home Server") text box. In the "Server name" column of the browse window, select the Instant Messaging Server that you created in step two of the Virtual Server setup. Then click OK.

6. When the server is displayed in the dialog box, click Next.

7. Click Finish and repeat steps 1-7 for all users for who you want to enable Instant Messaging.

After you have enabled all users, you will be ready to install the IM client and try to log in. If you are having difficulty logging in, check the IIS log file, located in the `winnt\system32\LogFiles\W3SVC1` directory. If you notice authentication issues, you can reference XCCC: Troubleshooting Authentication Failures in Instant Messaging (Q278974) from the Microsoft Knowledge Base. You can also try entering *domain\username* in the username text box when prompted to log in, with the domain text box left empty, or using the short domain name instead of the FQDN.

Programming with Instant Messenger

Two client components are available to programmers for programming against the Exchange IM service: `MSIMCntl.dll` and `msimhost.exe`. If these components are not registered or installed on the client machine you can download them from this book's companion Web site.

Once you download them you will need to copy them to a directory of your choice on the client machine and then register each component. Follow these steps to register a component:

1. Select Start → Run.

2. Type in **cmd** and press the Enter key. This should open a command prompt.

3. In the command prompt, change to the directory to which you copied the two components.

4. For each component you wish to register, type **regsvr32** followed by the component name. For example:

```
regsvr32 msimcntl.dll
```

5. Repeat Step 4 for `msimhost.exe`.

Table 15-1 lists each component and its features.

TABLE 15-1 CLIENT COMPONENTS FOR PROGRAMMING WITH
THE EXCHANGE IM SERVICE

Type Library Display Name	Type Library Name	Component	Features
MSIM Control 1.0 Type Library	MSIMCNTLLib	MSIMCntl.dll	This library exposes the Contact View interface and the Message View interface. To include either of these interfaces in your application, include this library.
Microsoft Exchange Instant Messaging Client 1.0 Type Library	MSIMCliSDKLib	msimhost.exe (msimhost.tlb)	Exposes interfaces for the IM Host, as well as for IM services, contacts, and message sessions

The MSIM Control 1.0 Type Library (`MSIMCntl.dll`) exposes two ActiveX controls as views: the *Contact View* and the *Message View*. The Contact View control deals with lists of contacts as well as with actions that can be performed against them. The Message View control deals with sending text-based messages between contacts. The Microsoft Exchange Instant Messaging Client 1.0 Type Library exposes a collection of interfaces used to manage contact, list, and session objects.

The ActiveX controls provide the user interface and the `msimhost.exe` provides access to the IM service. This is the basic architecture for the IM service (Figure 15-7).

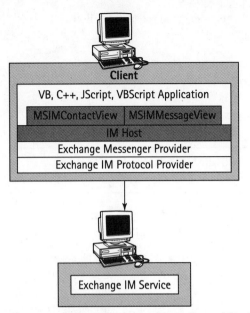

Figure 15-7: The basic Instant Messaging architecture

The IM Contact View control (MSIMContactView)

The IM Contact View control manages and displays contacts. The contacts are categorized into four lists:

♦ *Contacts* – The collection of contacts that a user can perform actions on and with which the user can monitor presence information. To reference this list, use $$Messenger\Contact with the List property.

♦ *Blocked* – The collection of contacts that are not allowed to send instant messages or see a user's presence information. Each user has only one Blocked list. To reference this list, use $$Messenger\Block with the List property.

♦ *Reverse* – The collection of contacts that have added the user to their contacts lists. The IM System maintains this list automatically. Each user has only one Reverse list. To reference this list, use $$Messenger\Reverse with the List property.

♦ *Allowed* – The collection of contacts that are allowed to send instant messages and see a user's presence information. To reference this list, use $$Messenger\Allowed with the List property.

The IM Contact View control also provides a context menu that enables the user to perform default actions against a contact, such as sending an instant message or an invitation to an online meeting. The context menu is context-specific: That is, if an action cannot be performed against a contact the action will not show up on the menu. The context menu can be customized through client-side VBScript or JavaScript.

The IM Contact View control also exposes an interface in which a programmer can program state change or how the control is displayed. Table 15-2 lists the IMSIMContactView interface elements. The Contact View control inherits several properties and methods from the _IUseIMBase interface. These properties and methods can only be accessed through the Contact View control or the Message View control.

TABLE 15–2 IMSIMCONTACTVIEW INTERFACE PROPERTIES

Property	Description
AcceptMessages	Property is marked Obsolete according to Microsoft documentation. You should not rely on this property as future versions of this interface may not support it. Instead, rely on the MSIMHost object to handle incoming messages.
AllowCollapse	Indicates whether or not the root nodes in the list can be expanded and collapsed by the local user. (This property can be set with an HTML <param> tag.)
ExtentHeight (read-only)	Returns the optimal height the control needs to display the list without scroll bars.
ExtentWidth (read-only)	Returns the optimal width the control needs to display the list without scroll bars.
FilterOffline	Indicates whether the offline contacts will be displayed in the list. (This property can be set with an HTML <param> tag.)
Group	Indicates whether the online and offline contacts will be grouped within the respective root nodes in the tree list. (This property can be set with an HTML <param> tag.)
HotTracking	Indicates whether the IM list will track the cursor as it is moved over contacts in the list. (This property can be set with an HTML <param> tag.)
List	The collection to be used in the list. (This property can be set with an HTML <param> tag.)

Continued

TABLE **15–2 IMSIMCONTACTVIEW INTERFACE PROPERTIES** *(Continued)*

Property	Description
OfflineCollapsed	Indicates whether the offline root node will be collapsed or expanded on load. (This property can be set with an HTML <param> tag.)
OfflineRootLabel	Indicates the label to be displayed for the offline sublist. (This property can be set with an HTML <param> tag.)
OnlineCollapsed	Indicates whether the online root node will be collapsed or expanded on load. (This property can be set with an HTML <param> tag.)
OnlineRootLabel	Indicates the label to be displayed for the online sublist. (This property can be set with an HTML <param> tag.)
SelectedMenuOptions (read-only)	Indicates which actions can be performed on a selected contact.
ShowIcons	Indicates whether or not the state icons are displayed. (This property can be set with an HTML <param> tag.)
ShowLogonButton	Indicates whether or not a login prompt is displayed if the local user is not already logged onto the IM service provider. (This property can be set with an HTML <param> tag.)
ShowSelectAlways	Indicates whether or not to continuously show the selection on the list. (This property can be set with an HTML <param> tag.)
Window (read-only)	Returns the handle of the IM window.
*AutoLogon	Indicates that the object should attempt to log on.
*HasService (read-only)	Indicates whether or not the object is connected to an IM service provider.
*LoggedOn (read-only)	Indicates whether or not the local user is logged on.
*Service	Returns and sets the service to be used by the control.

These properties are inherited from the _IUseIMBase interface.

Table 15-3 lists the methods of the IMSIMContactView interface.

TABLE 15–3 IMSIMCONTACTVIEW INTERFACE METHODS

Method	Description
Add	Adds a contact or a list of contacts to the IM list
AddMenuItem	Adds a menu item to the context menu displayed when a selected contact is right-clicked
BlockSelected	Adds the selected contact to the block list
EMailSelected	nitiates an e-mail message to the selected contact on the IM list
IMSelected	Initiates an IM session with the selected contact on the IM list
InviteSelected	Initiates an invitation to join an application to the selected contact on the IM list
Remove	Removes the selected contact from the IM list
UnblockSelected	Removes the selected contact from the block list
*GetLocalState	Indicates the local user's current state
*Logoff	Logs a local user off IM
*Logon	Logs a local user onto IM
*SetLocalState	Sets the local user's current state
*SetService	Gives an object a pointer to a currently active IM service

These methods are inherited from the _IUseIMBase interface.

Using the IMSIMContactView control on a Web page is very easy. Simply use the <object> tag referencing the CLSID of the control and then set the properties of the object that are exposed via the <param> tag. Refer to Table 15-2 for a list of the properties that are exposed. Listing 15-1 is an example of how to embed the IM Contact View control on a Web page.

Listing 15–1: Embedding the IM Contact View Control on a Web Page

```
<OBJECT
  classid=CLSID:B06EDBC7-287D-405C-A899-9C7F8358EF26
  codeType=application/x-oleobject
  width="100%"
```

Continued

Listing 15-1 *(Continued)*

```
        height="100%"
        id=MSIMContactView
        name=MSIMContactView VIEWASTEXT>
        <PARAM name="Service" value=0>
        <PARAM name="List" VALUE="$$Messenger\Contact">
        <PARAM name="FilterOffline" value=False>
        <PARAM name="Group" value=True>
        <PARAM name="ShowLogonButton" VALUE="1">
        <PARAM param name="OnlineRootLabel" value="On Line">
        <PARAM name="OfflineRootLabel" value="Off Line">
        <PARAM name="OfflineRootLabel" value="Off Line">
        <PARAM name="OfflineCollapsed" value="True">
        <PARAM name="AllowCollapse" value="1">
    </OBJECT>
```

Figure 15-8 shows the Contact View control embedded in a Web page.

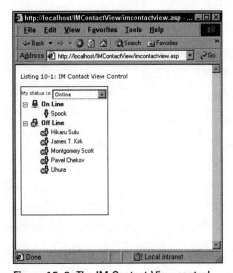

Figure 15-8: The IM Contact View control

The Content View control also exposes, through the DMSIMContactViewEvents interface, a series of events that can be scripted against. The events fire on the client-side and are referenced by the `id` of the `<object>` tag. To register for an event you must include the event in a `<script>` block. Types of events you may want to program against include a user logging on, a user logging off, the context menu being shown, and the user's state changing. Table 15-4 lists the events in the DMSIMContactViewEvents interface.

TABLE 15-4 DMSIMCONTACTVIEWEVENTS INTERFACE EVENTS

Event	Description
OnAddContactUI (pfEnableDefault As Variant)	Indicates that the add contact user interface (UI) is starting
OnAddResult(lResult As Long, bstrContact As String)	Indicates that a contact has been added, or that an addition was attempted
OnEMailContact(bstrContact As String,pfEnableDefault As Variant)	Indicates that the user has requested to send e-mail to a contact using a mailto: URL
OnExtentsChange(nWidth As Long, nHeight As Long)	Indicates that the size of the list has changed
OnLocalStateChange(lLocalState As Long, bstrDescription As String, pVarData as Variant)	Indicates that the state for the local user has changed, or that a state change was attempted
OnLaunchMessageUI(bstrContact As String,lFlags As Long,pfEnableDefault As Variant)	Indicates that the local user has requested a new IM session or a Microsoft NetMeeting session with a contact
OnLogoff(lResult As Long)	Indicates that the local user has logged off from an IM service provider
OnLogon(lResult As Long)	Indicates that the local user has attempted to log onto an IM service provider
OnMenuRequest(bstrContact As String,pbfDefaults As Variant)	Indicates that a context menu is about to be displayed
OnMenuSelect(bstrContact As String,lCmd As Long)	Indicates that a custom context-menu item has been selected
OnReady()	Indicates that the IM list UI is initialized
OnRemoveResult(lResult As Long,bstrContact As String)	Indicates that a contact has been removed, or that a removal was attempted
OnSelect(bstrContact As String)	Indicates that a root label or a contact on the IM list has been selected
OnShutdown()	Indicates that the IM list control is shutting down

Using the OnMenuRequest and OnMenuSelect events, you can programmatically add and respond to context-menu items. Listing 15-2 provides an example using these two events.

Listing 15-2: Using the OnMenuRequest and OnMenuSelect events to Change the Menu Context

```
... <!--Embedded IM View Control Above Code -->
<SCRIPT language='VbScript'>
Dim Cmd1
Dim Cmd2
Sub MSIMContactView_OnMenuRequest(BYVAL vSelected, BYREF pfDefaults)
    Dim Sep
    Cmd1 = MSIMContactView.AddMenuItem("Hello World")
    Sep  = MSIMContactView.AddMenuItem("")      'Inserts a menu break
    Cmd2 = MSIMContactView.AddMenuItem("Are you ready")
End Sub

Sub MSIMContactView_OnMenuSelect(BYVAL vSelected, BYVAL lCmd)
    If lcmd = Cmd1 then
        msgbox "You selected Hello World"
    elseif lcmd = Cmd2 then
        msgbox "You selected Are you Ready"
    end if
End Sub
</SCRIPT>
...
```

Figure 15-9 shows the modified context menu.

You can also keep track of and change the local user's state through the use of the onLocalStateChange event, and the setLocalState and getLocalState methods. A local user's state can be changed to one of eight states from the IM_STATE enum. Table 15-5 lists the eight possible values for the setLocalState method.

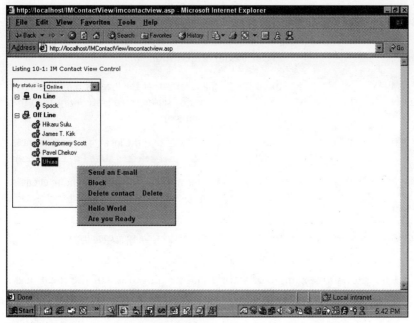

Figure 15-9: The modified context menu

TABLE **15-5** POSSIBLE VALUES FOR THE SETLOCALSTATE METHOD

Enum State	Enum Value	Description
IM_STATE_UNKNOWN	0x000	Indicates that the local or remote client is in an unknown state
IM_STATE_ONLINE	0x0002	Indicates that the local or remote client is online
IM_STATE_INVISIBLE	0x0006	Indicates that the local or remote client is in the user-selected state Invisible to other users
IM_STATE_BUSY	0x000A	Indicates that the local or remote client is in the user-selected state Busy
IM_STATE_BE_RIGHT_BACK	0x000E	Indicates that the local or remote client is in the user-selected state Be Right Back

Continued

TABLE 15-5 POSSIBLE VALUES FOR THE SETLOCALSTATE METHOD *(Continued)*

Enum State	Enum Value	Description
IM_STATE_AWAY	0x0022	Indicates that the local or remote client is in the user-selected state Away from the computer
IM_STATE_ON_THE_PHONE	0x0032	Indicates that the local or remote client is in the user-selected state On the Phone.
IM_STATE_OUT_TO_LUNCH	0x0042	Indicates that the local or remote client is in the user-selected state Out to Lunch.

Not all state values are shown. Please refer to the Web Storage System SDK for a complete list.

Listing 15-3 shows an example of setting and keeping track of the local user's state.

Listing 15-3: Setting and Keeping Track of the Local User State

```
...
<SCRIPT language='VBScript'>
Sub GetState()
  DIM strState, strDescr
  DIM iState
  on error resume next

  'get the current state
  MSIMContactView.GetLocalState iState, strState, strDescr

  'Read the iState return value
  if iState = 1 then
    localstate.innerHTML = "not <SPAN
onClick='MSIMContactView.logon()'> <U>logged in</U></SPAN>."
    localstate.style.display = "inline"
    lstLocalState.style.display = "none"
  else
    localstate.innerHTML = ""
    localstate.style.display = "inline"
    lstLocalState.style.display = "inline"
    lstLocalState.value = iState
```

```
      end if
end sub

Sub MSIMContactView_OnLogoff(lResult)
  GetState
End Sub

Sub MSIMContactView_OnReady()
  GetState
End Sub

Sub lstLocalState_onchange()
  On Error Resume Next

  MSIMContactView.SetLocalState CInt(lstLocalState.value), "", ""

  If Err.Number <> 0 Then
    MsgBox "An error occurred: " & err.description
      Err.Clear
  End If
End Sub
</SCRIPT>
```

Looking at Listing 15-3, you can see that the GetState procedure checks the local user's state by calling the getLocalState method. If the state returns 1 or IM_STATE_OFFLINE, the code changes the list box to a text message saying that you are not online. If you are online, the routine sets the list-box value to that of the current state. The onLogoff event fires after you have logged off and calls the GetState procedure, which will determine that you are logged off and display the logged-off message. The lstLocalState change event is triggered whenever you change the local user's state from the list box. To change your state, simply call the setLocalState method and pass the value from the list box. The state value must be a valid value from the IM_STATE enum (refer to Table 15-5 for possible values). Figure 15-10 shows an example.

The IM Contact control is one example of real-time collaboration. This control enables you to manage and keep track of contacts grouped into lists and view real-time presence information such as the state of a contact. It also exposes properties, methods, and events so that programmers can extend an application's functionality.

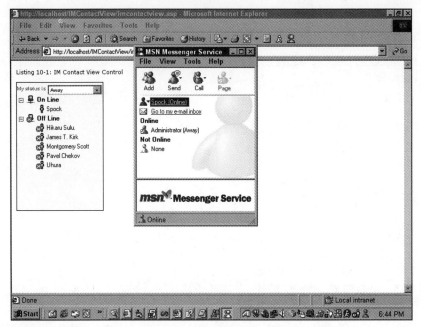

Figure 15-10: Showing a user's state set by the setLocalState method

The IM Message View control (MSIMMessageView)

The IM Message View control handles creating sessions for sending and receiving messages between contacts. The IM Message View control displays the following elements:

◆ *Current Participants* shows all the contacts participating in the current conversation. (The control handles this by default.)

◆ *Available Participants* shows all the contacts available to join the current session. Typically these are the user's default contacts. (Can be a list provided by another application.)

◆ *Conversation History* shows the message history from the time the user joins a session. If a user joins in the middle of the session the window will keep a history from that point forward.

◆ The *Outgoing Message pane* shows the message text that the user types. The window enables the user to set font style, color, and size, and also to send the message.

◆ The *Status Message pane* shows when the last message was received and who is currently typing.

The IM Message View control can be embedded into Web pages or custom applications. Figure 15-11 shows a picture of the IM Message View control.

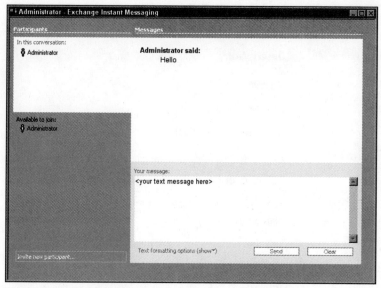

Figure 15-11: The IM Message View control in a VB Application

The IM Message View control also exposes the IMSIMMessageView interface and the DMSIMMessageViewEvents interface. The IMSIMMessageView also extends the _IUseIMBase interface. Table 15-6 lists the properties for the MSIMMessageView interface.

TABLE 15-6 IMSIMMESSAGEVIEW INTERFACE PROPERTIES

Property	Description
Appearance	Reserved for future use
AvailableList	Sets and retrieves the list displayed as the "Available to Join" list for the session
HideStatus	Reserved for future use
MessageHistory	Returns the contents of the Conversation History pane (read-only)
MessageText	Sets and retrieves the contents of the Outgoing Message pane, but does not send the text (read-only)

Continued

TABLE 15-6 IMSIMMESSAGEVIEW INTERFACE PROPERTIES

Property	Description
ShowAvailable	Reserved for future use
ShowEdit	Reserved for future use
ShowMembers	Reserved for future use
ShowMessageHistory	Reserved for future use
ShowParticipants	Reserved for future use
SourceURL	Sets the Uniform Resource Identifier (URI) of the HTML page to be loaded
StatusText	Sets and retrieves the contents of the Status Message pane
Window (Read-Only)	Returns the handle of the Instant Messaging Service (IM) window
*AutoLogon	Indicates that the object should attempt to log on
*HasService (Read-Only)	Indicates whether or not the object is connected to an IM service provider
*LoggedOn (Read-Only)	Indicates whether or not the local user is logged on
*Service	Returns and sets the service to be used by the control

*These properties are inherited from the _IUseIMBase interface

Table 15-7 lists the IMSIMMessageView interface methods.

TABLE 15-7 IMSIMMESSAGEVIEW INTERFACE METHODS

Method	Description
AddToAvailable	Adds a contact to the Available To Join list by implementing the Add Method of the IMSIMContactView interface
EndSession	Removes the local user from the current IM session
Invite	Associates an existing IMSession with the Message View or invites a contact to the current IM session

Method	Description
InviteNetMeeting NetMeeting session	Invites all the members of an IMSession to a NetMeeting session
NetMeetingInvite	Forwards the OnNetMeetingInviteReceived method event to a new message window and requests that the window manage the session
RemoveFromAvailable	Removes a contact from the Available To Join list by invoking the Remove method
*GetLocalState	Indicates the user's current state
*Logoff	Logs a local user off IM
*Logon	Logs a local user onto IM
*SetLocalState	Sets the local user's current state
*SetService	Gives an object a pointer to a currently active IM service

*These methods are inherited from the _IUseIMBase interface.

Table 15-8 lists the events exposed by the DMSIMMessageViewEvents interface.

TABLE 15-8 DMSIMMESSAGEVIEWEVENTS INTERFACE EVENTS

Event	Description
OnAddResultOnAddResult (lResult As Long,bstrContact As String)	Indicates that a contact has been added to a list, or that an addition was attempted
OnLaunchMessageUI (bstrContact As String, lFlags As Long, pfEnableDefault As Variant)	Indicates that the local user has requested a new IM or Microsoft NetMeeting session with a contact
OnLocalStateChange (lLocalState As Long,bstrDescription As String,pvarData As Variant)	Indicates that the state for the local user has changed, or that a state change was attempted
OnLogoff(lResult As Long)	Indicates that the local user has logged off an IM provider

Continued

TABLE 15-8 DMSIMMESSAGEVIEWEVENTS INTERFACE EVENTS *(Continued)*

Event	Description
`OnLogon(lResult As Long)`	Indicates that the local user has logged onto an IM provider
`OnNewSession()`	Indicates that a new IM session has started in the Message View
`OnReady()`	Indicates that the IM list user interface (UI) is initialized
`OnRemoveResult(lResult As Long,bstrContact As String)`	Indicates that a contact has been removed, or that a removal was attempted
`OnSessionEnd()`	Indicates that the IM session in the Message View has ended
`OnShutdown()`	Indicates that the IM list control is shutting down

You can use the Message View control with very minimal coding. Just use the `<object>` tag to include the ActiveX control in a Web page, use the `<param>` tag to set a few properties, and launch the Web page. Listing 15-4 provides a code sample that embeds the MS View control in a Web page.

Listing 15-4: Embedding the MS View Control on a Web Page

```
<OBJECT classid="clsid:528B6917-4DED-43F1-B56C-35A1519129CA"
  codeType="application/x-oleobject"
  id="MSIMMessageView"
  style="BORDER-BOTTOM: 2px inset; BORDER-LEFT: 2px inset; BORDER-
RIGHT: 2px inset; BORDER-TOP: 2px inset; HEIGHT: 457px; WIDTH:
625px" VIEWASTEXT>
  <PARAM name='Service' value='1'>
  <PARAM name="AvailableList" value="$$Messenger\Contact">
  <PARAM name='MessageText' value='Your Text Here'>
  <PARAM name='StatusText' value='Initial Status'>
</OBJECT>
```

Figure 15-12 shows the MS Message View object embedded on a Web page without code modifications.

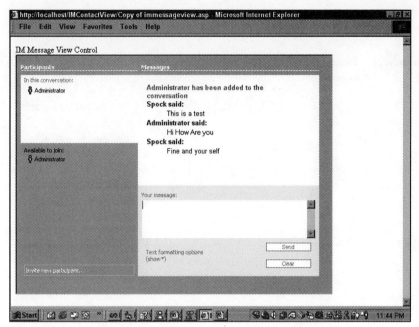

Figure 15-12: The IM Message View control embedded in a Web page

You can create a custom HTML page with all the elements from the IM Message View control by setting the SourceURL property of the control to a URL. The SourceURL can be a relative path, but it will be relative to the location where the MSIMCntl.dll is registered. Each element of the Message View control is bound to an HTML element with the ID attribute set to a predefined value. Table 15-9 lists the Message View element types, the HTML ID attribute, and a description of the element.

TABLE 15-9 MESSAGE VIEW ELEMENT MAPPINGS FOR THE SOURCEURL

Message View Element	Element Mapping	ID Attribute	Description
Current Participants	Object	ParticipantsList	The IM Contact View control used to display the contacts currently active and participating in the session associated with this message instance

Continued

TABLE 15-9 MESSAGE VIEW ELEMENT MAPPINGS FOR THE SOURCEURL *(Continued)*

Message View Element	Element Mapping	ID Attribute	Description
Available Participants	`Object`	`AvailableList`	The IM Contact View control used to display the contacts currently in the available list as specified with `MessageView.Available List` (or the `$$Messenger\Contact` list if none is specified)
Conversation History	`iFrame`	`history`	Used to display the ongoing message conversation. This object is optional, and can be omitted if the message view is to be used only for sending, since no incoming messages would be displayed.
Outgoing Message pane	`textarea`	`chat`	The input area for the text that is sent when the send button is clicked or activated. The `<textarea>` value is sent, including its current formatting, when the send action is initiated.
Outgoing Message pane	`any element with an OnClick event`	`btnSend`	Used to initiate the sending of the chat `textarea` contents to the message-session participants. The Message View control captures the Enter keystroke as the keyboard accelerator to initiate sending text, which cannot be overridden by the UI.
Status Message pane	`div or span`	`status`	Used by the control to display incoming status messages including the `isTyping` message

The ParticipantsList and AvailableList objects can be modified further on the page that hosts the objects. Listing 15-5 shows a code example of a custom IM Message View control. The code in Listing 15-5 shows two separate pages: The first page is the IM Message View control showing the SourceURL property setting, and the second page is the actual custom HTML.

TIP The status element is replaced with the StatusText property of the Message View control and an <image> tag; however, the image src property doesn't exist anywhere. The name of the image is uTyping.gif and can be any image you want. Just include it in the same folder as the custom HTML page and name it uTyping.gif.

Listing 15-5: Building a Custom HTML Message View

```
immessageview.asp
  ...
<OBJECT classid="clsid:528B6917-4DED-43F1-B56C-35A1519129CA"
  codeType="application/x-oleobject"
  id="MSIMMessageView"
  style='HEIGHT: 360px;      WIDTH: 300px;"'
  VIEWASTEXT>
  <PARAM name='Service' value='1'>
  <PARAM name="AvailableList" value="$$Messenger\Contact">
  <PARAM name="SourceURL"
    value="http://localhost/IMContactView/msgviewelements.htm">
</OBJECT>
  ...
msgviewelements.htm
<DIV class='IMWnd' style='width: 300px'>
  <SPAN class='imcontactlist'>
  <!-- Setup AvailableList -->
<OBJECT classid=CLSID:B06EDBC7-287D-405C-A899-9C7F8358EF26
        codeType=application/x-oleobject id=AvailableList
        style="margin: 0px; HEIGHT: 100px; WIDTH: 150px" VIEWASTEXT>
        <PARAM NAME="AcceptMessages" VALUE="0">
        <PARAM NAME="ShowIcons" VALUE="-1">
        <PARAM NAME="HotTracking" VALUE="0">
        <PARAM NAME="AllowCollapse" VALUE="-1">
        <PARAM NAME="ShowSelectAlways" VALUE="0">
        <PARAM NAME="OnlineRootLabel" VALUE="On Line">
        <PARAM NAME="OfflineRootLabel" VALUE="Off Line">
```

Continued

Listing 15-5 *(Continued)*

```
            <PARAM NAME="ShowLogonButton" VALUE="-1">
            <PARAM NAME="List" VALUE="">
            <PARAM NAME="OnlineCollapsed" VALUE="0">
            <PARAM NAME="OfflineCollapsed" VALUE="0">
            <PARAM NAME="Group" VALUE="-1">
            <PARAM NAME="FilterOffline" VALUE="0">
            <PARAM NAME="Service" VALUE="-1">
            <PARAM NAME="AutoLogon" VALUE="0">
</OBJECT>
</SPAN>
<BR>
<SPAN class='imcontactlist'>
<!-- Setup ParticipantsList -->
<OBJECT classid=CLSID:B06EDBC7-287D-405C-A899-9C7F8358EF26
        codeType=application/x-oleobject id=ParticipantsList
        style="margin: 0px; HEIGHT: 100px; WIDTH: 150px" VIEWASTEXT>
            <PARAM NAME="AcceptMessages" VALUE="0">
            <PARAM NAME="ShowIcons" VALUE="-1">
            <PARAM NAME="HotTracking" VALUE="0">
            <PARAM NAME="AllowCollapse" VALUE="-1">
            <PARAM NAME="ShowSelectAlways" VALUE="0">
            <PARAM NAME="OnlineRootLabel" VALUE="Participants">
            <PARAM NAME="OfflineRootLabel" VALUE="">
            <PARAM NAME="ShowLogonButton" VALUE="0">
            <PARAM NAME="List" VALUE="">
            <PARAM NAME="OnlineCollapsed" VALUE="0">
            <PARAM NAME="OfflineCollapsed" VALUE="0">
            <PARAM NAME="Group" VALUE="-1">
            <PARAM NAME="FilterOffline" VALUE="-1">
            <PARAM NAME="Service" VALUE="-1">
            <PARAM NAME="AutoLogon" VALUE="0">
</OBJECT>
</SPAN>

<!-- Setup History Window -->
<IFRAME class='imHistory' ID="history" SRC=""></IFRAME>

<DIV align='Center'>
<!-- Setup Chat Window -->
<TEXTAREA id=chat cols=55 rows=5 style="FONT: 10pt Arial">type your
message here</TEXTAREA>
</DIV>

<!-- Outgoing Message Pain -->
```

```
<TABLE width='350' cellpadding='0' cellspacing='0'>
  <TR>
    <!-- Setup Status Pain -->
    <TD class='status' Align='Left' id='status'></TD>
    <!-- Setup Send Button Pain -->
    <TD Align='Right'><INPUT Type="button" ID=btnSend
Value="Send"></TD>
  </TR>
</TABLE>

</SPAN>
```

Figure 15-13 shows the custom Message View control created by Listing 15-5.

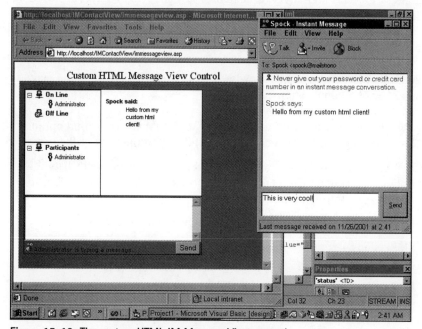

Figure 15-13: The custom HTML IM Message View control

The IM Host object

At the foundation of the Instant Messaging architecture is the IM Host object. The
IM Host object provides all the COM interfaces necessary for creating client applications that can access Instant Messaging servers. Client applications can be built
in C++ or Visual Basic.

Through the IM Host object, client applications can perform the following operations:

- ◆ Connect to IM servers

- ◆ Establish and manage sessions between contacts

- ◆ Provide access to contacts

- ◆ Invite users to join NetMeetings

- ◆ Register for events such as status changes, incoming messages, incoming invitations, or service-state changes

- ◆ Create in-process windows to host controls and user interfaces

The IM Host object is an ActiveX executable (msimhost.exe) that is deployed on a client machine. When running, the IM Host object displays in the Windows task tray an icon with which the user can log onto and off of the IM Service, receive message and status notifications, change options, and open the Message View control.

The IM Host object exposes the following six interfaces for creating and managing Instant Messaging applications:

- ◆ IIMService – Responsible for connecting to the IM server, setting options for creating contacts and contact lists, and setting the state of the user

- ◆ IIMContacts – Provides properties and methods to the contact's lists collection; if a contact is added to a contacts list, the contact subscribes to the Presence Information for that contact

- ◆ IIMContact – Provides properties and methods for the contact object

- ◆ IIMSessions – Provides properties and methods for managing session objects

- ◆ IIMSession – Provides properties and methods for managing the actions performed in the IM session, such as inviting a contact to join a session or sending text to a contact

- ◆ IISIMWindow – Provides properties and methods to a host window for determining the appearance of an action; the host window can host the MS IM Contact View control or the MS IM Message View control or any custom ActiveX control

Figure 15-14 is a graphic representation of the IM Host object interfaces.

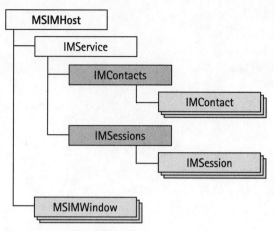

Figure 15-14: The IM Host object interfaces

Take a closer look at some of the interfaces and examine how you might go about creating a custom tree-view control. Listing 15-6 is written in Visual Basic and is not meant to be a complete application, but rather to make you think about how you might approach the task. All of the code is written on a single VB form using the IIMService, IIMHost, IIMContacts, and IIMContact interfaces. This example illustrates how to establish a connection to the IM Service from the IMMHost object, get a contacts list, filter that list, and create a tree view with the list of contacts. The form contains two buttons, one to log on and one to log off. You could compile the completed application as an ActiveX control and embed it on a Web page in place of the MS IM Contacts View control.

Listing 15-6 is the complete code listing with comments.

Listing 15-6: Creating a Custom Contacts Tree-View Control

```
Option Explicit

Public WithEvents MSIMApp As MSIMCliSDKLib.MSIMHost
Public WithEvents MSIMServ As MSIMCliSDKLib.MSIMService

Private Sub cmdLogoff_Click()
    Dim pVar As Variant
    Dim sVar As Variant

    '* Get local state to determine if we are still logged in
    MSIMServ.GetLocalState pVar, sVar

    If Not (pVar = IM_STATE_OFFLINE) Then
```

Continued

Listing 15-6 *(Continued)*

```
            MSIMServ.Logoff
            cmdLogon.Enabled = True
            cmdLogoff.Enabled = False
            tvContacts.Nodes.Clear
            StatusBar.Panels("Status").Text = "Offline"
        End If
End Sub

Private Sub cmdLogon_Click()
    Dim oList As IIMContacts
    Dim lLocalState As Variant
    Dim bstrDescription As Variant

    '* Call Logon; Pass no parameters to prompt user to logon
    MSIMServ.Logon

    '* Get the user contacts and write the tree view
    '$$Messenger\Contact
    '* Make Sure that the Local State is Logged on Not in transition
    Do Until (lLocalState = IM_STATE_ONLINE)
      MSIMServ.GetLocalState lLocalState, bstrDescription
    Loop

    '* This is needed as a delay, if not here the contacts list
    '*doesn't get returned correctly from the MSIMServ.List Call
    MsgBox bstrDescription
    '* Init the TV
    Call InitTV
    '* Get the list
    Set oList = MSIMServ.List("$$Messenger\Contact")
    '* Populate the tree
    Call SetTVNode(oList, "Contact")
    '* Set status bar to status description
    StatusBar.Panels("Status").Text = bstrDescription
    cmdLogon.Enabled = False
    cmdLogoff.Enabled = True
End Sub

Private Sub Form_Load()
    Dim pVar As Variant

    '* Create Host Object
    Set MSIMApp = CreateObject("MSExchangeIM.MSIMHost")
    '* Create Service
```

```
    Set MSIMServ = MSIMApp.CreateContext("Default", 0)

    '* Check Local State to see if we are online
    MSIMServ.GetLocalState pVar

    If pVar = IM_STATE_OFFLINE Then
        cmdLogon.Enabled = True
        cmdLogoff.Enabled = False
    Else
        cmdLogon.Enabled = False
        cmdLogoff.Enabled = True
        cmdLogon_Click
    End If

End Sub

Sub InitTV()
    tvContacts.Nodes.Add , , "Online", "Online"
    tvContacts.Nodes.Add , , "Offline", "Offline"
End Sub

Sub CheckState()
    Dim pVar As Variant
    Dim sVar As Variant

    '* Get local state to determine if we are still logged in
    MSIMServ.GetLocalState pVar, sVar

    If Not (pVar = IM_STATE_OFFLINE) Then
        MSIMServ.Logoff
    End If
End Sub

Private Sub Form_Unload(Cancel As Integer)

    Call CheckState

    Set MSIMServ = Nothing
    Set MSIMApp = Nothing
End Sub

'* Routine to Populate Tree View with Contacts
```

Continued

Listing 15-6 *(Continued)*

```
Public Sub SetTVNode(ByRef List As IIMContacts, ByVal ListName As
String)
    Dim oContact As IIMContact
    Dim oNode As Node
    '* loop through contacts list
    For Each oContact In List
        '* Check the state property of the contact to see if this
        '* contact is online
        If oContact.State <> IM_STATE_OFFLINE Then
            '* Add to Online
            '* Enhancement: check each contacts status and set
            '* the presence information on the tree view.
            tvContacts.Nodes.Add "Online", tvwChild,
oContact.EmailAddress, oContact.FriendlyName
        Else
            '* Not Online
            tvContacts.Nodes.Add "Offline", tvwChild,
oContact.EmailAddress, oContact.FriendlyName
        End If
        '* Expand tree view by default
        tvContacts.Nodes("Online").Expanded = True
        tvContacts.Nodes("Offline").Expanded = True
        '* release contact when done
        Set oContact = Nothing
    Next
End Sub
```

For more detailed information on the interfaces of the Host object, refer to the MSDN or the Web Storage System SDK at http://msdn.microsoft.com. Figure 15-15 shows the tree view running on the VB Form.

Figure 15-15: Application using the tree view with the MS IM Host objects

Summary

In this chapter we looked at real-time collaboration with Exchange and Instant Messaging. Several examples of using existing ActiveX controls that can enable you to extend custom Instant Messaging applications to the Web were provided. We also looked at the foundation of these controls in brief and examined the potential for building your own ActiveX controls or including instant messaging in your applications. Instant messaging is just one example of the real-time collaboration for which Exchange provides support. Exchange also provides support for conferencing applications through the Conferencing Technology Provider (CTP) and the Microsoft Conferencing Server. For more information on the CTP and Conferencing server, please refer to the MSDN.

Part V

Workflow Applications

Chapter 16

Overview of Workflow

IN THIS CHAPTER

- ◆ Introducing Exchange workflow
- ◆ Introducing the application architecture
- ◆ Introducing the workflow components
- ◆ Using different types of workflow

WORKFLOW IS THE SET OF RELATIONSHIPS that define the processes of controlling business logic in a series of steps for the purpose of sign-off, evaluation, performing activities in a process, and co-writing. Collaborative Data Objects (CDO) workflow is a built-in functionality in Exchange 2000 Server. CDO workflow simplifies the process of building workflow applications by providing a set of components that make it easier to write the fundamental code for accessing, modifying, and controlling data flow. The purpose of this chapter is to provide you with a brief overview of the workflow model and its components.

Introduction to Exchange Workflow

The Exchange workflow mechanism consists of three basic tools: the *workflow designer for Exchange 2000*, a tool that simplifies the process of creating and building workflow applications, the *workflow engine*, and *event sinks*.

The workflow designer enables you to create the different states and transitions that your item undertakes as part of an action. You create an action using Visual Basic Scripting (VBScript) within the workflow designer. The workflow designer also creates the default process definition, which associates a processing instance with a folder. When an action occurs within the folder, the event sink calls the workflow engine, which executes and manages the processing instance from the process definition.

CDO plays an integral part in the Exchange 2000 workflow model, providing the built-in workflow engine and exposing its object model to the developer to program against. The workflow engine evaluates the process definition, which is made up of an action table, to determine which action needs to run. The action table stores your business logic in the form of states and transitions. Once an action is triggered, the workflow engine executes the scripts to perform your business-logic tasks.

The CDO event sink acts as the listener. You register the event sink in a folder: When the specified event is triggered it calls the workflow engine automatically.

Workflow applications are built in Exchange Public Folders and execute as server-side components.

As with any application, security is always a concern. Organizations must decide who will be authorized to register workflow applications and decide who will write unlimited workflow scripts. The Exchange Administrator must grant those users owner rights over the workflow applications folder.

Exchange 2000 also supports Exchange 5.5 routing objects, which differ from Exchange 2000 CDO workflow objects in that they were specifically designed for MAPI and e-mail routing and don't take advantage of the Web Storage System. If you are running in a mixed-mode environment in which you have Exchange 5.5 as well as Exchange 2000, and you need your workflow application to run in both environments, you need to use Exchange 5.5 routing objects. On the other hand, if you're planning on taking advantage of the Web Storage System and don't require Exchange 5.5 support, you are better off using the CDO workflow objects.

Application Architecture

A workflow application is made up of forms or documents that users interact with, as well as components on the server that manage processes based on actions and rules. If we examine the workflow application components, they can be separated in two discrete layers. This is known as *two tiers*, the Presentation and Business Logic layers.

The Presentation Layer consists of the items that make up the user interface. These items can be documents, forms, Web pages, e-mail, or some other interface. All these interfaces work because workflow is triggered by some action (save, delete, or timer event) within a Public Folder. The Presentation Layer has no direct relationship with the Business Logic Layer, and so the Presentation Layer is independent of the CDO workflow objects. The Presentation Layer runs on the client machine.

The Business Logic Layer maintains the business rules that control your workflow process. This layer is made up of the CDO workflow objects and any other COM component with which the CDO objects interact. The Business Logic Layer executes its code on the Exchange server in an isolated process space different from the one in which the Web Store executes and can be written in any programming language. Figure 16-1 shows a diagram of the Workflow Application Architecture.

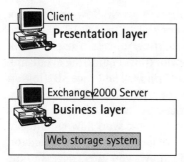

Figure 16-1: Workflow Presentation
and Business Logic layers

Workflow Components

The Exchange workflow components are made up of the workflow engine and event sink, and are installed automatically during the Exchange setup. The workflow designer is part of the Office XP Developer kit and is installed separately. The designer can be installed on the server or the client. The scripting host is the VBScript runtime engine that executes your VBScript.

The workflow engine and the scripting host run in the event-sink process space, isolating it from the Web Storage System process. This allows the scripting host to interact with the workflow engine without crossing process spaces. Figure 16-2 illustrates the workflow process isolation.

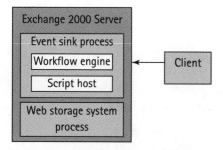

Figure 16-2: Workflow process isolation

Overview of the CDO workflow engine

The workflow engine is an in-process server (CDOWF.DLL) that implements the `Advance` method of the IProcessInstance interface. Unless you are creating a custom event sink or some other middle-tier COM object you do not need to make direct calls to the `IProcessInstance::Advance` method.

When an event triggers on a folder that is workflow-enabled, a `ProcessInstance` is created and passed to the event sink (CDOWFEVT.DLL). The *ProcessInstance* is a model of the work item in the workflow process. The event sink calls the workflow engine and during the call to the workflow engine the event sink locates the ProcessInstance rule from the *ProcessDefinition*. The ProcessDefinition is the encapsulated logic for advancing the state of your item through its workflow. When the event sink finds a match from the ProcessDefinition, it forwards the `WorkflowSession` object to the workflow engine so that the workflow engine can execute the associated action. The `WorkflowSession` object has a `Fields` collection representing the ProcessInstance in transition, which allows you direct access to the ProcessInstance and the user context. You can't change the `status` property of the *ProcessInstance* through code because only the workflow engine has permissions to directly modify the `ProcessInstance.status`.

Overview of the CDO event sink

The event sink is a COM+ application package that is installed and configured automatically by Exchange setup. The event sink is the interface between the Web Storage System process and the workflow engine. The event sink receives notification of events from an action within a workflow-enabled Public Folder.

In order to use the CDO event sink you must create an event registration in the workflow folder.

Event registrations will be covered in Chapter 18, "Web Storage System Events."

Your workflow application can register to receive notification of three different events:

- ◆ *OnSyncSave*: Triggers when an item is saved to the folder
- ◆ *OnSyncDelete*: Triggers when an item is deleted from the folder
- ◆ *OnTimer*: Triggers based on a system time interval

If you are using the workflow designer to create your workflow application, the designer will create the event registrations for you. Figure 16-3 shows a picture of the COM+ CDO event sink–application package.

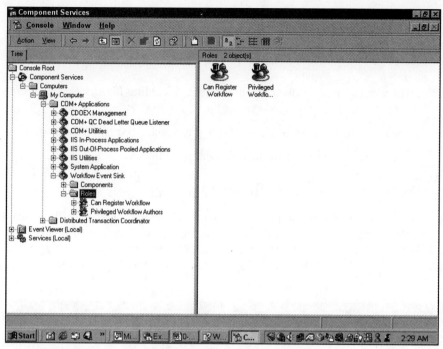

Figure 16-3: CDO event sink (CDOWFEVT.DLL) COM+ application

Two roles are associated with the CDO event sink (CDOWFEVT.DLL) COM+ application that enable security on the event sink. If a user is going to design workflow applications, he or she must at least be added to the can register workflow role, also known as Restricted mode. If an author is added to the Restricted role, he or she will have the following permissions:

◆ They cannot execute workflow scripts within their own user context. The user context for executing scripts is the Workflow System Account.

◆ They cannot make calls to the CreateObject function from within their scripts, known as *sandboxed* scripts. Sandboxed scripts are scripts where access to objects outside the currently executing script is denied.

◆ They are allowed only limited access to the intrinsic WorkflowSession object.

◆ They are allowed only limited access to the Active Directory through the WorkflowSession::GetUserProperty method.

◆ They cannot set the scripts action property to the classID of a COM object.

The `PrivilEgedWorkflowAuthors` role, also known as `Privilege` mode, is a super-user role and allows users to interact with separate systems such as Active Directory, SQL Server, and other business systems, by granting the following permissions:

◆ The user can make calls to `CreateObject`, including file-system objects, such as `Scripting.FileSystemObject`.

◆ The user can set the scripts to execute any valid `classID` on the system.

◆ The scripts run as the Workflow System Account.

Overview of the workflow designer

The workflow designer is a tool used by developers to create Exchange 2000 workflow applications. You can install it from the Office XP Developer CD; first you must make sure that you have installed Office XP and the Windows Component Updates 1.0 for Office XP Developer. Figure 16-4 shows the workflow designer.

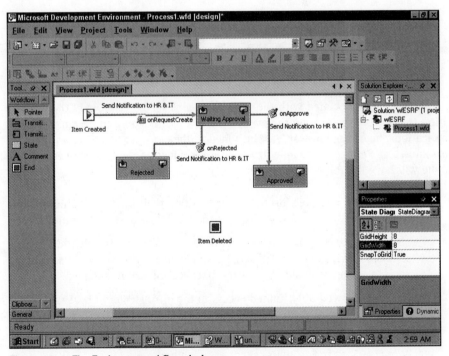

Figure 16-4: The Exchange workflow designer

The `ProcessDefinition` is created from your workflow diagram as you add transitions, business logic, and rules, which make up your workflow application.

The designer creates and maintains your `ProcessDefinition` in the Public Folder in which the workflow application is running.

The `ProcessDefintion` also automatically maintains the `Action` table as well as event registrations for the CDO event sink. An `Action` table contains the state-transition and rules for a workflow `ProcessDefinition`. Table 16-1 shows what a partial `Action` table row might look like.

TABLE 16–1 PARTIAL LISTING OF ACTION TABLE FIELD VALUES

ID	Caption	State	NewState	EventType	Condition
1	Rejected	stWaiting	stApprove	OnApprove	IsApproved

Table 16-2 contains a complete list of field names and descriptions for an `Action` table row. The row consists of the 14 fields listed.

TABLE 16–2 ACTION TABLE FIELD AND DESCRIPTION LISTING

Field Name	Data Type	Description
ID	String	Row identifier
Caption	String	Display name for the step
State	String	The current state of the `ProcessInstance`
NewState	String	The new state of the `ProcessInstance` upon successful completion of this step.
EventType	String	The type of event this step represents; `CDOWFEventType` enum lists possible values
Condition	String	A script expression common script call or COM-object `ProgID` whose result is Boolean
EvaluationOrder	String	The position of a row in the order in which conditions will be evaluated if there are multiple matching rows in a call to advance

Continued

TABLE 16-2 ACTION TABLE FIELD AND DESCRIPTION LISTING *(Continued)*

Field Name	Data Type	Description
Action	String	A script expression common script call or COM-object ProgID that executes if the row of the Action table matches the process instance and the condition is true
ExpiryInterval	String	The duration in minutes before a state will expire and trigger the OnExpiry event
RowACL	String	Must be empty, reserved for future use
TransitionACL	String	The ACL to use to override the default ACL role of the folder owner
DesignToolFields	String	Reserved for workflow designer tools
CompensatingAction	String	A script expression common script call or COM-object ProgID to run if the workflow transaction is aborted
Flags	String	Bitwise OR of cdowfTransitionFlags

The ProcessDefinition also enables you to set the AuditTrailProvider property, which determines which provider you use to handle logging information, warnings, and error messages. By default, the audit-trail provider that comes with Exchange writes to the Windows 2000 event log.

Types of Workflow with Exchange

Users can build two types of workflow applications in Exchange using e-mail or Web-based applications, with the Web Storage System as the primary medium.

Using the Web Storage System as your primary medium

If you are using the Web Storage System for Web-based workflow you use e-mail as a means of notification. Embedded within the message is a hyperlink allowing the user to open the original item and take an action.

For example, a manager can use this type of workflow to approve a request for time off. An employee fills out a request form via the Web, and when he or she saves the request a notification is sent to the manager via e-mail with an embedded link to the original item. The manager opens the original item via the link and either approves or rejects the item. When the manager approves or rejects the item, the workflow engine allows the item to move to the next state and notifies the employee of the end result.

In this scenario, both end users are authenticated by the corporate network, and therefore the CDO workflow engine can restrict or deny user access to items. Restricting or denying access is achieved from the `ItemReaders` and `ItemAuthors` collections.

Using e-mail as your primary medium

Using e-mail as the primary medium allows remote users to participate in workflow applications via e-mail. This means that you have no way to directly authenticate an end user.

In this scenario, the CDO workflow engine updates the workflow process when an e-mail is received that correlates to an existing workflow-process instance. If the e-mail doesn't correlate to an existing process instance, the e-mail is treated as a new process instance and creates a new workflow.

When creating the process instance, Exchange grants a unique correlation ID, but in order to support the correlation ID you must use Outlook as your mailer. Exchange uses its own correlation ID, because SMTP lacks the guarantee of a unique ID. If messages cannot be correlated, then this process will fail.

Specifying ad hoc and default workflows

The Exchange workflow process supports both ad hoc and default workflows. You can define your workflow definitions in four different ways:

- ◆ A client uses the default workflow for the folder.

- ◆ Based on the class of the document, a client chooses from one of many processes installed for the folder. The process can only run in `Restricted` mode and must be hidden to prevent unintended modifications.

- ◆ Based on the class of the document, a client picks a process from another folder. The process can only run in `Restricted` mode and must be hidden to prevent unintended modifications.

- ◆ A client submits an item with its process embedded. The process can only run in `Restricted` mode.

In a default scenario, all the items in a workflow folder use the same process definition. The process definition is stored at the folder level and is set by the `http://schemas.microsoft.com/cdo/workflow/defaultprocdefinition` property on the `OnSyncSave` registration item in the workflow folder.

In the second and third scenarios in the preceding list, the client chooses the workflow process definition from the current folder (or from another folder) based on the documents class, called a semi ad hoc workflow, and allows the end user to decide the workflow based on a given set of rules that you define ahead of time.

For an item to be completely ad hoc, the user must also determine how the item is to be reviewed when saved.

In order for a workflow to be considered semi ad hoc, you must set the `http://schemas.microsoft.com/cdo/workflow/adhocflows` property on the `OnSyncSave` registration item in the workflow folder to one of the `CdoWfAdhocFlows Enum` values, which are as follows:

- `PreventAdhocFlows` (0) — Only the default process definition can apply to each process instance in the workflow folder.

- `PermitAdhocFlows` (1) — Each process instance can use its own process definition. (The default is still used if a process instance declares no process definition.)

- `OnlyAdhocFlows` (2) — Each process instance must declare its own process definition.

Summary

In this chapter you have seen an overview of Exchange's workflow model, the components that make up that model and how they interact, as well as the types of workflow media. Exchange gives you the ability to create complex and advanced applications by exposing the CDO workflow object model, which enables you to build applications within the Exchange workflow designer. Together with Exchange and the Web Storage System, CDO workflow makes for a powerful platform for building workflow applications.

Chapter 17

CDO Workflow for Exchange

IN THIS CHAPTER

- ◆ The CDO Workflow Object Model
- ◆ Building a simple workflow application
- ◆ Debugging workflow applications

THE COLLABORATION DATA OBJECTS (CDO) workflow objects are the building blocks for workflow applications in Exchange 2000. The CDO workflow objects provide the built-in workflow engine and the event service used to monitor and process workflow applications. This chapter will show you the fundamental objects that comprise the object model, demonstrate how to build a simple application using the Workflow Designer, and show you how to debug your workflow applications.

The CDO Workflow Object Model

The CDO Workflow Object Model is exposed through the cdowf.dll and includes three main objects: the WorkflowSession, the ProcessDefinition, and the ProcessInstance. Each object contains a subset of objects and collections that comprise that object's structure. Figure 17-1 illustrates the entire CDO Workflow Object Model.

The following sections discuss each object in detail.

The WorkflowSession object

The WorkflowSession object implements the IWorkflowProcess interface and provides intrinsic access to the workflow item during the workflow process through the IWorkflowSession::Fields collection. The Fields collection is the ProcessInstance during workflow process. The WorkflowSession object also provides access to properties StateFrom, StateTo, ErrorDescription, and ErrorNumber. Table 17-1 lists the properties and methods that make up the IWorkflowSession interface.

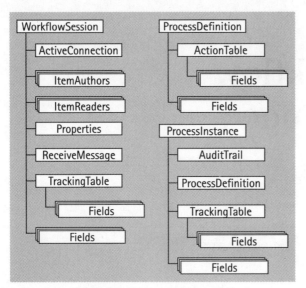

Figure 17-1: The CDO Workflow Object Model

TABLE 17-1 THE CDO IWORKFLOWSESSION INTERFACE PROPERTIES

Property	Description
ActiveConnection	Contains the Session object of the user that initiated the event. Only available during privileged Workflow. (Read-only).
Domain	Contains the server Domain Name. (Read-only).
ErrorDescription	Provides details of the error to be reported back to the AuditTrail object.
ErrorNumber	Stores the error number for the AuditTrail log and to be returned to the calling client.
Fields	The property collection for the ProcessInstance object. (Read-only).
ItemAuthors	Collection of users allowed to modify an item. Each ItemAuthor is an IMember interface. Used in item security. (Read-only.)
ItemReaders	Collection of users allowed to read an item. Each ItemRead is an IMember interface. Used in item security. (Read-only.)
Properties	Returns the ISessionProps interface for the WorkflowSession. (Read-only.)

Property	Description
ReceiveMessage	Returns a pointer to the IWorkflowMessage interface for correlated messages that initiate state transitions.
Sender	Contains the SMTP address of the user that initiated the state transition. (Read-only.)
Server	Contains the server name. (Read-only.)
StateFrom	Contains the current state of the ProcessInstance. (Read-only.)
StateTo	Contains the state of the ProcessInstance after the current transition. (Read-only.)
TrackingTable	Returns a pointer to the recordset object containing data related to the ProcessInstance that initiated the state transition. (Read-only.)

Table 17-2 lists the methods of the IWorkflowSession interface.

TABLE 17-2 THE CDO IWORKFLOWSESSION INTERFACE METHODS

Method	Description
AddAuditEntry(bsDescription As String, [hResult As Long])	Adds an audit-trail entry to the AuditTrailProvider
DeleteReceivedMessage()	Deletes the message correlated with the ProcessInstance item
DeleteWorkflowItem()	Deletes the ProcessInstance item
GetNewWorkflowMessage()	Returns an IMessage interface for sending e-mail from the Workflow engine
GetUserProperty(bsUser As String, bsAttrName As String, bIsEmail As CdoWfUserIDType)	Used to retrieve an Active Directory–attribute property for a user
IsUserInRole(bsUser As String, bsRole As String) As Boolean	Used to authenticate a user against a role

You can use the `WorkflowSession` object to do the following:

◆ Manage runtime errors through the `ErrorDescription` and `ErrorNumber` properties

◆ Cache properties between transitions using the `set` and `get` methods of the Properties collection

◆ Access Active Directory properties through the `getUserProperty` method

◆ Validate item security with the `ItemAuthors`, `ItemReaders`, and `IsUserInRole` methods

◆ Add audit-trail entries to the audit-trail provider with the `AddAuditTrail` method

◆ Delete workflow items with the `DeleteWorkflowItem` method

◆ Work with correlated messages from e-mail applications with the `ReceiveMessage` property and the `DeleteReceivedMessage` method

◆ Send e-mail using the `getNewWorkflowMessage` method

◆ Access and modify the ProcessInstance through the Fields collection

The ProcessDefinition object

The `ProcessDefinition` object is stored as an item in a public folder. Use `IDataSouce.save`, `IDataSource.saveto`, or `IDataSource.open` to access or save a `ProcessDefinition` item to a public folder.

The `ProcessDefinition` object provides access to the `ActionTable`, which is stored as a `recordset` object. Each row of the `ActionTable` is made up of 14 fields, which define the rules, script, and state for the workflow process.

Refer to Chapter 16, Table 16-2, for a complete list of `ActionTable` record fields and definitions.

Table 17-3 lists the properties of the IProcessDefinition interface.

TABLE 17-3 CDO IPROCESSDEFINITION PROPERTIES

Property	Description
ActionTable	Stores the script, state, and rules for the Workflow process; stored as an `ADODB.Recordset` object
AuditTrailProvider	Keeps track of the `ProgID` of the COM class that will be logged
CommonScriptUrl	Contains a URL to the item containing the shared script functions referenced in the `Condition` and `Action` scripts
DataSource	Returns the IDataSource interface for the object
DesignTool	Stores the name of the Workflow design tool used to create the process definition (if one was used)
Fields	Specifies the properties collection for the object
Mode	Sets the type of security checking done for the Workflow engine

You can use the `ProcessDefinition` object to do the following:

◆ Transfer work items between people

◆ Track the state of individual work items

◆ Take server-side control of work item status changes

◆ Handle work-item exceptions automatically

The ProcessInstance object

`ProcessInstance` models a workflow item from the Web Storage System. It contains the workflow item's state, its relationship to e-mail, and what happens when a workflow item exceeds the allotted amount of time for its current state.

You do not need to use this object explicitly, unless you are creating your own event sinks. You can access and change the `ProcessInstance` properties through the Fields collection of the `WorkflowSession` object. To save field modifications call the field's `Update` method.

`ProcessInstance` is responsible for moving a workflow to its next state by means of its `Advance` method. Table 17-4 lists the properties of the IProcessInstance interface.

TABLE 17-4 CDO IPROCESSINSTANCE PROPERTIES

Property	Description
AuditTrail	Returns the IAuditTrail object interface
CurrentState	Returns the current state of the process instance set by the Workflow engine
DataSource	Returns the IDataSource object interface
Fields	Specifies the properties collection for the object
ProcessDefinition	Returns the IProcessDefinition object interface
ProcessDefinitionUrl	Returns the absolute URL of the ProcessDefinition row; allows a new ProcessInstance that can specify which ProcessDefinition to use
TrackingTable	Contains records of all messages correlated with ProcessInstance in an e-mail-based Workflow

Table 17-5 lists the associated methods for the IProcessInstance interface.

TABLE 17-5 CDO IPROCESSINSTANCE METHODS

Method	Description
Advance(eEventType As CdoWfEventType, varReceived, varUserID,[pConnection As Connection]) As Boolean	Evaluates the action table for the current process instance and executes appropriate actions. This method is called internally by CDO workflow event sink and is not invoked by most applications.
DisableSuccessEntries (bDisable As Boolean)	Configures entry types for the AuditTrail. Can be set to True or False. When using the Workflow designer you do not need to invoke this method.
EnableDebug(bDebug As Boolean)	Enables JIT debugging
OnAbort(varReceived, varUserID)	Runs compensating action scripts and cleans up when a Workflow transaction is aborted

You can use the `ProcessInstance` object to control, record, and monitor the status of a workflow item.

Creating a Simple Workflow Application

This section will demonstrate how to use the Workflow Designer to build a simple approval application. The application we will build will act as an example of how to use Exchange to facilitate the processing of employee data to create and modify user accounts in Active Directory. The application that we will build is based on the hiring process of a fictitious company named Bebian Rugs.

Bebian Rugs hiring manager and Human Resources department (HR) have agreed to make a new hire, so they need to do several things in order to prepare for the new employee's start. For example, they must collect personal information about the employee and populate it into the Active Directory, they must create user and e-mail accounts on the network, and the hiring manager must be notified of the username, password, and e-mail address of the new employee.

The company uses the following process to do all of this:

1. The hiring manager submits new hire information.

2. HR is notified of the request via e-mail.

3. HR verifies employee data and approves or rejects the request.

4. If HR rejects the request, the hiring manager is notified and will have the option to make corrections and re-submit the request.

5. HR is notified of resubmission and again has the opportunity to approve or reject the request.

6. If HR approves the request, the hiring manager is notified of the approval.

7. An automated process is initiated, creating and updating user-account information in the Active Directory and then creating an associated e-mail account.

8. Once the process is complete, the Hiring Manager is notified via e-mail and provided with the new employee's username, password, and e-mail address.

Creating the folder and setting up security

To build this application using the Exchange Workflow Designer, you must first create a directory in the Web Storage System for the application, grant yourself owner permissions, and add yourself to the correct security roles for the workflow event sink. You can create the directory through the Exchange System Manager, through Explorer by using the M:\ drive, or by using any other method you are familiar with. When creating the directory name, you should name it wfESRF.

For a detailed explanation of how to create the directories in the Web Storage System, please refer to Chapter 3, "Overview of the Web Storage System."

Once the directory is created, you need to add yourself to the COM+ roles for the workflow event sink. Follow these steps to:

1. Open the MMC by selecting Start → Settings → Control Panel.

2. When the Control Panel opens, double-click the Administrative Tools icon, and then double-click the Components Services icon.

3. When the Component Services MMC snap-in opens, navigate to the Workflow Event Sink COM+ Application package by expanding the following containers: Component Services → My Computer → COM+ Applications → Workflow Event Sink.

4. Now expand the Roles and Users containers by selecting Roles → Can Register Workflow → Users and Privileged Workflow Authors → Users.

Figure 17-2 shows the MMC Component Services snap-in with the Workflow Event Sink Roles and Users expanded.

Repeat the following steps once for each role you wish to add yourself to:

1. Select the Users container under the Role and right-click.

2. From the pop-up menu, select New → User.

3. From the Users and Groups window, find your user account and double-click it to add it to the lower pane.

4. Click OK.

When you're done, your user account should exist under both Roles.

For more information on each Role and how they differ, refer to Chapter 16, "Overview of Workflow."

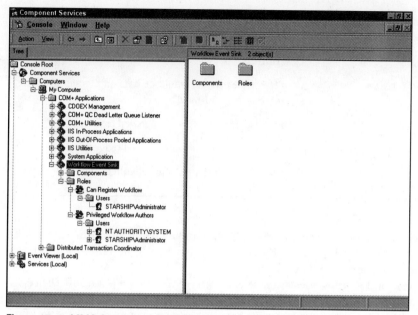

Figure 17-2: MMC Component Services snap-in with the Workflow Event Sink Roles and Users expanded

Building the user interface

Once you have set up the directory and security for the workflow application, you will need to Web-enable the folder with the FrontPage Extensions for the Web Storage System, and you will also need to build the custom Web forms, custom Properties, and form-registration items using FrontPage 2000.

For more information on creating custom forms with the FrontPage Extensions and the Web Storage System, please see Chapter 10, "Web Storage System Forms."

Table 17-6 lists the forms used in the user interface and their descriptions.

TABLE 17-6 WFESRF APPLICATION FILES

File	Description
emp_form.htm	Used to create new requests and edit existing employee data

Continued

TABLE **17-6** WFESRF APPLICATION FILES *(Continued)*

File	Description
`formreview.htm`	Used to review existing employee data and to approve or reject requests (read-only)
`vapproved.htm`	Used to display a list view of approved requests
`vrejected.htm`	Used to display a list view of rejected requests
`vpending.htm`	Used to display a list view of pending requests

The completed source code for these forms can be downloaded from this book's companion Web site. Figure 17-3 shows `emp_form.htm` in design view inside the FrontPage development environment.

To open the Workflow Designer, select Start → Programs → Microsoft Office XP Developer → Microsoft Development Environment.

Once the Designer is open, you will have to create a new project. The Workflow Designer stores each workflow application as a solution. The solution can have multiple projects and each project can consist of multiple process definitions; however, projects are stored in the directory that is being workflow-enabled, and each directory can have only one project. A workflow solution consists of the flowing elements:

- A Workflow Solution file (`*.sln`), stored at `<your drive>:\Office Developer Projects\`

- A Workflow Project file (`*.epw`), stored in the Workflow folder

- A Workflow ProcessDefintion (`*.wfd`), stored in the Workflow folder

- Event Registrations, stored in the Workflow folder

  - `OnTimerEventRegistration`

  - `OnSyncSaveDeleteEventRegistration`

Before you can create your Workflow project, you need to make sure that the folder exists, that it is Web-enabled, and that you have set up the security appropriately. Please review the "Creating the Folder and Setting up Security" section earlier in this chapter.

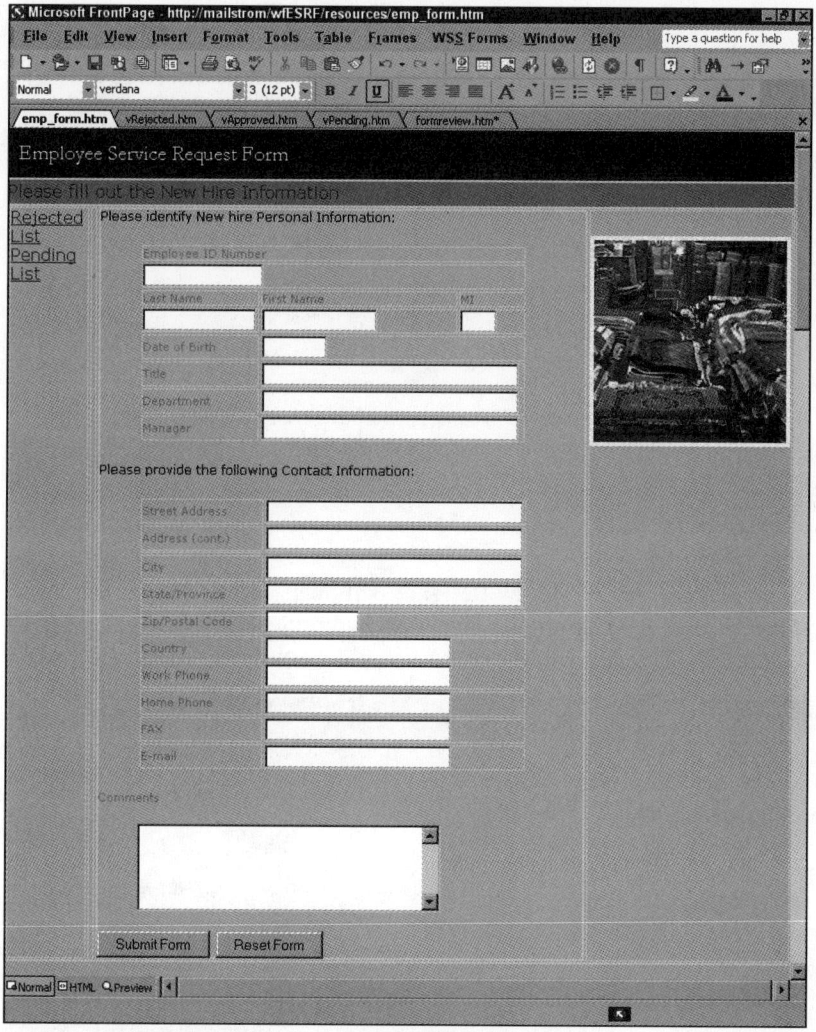

Figure 17-3: The emp_form.htm shown in design view

The forms have a hidden field called wfState, which is used to track the state of the form through the workflow process. This property is updated by the workflow process as the form moves in and out of certain states.

Creating the workflow solution

The workflow process definition and related event registrations are created with the Office XP Developer version of the Exchange Workflow Designer version 7.0. For the purpose of this section we assume that you have already installed Office XP, Office XP Developer, and the Exchange Workflow Designer.

To create the workflow project wfESRF, complete the following steps:

1. From the file menu open the New Project dialog box by selecting File →
   New → Project.

2. From the Templates pane choose the Exchange Workflow Project template.

3. Enter the name of the project (wfESRF) in the name text box, and enter
   the URL of the Web-enabled folder (http://<your server>/wfESRF/) in the
   location text box.

4. Click OK.

 You cannot browse over HTTP unless you have created a Web folder.

After a few seconds, the Workflow Designer will open with a new project and a
blank designer. Figure 17-4 shows the newly created project.

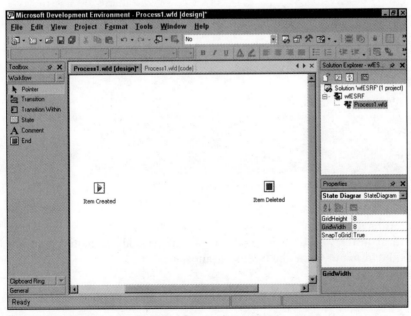

Figure 17-4: The newly created Workflow project wfESRF.

Getting familiar with the Workflow Designer

The Workflow Designer is made up of the Design window, the Code window, the Solution Explorer window, the Properties window, and the Toolbox window.

The Design window is where you create the Process Flow using the shapes from the Toolbox. The Code window is where you write your scripts against the workflow process. To enter the Code window, double-click a shape or use the View Code button in the Solution Explorer. From the Solution Explorer window you can enable and disable a workflow process, switch to the Code window, refresh the process workflow, open the process workflow, view the solution's Properties, and add new process definitions to the Solution Explorer. The Properties window displays the Properties for the object that you are viewing.

The Toolbox is made up of six shapes that can be used in creating a workflow process: Pointer, Transition, Transition Within, State, Comment, and End. A shape is simply an element. A workflow process contains two types of shapes: transitions and states. The Transition and Transition Within define the events that determine the flow of execution from one process to another. The Transition Within does not change the state. Use the state shape to create new states within your workflow process. A state is the outcome of a Transition.

When the project is created, two shapes are on the Workflow Design sheet: the Item Created and Item Deleted shapes. Item Created is the initial state of an item and triggers the Item Created event. You cannot have more than one Item Created per design; however, you can have more than one Transition coming from the Item Created or from any other state.

Item Deleted is the default Ending shape for all workflow items. The Pointer switches the mouse pointer to the default pointer. The Comment shape enables you to add comments to your workflow design.

To add shapes to the Design window, you may use any of the following methods:

◆ Double-click the shape

◆ Drag it onto the Design window

◆ Select the shape and the use the mouse to draw it on the Design window. Each shape has its own set of Properties. To view a shape's Properties, complete the following steps:

1. Select the shape with the mouse so that the shape is outlined.

2. Right-click, and select Properties.

Creating the workflow process

You start creating the workflow by building the workflow process in the Design window. The process is created by adding states and building transitions between them and then scripting the business rules. Based on Bebian Rugs' hiring process, we'll need these four states: stWaitingApproval, stApproved, stRejected, and stComplete.

Each state within a workflow has two main event types that can fire: Enter and Exit. Each event type has three events associated with it: Validate, Main Procedure, and Rollback. The Validate event is the condition or rule that determines whether the Main Procedure executes. If the Validate event returns True the Main Procedure executes; if it returns False the Main Procedure doesn't execute. The Rollback event triggers if the Main Procedure is aborted. The following list outlines the Enter and Exit event types:

- ◆ Enter: Fires when the workflow item is entering the current state and triggers the following events:

  - ■ OnEnterValidate: Fires to validate your business rules. This is the condition rule. Must return True to fire the OnEnter event.

  - ■ OnEnterRollback: Fires when the workflow ErrorNumber is set to a negative number.

  - ■ OnEnter: Fires if the OnEnterValidate returns True. This is the main workflow procedure.

- ◆ Exit: Fires when a workflow item is exiting the current state and triggers the following events:

  - ■ OnExitValidate: Fires to validate business rules. This is the condition rule. Must return True to fire the OnExit event.

  - ■ OnExitRollback: Fires when the workflow ErrorNumber is set to a negative number.

  - ■ OnExit: Fires if the OnExitValidate returns True. This is the main workflow procedure.

Create the four states needed by the application by adding each new state shape to the Design window and setting its properties. To add a new state to the Design window, complete the following steps.

1. Double-click the state shape from the toolbox.

2. Set the properties for the shape by selecting the newly created shape and right-clicking it.

3. From the popup menu select Properties to open the Properties window. Fill in the Properties according to the appropriate table listing. Figure 17-5 shows the stWaitingApproval state Property window.

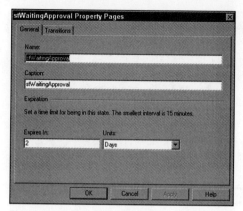

Figure 17-5: The stWaitingApproval state Property window

On the Properties window you will also notice the Transitions tab. You will come back to this tab after completing all four states. Certain states set the Expires In property to 2 and the Units to Days. This sets the OnTimer event to fire for that state when the duration expires. This configuration will be used as a reminder to a user if he or she does not respond to a request within a certain amount of time.

Tables 17-7, 17-8, 17-9, and 17-10 list each state's properties. Table 17-7 lists the properties for the stWaiting state.

TABLE 17-7 PROPERTY SETTINGS FOR STWAITING STATE

Property	Value
Name	stWaitingApproval
Caption	stWaitingApproval
Expires In	2
Units	Days

Table 17-8 lists the properties for the stApproved state.

TABLE 17–8 PROPERTY SETTINGS FOR STAPPROVED STATE

Property	Value
Name	stApproved
Caption	stApproved
Expires In	-N/A
Units	Days

Table 17-9 lists the properties for the stRejected state.

TABLE 17–9 PROPERTY SETTINGS FOR STREJECTED STATE

Property	Value
Name	stRejected
Caption	stRejected
Expires In	2
Units	Days

Table 17-10 lists the properties for the stComplete state.

TABLE 17–10 PROPERTY SETTINGS FOR STCOMPLETE

Property	Value
Name	stWaitingApproval
Caption	stWaitingApproval
Expires In	-N/A
Units	Days

Once you have completed adding and naming the four states, you must create the transitions between each state.

Every Transition has three events that fire when the workflow triggers that Transition: the Validate, the Rollback, and the Main Procedure events for that event type. The five event types are:

- Create
- Delete
- Change
- Expire
- Receive

The order in which the events fire is as follows:

1. Validate
2. Main Procedure
3. Rollback (if event is aborted)

The Validate event is the rule or condition that tells the Main Procedure whether to fire or not. If the Validate event returns True, the Main Procedure will fire. If it returns False, the Main Procedure will not fire. The Rollback event fires when a Main Procedure aborts a transaction, and should undo any actions the Main Procedure may have done.

If a state contains more than one Transition the transitions are evaluated in the order in which they appear on the Transitions tab until one of the Validate events returns True.

The following is a list of each of the four event types from the Transition window and the associated event procedures.

- Delete: Fires when the item is deleted. Triggers the following events:

  - OnDeleteValidate: Fires to validate your business rules. This is the condition rule. Must return True to fire the OnDelete event.

  - OnDeleteRollback: Fires when the workflow ErrorNumber is set to a negative number.

  - OnDelete: Fires if the OnDeleteValidate returns True. This is the main workflow procedure.

- Change: Fires when an item in the workflow is modified. Triggers the following events:

  - OnChangeValidate: Fires to validate business rules. This is the condition rule. Must return True to fire the OnChange event.

- ■ OnChangeRollback: Fires when the workflow ErrorNumber is set to a negative number.

- ■ OnChange: Fires if the OnChangeValidate returns True. This is the main workflow procedure.

- ◆ Expire: Fires when a workflow item exceeds the allotted time constraint. Triggers the following events:

  - ■ OnExpireValidate: Fires to validate business rules. This is the condition rule. Must return True to fire the OnExpire event.

  - ■ OnDeleteRollback: Fires when the workflow ErrorNumber is set to a negative number.

  - ■ OnExpire: Fires if the OnExpireValidate returns True. This is the main workflow procedure.

- ◆ Receive: This Transition is used for e-mail-only workflow. Fires when an item is received to a workflow-enabled folder and triggers the following events:

  - ■ OnReceiveValidate: Fires to validate business rules. This is the condition rule. Must return True to fire the OnReceive event.

  - ■ OnReceiveRollback: Fires when the workflow ErrorNumber is set to a negative number.

  - ■ OnReceive: Fires if the OnReceiveValidate returns True. This is the main workflow procedure.

The Property Transition window for the Item Created shape is slightly different from that of the other state shapes. You cannot choose the type of Transition. This is because the Item Created shape is the starting point for all workflow processes and only one event can fire: This is the OnCreate event. To add new transitions from the Item Created Transition window, simply select the Next State and click Add. The following is a list of the Item Created event and its associated event procedures:

- ◆ Create: Fires when a workflow item is created in the Workflow folder and triggers the following events:

  - ■ OnCreateValidate: Fires to validate business rules. This is the condition rule. Must return True to fire the OnCreate procedure.

  - ■ OnCreateRollback: Fires when the workflow ErrorNumber is set to a negative number.

  - ■ OnCreate: Fires if the OnCreateValidate returns True. This is the main workflow procedure.

To add the transitions between each state, complete these steps:

1. Open the Properties window for the desired state. Start with the from state or the state in which the Transition begins.

2. When the Property window opens, click the Transitions tab (Figure 17-6).

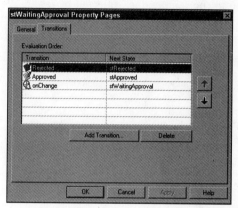

Figure 17–6: The Transitions tab of the Properties window

Follow these steps to create a new Transition from the Transitions tab:

1. Click the Add Transition button to open the Add Transition window (Figure 17-7).

2. Choose one of the four option buttons listed in Transition types (Delete, Change, Expire, or Receive).

3. Select the Next State pull down and choose the state you are transitioning to.

4. Click OK.

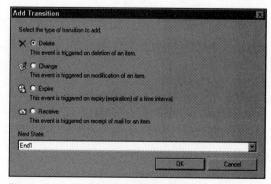

Figure 17–7: The Add Transition window

Follow these steps to modify the Transition name and caption properties:

1. Select the Transition line on the design window by clicking it.

2. Right-click and choose Properties to open the Transition Properties window (Figure 17-8).

3. Set the name and caption to the same value, reflected in Tables 17-11 to 17-15, respectively.

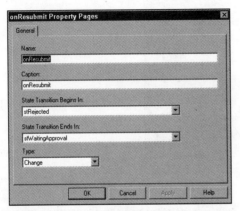

Figure 17–8: The onResubmit Property Pages

Table 17-11 lists the Transition to create for the Item Created state.

TABLE 17–11 TRANSITION FOR THE ITEM CREATED STATE

Transition Type	Transition Name	Next State
Create	OnCreate	stWaitingApproval

Table 17-12 lists the transitions to create for the stWaitingApproval state.

TABLE 17–12 TRANSITIONS FOR THE STWAITINGAPPROVAL STATE

Transition Type	Transition Name	Next State
Change	Rejected	stRejected

Transition Type	Transition Name	Next State
Change	Approved	stApproved
Expiry	OnChange	stWaitingApproval

Table 17-13 lists the transitions to create for the stApproved state.

TABLE 17-13 TRANSITIONS FOR THE STAPPROVED STATE

Transition Type	Transition Name	Next State
Expiry	Complete	stComplete
Change	OnReset	stWaitingApproval

Table 17-14 lists the Transition to create for the stRejected state.

TABLE 17-14 TRANSITION FOR THE STREJECTED STATE

Transition Type	Transition Name	Next State
Change	OnResubmit	stWaitingApproval

Table 17-15 lists the Transition to create for the stComplete state.

TABLE 17-15 TRANSITION FOR THE STCOMPLETE STATE

Transition Type	Transition Name	Next State
Change	UserMod	stWaitingApproval

Once you are done creating all the states and transitions, your workflow should look like the one shown in Figure 17-9, which is the completed workflow model.

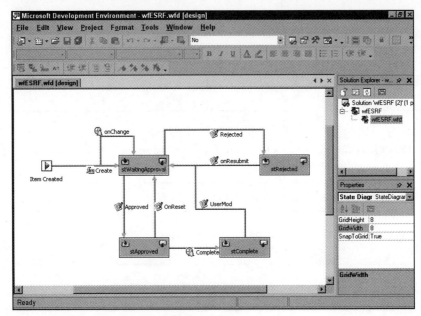

Figure 17-9: The completed workflow model

Adding the code to the workflow model

Now that the workflow model is completed, you need to add the business rules and logic to the transitions and states.

Look at the following process and compare it to your model:

1. The hiring manager submits new hire information.

2. HR is notified of the request via e-mail.

3. HR verifies employee data and approves or rejects the request.

4. If HR rejects the request, the hiring manager is notified and has the option to make corrections and resubmit the request.

5. HR is notified of resubmission and again has the opportunity to approve or reject the request.

6. If HR approves the request, the hiring manager is notified of the approval.

7. An automated process is initiated, creating and updating user-account information in the Active Directory, and then creating an associated e-mail account.

8. Once the process is complete, the hiring manager is notified via e-mail and provided with the new employee's username, password, and e-mail address.

Step 1 is completed through the submission of a form from the Web site. Step 2 is where the workflow process needs to send a notification to HR indicating that the item was created and is awaiting approval. The process achieves this by utilizing the Enter event type of the stWaitingApproval state. No rules apply to an item as it transitions to this state, so the Validate event just returns True to allow the item to enter this state.

Listing 17-1 shows the code for the stWaitingApproval_OnEnterValidate, stWaitngApproval_OnEnter event and the SendMail procedure, used by all the procedures to send notifications. The SendMail procedure uses the WorkflowSession. GetNewWorkflowMessage method to create a new message object and send the message to the appropriate person.

Listing 17-1: Sending Notifications

```
'* ------------------------------------------------------
'* Validation Event for Entering State Waiting Approval
'* Executes when entering State Waiting Approval
Function stWaitingApproval_OnEnterValidate
  '* Just return True, we have no rule to apply
  stWaitingApproval_OnEnterValidate = true
End Function


'* ------------------------------------------------------
'* Event Type: Enter
'* Main Procedure for State Waiting Approval
'* Executes if stWaitingApprocal_OnEnterValidate = true
'* Send a notification email to HR notifying them
'* of the new/edited Request
Sub stWaitingApproval_OnEnter
 If WorkFlowSession.StateFrom = "stRejected" Then
   SendMail("Employee Service Request Form" & _
       " - Reviewed Waiting Approval")
 Else
   SendMail("Employee Service Request Form - Waiting Approval")
 End If
 Workflowsession.Fields("wfState").Value=Workflowsession.StateTo
 Workflowsession.Fields.Update
End Sub


'* ------------------------------------------------------
'* Mail Routine to Route Email
'* Name:    SendMail
'* Parameter: MySubject - Subject of email
Sub SendMail(MySubject)
```

Continued

Listing 17-1 *(Continued)*

```
Dim msgbody

'* Get New Workflow Message
Set WFMsg = WorkflowSession.GetNewWorkflowMessage()

'* Allows for both HTML and Text Bodyparts
WFMsg.MimeFormatted = True

'* Read Subject to determine which email to send
If Instr(MySubject,"Rejected") Then
 msgbody = "Employee Service Request Form for " & _
 WorkFlowsession.Fields("Personal_FirstName").Value & _
 " " & _
 WorkFlowsession.Fields("Personal_LastName").Value & _
 " has been Rejected by " & WorkFlowsession.Sender & _
 " and is awaiting your corrections. Please follow " & _
 " thefollowing link to correct the " & _
 "request.<BR>" & _
 "<A href='" & "http://mailstrom/wfESRF/" & _
 WorkflowSession.Fields("DAV:displayname").value & _
 "?cmd=edit'>" & _
 WorkFlowsession.Fields("Personal_FirstName").Value & _
 " " & _
 WorkFlowsession.Fields("Personal_LastName").Value & _
 "</A><BR>"
Elseif Instr(MySubject,"Approved") Then
 msgbody = "Employee Service Request Form for " & _
 WorkFlowsession.Fields("Personal_FirstName").Value & _
 & " " & _
 WorkFlowsession.Fields("Personal_LastName").Value & _
 " has been Approved by " & WorkFlowsession.Sender & _
 " No further action is required.<BR>"
Elseif Instr(MySubject,"Reviewed") Then
 msgbody = "Employee Service Request for " & _
 WorkFlowsession.Fields("Personal_FirstName").Value & _
 " " & _
 WorkFlowsession.Fields("Personal_LastName").Value & _
 "  has been reviewed by " & WorkflowSession.Sender & _
 " and re-submitted for your review. Please click on the " &_
 "following link to review the " & _
 "request.<BR>" & _
 "<A href='" & "http://mailstrom/wfESRF/" & _
 WorkflowSession.Fields("DAV:displayname").value & _
 "?cmd=review'>" & _
```

```
          WorkFlowsession.Fields("Personal_FirstName").Value & _
          " " & _
          WorkFlowsession.Fields("Personal_LastName").Value & "</A><BR>"
       Else
          msgbody = "A New Employee Service Request Form has been " & _
          "submitted by " & WorkFlowsession.Sender & _
          " and is awaiting your review. Please click on the" & _
          " following link to review the " & _
          "request.<BR>" & _
          "<A href='" & "http://mailstrom/wfESRF/" & _
          WorkflowSession.Fields("DAV:displayname").value & _
          "?cmd=review'>" & _
          WorkFlowsession.Fields("Personal_FirstName").Value & _
          " " & _
          WorkFlowsession.Fields("Personal_LastName").Value & _
          "</A><BR>"
       End If

       '* Default Signature
       msgbody = msgbody & "<BR>Thank you,<BR> " & _
       Exchange 2000 Workflow Engine" & _
       "<BR><HR>" & WorkflowSession.StateFrom & "-" & _
       WorkflowSession.StateTo

       '* Prepare to send Mail
       With WFMsg
         .From = WorkflowSession.Sender
         .To = "hr@mailstrom"
         .Subject = MySubject
         .HTMLBody = msgbody
         .SendWorkflowMessage 0 'cdowfNoTracking
       End With
    End Sub
```

Steps 3–6 of the approval process deal with approving or rejecting the request. If the request is rejected, you need to notify the hiring manager and give him or her the opportunity to resubmit it. You also want to notify the hiring manager if the request is approved.

To do these things, use the approved and rejected transitions. Each transition fires when the request is changed from the stWaitingApproval state. So to determine which transition should be executed you need to set up the Validate events for both transitions. You can use the wfState property from the submitted form to determine whether the request was rejected or approved. You can read the wfState property by using the Fields collection of the WorkflowSession object. Listing 17-2 shows the code you use to approve or reject the workflow item by checking the wfState property.

Listing 17-2: Approving or Rejecting the Request

```
'* ----------------------------------------------------
'* Validation Event for Transition Rejected
'* Executes when Transitioning from stWaitingApproval
'* to stRejected
Function Rejected_OnChangeValidate
 Rejected_OnChangeValidate = _
    CBool(WorkflowSession.Fields("wfState").Value = REJECTED)
End Function


'* ----------------------------------------------------
'* Validation Event for Transition Approved
'* Executes when Transitioning from stWaitingApproval
'* to stApproved
Function Approved_OnChangeValidate
 Approved_OnChangeValidate = _
    CBool(WorkflowSession.Fields("wfState").Value = APPROVED)
End Function


'* ----------------------------------------------------
'* Main Procedure for Transition Approved
'* Excutes if Approved_OnChangeValidate = true
Sub Approved_OnChange
 '* set wfState to approved
 WorkflowSession.Fields("wfState").Value = ST_APPROVED
 WorkflowSession.Fields.Update
 '* send notification email
 Call SendMail("Employee Service Request Form - Approved")
End Sub


'* ----------------------------------------------------
'* Main Procedure for Transition Rejected
'* Excutes if Rejected_OnChangeValidate = true
Sub Rejected_OnChange
 '* set wfState to rejected
 WorkflowSession.Fields("wfState").Value = ST_REJECTED
 WorkflowSession.Fields.Update
 '* send notification email
 Call SendMail("Employee Service Request Form - Rejected")
End Sub
```

The last two steps of the Employee Service Request Form involve invoking a COM object to create or update user-account information into the Active Directory if the request is approved. You do this by using the Enter event of the stApproved state. No rule is necessary when the item is transitioning to this state, so the item just returns True for the Validate event.

This step also requires that the workflow process run in the privileged author's process space. Here's how to enable this:

1. Select the workflow process from the Solutions Explorer and right-click it.

2. Choose Properties to open the Properties page for the workflow process (Figure 17-10).

3. Check the "Run workflow script in privileged author context" checkbox.

 To invoke a COM object, you must also make sure that you are a member of the Privileged Workflow Authors role in the COM+ Workflow Event Sink.

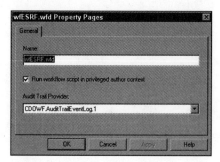

Figure 17-10: The workflow process Properties window

Listing 17-3 shows the Enter event of the stApproved state.

Listing 17-3: Enter Event of the stApproved State

```
'* ---------------------------------------------------
'* Validation Event for State Approved
'* Executes when entering State Approved
Function stApproved_OnEnterValidate
  stApproved_OnEnterValidate = true
End Function

'* Main Procedure for State Approved
'* Excutes if stApproved_OnEnterValidate = true
Sub stApproved_OnEnter
  Dim oAutoMgr
  Dim oMsg
```

Continued

Listing 17-3 *(Continued)*

```
Dim sMsgBody
Dim sUserName

On Error Resume Next

'* To break into application for debugging
'* use a stop statement.
'* stop

Set oAutoMgr = CreateObject("AutoEmployee.clsNetMgr")

If Err.number <> 0 Then
  WorkflowSession.ErrorNumber = -1
  '* Setting Error Number to - Number Does A Roleback
  SendMail("Employee Service Request Form - " & _
      " Create User Account Failed")
  Exit Sub
End If


Call oAutoMgr.CreateUserAccount(WorkflowSession)

If Err.number <> 0 Then
  '* Setting Error Number to negative value
  '* Aborts
  WorkflowSession.ErrorNumber = -1
  SendMail("Employee Service Request Form - " _ &
  " Create User Account Failed")
  Exit Sub
End If

'* Create User Name
sUserName= _
Left(WorkflowSession.Fields("Personal_FirstName").Value, 1)

If Len(WorkflowSession.Fields("Personal_LastName").Value) _
<= 7 Then
 sUserName = sUserName &_
  WorkflowSession.Fields("Personal_LastName").Value
Else
 sUserName = sUserName & _
  Left(WorkflowSession.Fields("Personal_LastName").Value, 7)
 End If
```

```
    Set oMsg = WorkflowSession.GetNewWorkflowMessage()

    oMsg.MimeFormatted = True

sMsgBody = "<B>" &
WorkflowSession.Fields("Personal_FirstName").Value & " " &
WorkflowSession.Fields("Personal_LastName").Value & "</B>" & _
        " was created in Active Directory.<BR>" & _
        "<B>User Name:</B> " & sUserName & "<BR>" & _
        "<B>Password:</B> password<BR>" & _
        "<B>Email:</B> " & _
WorkflowSession.Fields("Contact Information_Email").Value & "<BR>"

    '* Default Signiture
    sMsgBody = sMsgBody & "<BR>Thank you,<BR>Exchange" &_
        " 2000 Workflow Engine" & _
        "<BR><HR>" & WorkflowSession.StateFrom & "-" & _
        WorkflowSession.StateTo

    '* Prepare to send Mail
    With oMsg
     .From = "Net Manager"
     .To = WorkflowSession.Fields("Employee_Manager").Value
     .Subject = "Employee Service Request Form - Complete"
     .HTMLBody = sMsgBody
     .SendWorkflowMessage 0 'cdowfNoTracking
    End With
End Sub
```

Once you have finished adding all the code to your workflow, you are done creating the workflow process. The last step before running your workflow is to enable the workflow. To enable or disable a workflow, complete these steps:

1. Select the workflow project from the Solutions Explorer and right-click it.

2. From the pop-up menu, choose Enable Workflow (Figure 17-11).

Figures 17-12 thru 17-22 demonstrate the Employee Service Request workflow process from start to finish.

Figure 17-12 shows the Employee Service Request Form (ESRF) being submitted for review. When the request is submitted the state is stWaitingApproval.

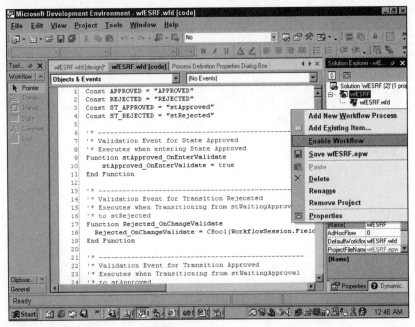

Figure 17-11: Enabling the workflow process

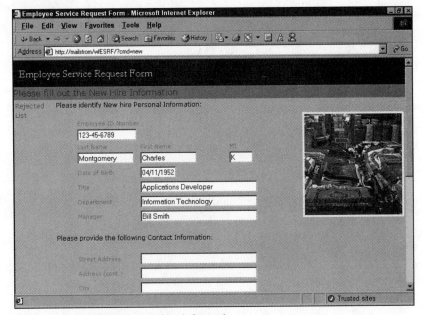

Figure 17-12: Submitting new hire information

Figure 17-13 shows the e-mail generated by the workflow process. The user (someone from the Human Resources department) will click the link provided to navigate to the request for review.

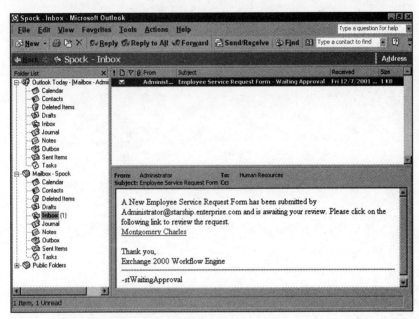

Figure 17-13: Initial HR e-mail notification

Figure 17-4 shows the request in review mode. From this screen, the Human Resource user can approve or reject the request.

Figure 17-15 shows the request being rejected. When the request is rejected, the wfState changes to stRejected and shows up in the Rejected list view. The state has changed to stRejected.

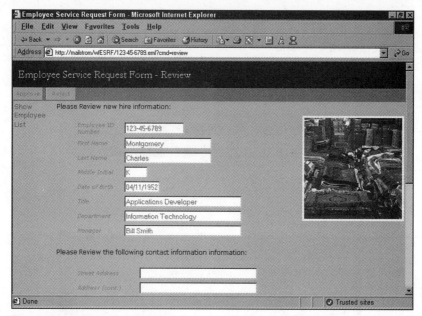

Figure 17-14: Reviewing the request

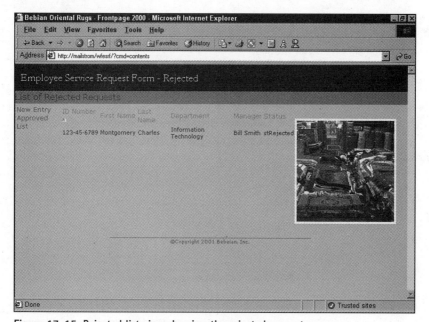

Figure 17-15: Rejected list view showing the rejected request

Figure 17-16 shows the rejected e-mail notification being sent to the person who originally submitted the request, who can then click the link to review the request and resubmit it.

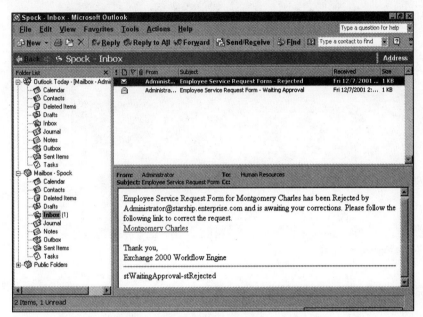

Figure 17-16: E-mail notification of rejected request

Figure 17-17 shows the request in review mode, being reviewed and resubmitted.

Figure 17-18 shows the notification of the resubmitted request. Its state has changed to `stWaitingApproval`.

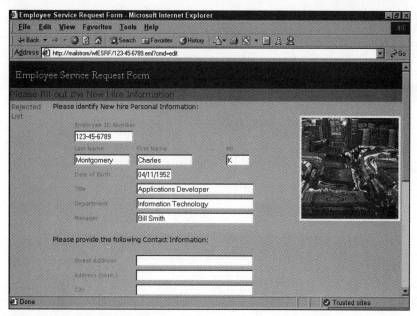

Figure 17–17: Resubmitting the request

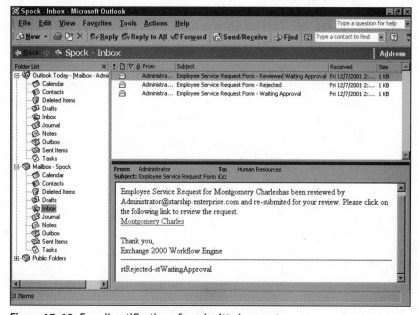

Figure 17–18: E-mail notification of resubmitted request

Figure 17-19 shows the request after it has been reviewed a second time and approved. The workflow engine has changed the wfState property to stApproved.

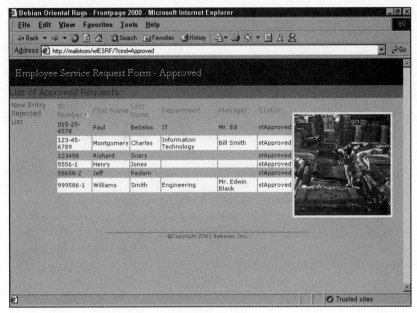

Figure 17-19: List view of approved requests

Figure 17-20 shows the e-mail notification generated by the workflow engine after an item has been approved.

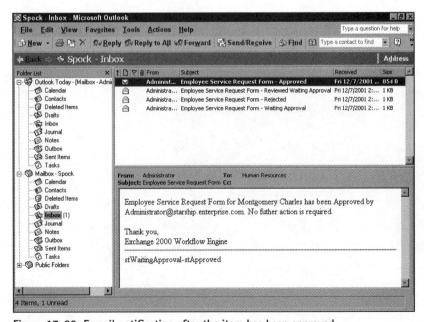

Figure 17-20: E-mail notification after the item has been approved

Figure 17-21 shows the e-mail notification that is sent after the user account has been created in the Active Directory.

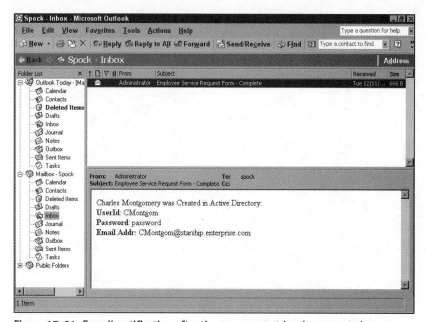

Figure 17-21: E-mail notification after the user account has been created

Figure 17-22 shows the new user properties populated from the Exchange global address book.

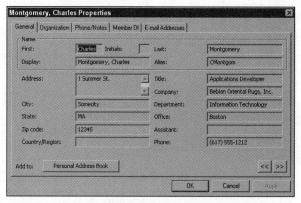

Figure 17-22: Exchange global address book populated after user account is created.

Figure 17-23 shows the Active Directory objects properties from the Active Directory Users and Computers MMC snap-in.

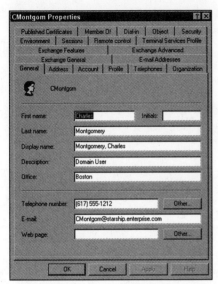

Figure 17-23: A new Active Directory object

Debugging Workflow Applications

The workflow components provide debugging capabilities through the use of the built-in audit trail provider and the Microsoft Script debugger.

The `AuditTrailEventLog` writes to the Windows 2000 application event log and is the default audit-trail provider. The `AuditTrailEventLog` provides insight into where your process succeeded or failed and also logs the nature of the transition. Figure 17-24 shows an error message from the Windows event log, logged by the `AuditTrailEventLog` provider.

You can build your own audit trail provider by implementing the `IAuditTrail` interface and then setting the `AuditTrailProvider` property of the `ProcessDefinition` to the `ProgID` of your component.

You can also use the Microsoft Script Debugger to debug your workflow application. To implement the Microsoft Script Debugger you need to enable Just-In-Time (JIT) script debugging. Follow these steps to enable JIT from the Workflow Designer:

1. Select the workflow project from the Solutions Explorer and right-click it.

2. From the pop-up menu, select Properties to open the Workflow Properties window.

3. Select the "Script debugging enabled for this folder" checkbox.

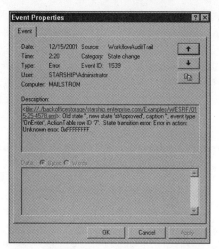

Figure 17-24: AuditTrailEventLog message
from Windows 2000 application event log

When this property is enabled you will be prompted to debug your application when errors occur. Figure 17-25 shows an example of the message you will receive when an error occurs in your application. To debug your application, choose Yes in the dialog box.

The script debugger launches on the server when debugging, so you will need to have access to the server.

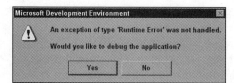

Figure 17-25: A debug error message

Your server environment also needs to be set up correctly in order to be able to debug your applications. To ensure that the server is set up for debugging, check the following three items:

◆ The workflow event sink COM+ identity must be set to Interactive User in component services. To change the identity of the workflow event sink complete the following steps:

1. Open the Component Services MMC snap-in.

2. Navigate to the workflow event sink and select the workflow event sink Component Package.

3. Right-click and choose Properties from the pop-up menu.

4. In the Properties window, choose the Identity tab (Figure 17-26).

5. Choose the Interactive User option.

6. Click OK. You will have to stop and start the component for your changes to take affect.

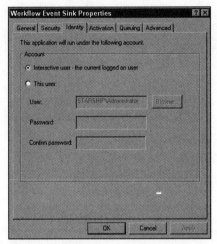

Figure 17-26: The COM+ Workflow Event Sink Properties dialog box

◆ The registry key HKCU/Software/Microsoft/Windows Script/Settings/ JITDebug must be set to REG_DWORD "1". This registry setting relates to the debugging checkbox on the project properties window in the Workflow Designer.

◆ If an event sink is installed on the server, JIT must be enabled in Tools → Options → Debugger → General Visual Studio Environment.

By default, a workflow script aborts after 15 minutes (900 seconds). You can configure the maximum time a script waits to execute using the registry key HKLM\SOFTWARE\Microsoft\Exchange\Workflow\Maximum. The value for this key is in seconds. The minimum supported execution wait time is 300 seconds (five minutes).

TIP To break into an application for debugging, use a stop statement at any point in your code (Figure 17-27).

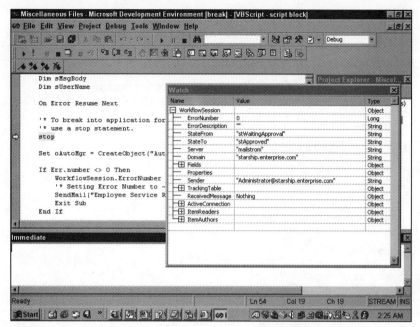

Figure 17-27: Using the stop statement to debug your application

Debugging is a critical step in building your applications. You should become familiar with the techniques we've covered in this section.

Summary

In this chapter, we have given you an in-depth look at the objects that constitute the CDO workflow object model and have looked at how to debug and build a simple workflow application using the Workflow Designer. The CDO workflow objects extend the developer's ability to interact directly with the workflow API to build powerful applications. The Workflow Designer is an easy-to-use graphical interface for building workflow applications within the Web Storage System using states and transitions. It provides all the fundamental elements you need to build basic workflow applications. The Workflow Designer, combined with the Exchange 2000 workflow platform, enables you to build workflow applications quickly and easily.

Chapter 18

Web Storage System Events

THE WEB STORAGE SYSTEM event model, as seen in Chapter 17, is a robust mechanism for building workflow applications. In this chapter, we are going to build upon what we have shown you so far and demonstrate how to use the Exchange event model to build custom event procedures. This chapter will introduce the different event types supported by the Exchange event model, and show you how to work with the event-sink interfaces and manage your event-registration items.

Introduction to Events

The Web Storage System provides a set of interfaces for responding to actions within the Exchange store. Types of actions you can respond to are items being created, modified, deleted, copied, or moved when time intervals elapse or when an Exchange store (MDB) is stopped or started. These actions are grouped into three types of events: *synchronous*, *asynchronous*, and *system*.

Synchronous and asynchronous events are triggered when items are modified, deleted, moved, or copied. Synchronous events fire before the item is committed to the Exchange store and are wrapped in transactions. Asynchronous events fire after the item is committed to the Exchange store and are not transactional. System events respond when the Exchange store is started or stopped or when a certain period of time has elapsed.

Synchronous and asynchronous events expose two events for responding to all actions dealing with creating, modifying, moving, coping, or deleting items in the Exchange store. These events are `save` and `delete`: Each one of the four actions is treated as some combination of the two. When a new item is created, Exchange triggers a `save` event on the folder in which the item is being created. When an item is moved, a `save` event is triggered on the folder to which the item is moving, and then a `delete` is triggered on the folder from which the item is moving. When an item is copied, a `save` event is triggered on the folder to which you are coping the item. When an item is modified within a folder, Exchange triggers a `save` event on the folder where the item resides; when an item is deleted, Exchange triggers a `delete` event in the folder where the item resides.

Asynchronous and synchronous events are guaranteed to execute under normal circumstances. If an event script fails, the event script will not be notified of that event in the future.

Code that is written to respond to one of these events is called an *event sink*. You can create event sinks using script files or as in-process DLLs. In order for Exchange to instantiate an in-process DLL, the DLL must be installed under COM+. Instantiating the in-process object under COM+ allows Exchange to use the security context of the user to connect to the Exchange store without logging on. If you create the event sink using a script file, the same process occurs; however, the script is executed by the Script Host (`exodbesh.DLL`). The Script Host is configured to run under COM+ and is not installed by default. The typical registration name is `ExOleDB.ScriptEventSink.1`.

In order for a folder to be notified about an event, you must create an event-registration item within the folder. An event-registration item is hidden by default and has its content class set to `urn:content-class:storeeventreg`. The event-registration item is made up of the properties from the `http://schemas.microsoft.com/exchange/events/` name space. Once an event-registration item has been created for a folder, that folder begins to receive notifications of the registered events.

Synchronous Events

Synchronous events are processed before the transaction commits the item to the Exchange store. Each event is fired in the context of the OLE DB transaction and is triggered twice, once for the initial post and once for the commit or abort. In situations in which multiple events are being fired for the same item, each event is fired in prioritized order. To set the priority for events, set the `Priority` property in the event-registration item to a number between 0 (the minimum) and 2147483647 (`0x7FFFFFFF` – the maximum). The default is 65535.

During the time it takes to execute the event sink, the item is locked under the control of the current event sink. No other process can access the item until the event sink is completed. These events do not fire when a folder registered for either event is moved or deleted. However, if the folder is copied, the event fires once for each item in the folder. When an event sink is processing an event, which has triggered from a move, and the event is aborted, then both the save and delete steps are aborted.

Synchronous events are supported by the IExStoreSyncEvents interface, which exposes the following two methods:

- OnSyncSave — Fires when an item is being saved to the Exchange store.

- OnSyncDelete — Fires when an item is being deleted from the Exchange store.

Table 18-1 shows the IExStoreSyncEvents::OnSyncSave and IExStoreSync Events::OnSyncDelete method parameters. Each method supports the same parameter interface.

TABLE 18-1 ONSYNCSAVE AND ONSYNCDELETE METHOD PARAMETERS

Parameter	Description
pEventInfo	A pointer to an IExStoreEventInfo interface that can be used to obtain further information related to the event
bstrURLItem	A string containing the URL of the item on which the event is occurring; this value is only valid if OLEDB or DAV created the item
lFlags	Bitwise AND of status values (see Table 18-2 for possible values)

Table 18-2 lists the possible values for the lFlags parameter, and shows which event supports which flags.

TABLE 18-2 DESCRIPTION OF LFLAGS VALUES FOR SYNCHRONOUS EVENTS

Decimal Value	Event Supported	Visual Basic Const	Description
1	OnSyncSave	EVT_NEW_ITEM	The item being saved is new
2	OnSyncSave		
	OnSyncDelete	EVT_IS_COLLECTION	The item being saved is a collection

Continued

TABLE 18-2 DESCRIPTION OF LFLAGS VALUES FOR SYNCHRONOUS EVENTS
(Continued)

Decimal Value	Event Supported	Visual Basic Const	Description
4	OnSyncSave		
	OnSyncDelete	EVT_REPLICATED_ITEM	The item is being saved as a result of replication
8	OnSyncSave	EVT_IS_DELIVERED	The item is being saved as the result of message delivery
16	OnSyncDelete	EVT_SOFTDELETE	The item has been moved to the dumpster (soft delete)
32	OnSyncDelete	EVT_HARDDELETE	The item has left the store MDB (hard delete)
64	OnSyncSave		
	OnSyncDelete	EVT_INITNEW	Set at the first firing of the event (useful for initialization purposes; it is set only once during the lifetime of a created event sink)
256	OnSyncSave		
	OnSyncDelete	EVT_MOVE	The item being saved is being moved
512	OnSyncSave	EVT_COPY	The item being saved is being copied
1024	OnSyncSave	EVT_DRAFT_CREATE	The item being saved is a newly created draft
2048	OnSyncSave	EVT_DRAFT_SAVE	The item being saved is a draft
4096	OnSyncSave	EVT_DRAFT_CHECKIN	The item being saved is a draft check-in
16777216	OnSyncSave	EVT_SYNC_BEGIN	Synchronous begin event
33554432	OnSyncSave		
	OnSyncDelete	EVT_SYNC_COMMITTED	Synchronous committed event

Decimal Value	Event Supported	Visual Basic Const	Description
67108864	OnSyncSave		
	OnSyncDelete	EVT_SYNC_ABORTED	Synchronous aborted event
536870912	OnSyncSave	EVT_INVALID_SOURCE_URL	The source URL could not be obtained during a move operation
1073741824	OnSyncSave		
	OnSyncDelete	EVT_INVALID_URL	The URL passed to the sink is invalid
2147483648	OnSyncSave		
	OnSyncDelete	EVT_ERROR	An error occurred in the event

When creating your event-registration item to register for the OnSyncSave event, set the EventMethod property to OnSyncSave. To register for the OnSyncDelete event, set the EventMethod property to OnSyncDelete.

The following properties are supported by the event registration:

◆ Criteria

◆ Enabled

◆ EventMethod

◆ MatchScope

◆ Priority

◆ ScriptUrl

◆ SinkClass

Asynchronous Events

Asynchronous events are processed after items are already committed to the Exchange store and do not support transactions. That is, if an item has been deleted, the item has already been removed from the Exchange store when the asynchronous event fires. Asynchronous events do not support a firing priority:

They are not processed in any particular order and no time limit determines when an asynchronous event should fire.

Asynchronous events are supported by the IExStoreAsyncEvents interface and expose the following two methods:

◆ OnSave — Fires after an item has been saved to the store.

◆ OnDelete — Fires after an item has been deleted from the store.

Table 18-3 shows the IExStoreAsyncEvents::OnSave and IExStoreAsync Events::OnDelete method parameters. Each method supports the same parameter interface.

TABLE 18-3 ONSAVE AND ONDELETE PARAMETER METHOD PARAMETERS

Parameter	Description
pEventInfo	A pointer to an IExStoreEventInfo interface that can be used to obtain further information related to the event
bstrURLItem	A string containing the URL of the item on which the event is occurring; this value is only valid if OLEDB or DAV created the item
lFlags	Bitwise AND of status values (see Table 18-4 for possible values)

Table 18-4 lists the possible values for the lFlags parameter and shows which event supports which flags.

TABLE 18-4 DESCRIPTION OF LFLAGS VALUES FOR ASYNCHRONOUS EVENTS

Decimal Value	Event Supported	Visual Basic Const	Description
1	OnSave	EVT_NEW_ITEM	The item being saved is new
2	OnSave		
	OnDelete	EVT_IS_COLLECTION	The item being saved is a collection
4	OnSave		
	OnDelete	EVT_REPLICATED_ITEM	The item is being saved as a result of replication

Decimal Value	Event Supported	Visual Basic Const	Description
8	OnSave	EVT_IS_DELIVERED	The item is being saved as the result of message delivery
16	OnDelete	EVT_SOFTDELETE	The item has been moved to the dumpster (soft delete)
32	OnDelete	EVT_HARDDELETE	The item has left the store MDB (hard delete)
64	OnSave		
	OnDelete	EVT_INITNEW	Set at the first firing of the event (useful for initialization purposes; it is set only once during the lifetime of a created event sink)
256	OnSave		
	OnDelete	EVT_MOVE	The item being saved is being moved
512	OnSave	EVT_COPY	The item being saved is being copied

When creating your event registration item to register for the OnSave event, set the EventMethod property to OnSave. To register for the OnDelete event, set the EventMethod property to OnDelete.

The following properties are supported by the event registration:

◆ Criteria

◆ Enabled

◆ EventMethod

◆ MatchScope

◆ ScriptUrl

◆ SinkClass

System Events

You can create event sinks for three different system events. The IExStoreSystemEvents interface exposes them:

- OnTimer — Fires after duration has expired.

- OnMDBShutDown — Fires when the Exchange store (MDB) shuts down.

- OnMDBStartUp — Fires when the Exchange store (MDB) starts up.

Each event fires asynchronously and in its own process. System events do not lock items in the store. System events are not tied to any particular folder, although it is good practice when using the OnTimer event to create the event registration in the folder in which the timer is going to execute. This helps with setting the OnTimer event context.

Table 18-5 outlines the IExStoreSystemEvents::OnTimer method parameters.

TABLE 18-5 ONTIMER METHOD PARAMETERS

Parameter	Description
bstrURLItem	A URL to the event-registration item
lFlags	Bitwise AND of status values (see Table 18-6 for possible values)

Table 18-6 lists the possible values for the lFlags parameter.

TABLE 18-6 DESCRIPTION OF LFLAGS VALUES FOR THE ONTIMER EVENT

Decimal Value	Event Supported	Visual Basic Const	Description
64	OnTimer	EVT_INITNEW	Set at the first firing of the event (useful for initialization purposes; it is set only once during the lifetime of a created event sink)

When creating your event-registration item to register for the OnTimer event, set the EventMethod property to OnTimer. The following properties are supported by the event registration:

◆ Enabled

◆ EventMethod

◆ ScriptUrl

◆ SinkClass

◆ TimerExpiryTime

◆ TimerInterval

◆ TimerStartTime

Table 18-7 outlines the IExStoreSystemEvents::OnMDBShutDown method parameters.

TABLE 18-7 ONMDBSHUTDOWN METHOD PARAMETERS

Parameter	Description
BstrMDBGuid	String containing the GUID of the MDB being stopped
LFlags	Bitwise AND of status values (see Table 18-8 for possible values)

Table 18-8 lists the possible values for the lFlags parameter.

TABLE 18-8 DESCRIPTION OF LFLAGS VALUES FOR THE ONMDBSHUTDOWN EVENT

Decimal Value	Event Supported	Visual Basic Const	Description
64	OnTimer	EVT_INITNEW	Set at the first firing of the event (useful for initialization purposes; set only once during the lifetime of a created event sink)

When creating your event-registration item to register for the OnMDBShutdown event, set the EventMethod property to OnMDBShutDown. The following properties are supported by the event registration:

◆ Enabled

◆ EventMethod

◆ SinkClass

Table 18-9 outlines the IExStoreSystemEvents::OnMDBStartUp method parameters.

TABLE 18-9 ONMDBSTARTUP METHOD PARAMETERS

Parameter	Description
bstrMDBGuid	String containing the GUID of the MDB being stopped
bstrMDBName	String containing the name of the MDB being started
lFlags	Bitwise AND of status values (see Table 18-10 for possible values)

Table 18-10 lists the possible values for the lFlags parameter.

TABLE 18-10 DESCRIPTION OF LFLAGS VALUES FOR THE ONMDBSTARTUP EVENT

Decimal Value	Event Supported	Visual Basic Const	Description
64	OnTimer	EVT_INITNEW	Set at the first firing of the event (useful for initialization purposes; set only once during the lifetime of a created event sink)

When creating your event-registration item to register for the OnMDBStartUp event, set the EventMethod property to OnMDBStartUp. The following properties are supported by the event registration:

◆ Enabled

♦ EventMethod

♦ SinkClass

Refer to the Web Storage System SDK for a complete listing of other support interfaces.

Working with Event Sinks

You can create event sinks in two ways: by creating scripts or by creating an in-process object. This section focuses on using Visual Basic to create an in-process event sink. When using Visual Basic to create in-process objects, you can either manually create and implement the interfaces or use the Exchange Web Storage System Event Wizard, which comes with the Exchange Web Storage System Tools.

To create an in-process event sink manually from Visual Basic, do the following:

1. Create a new ActiveX DLL project by selecting Start → Programs → Microsoft Visual Studio → Microsoft Visual Basic 6.0. The New Project dialog box will open.

2. Double-click the ActiveX DLL project icon (Figure 18-1) in the New Project dialog box.

Figure 18-1: Creating a new ActiveX DLL

3. Set a reference to the EXOLEDB Type Library by selecting Project → References to open the References dialog box.

4. Within the References dialog box, set a reference to the EXOLEDB Type Library by searching through the references list and checking the checkbox next to the item, as shown in Figure 18-2.

5. Click the OK button to exit the References dialog box.

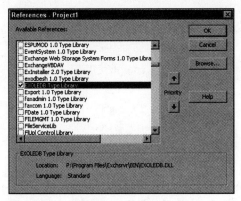

**Figure 18-2: Setting a reference to the
EXOLEDB Type Library**

6. Use the **Implements** keyword to implement the appropriate interface. Listing 18-1 shows the **Implements** keyword being used to implement `IExStoreAsyncEvents`.

Listing 18-1: Using the Implements Keyword to Implement IExStoreAsyncEvents

```
Option Explicit

Implements IExStoreAsyncEvents

Private Sub IExStoreAsyncEvents_OnDelete( _
  ByVal pEventInfo As Exoledb.IExStoreEventInfo, _
  ByVal bstrURLItem As String, _
  ByVal lFlags As Long)

 '* Need to Include method even if you are not going to code it.

End Sub

Private Sub IExStoreAsyncEvents_OnSave( _
  ByVal pEventInfo As Exoledb.IExStoreEventInfo, _
  ByVal bstrURLItem As String, _
  ByVal lFlags As Long)

'* Add your code here

End Sub
```

You can also use the Web Storage System Event Wizard to create a full set of templates for developing your event sink. The Wizard comes with the Web Storage System Tools and can be downloaded from this book's companion Web site. If you have installed the Web Storage System Tools, follow these steps to create the event sink using the Web Storage System Wizard:

1. Open Visual Basic and select Add-Ins → Web Storage System Wizard. If the option is not in the Add-Ins menu, choose the Add-In Manager option and see if the Web Storage System Wizard is located in the list of available add-ins. If it is not listed, you will need to register the mxeswiz.dll manually. The DLL is located in Program Files → Web Storage System → Tools → EventSinkWizard. Follow these steps to register the object:

    1. Open a command prompt.

    2. Navigate to the Program Files → Web Storage System → Tools → EventSinkWizard folder.

    3. Use the regsvr32 utility to register the mxeswiz.dll object. Figure 18-3 shows the object being manually registered.

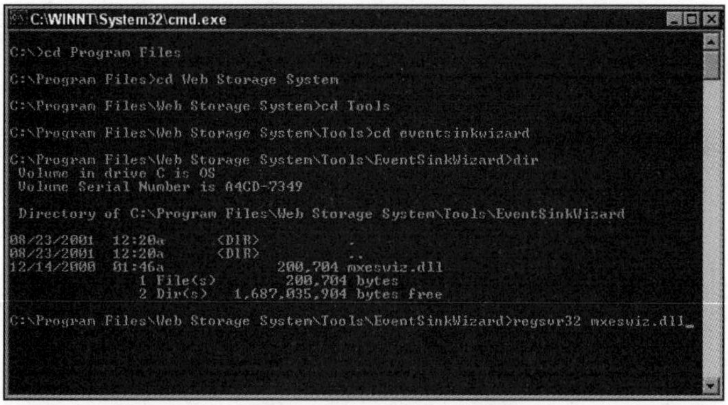

Figure 18-3: Using regsvr32 to manually register the mxeswiz.dll (Event Sink Wizard)

    4. Close and re-open Visual Basic and the Web Storage System Event Wizard should now be listed in the Add-Ins menu.

2. Start the Wizard by choosing the Web Storage System Wizard from the Add-Ins pull-down menu. Figure 18-4 shows the Web Storage System Event Sink dialog box.

Figure 18-4: Opening the dialog box for the Web
Storage System Event Wizard

3. Click Next to open the Selection of Events screen (Figure 18-5). Here you
   choose the type of events you want to create. You can include more than
   one set of events.

4. Check the Asynchronous Events checkbox (Figure 18-5) and then click
   Next to open the Selection of Options dialog box.

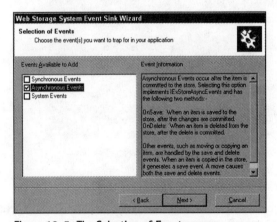

Figure 18-5: The Selection of Events screen

5. The Selection of Options dialog box enables you to add three different
   options to your event sinks. After selecting the options you want, click
   Next to open the Finish screen. The options provided are as follows:

   ■ Insert file logging code into each event – Adds a file-logging routine to
     your event sink. You have the option of changing the filename and
     location.

> **TIP**
>
> To increase performance, after debugging is complete or when logging is no longer needed, disable the file-logging option by setting the `PERFORM_FILE_LOGGING` constant to `False` in the project's code module.

- Insert a breakpoint into each event – Adds breakpoints to each event for debugging. Breakpoints are ignored after projects are compiled.

- Allow public registration of event sink – Adds the ICreateRegistration interface, which enables you to trap event-registration events and allow or disallow registration.

Figure 18-6 shows the Selection of Options screen with all options checked.

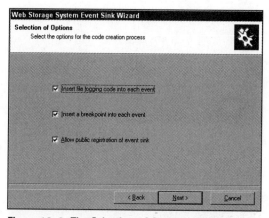

Figure 18–6: The Selection of Options screen

6. On the last screen click Finish.

Once you have stubbed out your project either manually or through the wizard you are ready to write your code. Each of the `save` and `delete` events in either the asynchronous or synchronous event interfaces receives the IExStoreEventInfo interface as the `pEventInfo` parameter.

The IExStoreEventInfo interface provides access to the item that triggered the event as an ADO `Record` object and the event transaction for synchronous events. The IExStoreEventInfo interface is not directly supported from Visual Basic or through scripting. In order for you to retrieve the item that triggered the event or the transaction for synchronous events you need to use the equivalent IExStoreDispEventInfo interface. Listing 18-2 shows how to retrieve the item that triggered the event as an ADO Record object through the IExStoreDispEventInfo interface.

Listing 18-2: Retrieving the Item that Triggered the Event as an ADO Record Object

```
Option Explicit

Implements Exoledb.IExStoreAsyncEvents

Private Sub IExStoreAsyncEvents_OnSave( _
 ByVal pEventInfo as ExevtsnkLib.IExStoreEventInfo, _
 ByVal bstrURLSource as String, _
 ByVal lFlags as Long _
)
 '* Get A compatible interface
 Dim iDispEvtInfo as IExStoreDispEventInfo

 '* QueryInterface the IExStoreEventInfo interface
 Set iDispEvtInfo = pEventInfo

 '* Get the item as an ADO Record
 Dim Rec as ADODB.Record
 Set Rec = iDispEvtInfo.EventRecord

 ' ********************
 '* Do Work
 ' ********************

 '* Set Rec = Nothing
 '* Set iDispEvtInfo = Nothing
End Sub

Private Sub IExStoreAsyncEvents_OnDelete( _
 ByVal pEventInfo as ExevtsnkLib.IExStoreEventInfo, _
 ByVal bstrURLSource as String, _
 ByVal lFlags as Long _
)
   '* Your Code Here
End Sub
```

The IExStoreDispEventInfo properties are listed in Table 18-11.

TABLE 18-11 IEXSTOREDISPEVENTINFO PROPERTIES

Property	Description
AbortChange	Aborts the transaction for synchronous events
EventConnection	Returns the OLE DB Connection object
SourceURL	Return the URL of the item's original location from a move. Only valid for an OnSyncSave event. During all other events this property returns Null.
UserGuid	Returns the GUID of the user from a synchronous event
StoreGuid	Returns the GUID of the store from a synchronous event
UserSid	Returns the Security Identifier of the user who caused the synchronous event
Data	Used to set and retrieve data for synchronous events during the Begin and Commit/Abort phases (equivalent to the IUserData interface)

Once you have completed writing your event sink and have compiled it you will need to register it as a COM+ application.

For complete instructions for creating and adding your object to a COM+ application, please refer to the "COM+ Applications" section in Chapter 6, "Web Storage System Management and Security."

For more information about debugging COM+ components, reference Q261871 from the MSDN (http://msdn.microsoft.com).

Once your object is compiled and registered as a COM+ Application, you need to create the event registration item, which is covered in the next section.

Managing Event Registrations

Event-registration items are stored in the Web Storage System, much like form-registration items. The registration item's content class is set to urn:content-class:storeeventreg and contains properties from the http://schemas.microsoft.com/exchange/events/ name space. Event-registration items do not require all properties to be populated. Each event supports a combination of the properties relevant to that event type. Event registrations must be created in the folder for which they are going to receive notification, and this determines their scope. Table 18-12 lists all the properties and descriptions of the http://schemas.microsoft.com/exchange/events/ name space.

**TABLE 18-12 HTTP://SCHEMAS.MICROSOFT.COM/EXCHANGE/EVENTS/
NAME-SPACE PROPERTIES AND DESCRIPTIONS**

Property	Description
Criteria	A SQL clause that specifies criteria for executing a particular event. Specified as a WHERE clause.
Enabled	Boolean value that specifies whether the event will fire. Needs to be True.
EventMethod	Specifies one of the 7 events to execute.
MatchScope	Deep or Shallow. Determines whether or not the event is recursive. If this property is set to Deep the event will trigger for each child folder relative to the folder in which the registration item is saved.
Priority	For synchronous events, set the priority of an event to fire.
ScriptURL	If the event is written as a script this property is set to the filename of the script. store the script in the same folder in which the event registration is stored.
Sinkclass	Prog ID of CLSID of a in-process DLL in which the event scripts are implemented.
TimerExpiryTime	Date and time that an OnTimer event will end
TimerInterval	Length of time for which the OnTimer event will fire
TimerStartTime	Date and time that the OnTimer event will start

There are several methods provided for creating an event-registration item. You can use the Web Storage System Explorer, RegEvent.vbs, or ADO. In this section we'll demonstrate how to create an event-registration item using the Web Storage System and RegEvent.vbs methods.

To create an event registration from the Web Storage System Explorer, do the following:

1. Open the Web Storage System Explorer by selecting Start → Programs → Web Storage System SDK → Web Storage System Tools → Web Storage System Explorer.

2. Enter the application root URL.

3. Once you have connected to the application, use the Web Storage System Explorer to navigate to the folder where you would like to create the even registration.

4. From the File menu, select Add Event Registration.

5. Enter the event's name (Figure 18-7) and click Next to open the Select the Category dialog box (Figure 18-8).

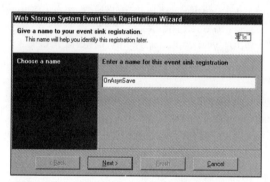

Figure 18-7: Web Storage System event registration

6. Choose Asynchronous from the list of events to register for (Figure 18-8) and then click Next to open the Pick the Event(s) dialog box (Figure 18-9).

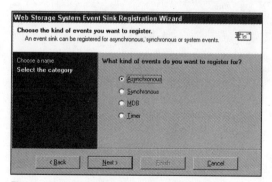

Figure 18-8: Choosing the registration type

7. Select the event you want to be notified of. Check both OnSave and OnDelete (Figure 18-9) and then click Next to open the Specify the Scope dialog box (Figure 18-10).

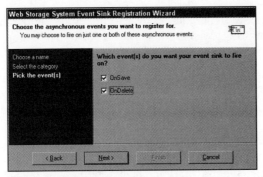

Figure 18-9: Choosing the event types

8. Leave the Scope and Criteria options at their default settings (Figure 18-10) and then click Next to open the Select the Sink Type dialog box (Figure 18-11). In the future you can specify any Criteria necessary, as well as the Scope.

For more information on creating a Criteria, using a SQL WHERE clause and setting folder Scope with DEEP and SHALLOW queries, please refer to Chapter 5, "Searching the Web Storage System."

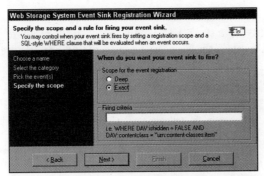

Figure 18-10: Setting Scope and Criteria for the event registration

9. Decide whether the event is a script or a COM event sink. For the purpose of this example, choose COM Event Sink (Figure 18-11) and then click Next to open the Choose the Class dialog box (Figure 18-12).

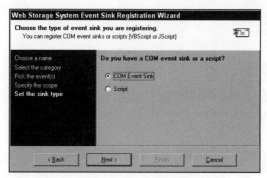

Figure 18-11: Choosing the event sink type

10. Enter the `ProgID` or `CLSID` of the COM+ event sink (Figure 18-12) and click Next to open the Review and Finish dialog box (Figure 18-13).

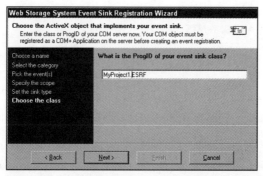

Figure 18-12: Entering the ProgID or CLSID of the COM+ event sink

11. The final screen will give you the opportunity to review your settings (Figure 18-13). When you are satisfied with your selections, click Finish.

Figure 18-13: Finishing up

RegEvent.vbs is a Visual Basic script used to create event registrations. The script is executed with the Windows Scripting Host **cscript.exe** from a command prompt. The following line shows the correct usage of RegEvent.vbs.

```
cscript RegEvent.vbs <add/delete/enum> <args>
```

Table 18-13 shows the possible RegEvent.vbs arguments and their descriptions.

TABLE 18-13 REGEVENT.VBS ARGUMENTS AND DESCRIPTIONS

Argument	Description
EventMethod	OnSave; OnDelete; OnSyncSave; OnSyncDelete OnTimer; OnMdbStartUp; OnMDBShutDown
Sinkclass	ProgID of sink Registration Item Name (scope) Event item name
StartTime	When to start the OnTimer event, such as 8/4/98 01:50:00 AM
Interval	Time between OnTimer events
-p [Priority]	0 (minimum) to 2147483647 (0x7FFFFFFF) (maximum). Default is 65535 (0xffff). Only decimal values are supported.
-m [MatchScope]	DEEP | SHALLOW | EXACT | ANY
-f [CriteriaFilter]	WHERE clause to restrict binding notifications
-file [ScriptFilePath]	Full (file or URL) path of the script

Argument	Description
`-url [ScriptUrl]`	Fully qualified URL of the event binding (registration message)
`-e [ExpiryTime]`	When to stop the `OnTimer` event

Listing 18-3 shows several examples of using the `Regevent.vbs`. The examples are: to add an event registration that is a script and a COM+ event sink, to delete an event registration, and to delete all event registrations in a folder.

Listing 18-3: Examples of Using the Regevent.vbs

```
To add an event registration that is a script
-----------------------------
cscript regevent.vbs ADD "onsave;ondelete" Exoledb.ScriptEventSink.1
file://./backofficestorage/STARSHIP.ENTERPRISE.COM\EXAMPLES\EventReg
s\wsserw\EventRegItem1 -file m:\
STARSHIP.ENTERPRISE.COM\EXAMPLES\EventRegs\wsserwtest.vbs

To add an event registration that is a COM+ Application
-----------------------------
cscript regevent.vbs add "onsyncsave" "regeventex.eventex"
"file://./backofficestorage/STARSHIP.ENTERPRISE.COM/EXAMPLES/EventRe
gs/wsserw/EventRegItem2" -f "WHERE $DAV:ishidden$ =
FALSE"

To delete an event registration
-----------------------------
cscript regevent.vbs delete "
file://./backofficestorage/STARSHIP.ENTERPRISE.COM/EXAMPLES/EventReg
s/wsserw/EventRegItem2"

To delete all registration items in a folder
cscript regevent.vbs delete "
file://./backofficestorage/STARSHIP.ENTERPRISE.COM/EXAMPLES/EventReg
s/wsserw/" -ALL
```

Summary

This chapter has extended your knowledge of the Exchange event services by demonstrating how to implement the Exchange event model into your in-process Visual Basic applications. You have been introduced to the types of events that the Exchange store exposes. You've also learned how to work with them and how to build event-registration items that allow your event sinks to be notified of events. By introducing synchronous events, guaranteed execution, and through the use of COM+ components for availability, scalability, flexibility, and faster code execution, the Exchange 2000 event model enhances your ability to programmatically respond to events within the Exchange store.

Appendix A

Deploying Applications for Exchange 2000

WITH EXCHANGE 2000 SERVER you can package and deploy your applications programmatically through the `IExAppInstallerEx` interface or by using the Microsoft Exchange Application Deployment Wizard that ships with the Web Storage System tools. This appendix provides step-by-step instructions for packaging and deploying applications with Exchange.

Microsoft Exchange Application Deployment Wizard

To launch the Microsoft Exchange Application Deployment Wizard, go to Start→ Programs→ Web Storage System SDK→ Web Storage System Tools→ Application Deployment Wizard (shown in Figure A-1).

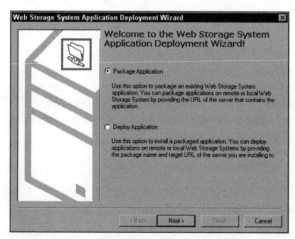

Figure A-1: The Application Deployment Wizard

Package an Application

The Application Deployment Wizard enables you to package your applications from the Web Storage System into a single CAB file or to a folder containing the application's contents. A CAB file is an efficient way to compress and package files to be distributed, very similar to a ZIP file. The Wizard uses the WebDAV protocol to package your application, so you will need to supply a valid http or https URL to your application and a username/password pair that will give you access.

 If your username fails to resolve, try appending the domain, as in starship\pbebelos.

The Wizard will package all files, including custom properties, content-classes, and schema references, within the current application folder and sub-folders if necessary, and will also create a package.xml manifest for deployment.

 The Wizard will package any file in the Web Storage System folder. However, when you deploy the package to a new server, if the file requires self-registration or needs to be set up as a COM+ application you will need to complete this step manually or use the Windows Installer Technology to package these components separately. For this reason you may not want to register your DLL files in the Web Storage System application folder.

You can exclude schema properties by using the samplefilter.xml file, which is located in the \Program Files\Exchsrvr\Tools\AppDeployWiz\ folder. The filter file excludes properties that are not relevant to the application during deployment. You can modify the filter file if necessary or use it as is.

To package an application, follow the following steps:

1. Open the Application Deployment Wizard.

2. Select the Package Application option. Click Next.

3. Enter the URL of the application to package. Click Next. Figure A-2 shows the Wizard at this stage.

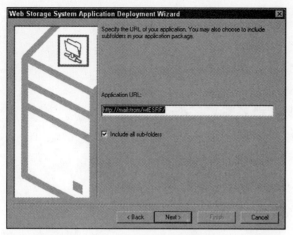

Figure A-2: Enter the URL of the application to package.

4. Enter a username and password. Click Next. Figure A-3 shows the Wizard at this stage.

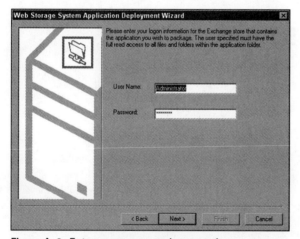

Figure A-3: Enter a username and password.

5. Select the type of package to create. Click Next. Figure A-4 shows the Wizard at this stage.

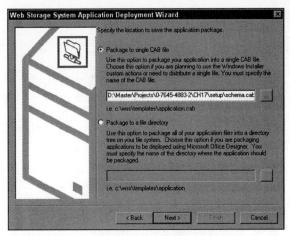

Figure A-4: Choose the type of package to create.

6. Set the Schema filter file to the xml filter file. (In typical situations you can leave this as is.) Click Next. Figure A-5 shows the Wizard at this stage.

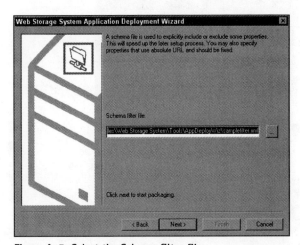

Figure A-5: Select the Schema filter file.

The Wizard will start to compile the package. Figure A-6 shows the Wizard at this stage.

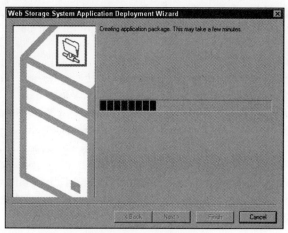

Figure A-6: The Wizard packaging files

7. When the Wizard is done, you will receive a message indicating that the Wizard has finished compiling the package. Click Finish. Figure A-7 shows the Wizard at this stage.

Figure A-7: The Wizard showing the finished dialog box.

Deploy an Application

You can deploy your applications from a packaged CAB file or a folder containing its contents. For simple applications, you can use the Application Deployment Wizard to deploy your application. To do this, supply the URL to the Web Storage System in which your applications will run. Then supply the path to the CAB file that the Application Deployment Wizard created, as well as a username and password. You cannot deploy a packaged application without the `package.xml` manifest.

 The Wizard will not self-register DLL files located in the `packaged application` or `Create COM+ application` packages. You will need to complete these steps manually or use the Windows Installer Technology.

For more complex applications containing event sinks and DLLs, you will need to use the Windows Installer Technology to deploy the package created by the wizard, followed by any items that run outside the Web Storage System.

 When packaging event sinks that are scripts, you will need to make sure that the `Exodbesh.dll` is registered as a COM+ application. Then use the Event Wizard from the Web Storage System Explorer to create the `Event` registration item choosing the `script` option.

The process for deploying the files packaged by the application Deployment Wizard is the same as the process for packing, with the following exceptions:

◆ In Step 3, enter the name of the destination where you want to deploy your application. Make sure that the folder doesn't already exist and that it is not a top-level root folder. Also make sure that you have permissions to create folders and items within the root folder you are deploying to.

◆ In Step 4, select the type of package to deploy — either a single CAB or folder contents.

The IExAppInstallerEx Interface

This section describes the Application Programming Interface (API) for programmatically packaging and deploying Microsoft Web Storage System applications as performed by the Application Deployment Wizard.

The filename and location of the interface DLL is `\Program Files\Web Storage System\Tools\AppDeployWiz\Exinstaller.dll`. To reference the object from Visual Basic, set a reference to the ExInstaller 2.0 Type Library.

Table A-1 lists the methods supported by the IExAppInstallerEx interface.

TABLE A-1   IEXAPPINSTALLEREX SUPPORTED METHODS

Method Name	Method Description
InstallAppEx	Installs a packaged application
InstallAppFromURL	Installs a CAB file from a Web URL
PackFolderEx	Packages an application

The InstallAppEx method

This method installs a packaged application. Listing A-1 shows the method in Visual Basic form.

Listing A-1: InstallAppEx Visual Basic Method Syntax

```
Sub InstallAppEx(ByVal bstrDstFolderURL As String, _
    ByVal bstrSrcFileFullPath As String, _
    ByVal bstrUserName As String, _
    ByVal bstrPassword As String, _
    ByVal lFileOption As Long, _
    ByVal lOverwriteOption As Long, _
    ByVal hInstall As Long, _
    ByVal lTotalTicks As Long)
```

The following list defines the input parameters for the InstallAppEx method:

◆ bstrDstFolderURL — The URL to the destination Web Storage System folder in which the application is to be installed. The folder and any of its parent folders that do not exist will be created.

◆ bstrSrcFileFullPath — The absolute path in the Microsoft Windows file system of the packaged application. This can either be the path and file-name for a CAB file or the path to a folder of a packaged application.

◆ bstrUserName — The username required for authentication.

◆ bstrPassword — The password required for authentication.

◆ lFileOption — Specifies whether to install from a CAB file (0) or from a folder (1).

◆ lOverwriteOption — Controls overwrite options if a CAB file or folder exists. Specify 0 to prompt a confirmation, 1 to fail, or 2 to overwrite without a confirmation.

◆ hInstall — Reserved. Specify 0.

◆ lTotalTicks: Reserved. Specify 0.

The InstallAppFromURL method

This method installs a CAB file from a Web URL. Listing A-2 shows the InstallAppFromUrl method in Visual Basic form.

Listing A-2: InstallAppFromUrl Visual Basic Method Syntax

```
Sub InstallAppFromURL(ByVal bstrSrcURL As String, _
    ByVal bstrSrcUserName As String, _
    ByVal bstrSrcPassword As String, _
    ByVal bstrDstFolderURL As String, _
    ByVal bstrDstUserName As String, _
    ByVal bstrDstPassword As String, _
    ByVal lFileOption As Long, _
    ByVal lOverwriteOption As Long, _
    ByVal hInstall As Long, _
    ByVal lTotalTicks As Long)
```

The following list defines the input parameters for the InstallAppURL method:

◆ bstrSrcURL — The URL to the CAB file.

◆ bstrSrcUserName — The username required for authentication to the source URL.

◆ bstrSrcPassword — The password required for authentication to the source URL.

◆ bstrDstFolderURL — The URL to the destination Web Storage System folder in which the application is to be installed. The folder and any of its parent folders that do not exist will be created.

◆ bstrDstUserName — The username required for authentication to the destination URL.

◆ bstrDstPassword — The password required for authentication to the destination URL.

◆ lFileOption — Specifies whether to install from a CAB file (0) or from a folder (1).

◆ lOverwriteOption — Controls overwrite options if a CAB file or folder exists. Specify 0 to prompt a confirmation, 1 to fail, or 2 to overwrite without a confirmation.

◆ `hInstall` — Reserved. Specify 0.

◆ `lTotalTicks` — Reserved. Specify 0.

The PackFolderEx method

This method packages an application. Listing A-3 shows the method in Visual Basic form.

Listing A-3: PackFolderEx Visual Basic Method Syntax

```
Sub PackFolderEx(ByVal bstrSrcFolderURL As String, _
    ByVal bstrPackageFullPath As String, _
    ByVal fIncludeSubFolders As Boolean, _
    ByVal bstrSchemaFilterFile As String, _
    ByVal bstrUserName As String, _
    ByVal bstrPassword As String, _
    ByVal lFileOption As Long, _
    ByVal lOverwriteOption As Long, _
    ByVal pfnCallBack As Long)
```

The following list defines the input parameters for the `PackFolderEx` method:

◆ `bstrSrcFolderURL` — The URL to the Web Storage System folder of the application to be packaged.

◆ `bstrPackageFullPath` — The absolute path and filename for the packaged application on the Microsoft Windows file system. This parameter can package to a CAB file or a folder containing the application's contents.

◆ `fIncludeSubFolders` — If `TRUE`, instructs the installer to include the application's sub-folders in the package.

◆ `bstrSchemaFilterFile` — A schema file with which to include or exclude properties and fix items with the correct URLs. The default file provided by the Application Deployment Wizard is `\Program Files\Exchsrvr\Tools\ AppDeployWiz\samplefilter.xml`. This file excludes properties that are not relevant to packaging an application.

◆ `bstrUserName` — The username required for authentication.

◆ `bstrPassword` — The password required for authentication.

◆ `lFileOption` — Specifies whether to install from a CAB file (0) or from a folder (1).

◆ `lOverwriteOption` — Controls overwrite options if a CAB file or folder exists. Specify 0 to prompt a confirmation, 1 to fail, or 2 to overwrite without a confirmation.

◆ `pfnCallBack` — Reserved. Specify 0.

Web Storage System Name Spaces

THE FOLLOWING NAME SPACES are defined and reserved for Microsoft Exchange. Each name space is listed with its associated properties. For a complete definition of the name space and properties, please refer to the Web Storage System SDK or the MSDN online at http://msdn.microsoft.com.

The DAV: Name Space

The following is a list of the DAV: name space properties.

- DAV:abstract
- DAV:autoversion
- DAV:checkintime
- DAV:childautoversioning
- DAV:childcount
- DAV:childversioning
- DAV:comment
- DAV:contentclass
- DAV:creationdate
- DAV:defaultdocument
- DAV:displayname
- DAV:getcontentlanguage
- DAV:getcontentlength
- DAV:getcontenttype
- DAV:getetag
- DAV:getlastmodified
- DAV:haschildren

- ◆ DAV:hassubs
- ◆ DAV:href
- ◆ DAV:id
- ◆ DAV:iscollection
- ◆ DAV:isfolder
- ◆ DAV:ishidden
- ◆ DAV:isreadonly
- ◆ DAV:isroot
- ◆ DAV:isstructureddocument
- ◆ DAV:isversioned
- ◆ DAV:lastaccessed
- ◆ DAV:lockdiscovery
- ◆ DAV:mergedfrom
- ◆ DAV:nosubs
- ◆ DAV:objectcount
- ◆ DAV:parentname
- ◆ DAV:resourcetype
- ◆ DAV:revisioncomment
- ◆ DAV:revisionid
- ◆ DAV:revisionlabel
- ◆ DAV:revisionuri
- ◆ DAV:searchrequest
- ◆ DAV:searchtype
- ◆ DAV:supportedlock
- ◆ DAV:uid
- ◆ DAV:visiblecount
- ◆ DAV:vresourceid

The http://schemas.microsoft.com/ cdo/configuration/ Name Space

The following is a list of the http://schemas.microsoft.com/cdo/configuration/ name space properties.

- http://schemas.microsoft.com/cdo/configuration/activeconnection
- http://schemas.microsoft.com/cdo/configuration/autopromotebodyparts
- http://schemas.microsoft.com/cdo/configuration/hardlinklist
- http://schemas.microsoft.com/cdo/configuration/languagecode
- http://schemas.microsoft.com/cdo/configuration/mailboxurl
- http://schemas.microsoft.com/cdo/configuration/nntpauthenticate
- http://schemas.microsoft.com/cdo/configuration/nntpserver
- http://schemas.microsoft.com/cdo/configuration/nntpserverport
- http://schemas.microsoft.com/cdo/configuration/postpassword
- http://schemas.microsoft.com/cdo/configuration/postusername
- http://schemas.microsoft.com/cdo/configuration/postusing
- http://schemas.microsoft.com/cdo/configuration/sendemailaddress
- http://schemas.microsoft.com/cdo/configuration/sendingusing
- http://schemas.microsoft.com/cdo/configuration/sendpassword
- http://schemas.microsoft.com/cdo/configuration/sendusername
- http://schemas.microsoft.com/cdo/configuration/smtpaccountname
- http://schemas.microsoft.com/cdo/configuration/smtpauthenticate
- http://schemas.microsoft.com/cdo/configuration/smtpserver
- http://schemas.microsoft.com/cdo/configuration/smtpserverport
- http://schemas.microsoft.com/cdo/configuration/smtpuserreplyemailaddress
- http://schemas.microsoft.com/cdo/configuration/timezoneid
- http://schemas.microsoft.com/cdo/configuration/urlproxyserver
- http://schemas.microsoft.com/cdo/configuration/usemessageresponsetext

The http://schemas.microsoft.com/ cdo/workflow/ Name Space

The following is a list of the `http://schemas.microsoft.com/cdo/workflow` name space properties:

- `http://schemas.microsoft.com/cdo/workflow/actiontable`
- `http://schemas.microsoft.com/cdo/workflow/adhocflows`
- `http://schemas.microsoft.com/cdo/workflow/audittrail`
- `http://schemas.microsoft.com/cdo/workflow/audittrailprovider`
- `http://schemas.microsoft.com/cdo/workflow/commonscripturl`
- `http://schemas.microsoft.com/cdo/workflow/currentstate`
- `http://schemas.microsoft.com/cdo/workflow/defaultprocdefinition`
- `http://schemas.microsoft.com/cdo/workflow/designtool`
- `http://schemas.microsoft.com/cdo/workflow/disablesuccessentries`
- `http://schemas.microsoft.com/cdo/workflow/enabledebug`
- `http://schemas.microsoft.com/cdo/workflow/expirytime`
- `http://schemas.microsoft.com/cdo/workflow/mode`
- `http://schemas.microsoft.com/cdo/workflow/parentprocinstance`
- `http://schemas.microsoft.com/cdo/workflow/processdefinition`
- `http://schemas.microsoft.com/cdo/workflow/response`
- `http://schemas.microsoft.com/cdo/workflow/trackingtablexml`
- `http://schemas.microsoft.com/cdo/workflow/workflowmessageid`

The http://schemas.microsoft.com/ cdo/nntpenvelope/ Name Space

The following is a list of the `http://schemas.microsoft.com/cdo/nntpenvelope` name space properties:

- `http://schemas.microsoft.com/cdo/nntpenvelope/newsgrouplist`
- `http://schemas.microsoft.com/cdo/nntpenvelope/nntpprocessing`

The http://schemas.microsoft.com/ cdo/smtpenvelope/ Name Space

The following is a list of the `http://schemas.microsoft.com/cdo/smtpenvelope/` name space properties.

- `http://schemas.microsoft.com/cdo/smtpenvelope/arrivaltime`
- `http://schemas.microsoft.com/cdo/smtpenvelope/clientipaddress`
- `http://schemas.microsoft.com/cdo/smtpenvelope/messagestatus`
- `http://schemas.microsoft.com/cdo/smtpenvelope/pickupfilename`
- `http://schemas.microsoft.com/cdo/smtpenvelope/recipientlist`
- `http://schemas.microsoft.com/cdo/smtpenvelope/senderemailaddress`

The http://schemas.microsoft.com/ exchange/ Name Space

The following is a list of the `http://schemas.microsoft.com/exchange` **name space properties:**

- `http://schemas.microsoft.com/exchange/adminfolderdescription`
- `http://schemas.microsoft.com/exchange/companies`
- `http://schemas.microsoft.com/exchange/contentexpiryagelimit`
- `http://schemas.microsoft.com/exchange/contentstate`
- `http://schemas.microsoft.com/exchange/defaultrevision`
- `http://schemas.microsoft.com/exchange/deleteditemsagelimit`
- `http://schemas.microsoft.com/exchange/extensionattribute1`
- `http://schemas.microsoft.com/exchange/extensionattribute2`
- `http://schemas.microsoft.com/exchange/extensionattribute3`
- `http://schemas.microsoft.com/exchange/extensionattribute4`
- `http://schemas.microsoft.com/exchange/folderadmingroup`
- `http://schemas.microsoft.com/exchange/folderproxy`
- `http://schemas.microsoft.com/exchange/foldersize`

- ◆ http://schemas.microsoft.com/exchange/mid
- ◆ http://schemas.microsoft.com/exchange/mileage
- ◆ http://schemas.microsoft.com/exchange/noaging
- ◆ http://schemas.microsoft.com/exchange/ntsecuritydescriptor
- ◆ http://schemas.microsoft.com/exchange/permanenturl
- ◆ http://schemas.microsoft.com/exchange/
  replicationmessagepriority
- ◆ http://schemas.microsoft.com/exchange/replicationschedule
- ◆ http://schemas.microsoft.com/exchange/replicationstyle
- ◆ http://schemas.microsoft.com/exchange/searchfolder
- ◆ http://schemas.microsoft.com/exchange/sensitivity
- ◆ http://schemas.microsoft.com/exchange/yomifirstname
- ◆ http://schemas.microsoft.com/exchange/yomilastname
- ◆ http://schemas.microsoft.com/exchange/yomiorganization

The http://schemas.microsoft.com/exchange/events/ Name Space

The following is a list of the http://schemas.microsoft.com/exchange/events/ name space properties:

- ◆ http://schemas.microsoft.com/exchange/events/Criteria
- ◆ http://schemas.microsoft.com/exchange/events/Enabled
- ◆ http://schemas.microsoft.com/exchange/events/MatchScope
- ◆ http://schemas.microsoft.com/exchange/events/Priority
- ◆ http://schemas.microsoft.com/exchange/events/ScriptUrl
- ◆ http://schemas.microsoft.com/exchange/events/SinkClass
- ◆ http://schemas.microsoft.com/exchange/events/TimerExpiryTime
- ◆ http://schemas.microsoft.com/exchange/events/TimerInterval
- ◆ http://schemas.microsoft.com/exchange/events/TimerStartTime

The http://schemas.microsoft.com/ exchange/security/ Name Space

The following is a list of the `http://schemas.microsoft.com/exchange/security/` name space properties:

- `http://schemas.microsoft.com/exchange/security/creator`
- `http://schemas.microsoft.com/exchange/security/lastmodifier`
- `http://schemas.microsoft.com/exchange/security/originalauthor`
- `http://schemas.microsoft.com/exchange/security/originalsender`
- `http://schemas.microsoft.com/exchange/security/originalsentrepresenting`
- `http://schemas.microsoft.com/exchange/security/originator`
- `http://schemas.microsoft.com/exchange/security/readreceiptfrom`
- `http://schemas.microsoft.com/exchange/security/receivedby`
- `http://schemas.microsoft.com/exchange/security/receivedrepresenting`
- `http://schemas.microsoft.com/exchange/security/reportdestination`
- `http://schemas.microsoft.com/exchange/security/reportfrom`
- `http://schemas.microsoft.com/exchange/security/sender`
- `http://schemas.microsoft.com/exchange/security/sentrepresenting`
- `http://schemas.microsoft.com/exchange/security/admindescriptor`
- `http://schemas.microsoft.com/exchange/security/descriptor`

The http://schemas.microsoft.com/ mapi/ Name Space

The following is a list of the `http://schemas.microsoft.com/mapi/` name space properties.

The http://schemas.microsoft.com/mapi/id/ name space

◆ http://schemas.microsoft.com/mapi/proptag/value

The http://schemas.microsoft.com/mapi/string/ name space

◆ http://schemas.microsoft.com/mapi/id/{propset GUID}/*value*

The http://schemas.microsoft.com/mapi/proptag/ name space

◆ http://schemas.microsoft.com/mapi/string/{propset GUID}/name

The urn:schemas-microsoft-com: datatypes Name Space

The following is a list of the urn:schemas-microsoft-com:datatypes name space properties:

◆ urn:schemas-microsoft-com:datatypes#type

The urn:schemas-microsoft-com: exch-data: Name Space

The following is a list of the urn:schemas-microsoft-com:exch-data: name space properties:

◆ urn:schemas-microsoft-com:exch-data:baseschema

◆ urn:schemas-microsoft-com:exch-data:closedexpectedcontent-classes

◆ urn:schemas-microsoft-com:exch-data:codebase

◆ urn:schemas-microsoft-com:exch-data:comclassid

◆ urn:schemas-microsoft-com:exch-data:comprogid

◆ urn:schemas-microsoft-com:exch-data:default

- `urn:schemas-microsoft-com:exch-data:dictionary`
- `urn:schemas-microsoft-com:exch-data:expected-content-class`
- `urn:schemas-microsoft-com:exch-data:iscontentindexed`
- `urn:schemas-microsoft-com:exch-data:isindexed`
- `urn:schemas-microsoft-com:exch-data:ismultivalued`
- `urn:schemas-microsoft-com:exch-data:isreadonly`
- `urn:schemas-microsoft-com:exch-data:isrequired`
- `urn:schemas-microsoft-com:exch-data:isvisible`
- `urn:schemas-microsoft-com:exch-data:propertydef`
- `urn:schemas-microsoft-com:exch-data:schema-collection-ref`
- `urn:schemas-microsoft-com:exch-data:synchronize`
- `urn:schemas-microsoft-com:exch-data:version`

The urn:schemas-microsoft-com: xml-data Name Space

The following is a list of the `urn:schemas-microsoft-com:xml-data` name space properties:

- `urn:schemas-microsoft-com:xml-data#element`
- `urn:schemas-microsoft-com:xml-data#extends`
- `urn:schemas-microsoft-com:xml-data#name`

The urn:schemas-microsoft-com: office:office Name Space

The following is a list of the `urn:schemas-microsoft-com:office:office` name space properties.

- `urn:schemas-microsoft-com:office:office#Author`
- `urn:schemas-microsoft-com:office:office#Bytes`
- `urn:schemas-microsoft-com:office:office#Category`
- `urn:schemas-microsoft-com:office:office#Characters`

- ◆ urn:schemas-microsoft-com:office:office#Checked_x0020_by
- ◆ urn:schemas-microsoft-com:office:office#Client
- ◆ urn:schemas-microsoft-com:office:office#Comments
- ◆ urn:schemas-microsoft-com:office:office#Company
- ◆ urn:schemas-microsoft-com:office:office#Created
- ◆ urn:schemas-microsoft-com:office:office#Date_x0020_completed
- ◆ urn:schemas-microsoft-com:office:office#Department
- ◆ urn:schemas-microsoft-com:office:office#Destination
- ◆ urn:schemas-microsoft-com:office:office#Disposition
- ◆ urn:schemas-microsoft-com:office:office#Division
- ◆ urn:schemas-microsoft-com:office:office#Document_x0020_number
- ◆ urn:schemas-microsoft-com:office:office#Editor
- ◆ urn:schemas-microsoft-com:office:office#Forward_x0020_to
- ◆ urn:schemas-microsoft-com:office:office#Group
- ◆ urn:schemas-microsoft-com:office:office#HeadingPairs
- ◆ urn:schemas-microsoft-com:office:office#HiddenSlides
- ◆ urn:schemas-microsoft-com:office:office#Keywords
- ◆ urn:schemas-microsoft-com:office:office#Language
- ◆ urn:schemas-microsoft-com:office:office#LastAuthor
- ◆ urn:schemas-microsoft-com:office:office#LastPrinted
- ◆ urn:schemas-microsoft-com:office:office#LastSaved
- ◆ urn:schemas-microsoft-com:office:office#Lines
- ◆ urn:schemas-microsoft-com:office:office#LinksUpToDate
- ◆ urn:schemas-microsoft-com:office:office#MailStop
- ◆ urn:schemas-microsoft-com:office:office#Manager
- ◆ urn:schemas-microsoft-com:office:office#Matter
- ◆ urn:schemas-microsoft-com:office:office#MultimediaClips
- ◆ urn:schemas-microsoft-com:office:office#NameOfApplication
- ◆ urn:schemas-microsoft-com:office:office#Notes

- `urn:schemas-microsoft-com:office:office#Office`
- `urn:schemas-microsoft-com:office:office#Owner`
- `urn:schemas-microsoft-com:office:office#Pages`
- `urn:schemas-microsoft-com:office:office#Paragraphs`
- `urn:schemas-microsoft-com:office:office#PartTitles`
- `urn:schemas-microsoft-com:office:office#PresentationFormat`
- `urn:schemas-microsoft-com:office:office#Project`
- `urn:schemas-microsoft-com:office:office#Publisher`
- `urn:schemas-microsoft-com:office:office#Purpose`
- `urn:schemas-microsoft-com:office:office#Received`
- `urn:schemas-microsoft-com:office:office#Recorded`
- `urn:schemas-microsoft-com:office:office#Recorded_x0020_date`
- `urn:schemas-microsoft-com:office:office#Reference`
- `urn:schemas-microsoft-com:office:office#Revision`
- `urn:schemas-microsoft-com:office:office#ScaleCrop`
- `urn:schemas-microsoft-com:office:office#Security`
- `urn:schemas-microsoft-com:office:office#Slides`
- `urn:schemas-microsoft-com:office:office#Source`
- `urn:schemas-microsoft-com:office:office#Status`
- `urn:schemas-microsoft-com:office:office#Subject`
- `urn:schemas-microsoft-com:office:office#Telephone_x0020_number`
- `urn:schemas-microsoft-com:office:office#Template`
- `urn:schemas-microsoft-com:office:office#ThumbNail`
- `urn:schemas-microsoft-com:office:office#Title`
- `urn:schemas-microsoft-com:office:office#TotalTime`
- `urn:schemas-microsoft-com:office:office#Typist`
- `urn:schemas-microsoft-com:office:office#Version`
- `urn:schemas-microsoft-com:office:office#Words`

The urn:schemas-microsoft-com: office:forms Name Space

The following is a list of the urn:schemas-microsoft-com:office:forms name space properties:

- urn:schemas-microsoft-com:office:forms#binding
- urn:schemas-microsoft-com:office:forms#browser
- urn:schemas-microsoft-com:office:forms#cmd
- urn:schemas-microsoft-com:office:forms#contentclass
- urn:schemas-microsoft-com:office:forms#contentstate
- urn:schemas-microsoft-com:office:forms#executeparameters
- urn:schemas-microsoft-com:office:forms#executeurl
- urn:schemas-microsoft-com:office:forms#formurl
- urn:schemas-microsoft-com:office:forms#language
- urn:schemas-microsoft-com:office:forms#majorver
- urn:schemas-microsoft-com:office:forms#messagestate
- urn:schemas-microsoft-com:office:forms#minorver
- urn:schemas-microsoft-com:office:forms#platform
- urn:schemas-microsoft-com:office:forms#request
- urn:schemas-microsoft-com:office:forms#version

The urn:schemas:calendar: Name Space

The following is a list of the urn:schemas:calendar: name space properties:

- urn:schemas:calendar:alldayevent
- urn:schemas:calendar:busystatus
- urn:schemas:calendar:contact
- urn:schemas:calendar:contacturl
- urn:schemas:calendar:created

- urn:schemas:calendar:descriptionurl
- urn:schemas:calendar:dtend
- urn:schemas:calendar:dtstamp
- urn:schemas:calendar:dtstart
- urn:schemas:calendar:duration
- urn:schemas:calendar:exdate
- **urn**:schemas:calendar:exrule
- urn:schemas:calendar:fburl
- urn:schemas:calendar:geolatitude
- urn:schemas:calendar:geolongitude
- urn:schemas:calendar:instancetype
- urn:schemas:calendar:lastmodified
- urn:schemas:calendar:location
- urn:schemas:calendar:locationurl
- urn:schemas:calendar:meetingstatus
- urn:schemas:calendar:method
- urn:schemas:calendar:rdate
- urn:schemas:calendar:recurrenceid
- urn:schemas:calendar:recurrenceidrange
- urn:schemas:calendar:reminderoffset
- urn:schemas:calendar:replytime
- urn:schemas:calendar:resources
- urn:schemas:calendar:responserequested
- urn:schemas:calendar:rrule
- urn:schemas:calendar:sequence
- urn:schemas:calendar:timezone
- urn:schemas:calendar:timezoneid
- urn:schemas:calendar:transparent
- **urn**:schemas:calendar:uid

The urn:schemas:contacts: Name Space

The following is a list of the urn:schemas:contacts: name space properties:

- urn:schemas:contacts:account
- urn:schemas:contacts:bday
- urn:schemas:contacts:billinginformation
- urn:schemas:contacts:businesshomepage
- urn:schemas:contacts:c
- urn:schemas:contacts:callbackphone
- urn:schemas:contacts:children
- urn:schemas:contacts:childrensnames
- urn:schemas:contacts:cn
- urn:schemas:contacts:co
- urn:schemas:contacts:computernetworkname
- urn:schemas:contacts:customerid
- urn:schemas:contacts:department
- urn:schemas:contacts:dn
- urn:schemas:contacts:email1
- urn:schemas:contacts:email2
- urn:schemas:contacts:email3
- urn:schemas:contacts:employeenumber
- urn:schemas:contacts:facsimiletelephonenumber
- urn:schemas:contacts:fileas
- urn:schemas:contacts:fileasid
- urn:schemas:contacts:ftpsite
- urn:schemas:contacts:gender
- urn:schemas:contacts:givenName
- urn:schemas:contacts:governmentid
- urn:schemas:contacts:hobbies

- urn:schemas:contacts:homeCity
- urn:schemas:contacts:homeCountry
- urn:schemas:contacts:homefax
- urn:schemas:contacts:homelatitude
- urn:schemas:contacts:homelongitude
- urn:schemas:contacts:homePhone
- urn:schemas:contacts:homephone2
- urn:schemas:contacts:homepostaladdress
- urn:schemas:contacts:homePostalCode
- urn:schemas:contacts:homepostofficebox
- urn:schemas:contacts:homeState
- urn:schemas:contacts:homeStreet
- urn:schemas:contacts:hometimezone
- urn:schemas:contacts:initials
- urn:schemas:contacts:internationalisdnnumber
- urn:schemas:contacts:l
- urn:schemas:contacts:language
- urn:schemas:contacts:location
- urn:schemas:contacts:mailingaddressid
- urn:schemas:contacts:mailingcity
- urn:schemas:contacts:mailingcountry
- urn:schemas:contacts:mailingpostaladdress
- urn:schemas:contacts:mailingpostalcode
- urn:schemas:contacts:mailingpostofficebox
- urn:schemas:contacts:mailingstate
- urn:schemas:contacts:mailingstreet
- urn:schemas:contacts:manager
- urn:schemas:contacts:mapurl
- urn:schemas:contacts:middlename
- urn:schemas:contacts:mobile

- urn:schemas:contacts:namesuffix
- urn:schemas:contacts:nickname
- urn:schemas:contacts:o
- urn:schemas:contacts:office2telephonenumber
- urn:schemas:contacts:officetelephonenumber
- urn:schemas:contacts:organizationmainphone
- urn:schemas:contacts:othercity
- urn:schemas:contacts:othercountry
- urn:schemas:contacts:othercountrycode
- urn:schemas:contacts:otherfax
- urn:schemas:contacts:othermobile
- urn:schemas:contacts:otherpager
- urn:schemas:contacts:otherpostaladdress
- urn:schemas:contacts:otherpostalcode
- urn:schemas:contacts:otherpostofficebox
- urn:schemas:contacts:otherstate
- urn:schemas:contacts:otherstreet
- urn:schemas:contacts:otherTelephone
- urn:schemas:contacts:othertimezone
- urn:schemas:contacts:pager
- urn:schemas:contacts:personalHomePage
- urn:schemas:contacts:personaltitle
- urn:schemas:contacts:postalcode
- urn:schemas:contacts:postofficebox
- urn:schemas:contacts:profession
- urn:schemas:contacts:proxyaddresses
- urn:schemas:contacts:referredby
- urn:schemas:contacts:roomnumber
- urn:schemas:contacts:secretarycn
- urn:schemas:contacts:secretaryphone

- urn:schemas:contacts:secretaryurl

- urn:schemas:contacts:sn

- urn:schemas:contacts:sourceurl

- urn:schemas:contacts:spousecn

- urn:schemas:contacts:st

- urn:schemas:contacts:street

- urn:schemas:contacts:telephoneNumber

- urn:schemas:contacts:telephonenumber2

- urn:schemas:contacts:telexnumber

- urn:schemas:contacts:title

- urn:schemas:contacts:ttytddphone

- urn:schemas:contacts:usercertificate

- urn:schemas:contacts:weddinganniversary

- urn:schemas:contacts:workaddress

The urn:schemas:httpmail: Name Space

The following is a list of the urn:schemas:httpmail: name space properties:

- urn:schemas:httpmail:attachmentfilename

- urn:schemas:httpmail:bcc

- urn:schemas:httpmail:cc

- urn:schemas:httpmail:content-disposition-type

- urn:schemas:httpmail:content-media-type

- urn:schemas:httpmail:date

- urn:schemas:httpmail:datereceived

- urn:schemas:httpmail:displaycc

- urn:schemas:httpmail:displayto

- urn:schemas:httpmail:expiry-date

- urn:schemas:httpmail:flagcompleted

- urn:schemas:httpmail:from
- urn:schemas:httpmail:fromemail
- urn:schemas:httpmail:fromname
- urn:schemas:httpmail:hasattachment
- urn:schemas:httpmail:htmldescription
- urn:schemas:httpmail:importance
- urn:schemas:httpmail:messageflag
- urn:schemas:httpmail:normalizedsubject
- urn:schemas:httpmail:outbox
- urn:schemas:httpmail:priority
- urn:schemas:httpmail:read
- urn:schemas:httpmail:reply-by
- urn:schemas:httpmail:reply-to
- urn:schemas:httpmail:savedestination
- urn:schemas:httpmail:saveinsent
- urn:schemas:httpmail:sender
- urn:schemas:httpmail:senderemail
- urn:schemas:httpmail:sendername
- urn:schemas:httpmail:special
- urn:schemas:httpmail:subject
- urn:schemas:httpmail:submitted
- urn:schemas:httpmail:textdescription
- urn:schemas:httpmail:thread-topic
- **urn**:schemas:httpmail:to
- urn:schemas:httpmail:unreadcount

The urn:schemas:mailheader: Name Space

The following is a list of the urn:schemas:mailheader: name space properties:

- urn:schemas:mailheader:approved
- urn:schemas:mailheader:bcc
- urn:schemas:mailheader:cc
- urn:schemas:mailheader:comment
- urn:schemas:mailheader:content-base
- urn:schemas:mailheader:content-class
- urn:schemas:mailheader:content-description
- urn:schemas:mailheader:content-disposition
- urn:schemas:mailheader:content-id
- urn:schemas:mailheader:content-language
- urn:schemas:mailheader:content-location
- urn:schemas:mailheader:content-transfer-encoding
- urn:schemas:mailheader:content-type
- urn:schemas:mailheader:control
- urn:schemas:mailheader:date
- urn:schemas:mailheader:disposition
- urn:schemas:mailheader:disposition-notification-to
- urn:schemas:mailheader:distribution
- urn:schemas:mailheader:expires
- urn:schemas:mailheader:expiry-date
- urn:schemas:mailheader:followup-to
- urn:schemas:mailheader:from
- urn:schemas:mailheader:importance
- urn:schemas:mailheader:in-reply-to
- urn:schemas:mailheader:keywords
- urn:schemas:mailheader:lines
- urn:schemas:mailheader:message-id
- urn:schemas:mailheader:mime-version
- urn:schemas:mailheader:newsgroups
- urn:schemas:mailheader:organization

- ◆ urn:schemas:mailheader:original-recipient
- ◆ urn:schemas:mailheader:path
- ◆ urn:schemas:mailheader:posting-version
- ◆ urn:schemas:mailheader:priority
- ◆ urn:schemas:mailheader:received
- ◆ urn:schemas:mailheader:references
- ◆ urn:schemas:mailheader:relay-version
- ◆ urn:schemas:mailheader:reply-by
- ◆ urn:schemas:mailheader:reply-to
- ◆ urn:schemas:mailheader:return-path
- ◆ urn:schemas:mailheader:return-receipt-to
- ◆ urn:schemas:mailheader:sender
- ◆ urn:schemas:mailheader:sensitivity
- ◆ urn:schemas:mailheader:subject
- ◆ urn:schemas:mailheader:summary
- ◆ urn:schemas:mailheader:thread-index
- ◆ urn:schemas:mailheader:thread-topic
- ◆ urn:schemas:mailheader:to
- ◆ urn:schemas:mailheader:x-mailer
- ◆ urn:schemas:mailheader:x-message-completed
- ◆ urn:schemas:mailheader:x-message-flag
- ◆ urn:schemas:mailheader:xref
- ◆ urn:schemas:mailheader:x-unsent

Non-Searchable Properties

The following properties cannot be searched because their values are only calculated when used and are not persisted in the Web Storage System:

- ◆ DAV:getetag
- ◆ DAV:href
- ◆ DAV:lockdiscovery

- DAV:parentname

- DAV:resourcetype

- DAV:searchrequest

- http://schemas.microsoft.com/exchange/content-href

- http://schemas.microsoft.com/exchange/ntsecuritydescriptor

- http://schemas.microsoft.com/exchange/oof-state

- http://schemas.microsoft.com/exchange/publicfolderemailaddress

- http://schemas.microsoft.com/repl/repl-uid

- http://schemas.microsoft.com/repl/resourcetag

- urn:schemas:contacts:proxyaddresses

- urn:schemas:httpmail:htmldescription

- urn:schemas:httpmail:subject

- urn:schemas:mailheader:subject

- urn:schemas-microsoft-com:exch-data:baseschema

- urn:schemas-microsoft-com:exch-data:schema-collection-ref

Appendix C

Web Storage System Content Classes

EXCHANGE DEFINES a number of content classes. The following appendix lists the predefined content classes and the associated name-space properties. For further information on any property of content class, please refer to the Microsoft Documentation at http://msdn.microsoft.com.

urn:content-classes:appointment

The urn:content-classes:appointment content class defines properties for items that are appointments. The following list defines the extended content-class, expected content-class, and associated properties if applicable.

Extends Content Class

- urn:content-classes:item

Properties

- http://schemas.microsoft.com/exchange/companies
- http://schemas.microsoft.com/exchange/mileage
- http://schemas.microsoft.com/exchange/sensitivity
- urn:schemas:calendar:alldayevent
- urn:schemas:calendar:busystatus
- urn:schemas:calendar:contact
- urn:schemas:calendar:contacturl
- urn:schemas:calendar:created
- urn:schemas:calendar:descriptionurl
- urn:schemas:calendar:dtend
- urn:schemas:calendar:dtstamp
- urn:schemas:calendar:dtstart

- urn:schemas:calendar:duration
- urn:schemas:calendar:exdate
- urn:schemas:calendar:exrule
- urn:schemas:calendar:geolatitude
- urn:schemas:calendar:geolongitude
- urn:schemas:calendar:instancetype
- urn:schemas:calendar:lastmodified
- urn:schemas:calendar:location
- urn:schemas:calendar:locationurl
- urn:schemas:calendar:meetingstatus
- urn:schemas:calendar:method
- urn:schemas:calendar:rdate
- urn:schemas:calendar:recurrenceid
- urn:schemas:calendar:recurrenceidrange
- urn:schemas:calendar:reminderoffset
- urn:schemas:calendar:replytime
- urn:schemas:calendar:resources
- urn:schemas:calendar:responserequested
- urn:schemas:calendar:rrule
- urn:schemas:calendar:sequence
- urn:schemas:calendar:timezone
- urn:schemas:calendar:timezoneid
- urn:schemas:calendar:transparent
- urn:schemas:calendar:uid
- urn:schemas:contacts:billinginformation
- urn:schemas:httpmail:hasattachment
- urn:schemas:httpmail:htmldescription
- urn:schemas:httpmail:normalizedsubject
- urn:schemas:httpmail:priority
- urn:schemas:httpmail:subject
- urn:schemas:httpmail:textdescription

urn:content-classes:calendarfolder

The `urn:content-classes:calendarfolder` content class defines a set of properties for a folder that primarily contains appointment items. The following list defines the extended content-class, expected content-class and associated properties if applicable.

Extends Content Class

- urn:content-classes:folder

Expected Content Class

- urn:content-classes:appointment

urn:content-classes:calendarmessage

The `urn:content-classes:calendarmessage` content class defines a set of properties for message items that contain meeting requests. The following list defines the extended content-class, expected content-class and associated properties if applicable.

Extends Content Class

- urn:content-classes:message

Properties

- urn:schemas:calendar:method

urn:content-classes:contactfolder

The `urn:content-classes:contactfolder` content class defines a set of properties for a folder that primarily contains contact items. The following list defines the extended content-class, expected content-class and associated properties if applicable.

Extends Content Class

- urn:content-classes:folder

Expected Content Class

- urn:content-classes:person

urn:content-classes:contentclassdef

The `urn:content-classes:contentclassdef` content class defines a set of properties for an item that defines a content class for the Exchange store schema. The following list defines the extended content-class, expected content-class and associated properties if applicable.

Extends Content Class

- `urn:schemas-microsoft-com:xml-data#ElementType`

Properties

- `urn:schemas-microsoft-com:exch-data:closedexpectedcontent-classes`
- `urn:schemas-microsoft-com:exch-data:codebase`
- `urn:schemas-microsoft-com:exch-data:comclassid`
- `urn:schemas-microsoft-com:exch-data:comprogid`
- `urn:schemas-microsoft-com:xml-data#element`
- `urn:schemas-microsoft-com:exch-data:expected-content-class`
- `urn:schemas-microsoft-com:exch-data:version`

urn:content-classes:document

The `urn:content-classes:document` content class defines a set of properties for an item that is a document, such as a Microsoft Word file. The following list defines the extended content-class, expected content-class and associated properties if applicable.

Extends Content Class

- `urn:content-classes:item`

Properties

- `urn:schemas-microsoft-com:office:office#Author`
- `urn:schemas-microsoft-com:office:office#Bytes`
- `urn:schemas-microsoft-com:office:office#Category`
- `urn:schemas-microsoft-com:office:office#Characters`

- urn:schemas-microsoft-com:office:office#Checked_x0020_by
- urn:schemas-microsoft-com:office:office#Client
- urn:schemas-microsoft-com:office:office#Comments
- urn:schemas-microsoft-com:office:office#Company
- urn:schemas-microsoft-com:office:office#Created
- urn:schemas-microsoft-com:office:office#Date_x0020_completed
- urn:schemas-microsoft-com:office:office#Department
- urn:schemas-microsoft-com:office:office#Destination
- urn:schemas-microsoft-com:office:office#Disposition
- urn:schemas-microsoft-com:office:office#Division
- urn:schemas-microsoft-com:office:office#Document_x0020_number
- urn:schemas-microsoft-com:office:office#Editor
- urn:schemas-microsoft-com:office:office#Forward_x0020_to
- urn:schemas-microsoft-com:office:office#Group
- urn:schemas-microsoft-com:office:office#HeadingPairs
- urn:schemas-microsoft-com:office:office#HiddenSlides
- urn:schemas-microsoft-com:office:office#Language
- urn:schemas-microsoft-com:office:office#LastAuthor
- urn:schemas-microsoft-com:office:office#LastPrinted
- urn:schemas-microsoft-com:office:office#LastSaved
- urn:schemas-microsoft-com:office:office#Lines
- urn:schemas-microsoft-com:office:office#LinksUpToDate
- urn:schemas-microsoft-com:office:office#MailStop
- urn:schemas-microsoft-com:office:office#Manager
- urn:schemas-microsoft-com:office:office#Matter
- urn:schemas-microsoft-com:office:office#MultimediaClips
- urn:schemas-microsoft-com:office:office#NameOfApplication
- urn:schemas-microsoft-com:office:office#Notes
- urn:schemas-microsoft-com:office:office#Office
- urn:schemas-microsoft-com:office:office#Owner

- urn:schemas-microsoft-com:office:office#Pages
- urn:schemas-microsoft-com:office:office#Paragraphs
- urn:schemas-microsoft-com:office:office#PartTitles
- urn:schemas-microsoft-com:office:office#PresentationFormat
- urn:schemas-microsoft-com:office:office#Project
- urn:schemas-microsoft-com:office:office#Publisher
- urn:schemas-microsoft-com:office:office#Purpose
- urn:schemas-microsoft-com:office:office#Received
- urn:schemas-microsoft-com:office:office#Recorded
- urn:schemas-microsoft-com:office:office#Recorded_x0020_date
- urn:schemas-microsoft-com:office:office#Reference
- urn:schemas-microsoft-com:office:office#Revision
- urn:schemas-microsoft-com:office:office#ScaleCrop
- urn:schemas-microsoft-com:office:office#Security
- urn:schemas-microsoft-com:office:office#Slides
- urn:schemas-microsoft-com:office:office#Source
- urn:schemas-microsoft-com:office:office#Status
- urn:schemas-microsoft-com:office:office#Subject
- urn:schemas-microsoft-com:office:office#Telephone_x0020_number
- urn:schemas-microsoft-com:office:office#Template
- urn:schemas-microsoft-com:office:office#ThumbNail
- urn:schemas-microsoft-com:office:office#Title
- urn:schemas-microsoft-com:office:office#TotalTime
- urn:schemas-microsoft-com:office:office#Typist
- urn:schemas-microsoft-com:office:office#Version
- urn:schemas-microsoft-com:office:office#Words

urn:content-classes:dsn

The urn:content-classes:dsn content class defines a set of properties for an item that is a Delivery Status Notification (DSN) message. The following list defines the extended content-class, expected content-class and associated properties if applicable.

Extends Content Class

◆ urn:content-classes:reportmessage

urn:content-classes:folder

The urn:content-classes:folder content class defines a set of properties for a folder in the Exchange store. The following list defines the extended content-class, expected content-class and associated properties if applicable.

Extends Content Class

◆ urn:content-classes:item

Properties

◆ DAV:searchrequest

◆ DAV:searchtype

◆ http://schemas.microsoft.com/exchange/adminfolderdescription

◆ http://schemas.microsoft.com/exchange/contentexpiryagelimit

◆ http://schemas.microsoft.com/exchange/deleteditemsagelimit

◆ http://schemas.microsoft.com/exchange/folderadmingroup

◆ http://schemas.microsoft.com/exchange/folderproxy

◆ http://schemas.microsoft.com/exchange/foldersize

◆ http://schemas.microsoft.com/exchange/replicationmessagepriority

◆ http://schemas.microsoft.com/exchange/replicationschedule

◆ http://schemas.microsoft.com/exchange/replicationstyle

◆ urn:content-classes:item

◆ urn:schemas:httpmail:special

◆ urn:schemas:httpmail:unreadcount

◆ urn:schemas-microsoft-com:exch-data:baseschema

◆ urn:schemas-microsoft-com:exch-data:expected-content-class

Expected Content Class

- `urn:content-classes:item`
- `urn:content-classes:folder`

urn:content-classes:freebusy

The `urn:content-classes:freebusy` content class defines a set of properties for an item that contains Free/Busy information. The following list defines the extended content-class, expected content-class and associated properties if applicable.

Extends Content Class

- `urn:content-classes:item`

urn:content-classes:item

The `urn:content-classes:item` content class defines a set of properties for an item in the Exchange store. The following list defines the extended content-class, expected content-class and associated properties if applicable.

Extends Content Class

- `urn:content-classes:object`

Properties

- `http://schemas.microsoft.com/mapi/proptag/0x001A001F`
- `DAV:abstract`
- `DAV:autoversion`
- `DAV:checkintime`
- `DAV:childautoversioning`
- `DAV:childcount`
- `DAV:childversioning`
- `DAV:comment`
- `DAV:contentclass`
- `http://schemas.microsoft.com/exchange/contentstate`

- http://schemas.microsoft.com/repl/contenttag
- DAV:creationdate
- DAV:defaultdocument
- http://schemas.microsoft.com/exchange/defaultrevision
- DAV:displayname
- urn:schemas:httpmail:expiry-date
- DAV:getcontentlanguage
- DAV:getcontentlength
- DAV:getcontenttype
- DAV:getetag
- DAV:getlastmodified
- DAV:haschildren
- DAV:hassubs
- DAV:href
- DAV:id
- DAV:iscollection
- DAV:isfolder
- DAV:ishidden
- DAV:isreadonly
- DAV:isroot
- DAV:isstructureddocument
- DAV:isversioned
- urn:schemas-microsoft-com:office:office#Keywords
- DAV:lastaccessed
- DAV:lockdiscovery
- DAV:mergedfrom
- http://schemas.microsoft.com/exchange/mid
- http://schemas.microsoft.com/exchange/noaging
- DAV:nosubs
- http://schemas.microsoft.com/exchange/ntsecuritydescriptor

- DAV:objectcount

- DAV:parentname

- http://schemas.microsoft.com/exchange/permanenturl

- urn:schemas:httpmail:read

- http://schemas.microsoft.com/repl/resourcetag

- DAV:resourcetype

- DAV:revisioncomment

- DAV:revisionid

- DAV:revisionlabel

- DAV:revisionuri

- DAV:supportedlock

- http://schemas.microsoft.com/repl/uid

- DAV:uid

- DAV:visiblecount

- DAV:vresourceid

urn:content-classes:journalfolder

The urn:content-classes:journalfolder content class defines a set of properties for a folder that primarily contains journal items. The following list defines
the extended content-class, expected content-class and associated properties if
applicable.

Extends Content Class

- urn:content-classes:folder

Expected Content Class

- urn:content-classes:item
- urn:content-classes:folder

urn:content-classes:mailfolder

The urn:content-classes:mailfolder content class defines a set of properties
for a folder that primarily contains messages. The following list defines the

extended content-class, expected content-class and associated properties if applicable.

Extends Content Class

◆ urn:content-classes:folder

Expected Content Class

◆ urn:content-classes:message

◆ urn:content-classes:calendarmessage

urn:content-classes:mdn

The urn:content-classes:mdn content class defines a set of properties for an item that is a Mail Delivery Notification (MDN) message. The following list defines the extended content-class, expected content-class and associated properties if applicable.

Extends Content Class

◆ urn:content-classes:reportmessage

urn:content-classes:message

The urn:content-classes:message content class defines a set of properties for an item that is a message. The following list defines the extended content-class, expected content-class and associated properties if applicable.

Extends Content Class

◆ urn:content-classes:item

Properties

◆ urn:schemas:mailheader:approved

◆ urn:schemas:httpmail:attachmentfilename

◆ urn:schemas:mailheader:bcc

◆ urn:schemas:httpmail:bcc

◆ urn:schemas:httpmail:cc

- ◆ urn:schemas:mailheader:cc
- ◆ urn:schemas:mailheader:comment
- ◆ urn:schemas:mailheader:content-base
- ◆ urn:schemas:mailheader:content-class
- ◆ urn:schemas:mailheader:content-description
- ◆ urn:schemas:mailheader:content-disposition
- ◆ urn:schemas:httpmail:content-disposition-type
- ◆ urn:schemas:mailheader:content-id
- ◆ urn:schemas:mailheader:content-language
- ◆ urn:schemas:mailheader:content-location
- ◆ urn:schemas:httpmail:content-media-type
- ◆ urn:schemas:mailheader:content-transfer-encoding
- ◆ urn:schemas:mailheader:content-type
- ◆ urn:schemas:mailheader:control
- ◆ urn:schemas:httpmail:date
- ◆ urn:schemas:mailheader:date
- ◆ urn:schemas:httpmail:datereceived
- ◆ urn:schemas:httpmail:displaycc
- ◆ urn:schemas:httpmail:displayto
- ◆ urn:schemas:mailheader:disposition
- ◆ urn:schemas:mailheader:disposition-notification-to
- ◆ urn:schemas:mailheader:distribution
- ◆ urn:schemas:mailheader:expires
- ◆ urn:schemas:mailheader:expiry-date
- ◆ urn:schemas:httpmail:flagcompleted
- ◆ urn:schemas:mailheader:followup-to
- ◆ urn:schemas:httpmail:from
- ◆ urn:schemas:mailheader:from
- ◆ urn:schemas:httpmail:fromemail
- ◆ urn:schemas:httpmail:fromname

- ◆ urn:schemas:httpmail:hasattachment
- ◆ urn:schemas:httpmail:htmldescription
- ◆ urn:schemas:httpmail:importance
- ◆ urn:schemas:mailheader:importance
- ◆ urn:schemas:mailheader:in-reply-to
- ◆ urn:schemas:mailheader:keywords
- ◆ urn:schemas:mailheader:lines
- ◆ urn:schemas:mailheader:message-id
- ◆ urn:schemas:httpmail:messageflag
- ◆ urn:schemas:mailheader:mime-version
- ◆ urn:schemas:mailheader:newsgroups
- ◆ urn:schemas:httpmail:normalizedsubject
- ◆ urn:schemas:mailheader:organization
- ◆ urn:schemas:mailheader:original-recipient
- ◆ urn:schemas:mailheader:path
- ◆ urn:schemas:mailheader:posting-version
- ◆ urn:schemas:httpmail:priority
- ◆ urn:schemas:mailheader:priority
- ◆ urn:schemas:mailheader:received
- ◆ urn:schemas:mailheader:references
- ◆ urn:schemas:mailheader:relay-version
- ◆ urn:schemas:httpmail:reply-by
- ◆ urn:schemas:mailheader:reply-by
- ◆ urn:schemas:httpmail:reply-to
- ◆ urn:schemas:mailheader:reply-to
- ◆ urn:schemas:mailheader:return-path
- ◆ urn:schemas:mailheader:return-receipt-to
- ◆ urn:schemas:httpmail:savedestination
- ◆ urn:schemas:httpmail:saveinsent
- ◆ urn:schemas:mailheader:sender

- ◆ urn:schemas:httpmail:sender

- ◆ urn:schemas:httpmail:senderemail

- ◆ urn:schemas:httpmail:sendername

- ◆ http://schemas.microsoft.com/exchange/sensitivity

- ◆ urn:schemas:mailheader:sensitivity

- ◆ urn:schemas:httpmail:subject

- ◆ urn:schemas:mailheader:subject

- ◆ urn:schemas:httpmail:submitted

- ◆ urn:schemas:mailheader:summary

- ◆ urn:schemas:httpmail:textdescription

- ◆ urn:schemas:mailheader:thread-index

- ◆ urn:schemas:mailheader:thread-topic

- ◆ urn:schemas:httpmail:thread-topic

- ◆ urn:schemas:httpmail:to

- ◆ urn:schemas:mailheader:to

- ◆ urn:schemas:mailheader:x-mailer

- ◆ urn:schemas:mailheader:x-message-completed

- ◆ urn:schemas:mailheader:x-message-flag

- ◆ urn:schemas:mailheader:x-unsent

- ◆ urn:schemas:mailheader:xref

urn:content-classes:notesfolder

The urn:content-classes:notesfolder content class defines a set of properties for a folder that primarily contains note items. The following list defines the extended content-class, expected content-class and associated properties if applicable.

Extends Content Class

- ◆ urn:content-classes:folder

Expected Content Class

◆ `urn:content-classes:item`

◆ `urn:content-classes:folder`

urn:content-classes:object

The `urn:content-classes:object` content class defines a property for a base object in the Exchange store. The following list defines the extended content-class, expected content-class and associated properties if applicable.

Properties

◆ `urn:schemas-microsoft-com:exch-data:schema-collection-ref`

urn:content-classes:person

The `urn:content-classes:person` content class defines a set of properties for an item that is a contact. The following list defines the extended content-class, expected content-class and associated properties if applicable.

Extends Content Class

◆ `urn:content-classes:item`

Properties

◆ `urn:schemas:contacts:account`

◆ `urn:schemas:contacts:bday`

◆ `urn:schemas:contacts:billinginformation`

◆ `urn:schemas:contacts:businesshomepage`

◆ `urn:schemas:contacts:c`

◆ `urn:schemas:contacts:callbackphone`

◆ `urn:schemas:contacts:children`

◆ `urn:schemas:contacts:childrensnames`

◆ `urn:schemas:contacts:cn`

◆ `urn:schemas:contacts:co`

- http://schemas.microsoft.com/exchange/companies
- urn:schemas:contacts:computernetworkname
- urn:schemas:contacts:customerid
- urn:schemas:contacts:department
- urn:schemas:contacts:dn
- urn:schemas:contacts:email1
- urn:schemas:contacts:email2
- urn:schemas:contacts:email3
- urn:schemas:contacts:employeenumber
- http://schemas.microsoft.com/exchange/extensionattribute1
- http://schemas.microsoft.com/exchange/extensionattribute2
- http://schemas.microsoft.com/exchange/extensionattribute3
- http://schemas.microsoft.com/exchange/extensionattribute4
- urn:schemas:contacts:facsimiletelephonenumber
- urn:schemas:calendar:fburl
- urn:schemas:contacts:fileas
- urn:schemas:contacts:fileasid
- urn:schemas:contacts:ftpsite
- urn:schemas:contacts:gender
- urn:schemas:calendar:geolatitude
- urn:schemas:calendar:geolongitude
- urn:schemas:contacts:givenName
- urn:schemas:contacts:governmentid
- urn:schemas:httpmail:hasattachment
- urn:schemas:contacts:hobbies
- urn:schemas:contacts:homeCity
- urn:schemas:contacts:homeCountry
- urn:schemas:contacts:homefax
- urn:schemas:contacts:homelatitude
- urn:schemas:contacts:homelongitude

- urn:schemas:contacts:homePhone
- urn:schemas:contacts:homephone2
- urn:schemas:contacts:homepostaladdress
- urn:schemas:contacts:homePostalCode
- urn:schemas:contacts:homepostofficebox
- urn:schemas:contacts:homeState
- urn:schemas:contacts:homeStreet
- urn:schemas:contacts:hometimezone
- urn:schemas:httpmail:htmldescription
- urn:schemas:contacts:initials
- urn:schemas:contacts:internationalisdnnumber
- urn:schemas:contacts:l
- urn:schemas:contacts:language
- urn:schemas:contacts:location
- urn:schemas:contacts:mailingaddressid
- urn:schemas:contacts:mailingcity
- urn:schemas:contacts:mailingcountry
- urn:schemas:contacts:mailingpostaladdress
- urn:schemas:contacts:mailingpostalcode
- urn:schemas:contacts:mailingpostofficebox
- urn:schemas:contacts:mailingstate
- urn:schemas:contacts:mailingstreet
- urn:schemas:contacts:manager
- urn:schemas:contacts:mapurl
- urn:schemas:contacts:middlename
- http://schemas.microsoft.com/exchange/mileage
- urn:schemas:contacts:mobile
- urn:schemas:contacts:namesuffix
- urn:schemas:contacts:nickname
- urn:schemas:contacts:o

- urn:schemas:contacts:office2telephonenumber
- urn:schemas:contacts:officetelephonenumber
- urn:schemas:contacts:organizationmainphone
- urn:schemas:contacts:othercity
- urn:schemas:contacts:othercountry
- urn:schemas:contacts:othercountrycode
- urn:schemas:contacts:otherfax
- urn:schemas:contacts:othermobile
- urn:schemas:contacts:otherpager
- urn:schemas:contacts:otherpostaladdress
- urn:schemas:contacts:otherpostalcode
- urn:schemas:contacts:otherpostofficebox
- urn:schemas:contacts:otherstate
- urn:schemas:contacts:otherstreet
- urn:schemas:contacts:otherTelephone
- urn:schemas:contacts:othertimezone
- urn:schemas:httpmail:outbox
- urn:schemas:contacts:pager
- urn:schemas:contacts:personalHomePage
- urn:schemas:contacts:personaltitle
- urn:schemas:contacts:postalcode
- urn:schemas:contacts:postofficebox
- urn:schemas:contacts:profession
- urn:schemas:contacts:proxyaddresses
- urn:schemas:contacts:referredby
- urn:schemas:contacts:roomnumber
- http://schemas.microsoft.com/exchange/searchfolder
- urn:schemas:contacts:secretarycn
- urn:schemas:contacts:secretaryphone
- urn:schemas:contacts:secretaryurl

- urn:schemas:contacts:sn

- urn:schemas:contacts:sourceurl

- urn:schemas:contacts:spousecn

- urn:schemas:contacts:st

- urn:schemas:contacts:street

- urn:schemas:mailheader:subject

- urn:schemas:httpmail:subject

- urn:schemas:contacts:telephoneNumber

- urn:schemas:contacts:telephonenumber2

- urn:schemas:contacts:telexnumber

- urn:schemas:httpmail:textdescription

- urn:schemas:contacts:title

- urn:schemas:contacts:ttytddphone

- urn:schemas:contacts:usercertificate

- urn:schemas:contacts:weddinganniversary

- urn:schemas:contacts:workaddress

- http://schemas.microsoft.com/exchange/yomifirstname

- http://schemas.microsoft.com/exchange/yomilastname

- http://schemas.microsoft.com/exchange/yomiorganization

urn:content-classes:propertydef

The urn:content-classes:propertydef content class defines a set of properties for an item that defines a property for the Exchange store schema. The following list defines the extended content-class, expected content-class and associated properties if applicable.

Extends Content Class

- urn:schemas-microsoft-com:xml-data#ElementType

Properties

- urn:schemas-microsoft-com:exch-data:default

- urn:schemas-microsoft-com:exch-data:dictionary

- urn:schemas-microsoft-com:exch-data:iscontentindexed
- urn:schemas-microsoft-com:exch-data:isindexed
- urn:schemas-microsoft-com:exch-data:ismultivalued
- urn:schemas-microsoft-com:exch-data:isreadonly
- urn:schemas-microsoft-com:exch-data:isrequired
- urn:schemas-microsoft-com:exch-data:isvisible
- urn:schemas-microsoft-com:exch-data:synchronize
- urn:schemas-microsoft-com:datatypes#type
- urn:schemas-microsoft-com:exch-data:version

urn:content-classes:propertyoverride

The urn:content-classes:propertyoverride defines a set of properties for overriding attributes on a property definition for a given content class. The following list defines the extended content-class, expected content-class and associated properties if applicable.

Extends Content Class

- urn:schemas-microsoft-com:xml-data#ElementType

Properties

- urn:schemas-microsoft-com:exch-data:default
- urn:schemas-microsoft-com:exch-data:dictionary
- urn:schemas-microsoft-com:exch-data:isrequired
- urn:schemas-microsoft-com:exch-data:propertydef
- urn:schemas-microsoft-com:exch-data:synchronize
- urn:schemas-microsoft-com:exch-data:version

urn:content-classes:recallmessage

The urn:content-classes:recallmessage content class defines a set of properties for a recall message. The following list defines the extended content-class, expected content-class and associated properties if applicable.

Extends Content Class

◆ urn:content-classes:message

urn:content-classes:recallreport

The urn:content-classes:recallreport content class defines a set of properties for an item that is a recall report message. The following list defines the extended content-class, expected content-class and associated properties if applicable.

Extends Content Class

◆ urn:content-classes:reportmessage

urn:content-classes:taskfolder

The urn:content-classes:taskfolder content class defines a set of properties for a folder that primarily contains task items. The following list defines the extended content-class, expected content-class and associated properties if applicable.

Extends Content Class

◆ urn:content-classes:folder

Expected Content Class

◆ urn:content-classes:item
◆ urn:content-classes:folder

Appendix D

Resources for More Information

UNLIKE COLLEGE, real life is one big open-book test. The answer to any question is readily available – if you know where and how to find it. There's no reason why you can't find the answer to any question using the Internet, even if the question is "What's the meaning of life?" – although you'll get as many answers to that question as you can find sources.

Getting many answers to your question is common. You need to know not only where information is stored, but how to use each resource to get the most it has to offer. And most importantly, you need to know how reliable that information is. You'll develop your own judgement over time and stick with what works for you. Continuously browsing these sites is critical for staying up to date on recent advancements and staying abreast of what others are doing.

Knowing Exchange is only one part of the necessary programming components of developing applications with Exchange Server. Many technologies come into play, so you'll spend time looking at Web sites that discuss ASP, VBScript, JavaScript, ADO, and CDO. Remember that in most of these examples, Exchange is being used as a database. Because Exchange 2000 can be accessed with commonly used database access technologies, look for examples that use VBScript to access databases like Access or SQL.

In some cases, the vendor isn't the best place to get information, but Microsoft has done an excellent job of providing information to developers. When you think about how much software comes out of Microsoft, it would be easy to think that they don't keep up with information for the public, but they do: They have Web sites, newsgroups, and the Exchange 2000 Server SDK.

Exchange 2000 SDK

The SDK is the ultimate source of information about Exchange 2000. We were impressed at the amount of sample code and the level of explanation of the technology. The SDK might seem overwhelmingly technical at first, but once you actually read the text and become familiar with it, it will become a place you return to often.

Download the SDK at `http://msdn.microsoft.com/downloads/default.asp?url=/downloads/sample.asp?_ url=/msdn-files/027/001/741/msdncompositedoc.xml`.

Another gem you'll find handy is the Exchange 2000 Server Developer Enablement Kit. In addition to the SDK, this kit includes training materials, examples, and white papers. You'll find a complete description of its contents at: `url:http://www.microsoft.com/exchange/techinfo/development/2000/enablekit.asp`.

You can order a CD version from `https://microsoft.order-1.com/ex_developer/`.

Web Sites

If someone would pay you, you could actually make a full-time job out of keeping up with the information provided by Microsoft Web sites. The ones we return to most are as follows:

◆ *Microsoft TechNet Online* (`http://Support.microsoft.com/directory`) — TechNet is your personal connection to support for all Microsoft products. This site contains technical articles, white papers, and responses to the questions most commonly asked of Microsoft Support. Almost every error message is explained here, as well as most "how-to" questions, and more.

◆ *Microsoft Exchange Server* (`http://www.microsoft.com/exchange`) — Visit this Web site often for updates to software, including development tools for the Microsoft Exchange Server platform. Links to all other Microsoft Web sites are also listed here. Use it as your starting point when you don't know where else to look. This site contains broad information (not necessarily related to development); but remember, in order to develop for Exchange Server, you need to know what Exchange Server can do.

◆ *Microsoft Developer Network* (http://msdn.microsoft.com) — Dedicated to the development of Microsoft BackOffice Applications, this site has plenty of information to get you moving when you're stumped.

Newsgroups

Newsgroups are a great way to stay in touch with what's going on in the field. It's like being in a college class: Everyone benefits when anyone asks a question. Some people choose to just observe what's going on, never asking a question, but taking in all the information they can. Others ask too many questions. The downside is that it's hard to wade through so much information to find what you want. Some users answer as many questions as they can, sometimes giving the wrong answer, sometimes not giving an answer at all. It's not unusual to see 300 messages a day on a busy group.

Accessing newsgroups

Use a newsgroup reader to access newsgroups. (You'll be grateful to not have newsgroups incorporated into your normal e-mail client when you see the traffic.) Once you have started your reader, subscribe to a newsgroup with the following steps:

1. From the Tools menu, select Accounts, and then select the News tab (Figure D-1).

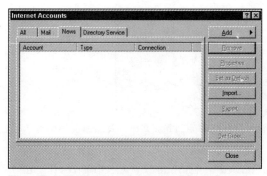

Figure D-1: The Internet Accounts dialog box

2. Click Add and choose News. After entering your name and e-mail address in the appropriate prompts, connect to news.microsoft.com (Figure D-2).

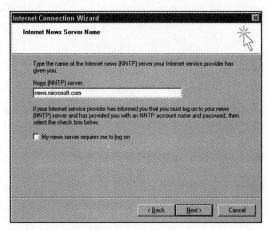

Figure D-2: Selecting an Internet news server

3. Select Finish to return to the Internet Accounts dialog box. Your news-group server will be listed here (Figure D-3). Select Close to connect.

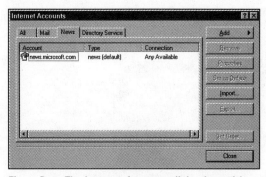

Figure D-3: The Internet Accounts dialog box with news server listed

4. Download the list of hosted newsgroups by selecting Yes (Figure D-4).

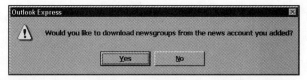

Figure D-4: Continuing the newsgroup download process

5. In the Newsgroup Subscriptions dialog box (Figure D-5), select the groups you would like to subscribe to. Highlight `microsoft.public.exchange.2000.development` and click Subscribe.

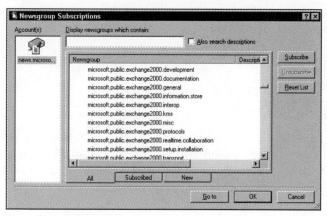

Figure D-5: Subscribing to a newsgroup

6. Click on the newsgroup you just added to start downloading the headers for all new messages in that group (Figure D-6), and you're done!

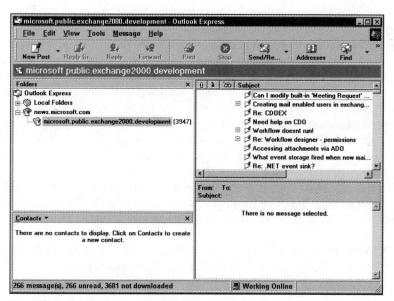

Figure D-6: Reading newsgroup headings

Microsoft-hosted newsgroups

Other newsgroups you should at least check into are:

◆ `microsoft.public.exchange2000.applications`

◆ `microsoft.public.exchange2000.development`

◆ `microsoft.public.exchange2000.realtimecollaboration`

Mailing Lists

I've seen a few mailing lists on the subject of Exchange Server, but most were catered to inexperienced users. Swynk has the best lists around in terms of being monitored by popular Exchange industry people. Visit `http://www.swynk.com/exchange` for more info.

Non-Microsoft Web Sites

Organization of the Internet is key and comes with practice. You may not always find the exact answer you're looking for on some magical Web page. Sometimes you just have to put together information from several places until you have the full story. That's why it's important to know what your sources are, and where to go to get the information you need. Thousands of Web sites exist on any topic. Finding and becoming familiar with the right ones will mean getting faster and better at answering your own questions. Looking in the wrong places will get you just enough information to become frustrated. To help get you started, we've put together a list of our favorite Web sites. We use these sites religiously and have come to trust the information they provide (for the most part).

One thing to keep in mind is that there are different types of questions. You may have a question that has an exact answer, and you may be able to find it. Or you may have a question that only experience can answer. In the latter case, you might find an example on the Web and reverse-engineer it.

Our experience is that the first place to look in most cases is the Web. First we start by searching our favorite development sites, and then we search the Web overall. Our favorite development sites include the following:

◆ Slipstick Systems (`http://www.slipstick.com`) — Probably the best non-Microsoft Web site for information on Exchange Server.

◆ Asp101 (`http://www.asp101.com`) — This Web site is filled with VBScript and ASP examples, from the simple to the complex. Many of these examples deal with accessing databases from ASP.

- ◆ 4GuysFromRolla (`http://www.4guysfromrolla.com`) — Another excellent ASP site.

- ◆ 15Seconds (`http://www.15seconds.com`) — Good development site.

- ◆ DevGuru (`http://www.devguru.com`) — Good Web-development site.

- ◆ XML Web site resources:

  - ■ TopXML (`http://www.topxml.com`) — Great XML reference site.

  - ■ MarrowSoft (`http://www.marrowsoft.com`) — Great XML debugger for building and testing XPath.

  - ■ DevX (`http://www.devx.com`) — Many "how-to" articles.

Appendix E

What's on the Web Site

WE THOUGHT HARD ABOUT including a CD-ROM with this book, but in the end we figured that a Web site would be a more fitting distribution vehicle. The Web site is available at `http://www.hungryminds.com/extras`. You can download the entire Web site to your server and begin using or studying the samples. In some cases, the samples will work without modification, but you should read through the comments in the code for variables that you may need to change, such as usernames, domain names, and so on.

Install the Sample Web Site

No installation is necessary for the sample Web site, except downloading all the code into one directory and creating a virtual directory in IIS pointing to that directory. Be sure to remove the Allow Anonymous Connection security setting. The Web site includes a `readme.txt` file that contains specific instructions.

Web Site Contents

All the code listings from the book are included in the sample Web site in the `\listings` directory. The name of each listing corresponds to its location in the book. So Listing 1-1 from Chapter 1 can be found in `\listings\listing1-1.asp`. We scoured newsgroups to find out what sample code people wanted to see and what technologies they were talking about, and we did our best to respond by creating examples that reflect the needs of real-life administrators and developers. As each of us is from one of the three main areas of Exchange — development, architecture, and project management — we think we bring a broad range of points of view to the book. We also developed a few cool utilities to include with it, and we promise you will find them useful. You'll have to download the Web site to see what they are.

Index

A

continued

continued

continued